Selected Letters of Conrad Aiken

Selected Letters *of* Conrad Aiken

EDITED BY JOSEPH KILLORIN

NEW HAVEN AND LONDON

YALE UNIVERSITY PRESS

1978

*Published with assistance from the foundation established
in memory of Calvin Chapin of the Class of 1788,
Yale College.*

*Designed by Sally Sullivan Harris
and set in VIP Sabon type.
Printed in the United States of America by
Vail-Ballou Press, Inc., Binghamton, N.Y.*

*Published in Great Britain, Europe, Africa, and
Asia (except Japan) by Yale University Press,
Ltd., London. Distributed in Latin America by
Kaiman & Polon, Inc., New York City; in
Australia and New Zealand by Book & Film
Services, Artarmon, N.S.W., Australia; and in
Japan by Harper & Row, Publishers, Tokyo
Office.*

Library of Congress Cataloging in Publication Data

*Aiken, Conrad Potter, 1889–1973.
  Selected letters of Conrad Aiken.*

  *Includes index.
  1. Aiken, Conrad Potter, 1889–1973—Correspondence.
2. Authors, American—20th century—Correspondence.
I. Killorin, Joseph, 1926–
PS3501.I5Z48   1978   818'.52'05 [B]   77-20620
ISBN 0-300-02180-1*

Contents

Illustrations

Edward Burra, 1976. Photo by Paddy Aiken.

Aiken in the attic at "41 Doors," Brewster, 1955. Photo by Eileen Darby, reproduced by courtesy of Graphic House, Inc., New York.

Conrad and Mary Aiken at "41 Doors," Brewster, 1955. Photo by Eileen Darby, reproduced by courtesy of Graphic House, Inc., New York.

Aiken at his desk in the Library of Congress, 1951

Aiken at 230 Oglethorpe Avenue, Savannah, 1965

Mary Aiken's map of Rye, 1938

Jeake's House, Rye. Photo by Paddy Aiken.

Aiken's two homes on Oglethorpe Avenue, Savannah

Aiken at the entrance to 228 Oglethorpe Avenue, with Mary Aiken at the entrance to 230 Oglethorpe Avenue, about 1963

"41 Doors." Photo by Fraser Bonnell.

The study at "41 Doors." Photo by Fraser Bonnell.

Mary Aiken's portrait of Aiken in his Jeake's House study, 1939

Mary Aiken's portrait of Aiken with Nipperty the cat, 1944

Aiken mowing the terraces at "41 Doors," 1955. Photo by Eileen Darby, reproduced by courtesy of Graphic House, Inc., New York.

Acknowledgments

Two hundred forty-five letters by Conrad Aiken have here been selected from a representative collection of over three thousand, a collection requiring the cooperation and labor of many people, not all of whom, alas, can be remembered here.

For a man who thrived on letters but was himself indifferent about saving them, Aiken's contribution (besides providing copies of his public letters and of some to Malcolm Lowry which he had made after Lowry's death) was to list his correspondents, though he always underestimated how many letters he had written to them and he seldom expected them to have saved any. Aiken made no suggestion about how to select or edit his letters. He neither reread them nor discussed them very much; there were newer things to talk about.

For eight years Mary Hoover Aiken has been working with me to discover and to photocopy letters. Without her ready help and sometimes ingenious detective work, the scope of the collection would be much less adequate.

Joan Aiken, Jane and Alan Hodge, and John and Paddy Aiken collected and copied Conrad Aiken's letters to a number of his English friends as well as to themselves. All those correspondents distinguished in this volume by the superscript [r] made letters available. In addition, the following people provided letters: Mrs. Lee Anderson, Anthony Bertram, Rufus Blanshard, Calvin Brown, Mrs. Gordon Cairnie, Huntington Cairns, Hugh Cecil, Maureen Connelly, Mrs. Harry H. Cooper, Richard Costa, Malcolm Cowley, Valerie Eliot, Maurice Firuski, Roy Fuller, Felicia Geffen, Isabelle Harrison, John Hay, Erich Heller, Eugene Istomin, Neva Kaiser, Elizabeth Killorin, Laura Knight, Roger Linscott, Margerie Lowry, Jerre

Mangione, Margaret Mackechnie, Grayson P. McCouch, William A. Murphy, Robert Overstreet, Norman Holmes Pearson, Houston Peterson, Charles Philbrick, Kathleen Raine, Charles Schlessiger, Mark Schorer, Suzanne Smith, Holly Stevens, Allen Tate, Kempton P. A. Taylor, Henrietta Waring, Barbara Wilbur, Richard Wilbur.

Librarians prepared lists and copies of letters from their manuscript collections; to them and to their libraries special thanks are due: Samuel A. Sizer, University Library, The University of Arkansas, Fayetteville; Howard B. Gotlieb, Mugar Memorial Library, Boston University; George Brandak, The Library of the University of British Columbia, Vancouver; Stuart C. Sherman, The John Hay Library, Brown University, Providence; K. C. Gay, Lockwood Memorial Library, State University of New York at Buffalo; Mary Janzen Wilson, The Joseph Regenstein Library, The University of Chicago; John C. Broderick, The Library of Congress; Rodney G. Dennis, The Houghton Library, Harvard University; Alexander P. Clark and Mrs. Mardel Pachero, Princeton University Library; Warren Roberts and David Farmer, Humanities Research Center, The University of Texas, Austin; Holly Hall, Washington University Libraries, St. Louis; Donald Gallup and Louis Martz, Beinecke Rare Book and Manuscript Library, Yale University. Gerald Sandy and the staff of The Lane Library, Armstrong State College, Savannah, have lightened with their interest and patient help many editorial tasks.

This volume is indebted to the forthcoming *Conrad Aiken: A Bibliography,* by Florence and Fraser Bonnell. Before their work was completed Mr. and Mrs. Bonnell generously provided me with a working checklist of Aiken's publications.

I am grateful to James Thorpe, Daniel Woodward, and The Huntington Library for the use of its new Conrad Aiken Collection. This volume was planned with Whitney Blake. It has taken shape under the editorial guidance of Ellen Graham and Charles Grench of the Yale University Press.

For time to complete this volume and to undertake a biography of Aiken I am indebted both to Armstrong State College and to the Callaway Foundation. I have relied on the understanding encouragement of Henry L. Ashmore, H. Dean Propst, Hugh Pendexter III, and the members of my department in Armstrong State College; of S. F. Johnson of Columbia University; and of Robert W. Mueller and Henrietta Waring.

The pleasant tasks of deciphering Aiken's script and of making daily editorial judgments have been shared with Harriet Davis Killorin; the labor of typing the manuscripts has been hers alone. To her I owe my greatest debt for this volume.

The selection of letters and passages of letters to be published has been made solely by myself.

The copyright in those letters of Conrad Aiken acquired from Mary Hoover Aiken for the Conrad Aiken Collection belongs to The Huntington Library. The copyright in all other letters of Conrad Aiken belongs to Mary Hoover Aiken.

July 1977   Joseph Killorin

Introduction

"Give yourself away, come clean!" If ever the root motive of a writer was meditated and clearly announced, it was this intention of Conrad Aiken throughout his thousand pages of poetry, his five novels, his short stories, and even his critical articles. "Get down to the real business of the poet," he wrote to his friend Malcolm Cowley, "consciously or unconsciously to give the lowdown on himself, and through himself on humanity. . . . What do you think or feel which is secretly you? shamefully you? intoxicatingly you, drunkenly or soberly or lyrically you?"[1]

Yet surely Malcolm Lowry was also right to wonder "how future generations would picture Aiken as a human being. . . . Because for a writer who has been accused of being 'subjective' as they say, Conrad Aiken has left . . . very little impression of himself . . . nor has Aiken himself ever pretended to be other than unhelpful."[2]

There were two reasons for this lack of a public picture of Aiken: the first was that he was insurmountably shy of public appearances; the second that—even in those works, like *Blue Voyage* and *Ushant,* where the autobiographical element is most obvious—Aiken saw an important distinction between the articulation of the poet's private awareness and the confession of the names, places, and dates of his private life. The poet's awareness makes him *"simply* indifferent . . . to temporal or social or fashionable or ephemeral distractions and disguises." Poets "are dateless; and precisely because they are themselves the most private and individualist of people, by articulating this extreme privacy of awareness they become themselves

---

1. C A to Malcolm Cowley, July 26, 1929[n] (see *Wake 11* [1952], p. 29).
2. "A Letter," *Wake 11* (1952), pp. 80–89.

universals." [3] The poet can reveal the poet's life only in an artifact:
"I can't feel any aesthetic or moral error in the casting of an autobiographical theme into the third person," Aiken wrote Cowley in
defense of *Blue Voyage,* "in fact, I believe it is possible to be more
detachedly honest in this form . . . than in straight confession. At
all events, I am much interested in *this*—the autobiography turned
novel, given shape and distance. And it seemed to me a useful thing
to do, at this point in my life: I mean to give myself *away*" [4] In
Ushant—subtitled "An Essay" to emphasize the new form of his *endeavor* or *attempt*—Aiken was taken by some, including his publishers, to be writing autobiography as a roman à clef; it is, he insisted, neither. He readily admitted to Jay Martin (Letters 222 and
224) that his *sources* ranged from "direct transcript from life" to
"pure invention." But autobiography as a transcription from life,
Aiken said, implies a self-revelation and self-disclosure "really on
the order of W[alter] Winchell gossip," which is at best "the fodder
of experience" and irrelevant to his aim from the beginning in all
his poetry and fiction: "*all the way* the aim has been to disclose the
psychic mechanism of the *artist and human being*—in the interest of
furthering self-knowledge." (Related to this aim, too, is Aiken's
rejection of a literary language "blindly and conceitedly idiosyncratic" [Letter 118].)

In a time when poets often survived by appearing before large audiences, chiefly academic, Aiken neither lectured nor taught. Unlike
Frost, Eliot, and many others, Aiken developed no *public* character;
he twice fled the country to avoid honors requiring his public appearance. His resignation from Harvard as class poet in 1911 was,
he said, "the forerunner of many such crucial decisions and avoid-
ances—it was the first time he had been forced to measure, and respect, the disturbing force of his share of the family *petit mal,*" by
which he meant the insanity which he had seen overcome his father,
and which all his life he feared would at last overtake him. "He had
known, instantly, that this kind of public appearance, and for such
an occasion [presenting the class poem], was precisely what the flaw
in his inheritance would not, in all likelihood, be strong enough to
bear. This was the kind of 'public' trial . . . which he must learn
how to circumvent: otherwise, the penalty might be tragic. . . . It

3. *Collected Criticism* (New York and London, 1968), p. 99.
4. C A to Malcolm Cowley, August 26, 1927[n] (see *Wake 11* [1952], p. 28).

was his decision that his life must be lived *off-stage,* behind the scenes, out of view."[5]

Nevertheless, the poet who avoided literary and political groups and movements *and* the man who shunned all public appearances had nothing in his nature of the solitary. From the age of twenty-three Aiken was never unmarried; in Boston, New York, and London he possessed circles of loved friends; and even farthest off-stage in Rye, Cape Cod, or Savannah, he steadily contrived to celebrate his rituals of friendship:

> At seven, in the ancient farmhouse,
> cocktails sparkle on the tray, the careful answer
> succeeds the casual question, a reasoned dishevelment
> ruffling quietly the day's or the hour's issue.[6]

R. P. Blackmur noted what evenings of conversation with Aiken were regularly like: one entered "the ambience of the vaudeville of the psyche."

> Anyone who has dined often with Aiken must have been struck a livening blow by his restless percipience of the casual that was going on about him in the midst of no matter what genuine preoccupation—of money or marriage or career—concerned both of you. Whatever the roving eye or cocked ear could report was in its circumfusion sponged into the preoccupation, and so becomes part of the declaration of the double self between you.[7]

Lowry suggested the qualities that, many of Aiken's friends agreed, caused his conversation to rise often to memorable effects:

> You couldn't, no matter who you were, have met Aiken, if only to pass the time of day with the exchange of a few words, without mysteriously feeling, as it were, that your system had been "toned up": possibly it would not be until you got around the next corner that you saw the joke he had inserted tangentially into this exchange, whereupon all at once the day too would take upon itself a new, brighter, or it might be a more bizarre, a more complex aspect, in any case, become a wholly

5. *Ushant* (New York and Boston, 1952), pp. 164–66.
6. "The Crystal," *Collected Poems 1916–1970* (New York, 1970), pp. 945–54.
7. "Introduction" to *The Collected Novels of Conrad Aiken* (New York, 1964), p. 5.

more amusing and sympathetic adventure: in some amazing way he had sensed *your* problem, made *your* own burden, whatever it was, seem lighter. In other words, to an extraordinary degree he possessed charity: in addition to this however he possessed a quality that, despite some richly comic scenes, and others savage and appalling, is not easily, or consistently at least, to be deduced from his works.[8]

There is no doubt that conversation was Aiken's favorite sport: minds at play with words, dishevelling, unravelling, modulating from comic to appalling and back, without signs of "overtraining," and always assuming that the play aimed at "coming clean." And also for Aiken—as his friends sensed—there was an unspoken solemnity in the rite of conversation:

> these and other aspects of the immortal moment
> glow into consciousness for laughter or tears,
> an instant of sympathy or misunderstanding, an exchange
> of human touch or tact, or agreement, soon silent.[9]

In "The Crystal" Aiken assumed that the conversation of the cocktail hour represents the communion of all friendly minds separated in time and in space:

> We pour for the gods, and will always,
> you there, we here, and the others who follow,
> pour thus in communion. Separate in time,
> and yet not separate. Making oblation
> in a single moment of consciousness
> to the endless forever-together.[10]

The quality of Aiken's voice in his intimate conversations was not, as Lowry said, "easily, or consistently at least, to be deduced from his works." But this quality, this voice, *is* heard in many of the letters in this volume. For his letters often seem a transcript of his conversation, a continuation of his speaking voice. He spoke in finished paragraphs, and waited eagerly for reply; so in many letters the "I" is not a "correspondent," again it is Conrad—as always—and he is listening for Jake Wilbur or Bob Linscott or Malcolm Lowry or Ed Burra to counterpoint, to return the serve.

8. "A Letter," *Wake 11* (1952).
9. "The Crystal."
10. Ibid.

Until the later years of his life Aiken never intended his letters—any more than his conversations—to become part of his published "work." He felt it a betrayal of the privacy of friendship even to make a carbon of letters he wrote to friends. In 1967 he suggested hesitantly to me that his letters might be collected—if anyone had kept some, and if they could be found. Though few letters possessed either the shape and distance—and therefore the truth—of art, and the self-revelation was often not above the level of gossip, they might conceivably, he thought, have interest as further—possibly unconscious—revelation of a life that had aimed to *reveal* itself, by making public at last those parts of the man which the family inheritance had determined must be, up to now, intensely private. Yet he was as skeptical as ever of attempts, which letters surely encourage, to root a writer's imaginative life in autobiographical facts; he had suffered too many theses, for instance, that purported to explain his works by the violent tragedy of his adolescence. In any case, whatever use the letters might have—not least that of reading for fun—required, he also insisted, no holding back now of anything he had said or done, no smoothing out or brightening of a life whose "maze-like pattern of persistence and devotion and infidelity" revealed him "over and over again unfaithful to pretty much everything" he loved,[11] a life that—perhaps more than his works—included "some richly comic scenes," but also "others savage and appalling."

And Aiken had another reason for publishing at last his letters, for—beyond the last conversation—letters are the food of that communion in which minds dead are made alive again in us;

> Somewhere beyond the Gorge Li Po is gone,
> looking for friendship or an old love's sleeve
> or writing letters to his children, lost,
> and to his children's children, and to us.[12]

In turn we "assume" Li Po in ourselves—as our inheritance of language and of mind. Aiken's preoccupation with the human race's inheritance of mind (the tradition of "letters" in the wide sense of civilization), as well as of body, led him to attach special meaning to the form of the *letter:* the poet is the letter-writer of the race.

This is why the form of direct address and the second person appear so often in his work: the prayer to his father and mother

11. *Ushant*, p. 301.
12. "A Letter from Li Po," *Collected Poems 1916–1970*, pp. 903–15.

concluding "Changing Mind"; "A Letter from Li Po," which poem is itself Aiken's letter answering Li Po's; "The Crystal," addressed to Pythagoras; "Hallowe'en," answering his Grandpa Potter's letter-journal; and *Dead Letters,* his partially completed project of letters to his ancestors. This is why he identified himself and his works with Li Po:

> Like him, we too have eaten of the word:
> with him are somewhere lost beyond the Gorge:
> and write, in rain, a letter to lost children,
> a letter long as time and brief as love.[13]

Next to conversation, all his life Conrad Aiken loved to receive and to write letters. At twenty-three, in late 1912 and 1913, in Europe on his honeymoon, Aiken began to write letters regularly, several days each week, mostly to close Harvard friends about his new outpouring of poems: outlining, defending, selling them, and high-spiritedly despairing of them. The quantity of letters diminished somewhat while he lived next in Cambridge and Boston, but on removing his family in 1919 to Cape Cod, distance and isolation increased all his various needs to write letters. Poverty largely determined this geographical withdrawal, but he had also by then sensed that his strength as a writer was protected by it. Thereafter, though he regularly felt compelled to migrate from one loved place to another, he lived and worked mostly, after South Yarmouth, in Winchelsea and Rye (Sussex), Brewster (Cape Cod), and Savannah. By the time Aiken, almost eighty-four, wrote his last letter on July 30, 1973, he had probably written about 12,000 letters. It is probable that more than 4,000 of these survive, and the present selection was made from almost 3,500 of those available to me, including almost all of the important correspondences to friends. Of those unpublished at least a thousand are as interesting as those included in this selection.

Even in the numerous letters required by the writer's trade or correspondence from readers, his voice never became impersonal. He replied at eighty to a note from a former receptionist for Oxford University Press:

Dear Rimsa Michel: Yes, I think I remember you and how nice of you to write to me. And yes, I'm still here, but showing

13. Ibid.

signs of wear and tear, naturally. How far off 114 Fifth Avenue now seems! I still remember my first visit to see Vaudrin—I needed a martini, and ordered one in Madison Sq., but c'dn't drink it, my hand was too unsteady—so I left it, and found a dark empty bar where I had a double gin in a TUMBLER, which I could surround with both hands—it was the solution. Hallelujah. Very best—Conrad Aiken[14]

But many a letter to a friend went a distance toward the transformation of the casual into art, as the first translation of the ephemeral into a form more accessible, which then constituted his best memory of it. Or at times a letter would try out as fantasy a work still seething: much of Letter 51, written in 1923, is a fantasy on characters in *Blue Voyage,* completed in 1926. To write a letter was a way to "fix" the hourly news of consciousness, the stuff of letters as well as of conversation:

> For we must hear and bear
> the news from everywhere: the hourly news,
> infinitesimal or vast, from everywhere.[15]

The day often began with news of dreams. He woke eager to tell and to hear of dream landscapes and voyages and, of course, of dream conversations and letters, as at eighty-two he woke to tell of Emily Dickinson's orchard.

John Hay and I were walking down Stony Brook Road, as it used to be, and in the fields beside it, and one of us said, It must be about here that Emily's apple orchard was. I looked down into the grass, and sure enough, there it was—rows of tiny apple trees, two inches high, each with a little red apple, size of a cranberry, on top, and I at once plucked one and popped it into my mouth, where I began to peel the skin off with tongue and teeth. As I did so, the taste of the little apple turned itself into language, in fact a poem, which went—

> Human, thou tastest
> Now in me
> A breath of
> Immortality

14. C A to Rimsa Michel, August 18, 1969.ʳ
15. "A Letter from Li Po."

I planted with my hands
This tree
And now
I give
It back to thee

I woke, got up, and put it down at two-thirty a.m., adding a note, She planted it on her way back to Dedham. In the dream I went back later to find the little apple-skin, to see if by any chance there might be hieroglyphics on the inside, but no—the taste had turned into the poem. Dedham (outside Boston) she never went to, as far as I know. Second time I've dreamt about her being dead! Some ghoul had been trying to dig up her grave, I found. And later, I looked at my hands, and there was dirt under my fingernails! Tiens. . . .[16]

Repetition in conversation to his wife Mary and then in a letter to his son-in-law Alan Hodge helped to "hold" such a dream, to record for reference this new exploration of an unknown landscape on the mind's map.

Aiken loved Emily Dickinson's poems, her "letter to the world"; he had edited the first English edition of her poems in 1924 and had later made *her* the quintessential American "Kid," "too intrinsic for renown."[17] What more in keeping than that *her* letter to him should have come as a translation of taste "into language, in fact a poem." The dream's very subject was the process of "translation" of landscape into language: an act of dream-imagination which describes *itself,* very like *Ushant's* central dream about the translators.

Aiken's precept that "the landscape and the language are the same"[18] implied that this work of inventing language is performed unbidden, it *presents* itself; "it simply lay there 'on the brush,' " he often said of a poem, as Emily's poem had lain on his tongue. The invention of dream or waking art presents itself as a teasing palimpsest, to be overheard, to be repeated, and at last—not too confidently, certainly not by orthodox doctrine—to be unravelled. "What do you make of that, Watson?" Aiken would demand.

And he listened intently for the reports of others. The news that

16. C A to Alan Hodge, March 14, 1971.ᵉ
17. The last lines of "The Kid," *Collected Poems 1916–1970,* p. 862, which echo Dickinson's "Lay this Laurel on the One / Too intrinsic for Renown" (*The Complete Poems of Emily Dickinson,* edited by Thomas H. Johnson [Boston, 1960], p. 597).
18. "A Letter from Li Po."

knocked daily with the postman (by breakfast, if possible)—newspapers aside, which must be devoured whole, down to comics, sports, and Wall Street—came in the day's catch of letters, each read and passed around for wonder and comment. He thirsted for the "soulnourishing" news of the infinitesimal, the pleasure of another's translation of his vital signs, of "ego." He wrote his son John in gratitude:

> Your letter, my lad, was a howling seething bloodletting hyper-pituitary masterpiece; I gargled over it like a drunken crow, it did me no end of good, for J's letters never tell me anything, never anything at all, I feel that Rye and Jeake's House and you and she and Jane and England don't exist, aren't there, that there's nobody home, that the Ship Inn never hung out a sign, nor Mr. Neeves never dug a potato, nor Mrs. Neeves never took her washing down the river's edge of a Monday, nor the milk-cans clanked on the cobbles at eight-fifteen of a morning in December, nor Squidge got a cobweb in his nose, and scuffed at it, rubbing anxiously with a hysterical paw, or, you know, any damned nonsense of that soul-nourishing sort. And your letter gave me such a lovely warm interior—I mean Dutch, not physical—but that's getting mixed, because there is also Dutch courage—I mean Pieter de Hooch, the grandfather of American gin. But that too doesn't seem to work, so we'll say Vermeer. I could almost hear the pingpong balls, or your tirelessly wearing out the wallpaper on the diningroom wall, and then the stone beneath it, and then working through the wisteria. —Hell. It was a lovely, lovely letter, and gave my umbilical cord such a deep and twingling twang as would be worth five pounds fine any day.[19]

Except for those surrounding the terrible nadir of 1932, the letters were usually touched by, sometimes rampant with, gaiety. Even his revelation of despair in the face of erotic or economic catastrophe leaned toward vaudeville hilarity. But the hilarity and the despair were shaped, controlled, by the movement of the language native to *this* landscape and to *this* voice, a voice "quiet, rapid, old Bostonian without the broad A, and always correctly punctuated—with some words audibly underlined and some phrases preceded

19. C A to John Aiken, November 14, 1933.[r]

and followed by pauses like parentheses." [20] It is from this careful voice that Aiken's beloved "quotidian" acquired its characteristic overtones of wonder, of vastness surrounding the infinitesimal.

> Wayfarer from afar
> why are you here? what brings you here? why here? [21]

In these letters that voice begins, without hesitation, its disclosures—as it did, once, while evening drinks were poured:

Dear Djones, Lovely adventure at the marina last night—we had a PRIVATE eclipse of the moon turned on for us—we parked the car under a tall bright harbor light, and just to the left, or east, of this, came the sickle of half-moon—and I said to Mary, Looks to me as if we might have an eclipse. Sure enough, they obliged: moon slid behind arc-lamp, vanished, the stars became brighter, and then, in about eight minutes, reappeared to the west. Delicious. Neither of them blemished—And tonight, under the same lamp, another oddity: a nightwalking seagull, who obviously liked to be in bright light, on the sand, by the edge of the seagrass, and was delousing and preening; we thought it might be ill, old, preparing to die. Not so. When Mary got out to take her stroll to the outer beach, he took off across the Dark River, happy as Larry. [22]

20. Malcolm Cowley, "Biography with Letters," *Wake 11* (1952), pp. 86–87.
21. "A Letter from Li Po."
22. C A to John Aiken, November 26, 1968.ʳ

Editorial Note

The principle of selection in this volume is not primarily what might serve the literary historian or critic seeking intentions or explanations of the author's works, hints of influences upon him, or even the autobiographical raw material of his art. These may all be found in this selection of letters, but many letters crucial to these interests remain to be published.[1]

Here the aim has been to include letters that reflect Aiken in the variety of his interests and styles, now as strategist defending his literary forts, now as psychologist in debate upon motive, now as rueful or comic historian of personal disasters (literary, domestic, economic), now as ironic "sassiety" gossiper, now as father or lover.

Omitted for the most part, not without occasional damage to the structure of a letter, are discussions of ordinary business, domestic and professional, and most repetition. It should be stressed that editorial deletions have been made seldom for the sake of discretion or to avoid embarrassment, but most often, and merely, to allow more letters to be printed.

All deletions, of whatever length, are indicated by three ellipsis dots. A few postscripts have been deleted silently. Where Aiken to indicate a change of subject used dashes or dots, the editor has used a dash only. When Aiken's spelling deviated from standard it was for the effect of dialect or pun (as, in Letter 51, "gaugin and van

---

1. The unity of this volume lies in the continuous arc—or "great circle"—of Aiken's life, which the letters were chosen to reflect. Against this biographical background, Aiken's letters on literary theory and technique (to Eliot, Allen Tate, John Davenport, John Freeman, J. G. Fletcher) and on psychoanalysis and the artist (to Wilbur, Murray, H.D.) should later be gathered, not to speak of his commentary on high and low life in his large correspondence with Edward Burra and Gordon Bassett.

gogh" should sound "go, gin! and *vin,* go!"). Therefore only obvious typographical slips are corrected—silently. Aiken's punctuation has been made regular, except for proper names (like NYorker, Lib Cong). The spacing of salutations and closings has been compressed. The occasional ampersand of the manuscript has been expanded to *and.* Dates or places of writing for a number of letters have been supplied by me in brackets from postmarks or contextual evidence.

By reading *Ushant* along with the letters, one can follow, from the perspective of 1950, Aiken's inner voyage—though calendar time is irrelevant to *Ushant*—through childhood (I), adolescence and Harvard (II and III), the "central summer of 1911" (IV), and moments in his career after 1914 (V and VI). C A approved my epigraphs from *Ushant,* which for part III required rearrangement of the order of passages and the addition of several phrases, because the Savannah passage in *Ushant* was written ten years before C A returned to live in that city, thus completing his "great circle."

The headnote that precedes each group of letters seeks to provide only the briefest biographical narrative needed to place Aiken in his irregular migrations and to note crucial events that may not be described in these letters. Footnotes usually aim to explain no more of passing references than the general reader will find necessary to follow Aiken's drift; nevertheless, oblique allusions abound, and, depending on the reader's taste, the annotations will sometimes have gone too far and sometimes not far enough. In headnotes and footnotes Aiken is designated as C A, his signet and frequent signature from youth.

The Cast of Correspondents at the end of the book identifies briefly each of the correspondents addressed by Aiken in this volume.

To save the reader greater interruption, editorial additions, particularly of names, have sometimes been made in brackets. However, the index of proper names includes names in all the forms that Aiken used. An index of Aiken's works similarly includes references in whatever form to each of his works.

The editor has transcribed each letter from Aiken's handwritten or typed original, or from a photocopy, or from Aiken's carbon or typed copy (except for Letters 4 and 21, which are transcribed from C A's copies of the newspapers). The present locations of the original letters are indicated after the name of the correspondents by these superscripts:

[a] University Library, The University of Arkansas, Fayetteville, Arkansas.

[b] The Library of the University of British Columbia, Vancouver, Canada.

[c] The Joseph Regenstein Library, The University of Chicago, Chicago, Illinois.

[ch] indicates that the present location of the original is unknown to me, but that Aiken's carbon or a typed or photographed copy of the original is in the Conrad Aiken Collection of the Huntington Library.

[h] The Huntington Library, San Marino, California.

[n] The Newberry Library, Chicago, Illinois.

[p] Princeton University Library, Princeton, New Jersey.

[r] in possession of the recipient or heirs.

[s] Lockwood Memorial Library, State University of New York at Buffalo, New York.

[t] Humanities Research Center, The University of Texas, Austin, Texas.

[u] The Houghton Library, Harvard University, Cambridge, Massachusetts.

[w] Washington University Libraries, St. Louis, Missouri.

[y] Beinecke Library, Yale University, New Haven, Connecticut.

Part I: 1898–1926

My father which art in earth
From whom I got my birth,
What is it that I inherit?
From the bones fallen apart
And the deciphered heart,
Body and spirit.

My mother which art in tomb
Who carriedst me in thy womb,
What is it that I inherit?
From the thought come to dust
And the remembered lust,
Body and spirit.

Father and mother, who gave
Life, love, and now the grave,
What is it that I can be?
Nothing but what lies here,
The hand still, the brain sere,
Naught lives in thee

Nor ever will live, save
It have within this grave
Roots in the mingled heart,
In the damp ashes wound
Where the past, underground,
Falls, falls apart.

["Changing Mind," Conclusion]

If it was the writer's business, or the poet's, to be as conscious as possible,
and his primary obligation, then wouldn't this impose upon him the still
deeper obligation of being conscious of his own workings, the workings
of his psyche, and of the springs and deficiencies and necessities and com-
pulsions, the whole subliminal drive which had made him a writer to

1

begin with, and along with the work itself, to present, as it were, the explication—? Wouldn't this be the next mandatory step, the artist's plain duty? that he take the machine apart, and show how it worked? . . . And at Troutbeck Bridge, on the honeymoon with Lorelei One, hadn't there been . . . that other fragment . . .

> *Was this the poet? It is man.*
> *The poet is but man made plain.*
> *A glass-cased watch, through which you scan*
> *The feverish fine small mechanism,*
> *And hear it ticking, while it sings:*
> *Behold, this delicate paroxysm*
> *Obedient to rebellious springs!*

. . . wasn't that visible now as the first succinct and lucid statement of what was to turn out to be the all-gathering preoccupation? even if, as seemed likely—though how could one be sure—?—one hadn't so conceived it at the time. But wasn't the fact that this fragment alone remained in one's memory, after upwards of three decades, and so many summers, so many loves, indicative of something at least prophetic? And in this had Jacob perhaps been right in his suggestion that an author's writings were very often in some degree an anticipation of attitudes yet to be formed, definitions yet to be made, actions yet to be taken? the work of art, of whatever category, itself, therefore, the conscious-unconscious process of arrival at this new point; and when completed, itself in a sense the catalyst which would precipitate the new attitude or action—?

Clearly, it was another definite facet of the whole disturbingly beautiful mechanism; and another aspect, therefore, of the off-and-on project, of all those years at Saltinge, or to and from it, driven by the twin winds of love and economics, the project of adding, to such work as he might undertake, or ever succeed in finishing, an exact statement about the nature and contents of the author, like the bill of lading of a ship.

[Ushant, pp. 246–48]

2

Letters 1–3: April 1898 to February 1904

On August 5, 1889, a night message was telegraphed from Savannah, Georgia, to Mr. and Mrs. William Lyman Akin in New York City and to Mr. William James Potter in New Bedford, Massachusetts:

> Arrived safely at six-thirty evening. Found Mother very comfortable. Signed, Conrad Potter Aiken.

Sending C A's first letter–to his grandparents–was Dr. William Ford Aiken, who two months before had brought his pregnant wife Anna, a distant cousin, on a stormy ocean voyage from New Bedford, where he had married her in November, to the southern town where he was beginning a medical practice in ear, eye, and throat diseases.

> His pa a doctor, painter, writer,
> his ma a beauty, but which the brighter? [1]

At twenty-five they were both brilliant creatures: gifted talkers, social and gay. They both came from homes alive to the new intellectual crosscurrents. Anna's father, a friend of Emerson, preached that the goal of all physical evolution is the higher evolution of human consciousness, of the Godhead in man. A founder of the Free Religious Association, he advocated "a worship purified of myth and of dogma." [2] Dr. Aiken's father had been for almost forty years a teacher of mathematics and the natural sciences and principal of a preparatory school in New York City.

C A early made himself an inheritor of these distant—and soon dead—grandfathers. At nine "he had, in pious imitation of grandfather Potter, written a series of sermons." [3] And he absorbed his father's own inherited passion for science as he observed Dr. Aiken operating on an eye, inventing medical instruments and photographic devices, and reading his papers on medicine and astronomy.

1. "Obituary in Bitcherel," *Collected Poems 1916–1970*, p. 1012.
2. *Ushant*, pp. 110–12. The lectures and sermons of William James Potter were collected in *Twenty-Five Sermons of Twenty-Five Years* (Boston, 1886) and in *Lectures and Sermons* (Boston, 1895).
3. *Ushant*, p. 108.

In a large house on Oglethorpe Avenue, Anna Aiken gave frequent parties and easily established the couple in the society of the old town. Three more children were born: Elizabeth in 1891, Kempton in 1893, and Robert in 1895, while Conrad roamed free between the lively house and the "rich and rancid" life of "that most magical of cities":

> I was allowed to run wild in that earthly paradise till I was nine—no school till nine . . . I can still remember that feeling every morning of having before one an infinity of freedom. Very nearly ideal for the boy who very early decided that he wanted to write. And write he appallingly did. Nothing could stop him.[4]

But in C A's eleventh year the mood of the Aiken house began to sour as Dr. Aiken became inexplicably suspicious and fierce, quarreling bitterly with his wife and then turning against Conrad:

> beaten he was: barebacked: crossed hands
> on bedstead knobs: trunk-straps, three bands:
> for something nobody yet understands.[5]

On the morning of February 27, 1901, he awoke about seven to hear his father and mother, in their bedroom, quarreling:

> And I heard my father's voice counting: "One, two, three." And a pistol shot, and then another shot. I got out of bed and walked through the children's bedroom, next to my parents' and where Elizabeth and Kempton and Robert were in their cribs, and opened the folding doors to my parents' room. I had to step over my father's body to go to my mother. But she was dead, her mouth wide open in the act of screaming. I came out, closed the folding doors, told the children to stay in their beds and that their nurse would come to them. I dressed myself, went downstairs and told the cook there had been an accident and to give the children breakfast downstairs, and to keep them in the dining room. Then I walked to the police station a block away and told them my father had shot my mother and himself, and they said: "Who is your father?" And I said: "Dr. Aiken." So they came with me and took command.[6]

4. "Some Important Authors Speak for Themselves," *Herald Tribune Books* (October 12, 1952).
5. "Obituary in Bitcherel," p. 1013.
6. C A in conversation with Joseph Killorin (February 1967).

*Murder and suicide by the socially prominent physician was re-
ported sensationally in the* Savannah Morning News. *Crowds outside the house observed the arrivals of Dr. Aiken's mother and of
Mrs. Aiken's brother and relatives from New England, and then,
two days after the deaths, the funeral cortege forming before the
house and Conrad being led to the black-plumed carriage. But already within the family a veil was being drawn over the horror and
guilt of William Aiken's act. It was to be years before C A would
speak about the event to anyone. Two days after the funeral, he was
encouraged to write Letter 2 to Uncle Will Tillinghast's son: "We
are all well here."*

> *Then we were taken to New Bedford. My brothers Kemp and
> Rob and my sister Elizabeth were adopted by the efficiency ge-
> nius Frederick Winslow Taylor in Philadelphia and I more or
> less lost touch with them. Uncle William Tillinghast became
> my guardian and took me in, but I never felt I had a home.*[7]

*C A went to school at first in New Bedford and then in Cam-
bridge and in 1903 entered Middlesex School in Concord. He was
an enthusiastic athlete and he formed fast friendships, particularly
with Grayson P. McCouch ("The Old Bird"). But preparatory
school for C A was overcast by loneliness; he was shy and he had
no real family (his relatives never once visited him at the school).
He felt marked by the whisperings around him about his family
tragedy—"the staining sense of guilt and shame";*[8] *and the "Boss,"
the headmaster, was hostile to him. His later attitude toward his
years at Middlesex was hardened by a humiliating episode mentioned in his last letter (244) to McCouch, written on his deathbed.*

1: TO EMILY FORD AKIN[h]   Savannah, Ga.
                                            April 27, 1898

Dear Grandma,   I hope you will soon be well. I have just written a letter to Aunt Kempton.[1] Uncle Alfred came to visit us.[2] I
hope we can come north this year. And if I do ill come to Cambridge to see you. I like the game that you gave me. I like to play

7. Ibid.
8. *Ushant*, p. 103.
1. Jane Delano Kempton ("Aunt Jean" in *Ushant*) was Anna Aiken's maternal great-aunt,
with whom C A was later to live for a year in New Bedford.
2. Alfred Claghorn Potter (see Cast of Correspondents).

with it all the time. I have a garden with panseys and four o clocks and sweet peas the sweet peas are not blooming.

[On back of folded sheet:] We are having a nice time at home. I have made a mistake by writing on the wrong side.

The United States is haveing a very bad time about war. Now I will have to stop so good by from your loveing   Conrad Aiken.

2: TO HAROLD TILLINGHAST[h]   Savannah, Ga.
                                                     March 3, 1901

Dear Harold: I am glad to hear that you are better and hope you will soon be well. We are all well here, and Uncle Alfred, and Uncle Will have arrived, and Uncle Alfred and I have great fun looking at my postage stamp album.

I have finished everything in my exams, and led my class in everything. Yesterday I had to climb up a telegraph pole to get the cat which was on the roof. Robert and Kempton held out a sheet and I dropped her in it, but Robert let go when he saw the cat coming as he thought it would land on his head, and the poor thing landed on the ground, but on his feet. Lately they have been digging up some of the old vaults in the old cemetery for the body of General Greene, but without success.[1]   Yours truly   Conrad Potter Aiken
P.S. We expect Cousin Julia tomorrow afternoon.[2]   C P Aiken

3: TO EMILY FORD AKIN[h]   Middlesex School
                                                 Concord, Mass.
                                                 Feb. 6, 1904

Dear Grandma;   —This morning when I got up it was snowing quite hard, but now it is almost raining. I wont stand anywhere

1. In fact, the search for the body of General Nathanael Greene, the Revolutionary War hero, in the old cemetery which the Aiken house faced, was made on the afternoon of March 1 at the very time the Aiken funeral cortege was forming—with a full view of diggers "tossing up the grewsome fragments of human frames." The *Savannah Morning News* (March 2) described "a ghastly feature of the effort to find the remains" in a lead column next to one describing the Aiken interment: "Before the procession had started for the interment of the murdered wife and the unfortunate suicide, the pick and shovel [across the street] began their work." Every moment of these days was sharp in C A's memory. But his letter permits mention only of another act of courage on his part and of another leading event in the news.
2. Miss Julia Delano, who, upon arrival in Savannah, conveyed the offer of Frederick Winslow Taylor (married to Anna Aiken's cousin, Lou Spooner) to adopt the three younger children.

nearly as high in my class this term as I did last, for my fourth french is pretty hard, and today, in Latin Composition I probably failed. Caesar is going quite nicely.

My story for the Anvil was not accepted [1]; but I hardly expected that it would be. Robert Wallace and I have built a little sort of cabin in the woods, chiefly composed of snow. All the club fellows are going home this afternoon, except Alfred de Forest and I,[2] so there will be no meeting.

About a week ago I had a little indigestion, but it was nothing at all compared with the attacks I had last year.

Tonight I am going to a candy-pull at Mrs. Chase's, and will probably have a very good time.

I am feeling rather down-hearted today; I am studying hard all the time these days, but french and Latin Comp. are pulling me down. However I probably won't drop more than three places. Otherwise I am feeling very well, and am gaining wait still;   Your loving grandson   Conrad P. Aiken (9:45 a.m.)

1. C A had already published a story ("The Making of the Trail," January 1904) in *The Anvil,* the school magazine; in his second year he became editor and by November 1905 had published five more stories and eighteen poems.
2. Alfred V. deForest (1888–1945; "Avvy" in *Ushant*) after Middlesex graduated from M.I.T. and later joined its faculty. An expert yachtsman, he taught C A to sail.

Letter 4: August 1908

C A entered Harvard in 1907. The work and gaiety of undergraduate life absorbed him gradually. By the end of the year he had met Tom Eliot, two years above him and also shy. C A's earliest memory of Tom was of "a singularly attractive, tall, and rather dapper young man, with a somewhat Lamian smile, who came reeling out of the door of the Lampoon, where a punch was loudly in progress, and catching sight of me, threw his arms around me. 'And that,' our friend Harry Wehle said, 'if Tom remembers it tomorrow, will cause him to suffer agonies of shyness.'" Tom convinced C A "about the necessity, if one was shy, of disciplining oneself, lest one miss certain varieties of experience which one did not naturally 'take' to." These included dances, parties, initiations, punches, meetings of the Signet ("a club with vaguely literary pretensions"), and editorial meetings of The Advocate.[1] *But what drew C A and Eliot into a fast friendship was their shared passion for writing poetry.*

Poets and poetry also drew Conrad, at eighteen, his freshman year done, on his first blue voyage to England, sailing steerage from Quebec with his classmate Ernest Oberholzer. "Naturally one would have *to go to England. . . . If Hawthorne saw to it that one took ship for Liverpool, Wordsworth and De Quincey insisted on one's going north to Coniston, Hawkshead, and Grasmere, and Burns that one press on to Dumfries and Ayr." As a "young American from Harvard, he rode his bicycle (with a loaf of bread strapped in a hat on the carrier) by day, or climbed mountains, or swam in the lake, and read Shakespere over his pint of half-and-half in the evening" and after two weeks in England sent a long letter to Mrs. Benjamin Anthony, whose husband published the New Bedford* Standard. *The first piece of C A's work to be publicly printed, the letter appeared in* The Sunday Standard, *August 16, 1908. The Lake District, this summer and again in 1909, 1911, and 1912, bound C A "more and more deeply and secretly and securely, to*

---

1. I have used an early draft of what became C A's contribution to: "King Bolo and Others," Richard March and M. J. Tambimuttu, eds., *T. S. Eliot: A Symposium from Conrad Aiken and Others* (London, 1948).

that island which he had learned, as a child, was where poets and heroes came from: Ariel's Island." [2]

4: TO MRS. BENJAMIN H. ANTHONY   Keswick, England
                                                                            August 1908

. . . Steerage passengers get the very best part of the boat. We had the run of the bow, and lots and lots of deck space—except when they were painting or washing; and below decks there was a kind of open hall around the hatches where any amount of games and amusements were continually in progress. . . . On the floor beneath this one were simply bunks—stacks and stacks of them, two deep, and "continuous as the stars that shine and twinkle on the milky way!" These were for the unfortunates who applied too late to get staterooms. This place was really quite terrible, and rather like my preconceived idea of the whole steerage. It smelt sea-sicky, was dark, and was full of unwashed humanity. In the middle of the bedlam a Bulgarian, squatting in an upper berth, was shrilling away on a bag-pipe, with stolid face and flying fingers. Around him stood all nations laughing and hooting, or swearing brokenly in English. After listening a little while to this strange music, I got out again.

Apparently the lesser breeds of the steerage were almost all in this hall of devils, below, and our floor was quite "la creme de la creme." From the very outset the people proved remarkably interesting and capable, and for the most part of praiseworthy cleanliness. There was a droll Englishman, whom we promptly dubbed "Sir Drollery," who could tell simple stories and make them absolutely side-splitting. I never heard anything in my life as funny as his comparison of English and American barbershop methods of shaving—a subject which certainly, on the surface, doesn't seem unusually humorous. He had come all the way to Vancouver, where his son is a house painter, and was now going home again, after having paid him a visit. He kept us laughing from Newfoundland to the Jersey. There was a Cockney, with a laughable accent, who was amazingly skillful at telling lies. He had spent the winter on a farm in Manitoba. To hear him talk, one would wonder that he was yet alive, for he had fought with wolves, bears, dysentery, cold, and starvation, hand to hand; and finally had to write to England to get

2. All quotations here are from *Ushant*, pp. 59–63.

money enough to come back. There was a Norwegian who had made his fortune in South Dakota, rising gradually from sheep herder to land owner; a Swede who was a silver mine worker, and aside from always having had misfortunes with his teeth (he opened his mouth) had also been unlucky enough to see his best friend blown to pieces with blasting powder; there was a fine looking, well-to-do Swedish minister, Nordstrom by name, who is endeavoring to unite seven creeds,—with his pretty wife, nineteen years old only, and their baby of seven weeks; there was a Norwegian woman, with fine gray eyes, leaving her husband behind in Sioux City for the summer, to see her home again; in spite of the fact that her only little girl died in April, I never saw a sprightlier individual; a Hindu who was going to get an audience of the king, in an endeavor to regain lands unjustly taken from him, for which he had charters from three Indian kings, dating back a hundred and fifty odd years—he was very tall and dignified, a preacher, and had beautiful soft dark eyes; then there was a Belgian, with his little boy whom we saved from sea-sickness by giving a lemon; a Cockney girl, quite pretty, who confided to Ernest that she would like to marry me, if she weren't already; and two families of "exports," driven out of Canada for stealing coal. These last certainly had a tough time of it. Coming to Canada in the winter, they could find no work. To keep their wives and children warm, they picked up coal in a train yard, and were put in prison for thirty days, family and all. During the thirty days, two of the children died from close confinement. After the thirty days, the others were exported to England. . . .

We have now been in the island almost two weeks. In that time we have come northward from Liverpool, getting along for as little as possible in pounds, shillings, and pence, and passing by all shops with cakes or confectionery therein displayed—for the English are a great people for cakes, tea, and ale. When we come to a river, we find us a secluded nook, and here take a bath, and wash our clothes, spreading the remnants out on the grass to dry; though often cows and sheep wander curiously about us, and the clothes take a good deal longer to dry than we do.

We are now in the lake district—a heavenly place! We have just come to Keswick from Windermere, where we spent a week; and we are both so enchanted with the whole region that I don't know whether we'll ever get out of it. We have circled about and about on our wheels, finding one delightful place after another, valleys, lakes, falls and mountains. We have dreamed dreams on Wordsworth's seat and moved quietly through his "Dove Cottage"; we have spent delicious minutes in the Ruskin Museum at Coniston, a beautiful little mountain village, and have looked with a kind of awe at the slender shaft that commemorates his life, his works, and his death. But I think, on the whole, we care less for these things than for the beauty of the place—and are rather inclined to run away from anything resembling an art gallery, or a Gothic cathedral. We like to see a quaint old village, with up and down cobbled streets and thatched roofs, and a peaceful church with a slanting graveyard; or a fine range of barren mountains, with a fertile valley beneath—cut up by the hedges into many different-hued fields of green, like a great, smooth, green patchwork-quilt; but the modern towns, and the places too inundated with trippers, we instinctively avoid. . . .

We procured a guide, in the shape of a little girl, who brought us here, to a place on the banks of the Greta, a pretty little river that flows through the town. I will try to describe it to you.

By walking along a board deck that overhangs the stream, you reach a row of whitewashed houses that stand like musing cattle, with their feet in the water. Over the deck is a glass roof, letting a pale green light through; and hanging from it, gently swinging, are many fern or moss pots, containing flowers. More flowers are on the benches and window sills—fine healthy red geraniums; a strange flower with beautiful clear yellow blossoms, like clusters of yellow grapes; a frail, delicate-leaved vine, with large purple flowers like violet butterflies with their wings outspread—hanging from the roof and faintly stirred by the breeze; huge green pots of ferns and cedars; and the drooping, crimson bells of the fuschia with their slender red stamens. It is like a garden in Old Japan! Across the Greta, which is a small and shallow, but rapid and lucent stream, are green meadows where children are romping and shouting, and a flock of sheep, with their heads down, browsing. Farther off, in the shadow of some dark trees that wood a hill, are tall swing-frames, with children swooping up and down beneath them. Skylarks are darting about over the water with shrill twitterings; occasionally they hurtle over in the air, and you see the flash of white spots on their backs. A few sea gulls, strayed inland, float silently past, amid a chorus of chirpings from sparrows in the trees that shade the opposite bank. It has rained heavily in the night and the sky is still grey with long clouds that hide even the nearest mountain. One shaggy shoulder of Mt. Skidda may be seen jutting upwards and disappearing in the mist. The horizon is very close, and the world seems very small, but complete. Just below, is a mill dam and a mill, where the water is wrestling. Now, it has begun to rain again, and on the darker, smoother surface of the stream above, the patter of the rain drops is like the flickering of a myriad tiny white moths. The water is already dripping from the eaves; the odor of the flowers is heavy and sweet; and still the little boys across the river are playing cricket and shouting and the sheep continue to browse. This is English placidity!   Conrad Potter Aiken

Letters 5–11: April 1911 to February 1913

In the spring of 1911, as graduation and his public performance as Class Poet drew near, C A resigned from Harvard and fled to Europe. With classmate Tom McCabe, he went first to Naples and then to Rome, where he spent a few tranquil weeks (reflected in his letter to McCouch). But that summer was to become "crucial, pivotal, all-generating, in the shaping of his destiny. . . . The change was in himself, and the roots of it were in that decision of his—to leave, and to come; and to begin, so to speak his own education" in sex and in art: the one leading him to "Irene," a prostitute in London, the other to Martin Armstrong in Florence and to Tom Eliot in Paris. (The outer and inner events of this summer are recounted in Ushant, *pp. 146–94.)*

In the fall he returned to Harvard and met Jessie McDonald, a senior at Radcliffe. They were married on August 25, 1912, at Cap à l'Aigle, Quebec, spent a cold autumn in England, and in December moved south to spend Christmas in Florence. All the while, C A was writing narrative poems, which he fired off to friends and publishers. Most of the poems that C A wrote on his honeymoon in England and Italy were never published and were lost or destroyed by him, but some—after cuttings and revisions—appeared in Earth Triumphant *(September 1914), among them the title poem and "Youth," "Youth Penetrant," and "Laughter." "Leicester Square," about "Irene" and the pavement artist (Letter 8) became "Parasite," published in* The Little Review *(December 1914).*

5: TO GRAYSON P. McCOUCH[h]   Müller's Hotel Bavaria, Rome
                                 Via Alibert—Piazza di Spagna
                                 [April 1911]

Dear Old Bird,   To begin with pleasantly—many thanks for Dame Care![1] I had never read it, naturally, for my knowledge of German literature is negligible. I enjoyed it tremendously; all I have

1. For the voyage McCouch had given C A Sudermann's novel *Dame Care* (*Frau Sorge*, 1887), in the translation of Bertha Overbeck, New York, 1891. It was inscribed "To Conradin in memory of the Monticure," which was a small group at Harvard that met to read works aloud.

to compare with it—and the comparison is true only in the most elemental matters such as Teutonic pathos, homeliness, and sentiment in the best sense—is Immensee,[2] of which I am very fond; and of course this is infinitely stronger and deeper than Immensee. Has Sudermann ever written any poetry? I should think he could. —I suppose it is pardonable to be irritated sometimes at the unplumbed stupidity of that hero! —The few love scenes—how I wished there were more—were simply idyllic; about as impalpable and ethereal as dreams against their sombre background. —Other parts were so depressing that I positively moped! —Blessings on you for the inspiration.

As to next summer,—it was tactless of you to call it a "business"—I think the honors are mine, and I hope the pleasures, too! By all means let us do it. My ideas, vague of course at such long range, were to spend most of the time just lolling around England,—loafing a little in London, walking a little in southern parts, Wales perhaps, or Sussex and Devonshire, or both, and dreaming a little in the Lake country. But I am of course ready to dovetail my plans with yours. Tom says you haven't been much in England,[3] so I entertain hopes that we can make that our battlefield—but France or anywhere else in reason would not break my heart! —At any rate, write me your preferences; and when the times are ripe, and my whereabouts at Class Day less in nubibus we can "make an appointment." The rest will then unfold itself.[4]

Tom and I get along pretty well together, considering we are both rather positivistic and "sot" in our ways—one or two tiffs is the total of bloodshed. I find that he hasn't the faintest understanding of my workin's! Nor have I of his, I reckon: he irritates me with his "sentimental Tommy"[5] and play-acting at times—and I probably do the same for him; but it's good for the young British soldiers. —Write again, and give us an epitome of the news, new and old. Don't let the Monticure die! —Oh, read Hewlett's Little Novels of Italy—and No 5 John Street, by Richard Whiteing. They

2. Theodor Storm's tale (1852), read by C A in the translation of G. P. Upton (Chicago, 1907).
3. Tom McCabe ("Wild Michael" in Ushant) was shortly to be arrested for assaulting a custodian of the Borghese Gallery and concealing a pistol. C A met him again briefly in Florence and in Venice, but differences led them to part, and Tom chose to take the Orient Express eastward when C A went on to Switzerland. A serious quarrel in 1912 ended their friendship.
4. C A remained in Europe, later met McCouch in London, and with Avvy deForest they spent two weeks on the Devon coast.
5. J. M. Barrie's popular character in his novel so titled (1896).

are in Tauchnitz, and both capital in their different ways. The former would do for Monticure—short stories, very pretty—and even the latter, piecemeal; though it really needs personal perusal of care—(loaded unexpectedly with philosophy). We are having warm blue weather after our cold spell, and I am again happy.   Love
C A.

6: TO GRAYSON P. McCOUCH[h]   16 Church Street
                                                 [Cambridge
                                                 Spring 1912]

Dear Old Bird: Don't think, because I've taken so long in answering, that egotistical letters aren't still in demand from the City of Somnambulists: [1] indeed far otherwise, for I enjoyed your last very much. Now go on and cultivate the first person singular habit, it's a good one—for *you*. —I must say, Old Bird, though the *tone* of your letter seemed cheerful enough, it seemed scant in cheerful *material:* this I don't say on my account but yours—for heaven's sake go on a tear occasionally, foster some kind of amusement in the shape of a hobby—in some way manage to hit life's funnybone once in a while! Your daily routine, per description, was as gray as a hospital in December. —All this does not mean that I don't want to *hear* about your daily routine—I do, surely. It's only on such evidence as this that it's possible for one man to project himself into the world of t'other—sententious observation but somewhat true. So let your irregular old pen sputter away, or use a pencil, damn your soul, but write with ever-waxing egotism, and so long as you write will I read, especially when your descriptions are as pungently realistic as those in your last, and such magic names as Chopin and Francis Thompson star the pages. Look at the rhetoric would you. —I've seen the old Sea-Cook [Alfred deForest] several times recently,— just last week he blew in with all sorts of news of Philly, and Elizabeth,[2] likewise, condescended me a letter with some slight gossips in it. I was sorry I couldn't get down during mid-year, but my exams were badly ordered, one the very first day and one the very last. So any jaunt (mere money questions aside) was out of the question.

1. Philadelphia, where in 1911 McCouch had entered the School of Medicine of the University of Pennsylvania.
2. Elizabeth Aiken Taylor, C A's sister, now twenty, also lived with her adopted parents in Philadelphia—close to McCouch's home.

—Avvy is certainly one of the most fascinating souls to talk with in this world. We've dined together twice and had long postprandial chats, which sounded earth and heaven and the human heart. The latter seems to be his strong point: his sympathies, hence what we vaguely term intuitions, are finer than any *woman's,* I think. I sometimes really wonder whether there's anything in such prate— woman's subtle subliminal perceptions etc.,—whether men aren't really—in the individual, of course, not the average—much more delicately tuned than the finest women. —I can point immediately to Myron Williams[3] and Tom Eliot as further evidence among my own acquaintance,—both are extraordinarily quick sensers of mood etc.—quicker infinitely than the average woman. Don't you think so? Perhaps you've been luckier in your experience of the other sex than I have,—If such intuitive analysis as this appeals to you, read some Meredith. Maybe you have got it already behind you. I've just finished The Egoist, Diana, and am now midway in Sandra Belloni. Oh what delicate tortures at times to see yourself turned inside out in a strong glare! You recognize yourself rather unwillingly when you see your deformities so plainly. For analysis of the sentimental impressionable youth who goads himself into believing himself in love, see Sandra. I get many a retrospective writhe, and Tom Mc-Cabe would ditto. (We are gradually welding again.) —Yet I find myself as sentimental as ever after the reading! Sentimentalism is its own life-buoy: give it imagination to feed on and it will thrive mightily. So I turn from Sandra to my simple meditations on Jessie McDonald without a jar. To be sure, there are times when senti-mentalism momentarily loses its serene self-trust and sets up a wail-ing, and surrounds itself with the blues like a squid,—but that is always brief. Given time, and a long enough absence from the girl, and perhaps some slight misunderstandings between Him and Her (possibly quite unperceived by the Her)—and Sentimentalism work-eth wizardry. —In this fashion I am at present keeping a tender thumb on my pulse (resigned at last to the belief that it will in no wise prevent there being a pulse) and hoping thereby to keep the warm realities close under my eyes as an antidote to impalpable dream. When I begin to think I'm passionately in love and in need of immediate hugging, I go and walk with this marvelous child and find that I'm perfectly happy and contented just with her com-

3. A Harvard classmate, Williams later taught at the Phillips Exeter Academy. They met until C A moved to England in 1921.

panionship: my perfervid fancies are all but dissipated before the tangible reality; and at bottom the tangible reality is so infinitely more satisfactory. When I'm with her, I shouldn't dare say that I'm in love with her, though it's a pleasure incomparable, one to which I run like an angel; when I'm away from her, behold, Sentimentalism gives me an image and a philtre, and my dreams are full of the lady, and my work woven with her and I say, I am in love. Then the walk again, and the aforesaid result.

I frequently wonder where the deuce I'm going at this rate: —will anybody here help Kelley? When I start out to see her I say incompletely with an internal murmur: "It's not impossible that if I go to see her in such a pitch of excitement I'll propose to her"; when I see her, and the flesh-and-blood wholesomeness of our play commences, I say "absurd," and absurd it is! A proposal, powerful sexual emotion of any kind around our wise intimate chatter and laughter, would be as queer as moonlight at noon. Like two characters in "Diana," of whom was hoped a match, we are "hopelessly friendly,"—at least very nearly so. (In this modifying appendix Sentimentalism can be detected.) —However, time is a sure hatcher of eggs, and I am developing patience,—or at any rate I am tonight. (You see how I always keep a door open at the back of the house, ready for a hurried escape.) —Enough that the child is lovely and wise and mirthful and a very tuneful companion. I think I should only fall in love with her if someone else started wishing her, or she threatened to go away, or if in any fashion I should be deprived of the pleasure of seeing her. Surely that ain't LOVE! I protest at the notion.

Now you can see how egotistical a letter may be. Profit by it. —Old Bird: the very fact that you liked Encomium[4] so much shows that you aren't happy enough. Read The Shaving of Shagpat please,—it will give you glee-lumbago!   Yrs   C A

7: TO GRAYSON P. McCOUCH[h]   [Cap à l'Aigle, Quebec July 29, 1912]

Dear Old Bird: More news—and devastating news! And before I tell it to you, I must bow and apologize as humbly as is possible for a proud person. Namely: that for various reasons, chiefly that it

4. A narrative poem, later abandoned by C A.

saves Mother [McDonald] a great deal of trouble and worry, Jessie and I have decided to be married down here at Cap à l'Aigle on the 25th of August. We shall then knock around this country (meaning by that a flying trip to Boston) and sail just as previously planned on the 6th of September for Liverpool. This makes it impossible for you to be present at the wedding, and I'm sorrier than I can say. —But you can see *us* just the same. . . . You can . . . await us in England—Liverpool best, and we could have a wild spree perhaps, or even London—or the English Lakes? . . .

Jessie's love comes with mine. She is frightfully eager to see you—so you *must* fix it somehow.   Conrad

8: TO GRAYSON P. McCOUCH[h]   [London
                                               December 1912]

Dear Old Bird   —I'm ashamed of myself for letting so much time dribble by—and that was such a peach of a letter. It came . . . curiously enough on the very evening when Jessie and I were celebrating the Anniversary of our meeting! So we had it, in lieu of cocktails, at dinner. Old Bird, you sound so merry and waggish and wise, so well-fed in body and mind, and so rag-time-musical of heart, that I grin with joy just to think of you. My only regret is that I can't see you. Just the other night I dreamed of reading a poem to you—our old friend suppressed desire, and I defy you to find trace of sex in *that!* —By the way, this letter is to wish you a merry Christmas, and it's going to be shorter than I would like it to be, because I've so damned many. So, *have* a Merry Christmas. —Sometime (I've been meaning to for God knows how long) I'll send you some of my works. I've done a lot. After Modernity, which I told you, I wrote a narrative poem about a pavement artist, 400 lines; ditto about a streetwalker, called Leicester Square—a girl who falls in love with one of her customers, lives with him for a time, then is drawn by circumstances and her conscience to give him up (she had looked forward to really marrying him), 460 lines; ditto about a hack-writer, shy, recluse, laborious, unfriended, lonely as the devil, who goes off on a bust, has a mistress, and falls in love with her only to be forced to leave her through his giving out of cash,—back to the old wife,—called Sanctuary, 400 lines; ditto, called Salvation, about a S. Army preacher and his wife; he, a reformed drunkard, falls in love (despite love for wife Jane) with a society girl doing settlement work, goes half-frantic, is rebuffed by her, and kills her in a black fit of passion, with an idea that he purifies himself by so doing, and frees himself to love Jane thenceforth; is hanged in consequence, Jane is left; 400+ lines; a number of short poems, lyric and philosophic (?), and a long narrative under construction, already over 600 lines,—a burglar is caught by a housemaid, who lets him off on condition that he quits; they fall in love; he quits thieving and whoring, becomes a street-car motorman; they go to Coney Island among other of their courting diversions (long and glorious description of Coney!); maid fired (she gets up late, day after), they are wed, financial troubles, he tries to become partner with an ex-thief (reformed) who kicks him out as a bad lot, is then tempted by a very alluring proposition for tunneling under a street into a jewelry store, does this with an accomplice, unknown to his wife, to be killed by a cave-in which results from the passing of a dray—Her child is born (perhaps with some congenital deformity owing to the father's former loose-living) and the mother becomes a charwoman. A sweet tale. It really is pleasant in the telling—up beyond the marriage where I've now taken it. The burglary scene forms part 1, realistic and rather good (!); part 2, lovemaking and the engagement,—becomes pseudo-poetical in excited moments, with diversions on the theme of love; part 3, scenes of kitchen love-making, *homely* realism; and Coney Island, *bang-whang-whong* realism, nothing whatever left out—smut and all; part 4, marriage, and description of domestic felicity on Staten Island. All these poems except the first two are in the Chaucerian 7-line stanza, those two being 6-line a b a b c c, but same metre. It's a fine narrative form. And all of them are attempts to make poetry of the commonplace and sordid. My idea is to keep an even tone of rough and ready realism in all the subordinate parts of a story, rising to the lyric, or impassioned when the event demands: at such moments permitting myself all the beauty I'm capable of. I allow myself slang, and all blunt, ordinary words that have meanings—do not at all restrict myself to the poetical vocabulary. It's frightfully interesting work, and I'm sure there are possibilities in it. Passages of *poetry* (in the generally accepted sense) gain greatly by their drab setting. I avoid moralizing as much as possible—allow the ethics of each tale to stand by themselves, though I generally make it pretty plain what the author thinks. The English Review refused Leicester

19

Square—they may have taken umbrage at its rather frank description of John and Mary in their nuptial bedroom, which Jessie and I both think rather engaging! Anyway, I *hope* that was the reason. I am now trying a publisher for the whole batch. Pray for them. Martin Armstrong[1] seems to like them, despite adverse disposition of mind, and Mr. Crist, the American composer here,[2] whose tastes are soundly plebeian, calls them MAGNIFICENT! GREAT POETRY! And is profoundly disturbed by them. If he represents the great unwashed, there is hope.

Are you coming abroad next summer? We are on the point of going to Italy—have cut out Spain, because I was in such good mood for work, and wanted to get some done.

I hope there won't be war. If there is, we may have to come scutling home, via Philadelphia (American Line) as War Despondents. Have you ever read Evelyn Innes by Moore? —Jessie has been in bed a week with pleurisy (slight attack) as a result of this drizzling draughty climate and unheated houses. She is up again in time to send you her love.   Yrs. Conradin

9: TO GRAYSON P. McCOUCH[h]   [Florence, Italy
                                                January 1913]

Beloved Old Bird   —Here is a marathon poem, "The Unregenerate Dust," for you to read and pass judgment on in your wisest manner, when you have the spare time to give it. Any changes which seem to you very obviously necessary, please make. And then dont send it back to me, but forward it to the Atlantic, or to the Forum, whichever you think better and when it has been refused in turn by each of these, you can send it back to its papa. . . . Will you be horrified, outraged, disgusted? I should like a full, free and frank criticism, Old Bird—go into details as much as you like—and don't be afraid of hurting my feelings, for I haven't any about it. Though I think perhaps this is the best of the kind that I have done, I am not yet so wedded to this kind that I cant modify it or drop it altogether. So I depend upon you. Read Masefield, Everlasting

---

1. "Chapman" in *Ushant* (see p. 172). C A met him in Florence the previous summer (1911); he became C A's "final course in English," as well as his guide to Italian art and to London itself. Armstrong remained a close friend until C A's divorce from Jessie (1929), whom Armstrong then married.
2. Lucien Bainbridge Crist, who a few years later became C A's neighbor on Cape Cod.

Mercy, Widow in the Bye Street, if you want analogies to judge by. I should like to know your idea as to the use of slang and idiom so freely—Isnt slang at bottom good stuff, the meat of the language instinct? Also, how about the philosophising, aside from your possible disagreement with it: does it retard too much, and does it give the desired feeling that the whole thing is only a string of accidents at best scantly motivated? I have been feeling lately that the power of the individual over his destiny has been absurdly exaggerated. —Tell me *exactly* what effect the poem has upon you at the first reading: to know that, as well as your matured opinion, would be an invaluable help to me.

We are in Florence, at the beginning of our second week. We came down from L[ondon] by easy stages, and are going on to Rome. . . .

Yours on a sunny day in Florence, looking down at the Arno, and up at cypresses on the hills opposite: Conradin

10: TO THE EDITOR OF *POETRY*ᶜ   [Florence, Italy
                                                  January 1913]

I wonder if Poetry is willing to listen for a moment to a benighted outsider—even if he be rude?[1] And whether it will listen tolerantly or cynically? Cynically, I fear; for though I must confess to having seen so far only four numbers, and to being therefore not a perfect judge, it has seemed to me that Poetry is, I wont say mistaking its aim (for that may not alas be true) but, by vehemently advancing one set of views on poetry and vehemently criticizing all others, at any rate missing an opportunity. I mean this: the Editor, or at least the Editor and Mr. Pound, are using Poetry too egotistically, in order to give expression and scope to their own personalities. Instead of at once putting this new magazine on a basis of broad and sympathetic tolerance towards all poetry, in a maternal attitude, without favoritism encouraging each of her children to develop as instinct suggests, the Editor, or the Editor and Mr. Pound, have

1. C A is protesting several statements in *Poetry* (first published in October 1912), particularly Ezra Pound's London report for January 1913, called "Status Rerum," which denied there was any important poetic activity except for Yeats and the—then unknown—"Imagistes." The entire "Georgian" revival, culminating in Harold Monro's publication of *Georgian Poetry 1911–1912* (London, December 1912), was ignored by Pound. Harriet Monroe did not publish C A's letter.

made it propagandist. And propagandism has no place in a magazine of this sort.

It is all very well for Mr. Pound to hold certain convictions: all young men do. I do myself! But that out of those convictions should be shaped a law, and that by these convictions should be established a magazine whose speech is as oracular as though it were the voice of an Academy—there I protest, and I am sure that poetry protests with me. Why must we accept Mr. Pound's views as final? Because his voice is loud and insistent, louder than ours? Or because Poetry was started to obtain a hearing for Pound—and incidentally for poetry? —Really, Mr. Pound becomes at times autocratic, high-handed. He writes good poetry, when he is not too intent upon writing good poetry, for which I am one among many who are grateful. But must we also have his opinions thrust down our throats? Must we agree with him, for instance, that Whitman is the poet most worth imitating, and that *vers libre* or some form evolved from it is the poetic form of the future? Must we share all of Mr. Pound's growing pains with him, pang by pang? And must we believe him when he says with lazy indifference (January number) that there is no new poetry in England at present—worthy of study—and that there are no new poets?

This last has annoyed me not a little. That Mr. Pound, in his self-created position of authority, should so abuse his authority, so deceive his audience! I have been following English poetry very keenly, as it happens, and I feel bound to say (and I hope you will give space to my say) that Mr. Pound has entirely misrepresented the state of things in the English world of letters. He mentions Lascelles Abercrombie,—whose "Emblem of Love" deserves very thoughtful study by all lovers of poetry,—casually, with a vague gesture of his left hand. He has once before sniffed at Masefield, if I remember rightly, and here he does it again. I imagine, because Masefield chose the effete Chaucerian stanza. But has that hindered him from saying his essential and valuable say—or from being something very like a great poet? Has the form not helped him, rather? —And there is no mention of the Pleiad of younger men, John Drinkwater, Walter de la Mare, James Stephens, Gordon Bottomley,—or W. H. Davies, the delightfully naif and refreshing poet of nature. And yet, these names are on many tongues!

In fact, Mr. Pound (stout American that he is) does his best to give the impression that poetry, or anything like a poetic renaissance, is not to be looked for in England (that worn out island); and many readers will accept his opinion, encouraged in their already well-rooted American insularity, when nothing could be farther from the truth. This is the kind of national spirit that courts derision. As a matter of fact, England is teeming with poetry. Every day seems to bring a new man of promise. So marked is this rebirth, that the Poetry Bookshop has published an anthology, "Georgian Poetry," drawn entirely from the works of men who have only made themselves heard within the last two years. And it is safe to say that no American anthology could even approach this volume in excellence—Mr. Pound to the contrary notwithstanding. Has America counterparts for Masefield, Abercrombie, Brooke, Davies, Gibson, de la Mare, Stephens, Drinkwater, that she should be so willing to ignore these men? Yet that is what Mr. Pound asks America to do! . . .

If I seem heated, it is for two reasons: I am an American, and self-styled a poet, and I have thought you were being a little unfair both to America and to poetry. And I have told you what I feel, frankly; though I may have to pay for it one day, when I come to you to be reviewed—with Chaucerian stanzas!   Conrad Aiken

11: TO GRAYSON P. McCOUCH[h]   Rome
                                                [February 1913]

Oh excellent Old Bird,   I had not expected to hear from you for a month or so yet—in fact, I thought you would be just about *getting* the poem now—so I was crazy with joy when your letter put in this morning. I cant tell you how glad I am that you like it in the main, and your remarks are all very illuminating and helpful, as your remarks always are. . . .

Well, I knew you would kick on the philosophy—hear me give vent to a resigned sigh! You never did like my philosophy, curse your soul. You are right in maintaining that it has no place in a narrative poem: I would say that myself if I were reading another man's poem. But for me, it was the philosophy that made the poem worth writing! I mean, mere narrative, for the sake of vividness, or clever imitation of life, mere putting of life on paper, in words, does not justify itself to me any longer. I want to have something more: that mere transcription seems aimless: there is no virtue in just being a pretty good kind of a mirror, because seeing life reflected in

23

little makes the monkey laugh. There ought to be something better than just making the monkey laugh! and that is where my poor philosophy comes in. I have vaguely in mind the composition of a whole cycle of tales, as varied as possible in tone and subject, for the mere purpose of putting forth a very tangible philosophy of life *in terms of life itself*. Well, you cant expect the run of folks to grasp this without being told. Who would look for a strong theory of life in a collection of short stories? Not that mine is as yet a strong theory of life, but give it time. . . .

This time I am sending you a couple: deal with them as with the other, to the Atlantic. The first reminiscent of London, the second a merry criticism of philosophy herself which I only dashed off last night. . . .   Both our loves. Conradin

Letters 12–18: February 1913 to October 1913

T. S. Eliot had also returned to Harvard in the fall of 1911, after his year in Paris. C A had seen "Prufrock" sometime in 1911 (possibly on his August visit with Eliot in Paris, for Eliot dated it July–August 1911)[1] *and thought it the masterpiece of the new "queer modern style of poetry," with which he himself had already experimented in "The Clerk's Journal" in the winter of 1910–11.*[2] *(C A suspected that his uncle, Alfred Potter, provided one model for Alfred Prufrock, as Bostonian Adeleine Moffat provided one for "Portrait of a Lady.") Eliot and C A met regularly for dinner and conversation during the school year 1911–12. C A thought Eliot "somewhat Europeanized" with his malacca cane and the sophisticated primitivism of his Gauguin "Yellow Christ" ("hoisted Jesus" in Letter 12) brought from Paris. C A made a "composite photograph" of Eliot as a "decadent" (Letter 12), partly used in "Parasitics: To Certain Poets," in* Earth Triumphant. *(C A, despite his deep affection for Eliot, made other caricatures: among them the "lamia" of* Preludes for Memnon, *XXXV, and "the minstrel fellow" of* Landscape West of Eden.*) But both were fascinated with "the first 'great' era of the comic strip, of Krazy Kat and Mutt and Jeff and Rube Goldberg's lunacies," and with American slang, an interest that C A said gave rise to Eliot's "series of hilariously naughty parerga which was devoted spasmodically to the singular and sterling character known as King Bolo, not to mention King Bolo's queen . . . a sort of derisive counterpoint to the study of Sanskrit and the treatise on epistemology."*[3]

Eliot remained at Harvard until the summer of 1914. Attracted partly by the promise of renewing their companionship, C A decided to return after his honeymoon to Cambridge. In March 1913 C A and Jessie went from Rome to Sicily; they suspected she was pregnant, and on their immediate return to Rome confirmed it. Home in June, they settled in a flat on Reservoir Street ("28 a

---

1. Lyndall Gordon, *Eliot's Early Years* (New York, 1977), p. 45.
2. *The Clerk's Journal, together with a memoir of Harvard, Dean Briggs and T. S. Eliot written in 1970 and a facsimile of the manuscript with Dean Briggs's comments* (New York, 1971).
3. "King Bolo and Others."

month, seven rooms and bath"), where on October 10, 1913, John Kempton was born. By the spring of 1914 Macmillan had agreed to publish C A's first book of poems.

12: TO T. S. ELIOT[r]   Rome
                                                    23 February, 1913

Dear Tom: If you are still in Cambridge—and if this ever gets to you, there or otherwhere, hail! (As Harold Bell once said to the Sun.) I sit in a rather cold room in Rome, smoking a cigar slightly too strong for one of my complexion, hearkening to the merry clack of the typewriter under my wife's nimble digits, and wonder why I have never obeyed my many inspirations to write to you. —What I most want to know is: Where are you going to be next winter? In Cambridge? As I am thinking of settling there myself, I begin to ponder upon the necessity for wise people to talk to,—of whom Harvard boasts few. —If not in Cambr., where?

I should like to spend a winter in London, but the climate there is too damnable for us. It drove us away to Italy last December. And Italy, on the other hand is no place for a live man: In Italy, no one thinks, not even the philosophers; they dream. —So, we are compelled, it seems, to return to good grey Boston. Unless—is Paris endurable in winter? Is it possible to be kept warm? —Even Italy is full of chills, so we flee tomorrow to Sicily.

What have you been writing—futurist poems? If you have a superfluous copy of the Love Song of J. Alfred Prufrock, any time, here is one who hath an appetite for it. Or anything new. —Pour moi, I have delivered some dozen or less of long narrative poems, realistic, rough, often smutty, occasionally impassioned, dealing always with humble folk. —One, I have written (totally different, I may say) as a caricature of T. S. Eliot Esq.,—O, a most seductively horrible pome—entitled "Decadence."—It is a caricature worthy of Beerbohm. It has you, and your poems (the earlier Lamia kind as well as the later Prufrock variety) and your hoisted Jesus, and all; a complete composite photograph. Tom posed as a decadent! I'm sure it would amuse you, but my last copy has just been sent away to a sister-in-law—. Anyway, it's rather childish.

Write and tell me about yourself, your latest meditations, and how Silk Hat Harry [Wehle] demeans himself,[1] and the others. —In other words, What's the Dope?   Yrs. C A

13: TO GRAYSON P. McCOUCH[h]   Palermo, Sicily
                                                March 5, 1913

Old Bird   —Whenever I lack anything immediate to do, as in the present instance, Jessie having retired to take a post-luncheon nap, I turn my typewriter loose on you with the latest flood of nonsense. By this time you ought to be fairly well tired of it. We are in Palermo, where we have been since last Sunday morning, basking in the most wonderful blaze of sun I ever saw—though it's very necessary, for the weather keeps strangely cool for this time of year—at least, here. We had a devil of a crossing by night from Naples, there was a wind blowing fit to capsize the stadium, and as we had already once put off the trip for premonitions, we started with misgivings. At an unearthly hour, when at last I had conquered the violent motion and was getting rid of turbulent nightmares for a deep and exquisite sleep, there came a roar and a crash and in the pitch dark I was drenched, drowned, suffocated and frozen by a torrent of sea which hit me in the back and poured like a ceaseless cataract out of the bunk above mine! Terrified is not the word. I sprang with unimaginable nimbleness, with the tremulous agility of the mountain goat, out of the very narrow and inaccessible berth on to a handy chair, where I stood like Robinson Crusoe, listening to the sound of many waters which skirled beneath me. I yelled to Jessie to turn on the light, which was beside her berth, and then was revealed to us the awesome sight of six inches of Mediterranean charging to and fro, as the ship rolled, bearing joyfully upon its crest my best brown hat! This, my cane having been handed to her, Jessie fished out—with delightfully sobriety. Meanwhile I had closed the port hole, whence had come the deluge, and we were then baled out by the stewards, who took up a collection of two buckets full, and bore off all our clothes to be dried and ironed. J. had to remain in bed for lack of them, but mine had been on a hook and so out of reach—except my shirt and drawers which I had on,

1. Harry B. Wehle ("Heinrich" in *Ushant*), C A's Harvard classmate and lifelong friend, became Curator of Painting in the Metropolitan Museum, New York. C A called him his first teacher in European art.

27

and wh. by the same token were wet as the sea itself. However I dressed and went up on deck in time to see the sun rise out of the Med. and *that* was nice.

We are going right back to Rome from here, because Jessie seems very tired and not very well, and I should feel easier if we could see a good doctor. . . .

Palermo is the most beautifully situated place I ever clapped eye on—mountains endeavoring to surround a piece of sea,—wonderful blue rugged mountains, some with snowy backs, and the little town rambling along the water, the houses huddled a little like a flock of sheep.   Yrs. with a sun-baked back, C A

14: TO GRAYSON P. McCOUCH[h]   Rome
                                                [March 1913]

READ POEM FIRST

Dear Old Bird   —From this day you are cursed with an affliction such as the mortals must endure, for I am in need of a critic, and you are the man, and I shall continue sending you poems till I am in the grave, and even then I may see fit to visit you in the guise of a fat manuscript from time to time. So, here is another of the things, one that is just hot from the brain, still slimy so to speak.[1] You will be pleased to observe that whatever philosophy lurks in it is expressed not on the author's part but in the person of the protagonist himself—I'm sure that ought to satisfy you. The poem is nevertheless a kind of philosophy as a *whole*—an allegory, if you like, merely a pessimistic remark to the effect that Youth is a glorious affair while it lasts, hit it up, hip hip hooray, it's your night to howl, and then when the shouting is over, well well, you are old and tame, but what does it matter—youth and age are equally useless, life is useless, sorrow and joy are useless, but thank god there are one or two things that can delude you into still thinking that life is beautiful, and above all that usefulness is beautiful—the main delusion of this kind being love. There you are! What virtue this attempt has is in its study of the psychology of youth in going from convention to wildness and from wildness back to convention again, the

1. Enclosed, noted McCouch on C A's letter, was a copy of "Youth"; it was revised and printed in *Earth Triumphant.*

28

transitory atavism taking him back to a very admirable and primitive state of mind, and his falling in love pulling him, alas, back again—I think the subject lends itself better to treatment in poetry than in prose from its singleness and its predominant emotional note—See what you think of it and then tell me with your utmost candor of soul—But dont shirk your work on this account, or hurry yourself uncomfortably because there is all the time in the world, and I dont want to encroach, as I fear I am already doing. Take your ease, Old Bird, eat it crumb by crumb, digest it ditto, and if you are compelled to reject from your bowels the whole thing unassimilated, in its virginal entirety, O lasso! I will spill an ash barrel on my head. Then, when the thing is no longer a torment to you, send it where you have sent the others, despite previous disasters.

Jessie and I are excited and overjoyed and pleasantly worried by the suspicion, which only needs a more complete confirming (the missing of a second period) that we are going to make you a godfather some time towards the end of next October! Isnt it great? I am growing a mustache so as to appear to my child properly parental. As a result of this, we are very seriously considering coming back and settling in Boston in the end of May or beginning of June, so as to be a little nearer our respective families. Hooray, we should thus be sure of seeing you. This is not to be passed on anywhere, needless to say. We are of the opinion that London, the only place where we might stay for the winter here with any patience, would not be too healthy—We shall know definitely in a very little. . . .   Love, Conradin

15: TO T. S. ELIOT[r]   Rome
                                                            [March 1913]

Dear Tom: Cheers for you. Not only that you're going to be in Cambridge next year, which is joyful news, but also that you have shunted Bergson down the hill. I struggled with the man last summer, a little in the original, but chiefly in a cheap and unintelligible compendium, and I was irritated with him. It seemed to me that he was not in contact with life: or if he was, in his first premises, he soon lost it in images of light and sound. And I always wax impatient with these withered little spiders who spin endless subtleties out of their own inner consciousness, merely using the external world as attacking-points, or points of suspension. —It has become one of my slogans that truth is not subtle, but simple: simple enough for the comprehension of animal nature! In other language, I would trust a dog or a waiter for philosophy that was healthy before I would trust a Bergson. —And I am of opinion that all philosophy should start with a study of biology, morphology, and such "literature" as The Origin of Species. From the last in particular would I have philosophy spring.

So you see what a base materialist I still am! Nevertheless, I'm eager to have wisdom from you *in re* these your Buddhistic and Indic mysteries. Did you know a weird ox-like Saxon in Harvard, one Otis McAllister? He used to read my soul to me, by Indic methods, and claimed to have developed his intuitional power by such. He adduced as evidence a line on his right palm which he said this development had put there! And tilting back his chair against my wall he would hold me spell-bound for hours with smooth talk of red, orange, yellow, green, blue, and violet purgatories, beyond which lay the perfect white light. Then you took a rest for 1,000 years (I guess you needed it after these chameleon feats of soul) and grubbed round on earth again, preparatory to another bath of psychic impressionism. It was a very serious business with Otis. I think it must have been his ambition to jump right into violet, first go off. —You will have to go some, as a salesman, to tempt my fastidious soul after that!

You remark with an enviable laconic sang-froid that poetry can do no harm, and summarize excellently my own opinion. At least, poetry justifies itself, pour moi, only in so far as it is philosophic. Mere wanton poetry seems to me both foolish and morbid. Only those emotions are healthy which in some way seek a practical end: emotion *per se* (as A. P. Baker is fond of saying, pronounced purr see) is a bastard thing, bad both for the author and the reader, for with both it is only a substitute for actual experience. It should be banned under the Pure Food and Drugs Act. —But then, for the matter of that, what good does philosophy do? I am interested, *myself,* in seeing life straight, myself in relation with it, but why bother seeing that anyone else should see it? What do I care about the other damn fools? Whether they live or die, mentally or physically, cannot matter. So why *write* a philosophy? Why indeed *study* philosophy? Why not instead study life,—and arrive at one's own conclusions, instead of "balancing libraries upon one's poll"? —To

30

study other men's theories of life, which you know from the outset can't possibly be right—what is it but antiquarianism? . . . But enough for now.   CPA

16: TO GRAYSON P. McCOUCH[h]   [Rome
                                            March 14, 1913]

Wise Ancient Fowl, or Owl   —Your letter and Ruth's came this morning, and with Ruth I am annoyed beyond measure;[1] I should use a stronger word about R. if I didn't like her so much. Now, I have just been waiting for some damned soul to cross their fingers at my poor little pomes and say "Masefield!" at them. For such a person has all the blackness of my wrath been bottling these many months—for I foresaw it from the beginning. And then to have it a womyan, whom I cant abuse to her face! so it has to be you, for agreeing with her to the extent of sending me her letter. Most annoying of all is the sad realization that I shall have a very hard time putting up any kind of defence of myself.

In the first place, I object with all my blood to being termed still "unconsciously imitative," as if I were a kitten who mewed with still unopened eyes. Who is Ruth that she should see more clearly than I? Shall he who composed The Unregenerate Dust with a copy of the Widow in the Bye Street in his left hand (and very glad to have it here) be called *unconsciously* imitative? Damn it, no; I knew perfectly well what I was doing, and I did it with malice prepense. I recognized in Masefield the kind of craftsmanship that was exactly suited to my needs. That I was already travelling on the same road with him you ought to know from the Clerk's Journal, the London Fugue—poor things, but they showed the trend of my wretched unconscious little mind. I wanted to tell stories in verse about the people of the lower orders, and I found in M. considerable valuable information as to the best way of doing it. With M.'s philosophy of life I did not agree, but that did not matter, for I would only borrow from his *method*. Well, that is what I tried to do. It is perfectly true, of course, that in the first two or three tries there is more than M.'s method about them: words, constructions, cadences, are often much as I should likely not have used had M. been unknown to me. But I claim, and unless I can seem right to you I shall be a discour-

1. Ruth McIntyre, the daughter of a physician in Cambridge.

31

aged man, that the resemblance stops there. My attitude towards the life I tell about is, so I see it at any rate, fundamentally different from M.'s. He is a gay optimist, he believes in providence, in God, in fate as a force exterior to our lives; i (for modesty's sake let me spell me with a small letter—this is embarrassing!) am a cheerful pessimist, as Myron [Williams] once called me, and believe in nothing but the blind physical laws of a senseless Nature. With Masefield a tragedy is a tragedy, he is very sentimental about it and is ready to shed a few tears with you when the story is done. On the other hand with me tragedy is only a spectacle, and a rather foolish one—when the story is done I should be very glad to laugh with you about it—no, *at* it. That is why I am so cranky about getting the philosophy in. I am certain at this minute that I have not put *enough* in. In The [Unregenerate] Dust, in Leicester Square, and in fact in all of these earlier ones, but not so much in the case of Youth, which by this time ought to have got to you, I checked the desire to make the philosophy explicit,—with purpose of adding to the completed group of tales a prologue or epilogue in which I should openly laugh at the whole series of tragedies. If that is not different from John then I don't know what is. In other words, I want very much to feel sure that people, in the unimaginable eventuality of my work's being published, will not be accusing me of burking another man's *vision*—if I have done that, or even if folk are going to *think* I have done that, I might better never have written these things at all. I may have imitated his craftsmanship, but I feel sure, pour moi, that my visual centre is my own, and virgin.

That you may understand me better, even, my whole idea is this: to make people see the foolishness of life, and its pettiness and insignificance, by showing them how foolish and little is that manifestation of life which seems to them most wonderful, most terrible, most profound of all,—tragedy; and in order to find tragedy at its best in this day and age I must turn to those parts of society which as yet are least civilized, most emotional, most unrestrained, most *active*,—the lower working classes. —Now Masefield turns to these classes because it is the fashion of the day to sympathize with the downtrodden, to explain them, to apologize for them, to show (as on the stage with monkeys) how extraordinarily human they are. He is a disciple of Christ, if you will. Whereas Aiken, on the other hand, is rather a Nietzschean, with this difference that he does not believe in the development of the human race as the summum bonum, nor very much in anything except that he is alive and that life is beautiful. Masefield is serious as a parson when he gives you the woes of the submerged tenth; but I am all the while enjoying the joke! —Now, nevertheless while I am busy telling one of these stories I am just as much concerned as the next—if I were not, I should be unable to do it. My laughter at the end comes just as much as a surprise to me as to you! because I am just as sentimental as you. Only, my nature seems at this point to become dual, and the instant the emotional side of me is through luxuriating in the passions of life, my mind scatters these passions with a gale of laughter—Could anything then be more totally unlike Masefield? —I dress in M. only to laugh the more harshly: the wolf in sheep's clothing! —He exploits the poor, sentimentally, I use them only because through them (since they are a more living form of life than we) I can better expode life's hollowness. And there you are.

As for Ruth's amateurish fears that I should mistake money-getting literature for true greatness—again, am I yon kitten, whose mouth must be thrust into the saucer because its eyes are still shut? And what is greatness that I should sacrifice my comfort for it? I have long since proved beyond all doubt to myself that art is an abnormal thing, a perversion, an illusion like all the other illusions that make life worth living. For over a year I could write nothing on this very account. If I write now, it is not because I believe in art for art's sake or in any such trash, nor with any desire to achieve perfection of form or to create something that is abstractly beautiful, or clever, or finely worked: none of these things attract me in the least. I write these poems in a spirit of impatient amusement,— they amuse me, but I cannot attach to them honestly any such importance or seriousness as would warrant my taking greater pains with them—or as Ruth says, with a kind of virtuous scorn, working them over once they are done. Why the deuce should I? The philosophy behind them is worth far more to me, as you know. If the poems irritate people, if people see this philosophy, if I could make a few folk temporarily angry with me or unhappy or discontented with their very smug little selves, and art, and christianity—that would afford me lots of fun, much more than to have the poems merely praised or condemned as poems—

Again, the wise Ruth casts shrewd doubts on my maturity. You are beginning to see that I am het up. Who is this Sphinx in the desert of her unwisdom that she should look asphinx on my maturity? It is my private, no, public opinion that youth is more mature than old age, that our youth is the best of us, that youth is the highest utterance of life—in fact, that youth is the very quintessence of life, and that whoever denies the sanity of youth is ipso facto unfit to judge—and of middle-aged mind. I foresee with painful clearness that I shall one day be one of the first to deny the sanity of youth—and I enclose a couple of poems written with this in mind. They ought at least to prove that I know myself better than Ruth knows me.

Old Bird, whom I cherish, all this vehement talk does not mean that I am angry with being criticised—not at all. What I regretted about your own letter, which as usual was a corker, was the very little you said about my poems yourself. I *was* peeved with Ruth, because in her remarks on my stuff, so extremely well meant, I recognized a complete expression of the amused tolerance, the paternal concern, which so many excellent friends of mine have always considered me with. I do hate to be considered a dreaming irresponsible! it seems as if my worthy friends were not going to let me grow up!—or if I am grown up, as I persist strangely in thinking, they will never, never admit it, because only as a kind of absurd child do I fit in with their ideas of what a poet should be. Isnt it distressing! . . .   Love, Conradin

17: TO GRAYSON P. McCOUCH[h]   [Cambridge, Mass.
                                             October 15, 1913]

Beloved Old Bird—   . . . Everything went beautifully. We werent expecting John quite yet, and had no nurse at the time, but happily knew her address and I was able to rout her out at one in the morning. Our next snag was the sudden illness of Doc. Mac, with septic poisoning of some sort, but a doc Goodrich was sent by Mrs. Mac, so by the time John actually came, the next evening at ten-ten, or rather, all the next evening, we were all fixed.

On the whole I think we got off easily. Jessie had only slight pains during the day, and they didnt become acute agony till about eight o'clock; from then on she paraded the floor with me pressing the base of her spine. She took to bed at nine, but was driven to her feet again by the anguish, and we paraded some more at greater speed, finally rousing John to action, at about nine thirty. The actual birth then took place pretty quickly, being all over at ten ten. The after-birth was slow, however, and took nearly an hour; and then she had to be etherized to sew up tears, and that was one hell of an ordeal, believe me! It took just an hour to get her under; for as soon as she was unconscious all her former self-control gave way and she ran through the whole scale of human emotions in her sleep, all the while keeping so rigid that we could do nothing with her. But finally that was over too. It was the most horrible experience of my life, as I continually felt certain she was strangling to death, and had no great confidence in the doctor. The worst of it was that I could do so little, only hold the ether cone. Whereas during the birth I could do a good deal to make her comfortable, pressing her back, bracing her etc. She was extremely brave, in fact did not even groan once, which misled doctor and nurse into thinking John not so imminent as he was.

As for John, he is a small thing, weighing only a trifle over six pounds. They insist that he looks like me, but the resemblance does not go beyond color of eyes and hair, as far as his father can see. He isnt so repulsive as I imagined they were, in fact is rather attractive, and seems to have a well shaped head. Methinks he is not so boiled looking as most. At first he was apparently without the instinct for nursing, but he is now beginning to do nobly in that line, and his hair groweth apace—

We are both fonder of this queer little animal than we thought we would be. When I saw him hauled out of his mother by the nape of his neck, oyster blue, I considered him only fit for the ashcan, a thing misshapen and putrid; but he improves on acquaintance, and is full of most delightful sounds and gestures. Though I must say he is selfish.

Jessie has been fine all along: had a good color and even pulse all through, and felt no after effects, next day. Her only trouble these days is enforced hunger.

Well well. Here we are.

. . . I have been writing again: did the story I told you, the steamer one,[1] with *fair* success, nothing brilliant, and some meditative sonnets,[2] ditto. There is no fulness of life in me at present, but I

1. "Romance," a narrative poem published in *The Poetry Journal* in May 1914 and, revised, in *Earth Triumphant*.
2. These meditative "sonnets" were a series of eighteen-line poems, titled "Earth Tedium" in *Earth Triumphant*.

suppose it will come. Maybe this storm and stress will act as an emotional cathartic.

How goes the routine? Write when the chance comes. And I will write a more general letter later on.

John squealeth for supper.   Conradin

18: TO HAROLD MONRO[u]   Cambridge, Mass.
Oct. 22, 1913

Dear Mr. Monro: At the risk of crossing letters with you I must write you none the less, hoping that you will not yet have completed your survey of my poem, Earth Triumphant. Mr. Martin Armstrong has just sent me your letter to him about it, in which you ask whether I would be willing to make alteration, and whether the poem was in its final form.

I must admit that on first thought I am decidedly opposed in principle to such "alteration to order." Minor changes, however, I should be glad to make,—to alter words possibly offensive, perhaps to omit a few lines that seem superfluous or weak, or to add a line or two where some explanation or preparation is needed. Further than this I think I should not want to go. The poem has been read as it stands to, or by, a number of people, and only one considerable change has been suggested: namely, that I curtail that part of the poem in which the man's grief at seeing things familiar or unfamiliar to his wife is expressed, where there is a certain amount of repetition. I am not sure, however, but what this repetition represents a very natural *recurrence* in the man's mind.

Mr. Armstrong thinks the death of the wife is too abruptly announced. I should be willing to introduce here a few lines indicative of what impends. Though invariably when read aloud this sudden news has failed to shock.

Of course, by suggesting changes in the poem, you put me in rather an awkward position. If I do not submit, I must defend the passages questioned, and inevitably such defence will smack of self-content, or conceit. At the risk of seming to be boasting, therefore, I am compelled to say in defence of the poem as it now stands that it was read and favorably passed upon by Macmillan's reader,—though on purely financial ground it was not accepted for publication. Whether this fact will be of any weight with you I dont know—I can only hope so!

I suppose that the truth of the matter is that no odds by whom suggested I should resist, with an entirely natural pride, all talk of extensive alteration. When we have created something we feel that the thing must be taken as it is, flaw with beauty, and that to change it to accord with another's taste would be a kind of insincerity, or duplicity, a posing for what one is not. We can all find faults in the work of the very greatest: some go so far as to edit these faults away. But I cannot escape the feeling that this is a mistake. This is a theory of egotism as opposed to pure art, and is I suppose unreasonable, like most matters of sentiment. . . . Yours sincerely, Conrad Aiken

Letters 19–38: June 1914 to August 1921

In June 1914, Jessie, pregnant again, joined her family in Canada, while C A went to London with the intention of "deliberately widening one's circle" (see chapter V of Ushant*). Advertising not only himself, he carried a typescript of "Prufrock" and "La Figlia Che Piange," "neither of which was I able to sell." But Ezra Pound served C A "tea, not so exquisitely, among his beautiful Gaudiers," and when at the end of the summer C A sent Eliot to him, Pound "recognized 'Prufrock' instantly, and this was the beginning for Eliot."* [1]

Eliot remained in London, but as war began C A rejoined Jessie and John in Boston. "My only service to my country was in bitterly opposing our entrance into the War at all, and in being the occasion of a decision by General Crowder that poets were usefully employed." Jane Kempton was born December 4, 1917, and by 1919 C A felt compelled "to find a cheaper way of living, two children having begun to strain our modest resources." [2] *He moved his family to the village of South Yarmouth on Cape Cod.*

His removal from the capitals of the "poetry renaissance," Boston and London, underscored the skeptical distance C A had chosen to put between himself and the "coteries." His critical writing since 1912 had centered on defense of a catholic variety of poetic voices and opposition to the doctrinal exclusiveness of groups like the "imagists" and "vorticists."

In his own work he continued to develop the long narrative poem as a symphonic tone poem (on the analogy of Richard Strauss's), where the poetic implications "will not be found in the particular phrase or line . . . but rather, as is true of music, in the totality of emotional and sensory effect, the balancing of episode and episode, mood and mood, overtone and overtone." [3] *Between 1914 and 1921, when he moved his family to England, C A published seven volumes of poetry, almost seventy-five critical articles and reviews, and a volume of selected criticism.* [4]

1. "King Bolo and Others."
2. C A's vita written in 1936 for the *Records of the Harvard Class of 1911.*
3. A "Preface" to *The House of Dust,* which was written in 1917 but never published.
4. Rufus Blanshard, in his edition of C A's *Collected Criticism* (New York and London, 1968) gives a virtually complete checklist of C A's critical writing.

o   o   o

Earth Triumphant and Other Tales in Verse (New York: Macmillan, September 1914).

Turns and Movies and Other Tales in Verse (Boston: Houghton Mifflin, March 1916; London: Constable, October 1916).

The Jig of Forslin: A Symphony (Boston: Four Seas, December 1916; London: Secker, January 1922).

Nocturne of Remembered Spring and Other Peoms (Boston: Four Seas, December 1917; London: Secker, January 1922).

The Charnel Rose; Senlin: A Biography; and Other Poems (Boston: Four Seas, October 1918).

The House of Dust: A Symphony (Boston: Four Seas, September 1920).

Punch: The Immortal Liar, Documents in His History (New York: Knopf, February 1921; London: Secker, October 1921).

Scepticisms: Notes on Contemporary Poetry (New York: Knopf, November 1919).

19: TO GRAYSON P. McCOUCH[h]   [Cambridge, Mass.
                                                June 2, 1914]

Dear Old Bird: . . . Why not be happy? and I think I will be happier if I waste no time in getting to London. There I shall do as much work as I can, and as much selling and self-advertising; in fact, I am hoping to obtain an opportunity of reading some of my works aloud at the Poetry Bookshop Readings, as I am taking letters and already know by correspondence the Prince of the place.   Yrs. ever, Conradin

20: TO GRAYSON P. McCOUCH[r]   Boston
                                                Jan. 15, 1915

Dear Old Bird   —The baby arrived last Monday morning at 8, but died at (or during) birth, owing to the fact that the cord came down in advance of the head, cutting off the circulation.

Jessie has taken it extremely well. She got off, otherwise, more easily than last time, if anything, and is mending very quickly.

When do you come up? I shall be here (I think) till the 20th.   Conradin

It was an excellent *boy.* Looked very like his father.

Cambridge, Mass.
January 17, 1915

Your correspondent, Mr. William D. Goold, will probably find few of the younger generation in letters to sympathize with his dirge for the Immortal Trio, Tennyson, Longfellow, and Whittier. I am not sure, moreover, that we will not find even the more discerning of the older generation aligned against him—Edmund Gosse, for example, and Edward Garnett, to name only two. Has not the former said that the future of English Poetry lies in American slang? Mr. Goold, however, raises an interesting question. Though it is obvious from his few quotations that he has a taste for the sentimental in poetry, ("But oh for the touch of a vanished hand," etc.) and it would, therefore, be very easy to dismiss his contentions as built upon deficient taste, the matter is not so simple as that. Has Mr. Goold read much modern American and English verse? If he has, and if he finds it barren reading (devoid of the sentimental) then he raises a serious issue. For the sentimental, I take it, may be defined as emotion banally expressed: the emotion is true, but the poet trying to convey or suggest it to his hearer lacks the power to give it other than commonplace voice. Mr. Goold, like most readers of poetry, wants to find this emotional element in it, and with justice. It is only, so to speak, by the accident of feeding when young on poets of rather commonplace mind that he cherishes a fondness for the Immortal Trio. But is it not none the less true that he would enjoy reading a poet of the first order? His desire for the emotional would be quite as well satisfied, and this time legitimately, because the emotion would be given a beauty of expression more nearly proportionate to its intensity. . . .

If there is anything that is conspicuous in current American poetry it is the lack of human warmth. Any one who judged us as a nation by our verse might reasonably conclude that, though clever, we were as cold as seaweed. For our magazine verse is, with sincere apologies to Mr. Braithwaite,[1] not worth a fig. All magazine verse may be divided into two classes: The prettified-sugary, artificial, decorative; and the modern, which may or may not be in vers libre, and which seizes in passionate embrace the locomotive, steam-

1. William Stanley Braithwaite had edited the *Anthology of Magazine Verse for 1913* (Cambridge, Mass., 1913).

shovel, and such. Neither sort has anything to say to the Average Man about his own life in his own language. . . .

. . . I am afraid the average man would find cold comfort in Percy MacKaye, George Woodberry, Amy Lowell, Vachel Lindsay, or Edwin Arlington Robinson. One and all they are intellectualists: and that is a serious charge against any poet. The last three have a certain exuberance, to be sure; they are novel, and, to the connoisseur, interesting. But has any of them that emotional power, simplicity, above all, warmth, which will lay hold of what Ford Madox Hueffer calls the peasant intelligence? Are they rooted in normal human nature?

This is not intended as an all-around estimate of the five poets in question. For the moment I am considering them from this one point of view, leaving all other qualities out of consideration entirely. And I have taken these names less absolutely than representatively. What I say about these particular poets could be said just as well about all American poets of today, bar none. It seems to be almost a national characteristic; we are conventional and derivative on the one hand, word-specialists and theorists on the other; but never, no matter whether we are old-fashioned classicists, or Imagists with Ezra Pound, do we feel things profoundly, or if we feel things profoundly then it never occurs to us to say so. . . .   Conrad Aiken

22: TO HARRIET MONROE[c]   Cuttingsville, Vermont
                                            September 4, 1915

Dear Miss Monroe: Your zeal for proving a case has apparently prevented you from reading my articles on Imagism very carefully, and from understanding them very clearly. You have read into them, and quoted from them, some things that are not there, and have seemingly not read at all things which *are* there. For example, you hold me up to scorn for my (imputed) inability to find word magic in any imagist verse—an inability to which I not only have nowhere pleaded guilty but which, moreover, I think I do not labor under. What I did say was that the Imagist *platform,* precisely construed, forbids the use of word magic: in other words, that if the Imagist employs word magic it is in spite of his avowed intentions, rather than because of them. As a matter of fact, I have always felt

41

keenly this quality in the best of Mr. Fletcher's work, and also sometimes in that of Miss Lowell, Mr. Aldington and others.

You also contrive throughout to give the impression that I am enlisted with the powers of conservatism, and cry out against the Imagists merely because they dare to challenge the accepted. This, I beg to state, is not the case. I do not object to radicalism (the return to roots) or to experiment, but on the contrary sympathize with them profoundly. I do however contend, and will always contend, that a mere breaking of bonds does not necessarily constitute originality: that genuine originality is a radicalism which is intelligent, or better still, intuitive. My objection to much of the current Imagism is that it is neither intelligent nor intuitive. I think in one of my articles[1] in the New Republic I made it clear that what I objected to was not newness of form, but formlessness: that many of the would-be radicals destroy, but do not create. It is also perhaps worth pointing out that some of those poets who contain the most amazing acrobatics as regards—shall I say?—method, are, as regards viewpoint and mental horizon, still with the last century.

If proof is needed that I am not so provincial a Victorian as you say, I may add that I was indirectly, and largely, responsible for the publication of Eliot's "Love Song of J. Alfred Prufrock" in your June issue, 1915. That poem was written, if I remember rightly, nearly four years ago, and I had a copy of it from the first; and as Eliot himself was heartlessly indifferent to its fate, it was I who sought publication for it. Four years ago! So you see, if I am suffering from a "culture" of radicalism—and I am sure you did not consider Eliot's poem precisely old-fashioned—I have been suffering from it rather longer than most of the Imagists.   Yours sincerely, Conrad Aiken

23: TO JOHN GOULD FLETCHER[a]   11 Walnut, Boston
                                             [April 1917]

Dear J. G. F.   . . . I had a long article on B[raithwaite], and contemporary poetry in general, in The Dial (Mch 8). I hereby apologize for any offense it might give you—I felt it necessary to qualify my attitude towards you somewhat to avoid any appearance

1. C A is responding to Monroe's editorial in *Poetry* (September 1915) defending imagism against his three attacks in the *New Republic*: "The Place of Imagism" (May 27); "Limits to Imagism" (June 26); "Imagism or Myopia" (July).

of nepotism! Incidentally, I had some good cracks at Untermeyer, Harriet [Monroe], Kilmer, and more mildly at Firkins and Mencken.[1] I think it right to clear the air a bit. If you have not seen it you will be pleased to hear that throughout I accepted as the major group of contemporary poets Frost, yourself, Amy [Lowell], Masters, and Robinson. Next time I shall drop Masters. And after "Merlin" (Robinson's latest—astonishingly Tennysonian and dull) I'm not so sure of him. Nor damn it all, of Monstrous Mistress Amy! —The tone of the article was destructive as regards Braithwaite, and mildly depreciating as regards American poetry in general. I have come to the conclusion that the best way to explode a lot of the current fallacies is to be persuasive, reasonable, temperate, but deadly—to *undermine*. It is far more discouraging to be told that one is a bad poet by a critic who appears serene, intelligent, sensitive, catholic-minded than to be overwhelmed with abuse (as I was, recently, at the hands of John L. Hervey, in Mirror—very amusing, quite in the Quarterly style!) I have sent the Dial also a review of Harriet [Monroe]'s anthology—I hope they'll take it.

On the whole it's been a bad winter for poetry. No one new has appeared, and almost without exception the old ones are falling off. Doesn't it strike you that way? Untermeyer has just got out two books—one his own, the other a translation of Heine—both shockingly bad. I've reviewed them for the Chicago Daily News.[2] —Amy has printed very poor stuff in the magazine latterly. For God's sake, Sir, stick by the Ship! Don't let the war get too deep into your heart—it's corrosive. Take your time, smoke your pipe, be tranquil—this is the dope. This is what I say to myself when discouraged with my latest labor, or disquieted by the shipwrecks of others. If we keep our heads, I think you and I can pull through and still be soundly radical ten years from now.   Yrs. Aiken

24: TO GRAYSON P. McCOUCH[h]   [Boston
                                                 1917]

Dear Old Bird   —How delightful to get a letter from you after so long a time, and with such delightfull news! I couldn't have been

1. Oscar W. Firkins was critic for *The Nation*, Mencken for *The Smart Set:* they "have an embarrassing tenderness for all that is sentimental, politely romantic, formal, ethically correct."
2. *These Times* and *Poems of Heine*, reviewed April 11.

43

more affected if I had heard a voice from among the friendly dead. I feel as if I had walked a long way from the time and place where I last saw you, I know I have changed. I am not sure that I am happier; and consequently to hear from you now, and in such a vein, is very much (to exaggerate a little) like hearing a spring-song in February. How joyful you sound and how glad I am to overhear it! Cécile (as I shall in time write her) is a very lucky girl; and I am eager to know that you are equally lucky. I hope too that you will find it not too difficult to get married very soon—in other words, that the war will not last much longer. —As for your war-work, congratulations,—provided you don't have too much thrust upon you. To be frank, my sympathies are not much in this war (particularly as regards our own entrance) and I am personally determined to avoid a belligerent part in it as long as I can. If I am drafted, I shall go, but under protest. —I suppose I can't hope you'll enjoy it, but at any rate I hope you'll find it fruitful.

I'm glad you liked Forslin at all—I was resigned to a belief that you wouldn't. —It *is* obscene, perhaps,—I think it even, to that extent, bound to be. I know you are quite right when you say that I have done violence to the true dream mechanism: What I aimed at was rather the presentation of a typical cycle of adventures, vicariously experienced, not solely as the individual would achieve them incoherently and abortively by his own imagination, but also, and preponderantly, as they would be supplied to him by society: that is, already worked up and rounded either as works of art, or as the gossip of the smoking-room, or as the smutty story. And to some extent I merely took the sum-total of this idea as an adequate theme for musical development: an excuse for writing a poem! Which might incidentally be true, or throw light.—

Are you expecting to get war-shock work? If so, it ought to be damned interesting as another aspect of this whole Freudian question. To that degree, I envy you your opportunity! Write me again if you get time, Old Bird—and don't write about me. Write about you.   Conradin

25: TO WILLIAM TAUSSIG[ch]   Cuttingsville, Vt.
                                               Aug. 24, 17

Dear Bill: Your solemn leave-taking brings tears to my eyes. How soon do you really expect to go? I hope not before I get back to town: I should like to see you—God knows what I shall do without you, in my financial career. . . .

Why in the name of God do WAR WORK unless or until it is thrust upon you? Breathes there a man with soul so dead? How quaintly gregarious is man: if they start dying in Europe it seems to him deeply improper that they should not be dying in America; he likes even to die in herds—The wise will wash their hands of it, or enter only to interfere. The foolish will take a very sentimental pleasure in washing their hands in blood—vicariously, 3000 miles away—Now, sisters, may I remind you, at this weekly meeting of our little club of Unselfish Workers, that every stitch keeps the lice from a hero's feet? —Etc., etc.—I hope I have persuaded you to stay in Boston.   Yrs. C A

26: TO HARRIET MONROE^c   Cambridge
                                            November 20, 1918

Dear Poetry;   Your editorial in the November issue does me too much honor. It would have been indeed quixotically courageous of me to have asked military exemption on the ground that I was a poet—it would even more, perhaps, have been presumptuous. That I did not do, however. It was not the real point at issue, for I was already in Class II. The question was whether under the Work-or-Fight Law the writing of poetry was to be classed as non-productive—along with billiard-marking, setting up candle-pins, and speculation in theatre-tickets—and whether artists in general would have to change their occupation. I merely submitted that poetry should not be so classed, and that it was not specifically implied in the terms of the law. Was the consequent decision more commercial, perhaps, than idealistic in motive? *Hac itur ad astra!*   Conrad Aiken

27: TO ROBERT N. LINSCOTT^w   S. Y. [South Yarmouth]
                                            Feb. 10/20

Congratulations on the safe arrival of R. Bourne. Helen's description of the arrival of the census-taker at the spot, and at the moment (for all the world as if he had been tipped off that whatever increase in population Winchester might boast would probably be discoverable at 135 Forest St.) was too delicious! I'm almost surprised that she didn't holler after him "Wait a minute! there may be another!" Pardon the levity: I become rather too rudely rural. Well, we had no trains and no mails and no new supplies of meat etc for three days last week, and had a taste of what it might be in a revolution. Rather nice: I submerged myself in Henery's golden bowl, and have now, since I finished it last night, come up shining. It's gorgeous. What a quartette. Not to mention the duet of Assinghams, as captivating as any in vaudeville. The book as a whole doesn't move one as much as the Wings of the Dove: hasn't, I think, the same bloom or whatever you want to call it, a lack traceable to the theme itself, the initial situation, which I cannot help feeling was a little too artfully arranged, as if Henry had said to himself "well, let's take four of the most cerebrally and emotionally complicated and self-conscious and passionately analytical and analytically passionate creatures we can think of, such creatures as Henry Adams might have imagined for his Ethereal Phase of Thought, except that *our* creatures will use the ether only in thinking of and about themselves, not for more general speculations; and let us then complicate the inter-relations of these creatures, who will inevitably be so sensitive to the terms of relation, in a subtlety of manner and obliquity and hopelessness of degree which will make the utmost attainments of the Borgias or Cenci look like a game of Jenkins Up on Beacon Street. Then we will listen to their exquisite tickings and strugglings."

Well, he gets away with it, all right, but ultimately it has a little the air of a magnificent tour de force, and although one entirely surrenders to Henry's baton *during* the symphony, one suspects that one's gullibility has been trifled with. This is a feeling that one does not at all have after the Wings of the Dove, which has its roots so much more deeply in probability, and which in spite of all its arabesques of analysis remains supremely lyrical. The Golden Bowl is almost never lyrical—perhaps was not intended to be—and since its beauty is rather that of scrutiny than of vision, its final quality seems to me to be power rather than magic, the reverse of the case of the Dove (though lord knows that was powerful!).

Of course I am speaking relatively: the Golden Bowl, compared to anything not by Henry, or not by George the Moore, is brimfull enough of beauty! Quite as colossal a thing as The Awkward Age or Wings, and in the same incomparable vein of what one might call *absolute* fiction, fiction raised several planes toward the plane of pure music. My god how frantic he makes one to know what's going on between the Prince and Charlotte during the 2nd volume! what's going on in Charlotte's poor anguished brain! I wonder whether he might have given us more of that without hurting his pattern or lowering the tension? I'm inclined to think he should, and that he has not *quite* seen the whole beauty of his own Galatea. A part of his opinion of the Ring and the Book might be turned against the golden bowl.

Luis Untermeyer writes me that Burt [Burton Rascoe] has walloped my Scepticisms in the Tribulation [*New York Tribune*]: if you have a copy I'd appreciate seeing it. I've written Burt for it, but I daresay he doesn't intend to send it to me. How delicious are the *expected* surprises of life. . . .

Festus—ah, poor Festus. I read him to Lucien [Crist], and Lucien's comment was—"Forslin is a masterpiece." —Festus is at present planting birches on clouds, and looking down at the sky through rocks. He has escaped from Buddha, Confucius, Christ, and Mephistopheles. But I foresee little freedom or comfort for the poor devil. . . .   Yrs. C A

28: TO ROBERT N. LINSCOTT[w]   [South Yarmouth, Mass.]
March 25/20

Dear Bob—   . . . . Thanks for the rose to pin on Senlin's breast—Festus is now engaged in a sluggish dialogue with his *alter ego:* à propos of God, epistemology, sea-pools, the laws of gravitation, crabs, and the remarkable instability of the universe. . . . The Eternal Feminine intrigued him for a moment, and he awoke finding himself with a stone in his hand. Heavenly sounds will presently be heard arising from the solitude of the Festus-Forest,—it is the music played by the Orchestra of Butchers. They have their aprons on, which are daubed with blood. On this harsh note of cymbalism Festus will begin to introvert, returning mentally into his past.

My lilacs are budding, Jake has brought his cat back, and Joy;[1] and Lucien is painting his kitchen grey and mushroom pink. When I look at it I feel like an all-day sucker.   C A

1. George B. Wilbur and his wife Joy (see Cast of Correspondents).

S. Yarmouth
April 14/20

. . . I am sending you Festus, with serious misgivings, for I have
just read the whole thing through for the first time and, as usual,
find myself wretchedly incapable of forming any sort of estimate of
it. For the first two hours after reading it I was unable to smoke a
pipe, for the reason that my chin was resting on the ground. Passages that I recollected as crystals of flawless beauty appeared to me
more spotted with rot than ancient banana-skins. I experienced a
desire to kick Festus in the tail. But no doubt a large part of my dis-
taste is the usual reaction, somewhat intensified owing to the un-
precedentedly long time it has taken me to write the thing, fifteen
months of suspended animation, a period long enough to have reduced Festus to the camembert condition of M. Valdemar. My specific perceptions I for the present conceal from you, so as not to
blur the tabula rasa of your mind. One thing I *will* say, though it
would in any case be perfectly plain to you, and that is that Festus
is of course my thus-far maximum development of the method of
implication. It might be regarded as little more than a spicy wind. I
should hesitate to carry the theory any farther, and I even wonder
whether it has safely been carried so far. It may well be the reductio
ad absurdum.

Let me have it back in two or three days if you can: Louis Untermeyer comes down next Thursday and has asked me to have it
ready for him. He's looking for material for his anthology. His visit
ought to be a diverting 24 hours.   Yrs. C A

S. Yarmouth
April 23/20

Who says you can't write? Festus is justified if only by having
roused vesuvius to this extraordinary outburst of purple and gold
lava, mixed with volcanic rocks—George [Moore] himself looks
kind of lame and grey by contrast. And Festus, where is he? buried,
with S. Yarmouth, under a mountain of saffron crocuses, and only
one visible moving thing, the taile of Festus, which feebly wags.
Well, then, I am astonished by many things. First, that you should
so like Part I, second that you should so little like Part II, third that
you "don't get" Part III, fourth that you don't find (or perhaps you

do) Part IV actually weak and bad. And to have your opinion so remarkably like and unlike the opinion of Louis, who has just left. . . .

why the hell do you want the 2nd part deleted? Festus must, after all, have his crack at temporal power, try the imperial gesture; must learn its futility and ephemerality. Part II contributes this phase of his experience. Good, bad, brilliant or dull, in tone with the rest or out of it, it is essential. As a matter of strict fact it is, I think, a little of all these things. Some of it I like and some of it I don't. Part III I am very fond of. The fourth movement of it is one of the best, I think, in the symphony. Is it obscure? alas, I fear it is; perhaps a subtitle will help it. Part IV is the one I sickly distrust. I shall try to rewrite it a little, or, that failing, I'll drop out some of it: though, for its treatment of the "problem of knowledge" (epistemology), i.e., the degree to which knowledge is conditioned almost to the point of valuelessness by the limitations of the knower, it certainly has its place in the poem.

I am prone to agree with you—as I said before—that Festus as a whole pushed the theory of implication and "absolute" poetry to or beyond the limit. . . .

Fletcher writes Louis that "all his poetry theories have been scrapped by the Peace Conference"! —And Burton [Rascoe] lifts his head again?   C A

31: TO ROBERT N. LINSCOTT^w   14 Greenwich Village Ave.
S. Yarmouth Mass.
[1920]

Dear Bob: The roots were prodigious. They arrived on a rainy day, so we immediately dug up our peas, which were at last on the point of rendering us a tributary pod or two, and thrust the roots at random into the earth, thus being spared the necessity of watering. Mosquitos were on hand to superintend the proceedings. After two days, the whole display looks singularly dead; but I have faith in them, as in my lord and master, Jesus, that they will in due season rise again. If they don't may the ghosts of those tender pea-pods make your nights a hooror. . . .

Peggy Baird, now Mrs. Malcolm Cowley, has invited herself to stay with us, and is here, dutch cut, morals and all. John Coffey and

Max Bodenheim and Mrs. Bod., and one Louise Bogan . . . who has her infant (the offspring of a lawful wedlock now in process of dissolution) have all blown in in the last 24 hours, rolling in money, and have hired a house not far away.[1] Lucien [Crist] beside himself and threatens to invoke the law against John, and for that matter may already have done so; in which case we are all in for ruined reputations. Jessie is frantic, and as for me I don't know what in hell to do. If John, restored once more to the familiar environment of the prisoner's bar, mentions his friends the Aikens, O Boy! Liberia for us.

Meanwhile Bob Sanborn[2] is going around N.Y. telling everybody he meets that I spend my entire life going around to movies in search of young ladies to hold hands with—that this is the secret of my existence! My god what a world it is.

Julius[3] says that you are both considering the 12th as the occasion of a jaunt to these parts. . . . Greenwich Village will, I imagine, unless Lucien has his way, still be here. Some town, South Yarmouth.   Yrs. C A

32: TO JESSIE McDONALD AIKEN[r]   37 Great Ormond Street
[London]
June 10, 1920

Sweet Kittikins: Just as I was beginning to despair your two letters came on successive days and greatly cheered me up. How delightful that the family has come, or started coming, and that you have a prospect of freedom at last for a visit or two. Do have a good time. And give my love to everybody you see. Today it is really raining for the first time since I landed, a persistent english

1. John Coffey's transient household—as well as his own life at this time in South Yarmouth—was transmuted by C A into the novel *Conversation*, written in 1939. Coffey, a well-known thief who stole furs from department stores, wrote C A in 1940: "You did a fine job in *Conversation*. . . . I was glad to have your description of me . . . although I felt somewhat chagrined by your repetition of Bodenheim's rationalization that I stole from a desire to support 'genius' like his, as a kind of Robin Hood esthete. My main aim at the time was to make myself more articulate; that was why I consorted with you litterateurs. . . . I stole to finance my education . . . I wasn't naively unaware that Bodenheim was acting as parasitically toward me as I was acting toward the department stores. . . . Less larcenously yours, John Coffey." Compare Letter 63.
2. Robert Alden Sanborn, well-known poet of the period, appearing in, for example, *Others* and *Little Review*.
3. Julius Clark ("Jules" in *Ushant*), a music critic and reporter for the Boston *Transcript*, was C A's guide to symphonic music.

feathery rain which soaks one's trousers in no time. Happily I foresaw the chance of it and took my beautiful new Burberry instead of borrowing a stick from Martin [Armstrong] when I set out for my morning's adventures: and the moment before it really started to pour I found myself in Leicester Square, close to the Leicester Galleries, to which I was bound, and darted in to spend an hour over the Pissarro exhibition, which was very nice: paintings, drawings and etchings. There were about six things which really delighted me, though my feeling is that Pissarro while charming is not great. Having done these, I had lunch with Tom (picked him up at Lloyd's bank) and discussed with him the advisability of spending the winter here, and kindred topics. I get along very nicely with him. Our discussions are grave, tinged here and there with just a glint of guarded humor. Quite unlike the often extravagantly foolish and irresponsible talks I have with Martin.

This finished, I am here, by bus up Holborn and over the viaduct. A pint of "bitter" is warming me (it has been outrageously chilly here for a week) and I start my weekly letter only one day behind schedule. I have the feeling of having been very busy all week without accomplishing much. I have prowled out a good deal, usually in the morning before coffee and in the afternoon after tea, on which occasion I often take the 19 bus to Hyde Park and sit on a penny chair till it's time for Martin to be home from work for dinner. For dinner we have been to Gourmet, Brice, Chantecler; I have also of course been several times to the Boulogne. —I have had two appointments with Brown's agents here,[1] neither of which they have kept, so that I am as far from getting a publisher as ever. Unless I hear from them in a day or so I shall go ahead without them and damn the consequences. It's very annoying. Last Wednesday I went to the Poetry bookshop squash and met [Richard] Aldington, [F.S.] Flint, [John] Freeman, and [John] Cournos, with the latter of whom I had a long talk. We had dinner together last Monday and then went out to see [Jean de] Bosschère,[2] where we found that Max [Bodenheim] had beaten us to it. Bosschère is delightful: looks very like Baudelaire, a trifle gnomish and pale and Napoleonic: long

1. Edmund Brown, whose Four Seas Company in Boston had published four of C A's books, had arranged for C A to meet his London literary agent.
2. Jean de Bosschère, Flemish poet and illustrator, whose volume of poems, *The Closed Door*, translated by F. S. Flint, C A had praised highly in the *Dial* (January 31, 1918): "de Bosschère seems like a maturer and more powerful Eliot."

thin, melancholy mouth, small head and face, eyes far apart like
Jake's, a man about forty-five. He has a very nice calm sense of
humor, talks english brokenly. Dulac, the artist was there, and his
wife and B.'s wife and another Russian and his mistress, and of
course Max and Cournos. The gathering was an awkward one with
little general talk. I did, however, have fifteen minutes of B. to
myself which was delightful: he observed that in my review (which
he saw for the first time six weeks ago, Fletcher showed it to him) I
"guessed" things which not even the french critics had guessed, at
which I was of course pleased! We got along delightfully, and he is
going to ask me round when he gets back from Paris next week,
and present me with all his earlier works. Isn't it nice: or am I
guileless? [Edward J. H.] O'Brien has translated his new book,
which B. isn't very keen on getting out in America. I think I weakened him about it however.

Friday night I called with Martin on Col. Wright[3] and had a nice
pianola concert of Bach and Chopin. Saturday night I went alone to
see Pavlowa's last performance in ballet, and it was heavenly. Sunday I drifted. Tuesday I had lunch with [John Middleton] Murry,
[J.W.N.] Sullivan (athenaeum's science reviewer: we argued
furiously about Henry Adams!) and an artist named Ferguson: I sat
and listened for the most part. Murry has taken, by the way, to Aesthetic Solipsism. Yesterday afternoon I went to the Old Vic, a battered old theatre across the river, to see a revival of old english
dances and music, in the company of the beautiful Miss Ormond.[4]
We were soon bored (the performance was amateurish) and went to
the National gallery, which was great fun. She is simply beautiful to
look at and extraordinarily intelligent and "fine." I was to have had
tea with her last Wednesday, but she called here with a lady named
Claire Mackail (granddaughter of Burne-Jones) to ask me to meet
her and go to a concert, which I did. This also we left early, while
we were still enjoying it, and then went to Cheyne walk, where she
lives, for tea. Mrs. Ormond is very charming. And the house, and
the view from it of the river are delicious. I have written four poems

3. Lt. Col. W. F. Wright ("the Noble Lord" in *Ushant*) was secretary to Keir Hardie, Labour
party leader in the House of Commons.
4. C A had just met Reine Ormond, the niece of John Singer Sargent, on their voyage to England; he was to meet her again on shipboard a year later. Reine and these meetings in 1920
and 1921 were the seed for Cynthia and the plot of *Blue Voyage*, written between 1922 and
1927 (see C A to Robert N. Linscott, Letters 40, 51, 60).

about the lady, from which one might almost suppose that I am in love with her! Isn't it shocking to behold. I do like her extravagantly, nevertheless, and hope to see her a good deal, if it can be done without my appearing to persecute her. She has an enormous acquaintance, and I have to be fitted in, I imagine, rather like a disagreeable duty.

I haven't seen the Old Bird again. Cecile had to have another operation and is still at hospital, and I am planning dinner with the Old Bird some time in the course of the next few days. Isn't it rotten luck. Our house-hunting expedition to Oxford has had to be postponed. But it will come.

How *do* you feel about the winter here? I consider quite seriously Oxford, London, and Rye. In London I think it would be possible to get a furnished apartment of five or six rooms for about four pounds a week, which with the exchange means sixteen dollars: we could manage it. We could get one, I think, near Hyde Park or in Chelsea not far from Battersea park and the Walk, either of which would give the children a chance for outings. Food is perfectly good, and rather cheaper than ours, except for fruits; help is rather scarce, but also much cheaper than ours; clothes are cheaper by a long shot. I am getting the best of serge suits for £8.10. Rye I haven't looked at yet, but Cournos and Martin both swear it is lovely; it is where Henry [James] lived. The Old Bird says that Oxford is a veritable lotus land. I must say I am very much tempted! Shall we try it out for a year, planning to spend the next fall and winter in S. Yarmouth? Would you like to plan to come over in September? Think it over carefully. My own mind is extremely uncertain: I am just powerfully, somewhat terrifiedly, tempted, that's all.

Perhaps the Wilburs and Crists are tempted also? Tell them that as far as living is concerned it's o.k. Perfectly calm and settled, no Bolshevism. Of Lucien's chances for work I have already written. Consult with them about the whole business and let me know what you think. I can come back, of course, though I think I might have a kind of cracking of the heart. Cournos says he will be willing to come back a year from now to try out America. Tom Eliot is here for life. I don't know how well I could work here, but it might be just worth trying. Even if it failed it might have been worth doing.

Did any of the fruit trees blossom, and how many of the lilacs did, and have they grown perceptibly, and how did the grass do at the back of the yard? I wish to god the atlantic could be crossed in five minutes.

Be deliberate about this business: do what you *like*. My own taste is as I say very uncertain and I am not sure that it is reliable. I would much rather be dictated to, and have it settled by you.

Give my love to Jonikins and Winks [John and Jane]! Tell them there is a school next door where a lot of little girls sing the Three Blind Mice.   By By! Conrad

33: TO JOHN FREEMAN^r   37 Gt. Ormond Street
                                                   [London]
                                                   Aug. 19/20

Dear Freeman: Forgive my characteristically American use of the typewriter: my handwriting is, if anything, even more indecipherable than yours. I was delighted to get your note. After several readings I believe I can say that I have translated every word of it! What you say about the House of Dust interests me extremely, both in itself and because it in one way is so much what I should expect. Do you remember at tea the other day our discussion of the relations of contemporary American and English poetry to the English poetic "tradition"? I remarked then, with secret misgivings, such as one has always in mid-flight of even the most plausible supposition, that it seemed to me that American poetry is not so "close" to the English tradition. For the moment I am not speaking so much of form as of tone. And I think I see—perhaps wrongly?—a sort of confirmation of this in the fact that of the episodes you have read you should like the Tokkei movement best. That movement, of course, not only is more formal, it is also much more in the traditional poetic "key": I won't be so presumptuous as to say that it sings, but it does have inevitably somewhat that air simply because the voices which come before and after it are so conspicuously voices which merely "talk." The tone of the poem in general is, indeed, colloquially realistic or "psycho-realistic"; only by implication and in overtones is the wretched reader given, here and there, the specifically "poetic" key. And it is this fact which will I fancy, most put off the English reader—perhaps, for that matter, the American too. I shall be interested to know, when you have finished the poem, if you ever do!—whether it still remains for you a mere series of episodes or whether it then falls together in your mind as one picture. . . .

Lyme Regis sounds charming. It whets anew my appetite for my own small village—which has, however, no hills; merely pine woods, salt marshes, tidal river, sand and sea. And half a dozen people.   yrs. Conrad Aiken

34: TO T. S. ELIOT[r]   37 Gt. Ormond Street, London
                                         [August 1920]

Dear Tom: Our notes appear to have crossed: I add to mine, therefore, this postscript.

My address is simply South Yarmouth Cape Cod Mass. Let us indeed attempt to write oftener.

I am sorry myself, in some respects, that I could not arrange to be in England this winter. It would have been pleasant. But on the whole I go unreluctantly back to the Cape, thankful for the prospect of clear skies, and of minds and manners as candid. I cannot work here. I find your adopted people unexpectedly stifling and sterile. It is a nation of "shut-in personalities." Taken as merely a kind of game, I find the effort to get at them, to conquer them, highly entertaining; but one is content with little of that, there are more important things, and one's energies are no longer unlimited. The literary crowd here, frankly, I dislike. I prefer the hearty simplicities of the Mercury to the supercilious and somewhat dishonest academicism of the Athenaeum. I come more sharply to the opinion that in the long run the former will prove more fruitful, though I can agree that the latter will also have served a purpose.

Whether I shall return next year or not I cannot now say. All I can say is that it is possible.

Let me know your new address when you move.   Yrs. Conrad

35: TO JOHN FREEMAN[r]   S. Yarmouth Mass U.S.A.
                                         Sept. 28/20

Dear Freeman: . . . I'm glad you liked the House of Dust better as you proceeded through it. But how your query as to its precise aim frightens me! Really, though it may appall you to have me confess it, I'm not sure that I can identify its precise aim. Of course you will have seen from a comparison of Senlin and the Charnel Rose and Forslin with the House of Dust that for some time this method, which I have arbitrarily called symphonic, has had an almost compulsory fascination for me. Did I, in the case of the House, choose the theme because it seemed so admirably to lend itself to that sort of method, or did I select the method because it seemed best suited to a theme which greatly attracted me? I rather think—and this will perhaps throw a light for you—that from the outset I regarded method and theme as ambivalent; as cooperating in the production (should I be fortunate) of a kind of absolute music, a music not so much intended to convey any single dominant idea or theme as to be, in itself, a small sort of world in which, inevitably, ideas are implicit. This, you will see, leaves the reader some latitude for "seeing" in the poem what he will: and you, for example, astonish me not a little by seeing in it a kind of moral. I do not mean, naturally, that the poem has not a general theme— "crowd" or "city." Nor do I mean to imply that the development of this theme has been wholly random. There *is* a sort of arrangement about it, a roughly orderly progression from the crowd to the individual, and again from the individual superficially seen (as a mere atom in the crowd) to the individual seen intimately, subjectively, at a moment when his consciousness is sharply focussed by an emotional crisis. There is, again, a gradation in degree of consciousness: it is lowest in Part I, in which the individual is given no identity save that which he has as part of a moving crowd, it is highest in Part IV, reaching a climax in the third movement of Part IV, "Palimpsest," in which the individual attempts to grasp consciousness itself. And in general I might add that, throughout, individual and crowd are used as contrasting themes with which one might play a species of counterpoint. —Does all this seem lamentably vague to you? Does the whole "aim" of the poem appear to you to be one which is perhaps not quite legitimate, or at any rate not satisfactorily to be compassed, in poetry? I shall be interested to hear. —What you say about the monotony of those parts in which feminine endings are too freely employed is, I think, quite just. I suppose I felt that a certain recurring unity of "tone" was essential in a work which was inevitably to be, in other respects, heterogeneous and episodic. I say "I suppose" because one is so seldom sure of having precisely weighed and calculated this sort of thing in advance: One does it subconsciously. Yet I agree with you wholly as to the resultant monotony, and have always feared for it. . . .   Yrs. Conrad Aiken

36: TO JOHN FREEMAN[r]   South Yarmouth
                                                        Massachusetts
                                                        March 2/21

Dear Freeman: It is very amusing, and a little disconcerting, in the light of my remarks on "loading every rift with ore," that in two recent reviews of the House of Dust, in the Dial and New Republic, I am attacked precisely for doing too much of it. Both reviewers assure me that I anaesthetized them with too insistently rich a "rhythm" or "harmony" or what not. I give it up! Of course, I don't for a moment agree with them! But there we are. Both critics share with a great number of my countrymen an insatiable appetite for the tone of the "actual." This appetite comes of the application, in the domain of poetry, of that theory of the "slice of life" which dominated so much fiction at the end of the nineteenth century. Certainly it is hard enough, in poetry, to achieve the tone of the actual and at the same time obtain any of what the aestheticians term "psychic distance": what is colloquial in fact must be also colloquial in tone if it is not to be false. The artist should find, I suppose, the maximum "height" of tone which his particular "actual" will stand, and there lies the difficulty. Browning steers as close to the actual as W. W. Gibson, yet keeps under his keel a greater and clearer depth. The dramatic poet has in this respect an advantage over the merely narrative poet. Most of our critics here want the actual at all costs, and resent any attempt at magnification of the actual by selection or elaboration: they would prefer Chekhov to Turgenev, Dreiser to Henry James. I stand, I fancy, half way between them and you, and tend, as I get older, to walk eastward.

I am delighted to hear that you are at work on a book on Moore. You asked me in your previous letter whether I was a Moore enthusiast—I am! I send you a brash review of Avowals which I wrote two years ago for the Chicago Daily News,—written "down" somewhat, therefore, and here and there written foolishly, but it will let you know how I feel about G.M. Only day before yesterday I acquired, at a frightful expense, the new edition of Memoirs of My

Dead Life (the new American edition is, I believe, more complete than any other). When I think of English criticism I think of Moore's Avowals and Henry James's Notes on Novelists, and I really don't know which I would more reluctantly surrender: and in fiction I should be equally torn between The Brook Kerith and The Golden Bowl, between Esther Waters and The Wings of the Dove. —Do let me have an early copy of your book so that I may review it for the Freeman? . . .   Yrs. Conrad Aiken

37: TO AMY LOWELL[u]   South Yarmouth Mass
                                                     August 3/21

My dear Miss Lowell: Well, to be frank, I *was* surprised, and perhaps still am; but my surprise isn't a half of my delight. It is extraordinarily generous of you to like Punch and to write and tell me so—it is you, now, who quite "bowl *me* over." I should, in any case, value your praise very highly, but I value it all the more in *this* case, first because we have so often, professionally, been at swords' points, and second because my own judgment of Punch has been, as it happens, and still is, singularly uncertain and wavering. I won't be so naive as to say that I had *no* faith in it: that would be ridiculous. I had, from the outset, faith in the "idea." But the composition of it was a series of melancholy dissatisfactions, and those dissatisfactions I have never wholly repressed: when, for a moment, I recover from them, and bless the poem as good, it is with the instant wonder whether I am not merely wishing away defects that are only too obvious. I submitted the book to Knopf with misgivings, and told him so, for I was genuinely afraid, as late as that, that the book was "bad." Now that it is out, and that Untermeyer and you and others prefer it so sharply to any of my other books, I begin to smile upon it, I read it with credulous interest, and my vanity begins to put on feathers! You see what you do to me!

What you say about the book in detail interests me very much. I am delighted that you think the characters are sustained (I had much anxiety over that), and that you like the epilogue and the general "arrangements." The latter business, as I wrote Louis Untermeyer only the other day, was the problem of problems: the poem grew slowly and irregularly, and not in its present order. When the parts were complete I found, after much trial and error, the present, and I think on the whole the right, arrangement. The only sections of which the positions were "fixed" were the Two Old Men and the Epilogue. The real question was as to whether the bombast (the illusion, rather) should precede the analysis, or vice versa. In this respect my final order was my first—the first things written were What Punch Told Them and He Conceives His Puppet to be Struggling with a Net (the two chief sections) and after that the poem was put aside for the writing of Senlin and then again taken up and slowly "filled out". I think it will be only honest of me to confess at this point that I myself prefer The House of Dust to Punch, and I think Senlin, and even perhaps Forslin; though I reserve the right to change my mind!

It is very kind of you to offer to review Punch.[1] . . .   Gratefully, Conrad Aiken

38: TO JOHN FREEMAN[r]   S. Yarmouth Mass
                                          August 14/21

Dear Freeman—   . . . Yes, American reviews are fearful things. What enthusiastic stupidities of blame or praise! The N.Y. Post is the best of the newspapers in that regard, the Dial and Freeman and New Republic and Nation the best of the magazines. But we have no good critic, unless we except Van Wyck Brooks. I wish we could have kept Eliot here; and how good for us Santayana might have been. When we procure a critic, like Santayana, capable of diagnosing Browning and Whitman as "barbarians," or capable, like Henry James, of withering at a breath the brightest blooms of Wells and Bennett and the younger novelists, it is only to lose them, alas. —But as you say, England is not much better off. The Times is goodish, but somewhat sclerotic, and certainly none of the Mercury critics is satisfactory: they whet one's appetite for the analytic and the wise but give one little to chew on. Murry would be a good critic if he could pay less attention to his own shadow as it falls across the page he reviews, or perhaps I should say, if he *liked* it less. (He has some appalling moments of this sort in his book on Dostoevsky.) Your one-man idea is a good one, but the really first-rate critic so seldom wants to preoccupy himself solely with the contemporary. It's a vile job, sifting the contemporary!

1. Lowell's review appeared in the *New Republic* (September 28, 1921): "The drama of the man Punch becomes the tragedy of blind, yearning, cheated humanity. The poet rises to his climax inevitably and with a high seriousness new to his work."

It was good of you to make inquiries about rooms for me. I am grateful to you, and apologetic; for it's a hopeless business. I shall simply leave the thing till I get there, if I do get there, and take my chances. Anerley sounds rather nice—I shall give it serious consideration. Two poets in it is perhaps just about right. God deliver me from a *crowd* of poets—nothing could be more dreadful! Boar's Hill makes me shudder, and England itself is rather a Parlement of Foules; I like, in this country, the feeling of hopeless isolation; one is more wretchedly aware here of time and space, and I daresay I make a mistake in taking flight from it, if for only a moment. Unhappy is the American who has visited England—neither country, thereafter, wholly satisfies him.

Did I thank you for your kind remarks on "Punch?" If I did not, I do. . . .   Yours, Conrad Aiken

Letters 39–53: November 1921 to January 1924

That first postwar voyage—solo—to London in 1920, May through August, had been in the interest of investigating where C A might interestingly settle his family to permit an English education for John and Jane, as well as to take advantage of the exchange rate. But, with shock, C A felt himself rebelling against the English literary scene, which in 1914 had seemed about to admit him.

Nevertheless, the path to London and Winchelsea and Rye (where Armstrong had taken him in 1920) seemed unavoidable. In the autumn of 1921 C A moved his family to London. In the late spring of 1922 the Aikens settled in Lookout Cottage, in Winchelsea, Sussex.

> *And the wonderful decade or more was to unravel itself as predestined—in the Arnault bookshop, at Soho restaurants, in the Bloomsbury tea-shops, Lyons or ABC's, and at Inglesee [Winchelsea] and Saltinge [Rye]. A time of blooming, of profusion, of hard work and endless debate; of good food, good drinks, and good living. But a time of competitive stress also, of unceasing literary* sauve-qui-peut. . . . *Which of them would survive? which of them wouldn't? The various cliques formed or fell apart, new coteries rose and fell; but central among them, and in the end omnipotent, was the group that erratically and fluctuatingly arranged itself, or rearranged itself, round the Tsetse's quarterly [The Criterion], and the luncheons and dinners that intermittently celebrated its appearances.* [Ushant, p. 232]

o   o   o

Priapus and the Pool (Cambridge: Dunster House, March 1922, a limited edition of 425 copies).

The Pilgrimage of Festus (New York: Knopf, July 1923; London: Secker, February 1924).

And an anthology to introduce new American poetry to England:

Modern American Poets, Selected by Conrad Aiken (London: Secker, October 1922), also published as *American Poetry 1922: A Miscellany* (New York: Harcourt Brace, 1922).

Notting Hill, London
                                   Nov 9 21

Dear Maurice: I was delighted to hear from you—even in so
melancholy a strain. I think the thing to remember in these situa-
tions, if one has any capacity left for "remembering," is that one
can always escape the worst moment of one's crucifixion by suddenly taking a detached view of the cross, the crucifiers, and the singular pains in one's hands and feet. If one can be amused by the
whole spectacle, so much the better. Laugh, and you will be healed.
Try laughing three times a day. Rock back and forth in the subway
(Harvard Central Kendall Park) observing the extraordinary fish
who sit opposite you: have a vision of all these idiot mouths simultaneously opening to receive food: observe how, as food enters the
mouths, light dies out of the eyes, and after that take seriously any
human affliction if you can. Would you believe it? I have had trials,
crucifixions myself—bewilderments of pain, outrageous dislocations
of the soul, and one of them, not a trifle, since I saw you. But I'm
becoming a very Buddha of callousness—I smile at my navel (I'm
not so fat but what it has to be done in a mirror) and thumb my
nose at heart, soul and pride. Let things go! They were never anything but a nuisance.

     Very little news here. "Punch" is out—a nice looking book Secker
has made of it, too. Forslin and Nocturne follow in January. I've
seen Fletcher, Freeman, Shanks,[1] Bosschere. —We've taken a flat,
and of all the refrigerating plants I've ever lived in, it's the best. My
teeth chatter, my hands are blue, I have to melt the ink drop by
drop to write to you. —I told Shanks to mention the "Journal" to
Virginia Woolf. (It is reported that she goes cuckoo every once in a
while and moos like a cow.) (Woolf, cuckoo, cow!)   Yrs. C A

40: TO ROBERT N. LINSCOTT[w]
                                   c/o Brown Shipley [and Company]
                                   123 Pall Mall London
                                   Dec. 3 21

Dear Bob: . . . Here we are—utterly miserable, fog-enclosed,
sunless, cold, and financially swamped. . . . The children have

---

1. Edward R. B. Shanks, a poet prominent in the "Georgian" movement.

colds, I am ill with indigestion which has the dimensions of pto-maine, we haven't seen the sun for three weeks—and we dont see many people nor get on very well with those we *do* see. The *genial* Fletcher is a lifesaver—him we see and like; his wife is a pleasant large Saxon, very simple and kind, his children—girl, artist, sixteen, pretty, charming; boy, fourteen, very amusing—are imposing. Armstrong also is as delightful as ever. But the English stagger me, paralyze me: facing these strange beings, so cold, so self-composed, so insensitive, so unimaginative, so little magnanimous, so often stupid, so well-informed, and so polite, I gradually lose human shape and become a rabbit small and meek, with a dazed and wist-ful expression and a conviction that I have neither tongue nor brain. I fail utterly with them, that much is clear; and what makes me wretched is that I haven't the vanity, au fond, to assume that the failure is theirs. Is it? God knows! But this much I am certain of: the English have no social gift, do not know how to be agree-able. When I get to see Secker, my publisher, he keeps me standing outside the barrier; never invites me in or to sit down, never himself puts a question or makes a remark of a sort calculated to put me at my ease as a visitor; he smiles constrainedly and to my struggling observations replies "Yes—Yes—Yes" till I turn tail and flee. . . . When this sort of thing occurs, I feel like hurling bombs. Have the English any feelings—or do they hide them on the theory that they are things which no civilized person would confess to? . . . En-gland would be so nice if it was inhabited by Americans! —As it is, I become every day more inclined simply to crawl into my hole and let them all go to the devil, which is really what I've begun to do. . . . "Punch," meanwhile, is sharing the ostracism of his author. It's been out over a month, with no sale and no reviews, save a tiny "note" in the Times which appeared day before yesterday. Other papers haven't even listed it as among books received. And the Times note observes that it's mostly in *rhymed decasyllabics* (there's not one in the book); and in the same issue devotes a column and a half to Freeman's new volume. O grief, frustration, and thoughts of suicide! Why on earth did I come here to begin all over again this abominable and hopeless struggle for *some* sort of recognition! What an idiot I am, what a preposterous biped wearing spectacles and an air of melancholy, a walking lamentation, a grief clad in a union-suit.

Meanwhile, until this last blow in the *Times* knocked the last breath of confidence out of me, I've been taking a shot at short stories and have completed three, commercial in intent, which I shall shortly send to you—begging you to ship them to the Century or what-not. One of them, you will observe, is an absurd extravaganza on the Linscott family. How I enjoyed doing it! If I recover my equanimity I shall go on and try to do enough for a book. Then, possibly, go off the deep end with a novel, or a play.

I have seen *Heartbreak House,* which was excellent, and the Andreyeff thing that came out in the Dial—here called *The Painted Laugh.* It was far finer on the stage than in print: really amazing. —Also I have heard some superb music—notably Scriabin's "Divine Poem," and two things that go far to remove my prejudice against Anglo-Saxon composers—"The Planets" by Holst, and "Norfolk Rhapsody No. 1" by Vaughan Williams; the latter a thing of singular beauty and feeling.

Fletcher lives in luxury in a large delightfully furnished house which backs onto the Crystal Palace Park. I was amazed.

Do you remember Reine Ormond, whom I met on the boat a year ago? Well, she turned up on the boat again, with her mamma and her huge black ruffian of an uncle, John Sargent. I prowled onto the first cabin deck one night early in the voyage. And there she was. But when it was discovered (1) that I was travelling 2nd Class, and sneaking thru into the 1st; and (2) that my family was going to be in London for the winter (and might be a social nuisamce), they proceeded thenceforth to "cut" me! It was frightfully funny; for on the landing-day we of course encountered one another at every turn—in the customs, on the way to the R.R. station, in the station, on the train, in the dining-car (Mrs. Ormond was forced by a lurch of the train to lean an embarrassed hand *on my table* as she walked blandly past!) and in the Euston Station in London. Next day I encountered a friend (who was also *with* Mrs. Ormond) even in Brown Shipleys! and remained grave only with an effort. Really, of all the disgusting bad manners, provincialism, conceit and snobbishness I've ever encountered, this is the worst. Sick transit glory Ormundi! I thought better of the lady than that.

Another light on English manners. They're so damned afraid of the great contaminating world: if one is friendly with them, they consider it an intrusion. Mrs. Ormond is the typical fatuous round-faced smug Beacon streeter raised to the Nth power by transplantation to Cheyne Walk. She draws her own portrait for you by terming G. Moore "an odious person." Isn't that heavenly! Well, it's a delicious comedy. It's a novel sensation and rather titillating, to be cut by one's inferiors.

Tom Eliot has had some sort of nervous breakdown and is at present in Lausanne: hybrid difficulties, I suppose, or else the severe strain of being an Englishman. He'll be back in January and then I hope to see him with interesting results—Reports conflict about Katherine Mansfield—by some she is said to be fatally ill with t.b., in Davos. Isn't that frightful! When idiots can live so long. A sequel to her "prelude" wil probably be in January "Mercury"—Have you seen "Broom"? 1st issue seems to me admirable—I hope you're getting it. Write! Merry Christmas! Regards to the entire regiment.   C A

I ran into Bosschere in the underground the other day—he's made a Chevalier by the Belgians.

41: TO MAURICE FIRUSKI[h]   Notting Hill, London
                                             Dec 31 21

Maurice.   You are much too generous to the poet errant: your letter was pleasure enough to one reduced to hands-and-bones by nostalgia; and your "Hardy" leaves me quite prostrate in debt. Thanks. Thanks! It's lovely and a joy to have. I was delighted that your ways don't appear quite so bass, and are becoming more of an even tenor(!). Did I advise you to sink heart and soul? Good advice! and not difficult to take. All you have to do is wait a little and daily life will sink them for you quite without charge. Part with them without a pang. They are the true *vermiform* appendices, heirs of the original serpent. Besides. I'm not sure that they exist. We have a sensibility, designed, as far as one can tell, chiefly for the feeding of the ego. Keep that well fed, all is well. The fatal thing is to feed it without knowing it or starve it without knowing it. However, I've just drunk so much stout that my ego is egg shaped and my brain liquefied. In other words, I am as I advise you to be—quite happy, pro-tem., and perfectly useless. Evoë! Oi! Oi! Bacchus! Have you heard, speaking of bacchusses (I presume the English would pronounce Backhouse Bacchus) who the bravest man in England is? Viscount Lascelles, who pinched the Queen's little Mary.[1] A good

1. Lascelles, forty, a sportsman and bon vivant, married the Princess Mary, twenty-five, in February 1922. What tale provoked C A's blushes he could not remember.

tale, and one that the English maidens think nothing of telling at tea-time, the only blushes provoked by it being those of Aiken—that little American poet, over there, whose hands are so raw and hairy, and who is so shy that he can't climb out of his tea-cup.

How comes Priapus? Has he gone to press? Are the forms locked? I'm delighted that Rogers likes it—Freeman sinks nearer and nearer the grave, lifting towards me a reproachful eye—his other book, out of which he left The Red Path and The Wounded Bird at my suggestion, is not very well received. Hurry! Speed! Pep, there, in Cambridge! —I have at last a card to George Moore, and am expected there any day—

I've given up poetry, Maurice—"alas, what boots it with incessant care"—The muse is indeed thankless, gives neither cash nor credit. So I flirt with the short story and the drayma—The Mercury still keeps me on as correspondent, and therefore, Maurice, I should be greatly beholden to you if once a month or so you'd send me the work for that period which strikes you, intrinsically or because of its reception, as most important. Could you do that? Put them on the bill and some day I'll pay you. American books, of course. *Make several notes of this!* . . .

I'm reading Wm James's letters—oh glorious. I wish the James who writes the preface wouldn't keep calling Milly Theale *Minny* Theale. If you ever see him, tell him his error.

Did I ask you if you'd like to do a book of Fletcher's? Well, I must quit, and let in the grocer's boy with the vegetables. O Brussels Sprouts! I love you.   Tiddledy Bung   C A

42: TO ROBERT FROST^c   c. Brown Shipley, 123 Pall Mall
                                    London
                                    April 2/22

Dear Frost: I am editing for publication by Secker in England an anthology of American verse, its aim being the presentation of the more important figures in American poetry. The profits are to be divided equally between poets and publisher. I myself in the capacity of editor get almost nothing—five pounds per edition of 1000 copies. The contributors will share their fifty per cent pro rata according to space. The major contributors will be: Emily Dickinson (the only dead one invited), Fletcher, Masters, Robinson, Amy Lowell, Eliot, Stevens, Kreymborg, Lindsay, and yourself. There will be a half-dozen lesser contributors, and a preface by myself. May I have your permission to use: The Road Not Taken, Home Burial, Woodpile, The Fear, Birches, The Sound of the Trees, Hyla Brook, The Oven Bird, and perhaps in addition either The Hill Wife or the Death of the Hired Man? —Louis tells me that you're unpredictable as a correspondent, and Flint, here, corroborates him. I implore you to make an exception of this, and to let me know immediately, if you can, whether I can go ahead; as Secker wants to set up in July, and writing across the ocean takes time. —Before you tuck this letter away, never to be seen again, write me!

I think the chances that this anthology will do something for American poetry here are excellent. And it may well be very profitable for the poets concerned—for them, at any rate, or nobody.   Yrs. sincerely   Conrad Aiken

43: TO F. S. FLINT¹   London
                                                     April 14, 22

Dear Flint: Thanks very much for "Otherworld": I am delighted to have it. I won't pretend that I like all of it, though I like some of it very much; nor do I agree with your preface, except to a slight extent. To say that Dante is of no importance in the history of prosody seems to me a little wild—he didn't invent the Terza rime, but he made it his. In general, your argument against rhyme and metre seems to me extraordinarily flimsy—not because you are not ingenious, but simply, au fond, because there is no argument! Is there any getting away from the fact that even the slightest step in literature, from the less to the more "poetic" is a step from the less to the more "arranged?" "Arranged" in the richest sense—embracing selection, order, emphasis. To "arrange" at all is, if you like, artificial: but it is an essential of all art; and it is logically impossible to dismiss metre and rhyme (which are extraordinarily efficient agents in this process of arrangement) because they are artificial, without also dismissing cadences, metaphor, selection, and, in short, every conceivable aspect of the exagerative process which we call style. I quite agree with you that the "less arranged" has its own cool sort of charm, adapts itself admirably to certain moods more colloquial and less intense; but I think its range is, in comparison with that of the "more arranged," infinitely small—Theoretically, one should seek in a work of art the utmost complexity, or arrangement, consistent with brevity—should one not? Or else give up art entirely and go back to the holophrase!   Yours sincerely Conrad Aiken

44: TO MAURICE FIRUSKI[h]   London
                                              June 7:22

Thanks, Maurice, for the letter and the book [*Priapus and the Pool*], which I believe I havent acknowledged, in the excitement of moving from London to Winchelsea. Its a superb thing: exquisite. I congratulate you with all my heart. Them golden flakes! that little label! that title page! —Do i correctly gather from this latest letter that you are feeling more chipper? you sound so, and I'm glad to believe it. I duly destroyed, as commanded, your other, after marvelling at its contents. My word, Maurice! So this is Cambridge! Well, keep your pecker up, and remember, as I once heard a man say (its true he was slightly cuckoo) that any woman can be captured if you will take a pink silk cushion on your knee and, while conversing with her about the weather or the price of kippers stroke it to and fro, suavely, pausefully, with the palm of your hand. That's what he said! I think you are supposed to keep it up indefinitely—eight or ten hours if necessary; but the lydy will eventually with a singular cry fall helpless on to the floor in a state of coma. —I never tried it; but I can well believe that the coma is real enough. —If your lady doesnt have pink silk cushions knocking about the sitting room, you'll have to take one along with you: tell her you're running for the D.K.E.

Thanks for the Legallienne review—what awful rubbish the old fool talks, and how disgustingly smacks his style of the nineties.[1] The god of love—ah Benedicite! says he forsooth; I'd like to kick him with hobnailed boots. I dont doubt he wears silk drawers and has a baby blue ribbon in his corset covers. No doubt his review will sell the book—that's all right; but it will tend to sell it to the wrong people, and will convince a lot of my professional enemies and despisers that I must be even rottener than they thought I was! and perhaps I am. —There are no comments on the book here—but it's not the custom to comment. Fletcher, with an evil gleam of the eye, remarked that the book was a beautiful piece of printing etc. —

1. Richard Le Gallienne reviewed *Priapus* in the *New York Times* (May 7, 1922).

Armstrong said he liked the "last poem" in it the best—etc tutti frutti. More and more I detest poets and literati and "literature" and the arts. "Literary people are shits," gravely observed Eliot to me at lunch this winter; he said a mouthful. I recognized myself instantly. I sometimes wonder whether I shall ever be able to outgrow the disease, and become normal: certainly, if you had seen me walking about on Epsom Downs the other day you might have thought there was hope for me. Nothing to eat from breakfast till four o'clock, and all the time walking and talking and doing other things. The buttercups and dandelions were wonderful; but there were too many caterpillars and beetles for *comfort*. That day, at least, I lived. Skylarks were bursting their bloodvessels all over the sky: I paid no attention—write me.   C A

45: TO G. B. WILBUR[r]   Harvard Club of Boston
                                          Sept. 26, 22

Dear Jake—   I was delighted to get your letter; but disappointed to find that you weren't going to be in this part of the world. However, such is life. Anyway, this old club isn't what it used to be: no drinks, no people. Porter Sargent still comes in occasionally with his air of mystery and his cynic smile, and I had lunch here with Zech Chaffee the other day, and dinner with Lucien [Crist]—but alas it ain't like the old times! Speaking of Lucien, he's put a still longer steering wheel on his Ford, and an automatic wind-shield wiper, and fifty other such improvements, and started off recklessly for Washington, where he seems to have decided to live. He looks Haggard, and Florence [his wife] has had a nervous breakdown (a very ingenious one—it did the trick, brought Lucien from South Yarmouth to Washington) and [son] Bainbridge has had his hair cut. —So much for the Crists. —I'm having the time of my life in Boston—weekend with the Linscotts (same old imitation of a boiler factory, a furious row going on all the time), dinner with bald Julius [Clark] (I'm damned near bald myself!), tennis with Maurice [Firuski] et al; staying in Trinity St. with Voorhis. Tonight I'm actually having dinner with Amy Lowell! Who'd a thunk it—I'm off to the Cape with Julius this week—my tenants get out on Sat, and I want like the devil to see what the house and garden look like. I'm taking down some more books and prints with me. —So you're going back to the Cape next summer? And will you

69

spend a winter there? If you're contemplating the latter let me know—it might bring us back from Europe. This winter we'll spend partly in the country (Sussex) and partly in London. Three of my books are now out in England and an anthology of American verse which I edited last spring: I am just beginning to have a sort of standing. Tom Eliot is starting a mag., The Criterion, which ought to be good. He, poor devil, cries out for analysis more than anyone I've ever seen. He's in a perfect Gordian knot—he thinks he's god. A passion for perfection—etc. His wife's an invalid. He still writes an occasional Boloism—Speaking of Boloisms, I hear that Waldo Peirce[1] has written a simply magnificent hymn in praise of THE BOSOM OF MRS. ISAAC RICE, his ex-mother-in-law. It begins:

> Breasts and bosoms have I known
> Of varied shapes and sizes,
> From poignant disappointments
> To jubilant surprizes.

It ends with something or other that would—

> —settle
> On Mrs. Isaac Rice's potent
> Popacatapetl!!!

I met an individual named Robert Hale on the boat (a delightful youth, incidentally, and somebody intelligent) who had been staying with Waldo in Paris, and he swore he'd send me a copy. It's really glorious. —I was sorely tempted to accept your offer of a ticket to Iowa City—but it can't be done. No time. I'm doing a scuttle. I don't think Jessie especially enjoys being alone in the continent of Europe, and I plan to start back just as soon as I've settled my financial and literary affairs.

Now that I've weathered the first front, I like England hugely. They're a damned intelligent family, and I could think of worse things than spending one's life there. —I was awfully sorry to hear that Joy had had such a rotten time of it with the son and heir—for whose picture, with his properly radiant papa, many thanks. Yes, kids are the finest of all entertainments—bar none. My eye not sufficiently professional or maternal to enjoy them when they're under six months; but from that time on they've got everything beaten,

---

1. A well-known painter and adventurer, Peirce, Harvard '06, met C A often in Boston and on Cape Cod.

from Aeschylus to the latest vaudeville. —I had some fine chess in the boat, with the aforementioned Hale, under the eye of a professor of higher mathematics who was an ex-tournament player, and had once won a game from Lasker. He knew a great many games by heart—could set the board up at any point in a given game. He told us we were pretty good players, and we felt like Gods. I played one game with him and managed to keep going for about 30 moves—after that the flood. —Your psychiatry work sounds extremely interesting—I'd certainly like to hear about it. Perhaps next fall. I don't think we'll be back before then. Jessie likes it now that we've got a cottage in the country; and I find I can work there. (Short stories at present; more lucrative, and incidentally amusing to do.) A dream for you to probe: I was walking down a vast beach crowded with people—all looking for amber washed in by the tide. It seemed to me frightfully important to find a small, precious, and perhaps exquisitely carved piece of amber. I heard that a man had found a piece—perhaps the only fragment there was. This news desolated me. —It should be noted that all through this dream the *word* amber was used, or was *present,* but the actual significance of it was *jade.*

Well, drop me a line now and then. Above all, let me know when you've fully formulated your plans for next year.   Love   Conrad

46: TO ROBERT N. LINSCOTT[w]   c B Shipley 123 Pall Mall
                                          Nov. 8:22

Dear Bob: A stormy passage with a lot of k[itchen] m[aids] and a monocled englishman and two bridge-fiends for company: ten days of it. Twenty dollars lost at bridge. Two sparrows, six finches, and a hawk, blown out to sea, boarded us and died. Reading matter: The Return, de la Mare, Books and Characters by Strachey, Europeans (pretty bad) by James. Chess with a neurasthenic.

I've sent you an anthology: it's being reviewed everywhere at great length: five columns a week. Also listed as a best seller, which is an irony, as I don't get anything out of it. Jesus. Fletcher and Kreymborg purring like lions, Eliot grinning like a cheshire cat. Secker tickled to death at the prospect of getting back some of the money he lost on Punch and Forslin, poor wretch. Monro is giving a reading from it tonight, wh. I shall not attend.

I've been in town for the last three days, buying coats, female hats, Ulysses (2nd edition: ten bucks: what's it worth in america?) and talking my head off with the boys. Eliot's mag. [*The Criterion* 1, no. 1 (October 1922)] is well received, and his poem ["The Waste Land"] called "great." Great it may not be, but it's certainly delicious. Am I cuckoo in fancying that it cancels the debt I owed him? I seem to detect echos or parodies of Senlin, House, Forslin: in the evening at the violet hour etc, Madame Sosostris etc, and in general the "symphonic" nature, the references to music (Wagner, Strawinsky) and the repetition of motifs, and the "crowd" stuff beginning "Unreal city." However, that's neither there nor here: it's the best thing I've seen in years. Get the Criterion. It also has an article on Ulysses by a french critic [Valery Larbaud], very interesting and clearly "inspired." . . .

Jessie and the kids are flourishing. Day before yesterday Jane exhaled the horse chestnut which, some months ago, she *in*haled. Marvelously retentive child. We had noticed that her M's and N's were like B's and D's. . . .

I like england better than ever on seeing it again. Here it is Nov. 8, a warm delicious blue day, chrysanthemums iceland poppies nastutuiums (you know what I mean) roses etc. blossoming blandly in the garden, and no necessity at all for the lovely furry Burberry winter coat I blew myself to the other day. You, meanwhile, poor devil, are very likely tunneling your morning way to the electrics and breaking icicles off your radiators. You dont have any beer either. Still, I see by the papers that you almost got rid of Lodge. . . .   Yrs. C A

47: TO ROBERT N. LINSCOTT^w   Lookout Cottage Feb. 6:23
                                                                                 [Winchelsea, Sussex]

Drinking beer, and listening to the north wind; looking through the north window at the Strand Gate, and recalling old times; I am sad, thinking how fleeting is life; I am cheerful, reflecting on its infinite diversity. You, greyguardian of the Tombstones, burier of beans in the old defilement of the earth: you, mad delighted tippler on heady rhymes; who smile as you take the wild path betwixt printed word and word; you send me a letter asking me to change the style of my poem; you ask me to cut the auricle from my heart. Many times have the heavens changed since then—what does it matter that thought injured thought? Now it is perhaps your conscience which has moved you; you send me a letter heavy with gold.

A yellow crocus was opening in the small garden when W. H. Davies married his young housekeeper; Armstrong was one of the witnesses; and the sad poet Aiken the other; the young housekeeper wore patent leather boots: Davies a frock coat; drinking port with the bridegroom shortly before the ceremony—the bridegroom observed that the rubbishy talk of the girl could not deter him from making poems; listening, in the frosty garden, to the sound of the gas engine in an adjacent printing press—the bridegroom answered that the sound could not break the rhythm of his thought.

Sunlight is beautiful, but how fortunate it is that the world also contains patent leather boots! The mind of an old peasant poet is beautiful, but how fortunate it is that there are also young housekeepers with sly smiles and pliant bodies! The old poet had incorrectly remembered his bride's name—and the registrar was disturbed; books were consulted: in which byelaws were engraved in old granite; the old poet trembled and licked his dry lips: the bride giggled and looked at Aiken with humid eyes. After all, thus spoke the old registrar, the name Matilda is not *wholly* unlike the name Elizabeth; let them be married. At lunch the old poet put his hand under the table—he tickled the young housekeepers knee. Armstrong and Aiken, noticing that the old poet refused beer (at first) remembered a rumor that he was not yet recovered from gonorrhea; strange, strange, they murmured; and took a train to London.

Life is short—alas that quarrels must darken the Way! Fletcher told me of his foolish letters to you—and showed me your wise letter to him. Then said I to the tygerpoet: an old friend is more precious than many poems; but the tygerpoet said nothing—he looked far away and sharpened his tooth against a lamp-post. Deep deep is the heart of man—devious the dark path that winds downward to its bottom; all my life have I trod that path—only one step have I gone. Looking into man's heart—I see a maelstrom of demons; looking into his mind—I see an abyss of silence.

Many things in your letter delight me—gladly would I see Hazel in a pink loveshawl. I note with joy what you say of Paul the Apistle—and Mrs. Horn Rash. With your kind words for Tetelestai, I have fed the lazy carp of my vanity. For the moment it sleeps —tomorrow again will be hungry.

73

For the prostitute, drugged, who suddenly stared at me with distended eyes—my heart was wounded. When I saw that she was being arrested, my tears fell like hot rain. For the armless man with the face of a kindly poet, who clutched with his right hand the cuff of his empty sleeve and held there all day, as on a little hammock, against his breast, a little girl—both of them staring for long with listless blue eyes at the unceasing traffic of Oxford Street: for them I was wheel-broken. Truly some are more called upon to endure than others: and they, though they know it not, know best the eternal way.   C A

Ulysses: Bloomsday: can be got for ten dollars, or a shade less. Thanks for the clippings: I've got a poem in No. 2 Rhythmus (so I'm told.)

I've reviewed the Waste Land for the Repube. They say nothing about my article, bad cess to them.

We've got a piano and player and taken the cottage for a year and a half longer.

48: TO MALCOLM COWLEY[n]   Lookout Cottage
                                            Winchelsea Sussex
                                            March 26:23

Dear Malcolm: I was delighted to hear from you—I've often in the last year wondered if you were here (Europe) or gone back again to e pluribus. What you were doing. Whether you would become, as Pound seems to think one should, an unnational being. Etc. I'm glad to hear that you are definitely going back, with roots pointed towards a farm or some such thing. A good idea: much better than living in a city, particularly New York, the last resort. Boston would be much better. It is at least not "alive" in the modern sense of the word—which comes close to meaning infested. But the country is best of all.

    As for myself, I really dont know what I shall do. We are comfortable here, it's a lovely place, rent is cheap, views and walks and tennis and beer are plentiful, it isn't far from London (only resemblance to Kew), the scrotumtightening sea is only a mile away, and it agrees with John and Jane even better than S. Yarmouth Mass. Still I dont feel settled here, yet, at any rate, and though I have been able to resume the deadly agonies of verse, thanks to its charm and

74

peace, for the first time in several years, I am restless, feel a little cramped and repressed, would like now and then to feel a hearty slap on the back, see and hear a peanut stand, or sit in the frontrow at the Orpheum. On the other hand, the virtues of England and the english are equally distinct, and I am sure I shall be hungry, in America, for the general high level of intelligence and good taste and wellinformedness of which in that country one can find only here and there a passable imitation. Not that I know or see many english—very few. There's some hitch—at bottom I dont get on with them, never can get anywhere near them, nor let them get anywhere near me. There are literally *no* english literary folk whom I have the very smallest desire to meet. (However, that's equally true of my beloved compatriots.) On purely literary grounds, they simply don't interest me. Eliot is the only creature whom I should like to see more of, and Eliot keeps me at arm's length: he has an invalid wife and social preoccupations and (I suspect) ambitions which make him as wary and guarded as a european. All of which restricts me, and will probably in time drive me home, for sheer need of human nature's daily food.

I liked immensely your things in 8 Mere [Eight More] Harvard Poets. Far and away the best in it: too good for it. Wheelwright sent me a copy and wrote me asking me to find sales and reviews for it in England. He seemed a little peeved when I told him that I have absolutely no "connections" which are of the slightest use in England for such things—peeved and incredulous. It's true, however, or rather it's true to say that I have a very very faint position which I only dare use for "special occasions." In other words, for something damned good, which this anthology as a whole is not! . . .

Do you see Joyce? Pound? and if so, I wonder what you make of them. Joyce is one of the remarkably few living writers whom I should like to know. Pound I should like sometime to see again just for the pleasure of quarreling with him. His articles in the dial infuriate me! —Other things that infuriate me are the poems and drawings of cummings, crane, loy, etc. Is "Broom" dead, dying? A cryptic note from Loeb refers to "funeral rites." Has secession ceased? seceded? and what is there, aside from advertising value, in the idea? (rhetorical question: no answer required.)

I am still, perhaps more than ever within the barren circle of love and death which you drew about me. My vocabulary grows smaller and purer every day. I shall end by reducing all speech to the mystical word OM; eye upon navel. . . .   Yrs. C A

Winchelsea
                                                                May 9:23

Yrs furiously received. Also a letter from Alfred [Kreymborg]. I find myself hopelessly in the dark, I give it up. I have just written Frost that I wont stand in the way, and that, if he will only come in provided that Louis [Untermeyer] does also, I will peacefully go out. I officially notify you to that effect, and beg you to act accordingly, and keep my stuff out if you hear from Frost or the others that Louis is to be "in." It cant be helped: it's a tragedy implicit in the situation. It's really better for the success of *New Leaves* that Frost should be in, even with Louis attached as a sinker, than that I should be in and Frost out. I regret it, but it is so, and I wont stand in the way, nor bear any grudges. Selah. Haec olim forsan nobis meminisse inuvabit. I do feel deeply that there's no use being in such a thing if it is not run on strictly impersonal basis. I trust to you, beloved Maurice, whom I have so much abused, to act decisively for me as the occasion dictates. Into thy hands, O Mus, my Mss.[1]

Have you been to the cape yet? o write and tell.

The cuckoo has arrived in england. One struck a hundred the other morning at half past four outside my bedroom window. And still they write poems about it. O cuckoo is it thee I hear? Yes, you bloody fool, what did you think it was.

A scotchman opened his purse and a moth flew out.

The prince of wales—darling boy—has had an unhappy love affair with an actress; he falls off his horse once a week, regularly, in hopes of death.

In the event of royal weddings, the royal doctor is called in be-

---

1. Fletcher and C A had proposed that Frost and E. A. Robinson join them in planning a poetry magazine, *New Leaves*, to be published by Firuski's Dunster House. Various other names for the nucleus of poets were put forth, and Frost suggested Untermeyer. C A replied that if Untermeyer was in, he was out. Frost had just written C A that a plan which had been stretched to take in Stevens, Kreymborg, and Williams "for you" wouldn't have to be stretched very much more to take in Untermeyer "for me" (May 12, 1923; in C A Collection, Huntington Library).

fore the ceremony and administers funkpowders to all the royal participants: taking the funk from function.

Many of the royal family have defective eyesight. When they need glasses, or a cinder or beam removed, they repair to . . . an expert with the lens and alphabet. —— [He] sends them no bill—no, he is paid in plate. Between ourselves, [he] has no rectum, having had some time a painful operation as a result of which he delivers his bowels through a tube in his left side. Flatulence is much to be feared. Some day, after too gaseous a dinner, four glasses of burgundy, suddenly will come to himmelfahrt.   Thine as ever
C A

50: TO ROBERT N. LINSCOTT[w]   Lookout Cottage Winchelsea
                                  June 20:23

Dear Bob: . . . I have an idea that I havent written you since we went up to town for our month's dissipation; which in my case resolved itself into two. It was very pleasant to trot on the pavements again, to go to shows, look at pictures, and meet a few people—no new ones of any moment, but the Freemans seen again, and the Flowers[1], and the Knights (Harold and Laura, both artists) and of course Armstrong. Tom Eliot was just going away for his holiday, with great air of secrecy to a place unknown (he cultivated a fine mystery about it—gave no address) so I saw him only once, for lunch; during which nothing was said on either side of my review of the Waste Land in the Republic. He's a strange creature. Full of protestations of friendliness, not to say affection; but makes no move to see me, beyond an occasional "You must have dinner with me one night next month, or the year after next." Consequently, I have tired of looking him up, much as I like him and enjoy seeing him; I cant carry the entire burden of the friendship alone. —[Edwin Arlington] Robinson turned up in June (I think it was) and I have had some delightful times with him—a journey to Canterbury, which ended in a superb debauch of whisky (he drinks whisky as if it were air). During one dash into a bar, a Lovely Young Whore smiled at me, and on being smiled at in return, swiftly crossed the pub and kissed me: a quite nice kiss. Father

1. Robin Flower, a curator of manuscripts in the British Museum and translator of Gaelic poetry, with whom C A had become friends.

Robinson was delighted: stepped nimbly back and observed "I fear I'm in the way!" —The young lady then suggested that I supply her and her four lydy friends with drinks; suggestion declined and acquaintance terminated; the pub-crawl resumed; more whiskies drunk; finally a dinner, at ten oclock of lobster, which Robinson conducted like roman rite. He's a charming creature—more of a being than any american litry person I've met.

Fletcher back, saddened by failure to sell a single poem in america. Daisy [Fletcher] liked the u s a. —How can I collect 119 dollars from Rhythmus? they invited me to contribute on those terms, but never a cent can I get: my last remaining saleable poem, too. Confound it! and me bankrupt at the moment through buying too many Kiyonagas, Utamaros, Harunobus, Hokusais, Shunyeis, Shunshos, Hiroshiges, Taitos, and a sixteenfoot long chinese painting of the Yuan dynasty—Immortals in the Mountains of Eternal Youth, painted by the Solitary Cloud Man.[2]

. . . New Leaves is dead: beheaded, as Emily somewhere puts it, by the blonde assassin, Frost. Maurice evidently feels (perhaps rightly) that the rest of us aint good enough. My last venture of the sort. Poets are fools and criminal and dont know what truth or honesty is. I dont say this only of Frost—Kreymborg and Fletcher were equally to blame, with their little behind-the-scenes machinations apropos the inclusion of Louis, whom they were afraid to offend. As for my own part, I was of course just mulish. And a damned good thing, too.

I have now had four cheese biscuits and a glass of beer. The cat, Nettle Trotzky Aiken, shared in the feast. —I dont see why D. Richardson should prevent one's enjoying V. Woolf. Any more than Chekhov spoils Mansfield. —I have done a selection of Dickinson and offered it to Cape. 160 poems—she comes off awfully well in selection. I cant remember whether you like her or not.   regards to the crew   Conrad

2. C A began collecting Japanese prints in London in 1914, and again in 1920, under the guidance of Lt. Col. W. F. Wright. He regularly visited the print shops, especially one in Holborn owned by "Kato," who taught him the signatures of the artists. His short story "Field of Flowers" mirrors C A's passion for these prints. (Twelve prints from his collection are now in the C A Collection, Huntington Library.)

Says Burton Rascoe, in the bookworm's nightmare,[1]—"Aiken is obese, coarse, porcine, negroid of feature, with thick lips, darwinian tubercles on his chocolate colored ears, a wart like a horse chestnut inside the left nosevalve, and a marked esquimau accent. He has a massive prognathous jaw, mounting a battery of windblown teeth, a low stupid brow, and eyes, small and beautiful as a pig's, set close together without lids or lashes. A thing of beauty is the boy forever. I asked Aiken what he thought of Stevens' book. Unhesitatingly Aiken replied, in his Greenlander's icy accent, 'I consider this book of Stevens to be greater than The Hunting of the Snark, as great as the first book of Euclid, almost as great as the fourth part of Espronceda's El Diablo Mundo, but deplorably inferior to the Orangotango.' Aiken had just returned from the annual game between Chatham High school[2] and the University of Honolulu, on the beech at waikiki. In his right hand he bore a feather of the blessed parakeet (in the beginning was the bird), in his left hand he treacly twangled a ukeliptus, a rat peeped out of his breast pocket, a flotilla of dachshunds, each answering to the name of a contemporary poet, belled at his heels. —On the ship, he had been hurriedly kissed by the irish cook, a highbreasted girl of considerably beauty who had touched his foot under the whist table. You ought not to, you, a married man! hard unyielding cheeks, odorless odalisque, blueyed, raven-locked. Five days she had been ill, foodless five days, and then resurrected saw Aiken, opening upon him bivalvular eyes of love: into which, lo Aiken empedocles opalescently plunged. Beauty! he cried, and on the deck in darkness walked loquaciously beside her, prattled, flattered, she silently and with overwhelming grace pacing up hill and down as the sea suggested, touching his arm as they turned the corner, locking knees with him as they sat, freezing, in the verandah cafe. And at Queenstown, three kisses passionately flung up to him from the dark red-and-greenlighted tender-farewell farewell—and a long night of whisky and smutty

1. The first half of this fantasy weaves events and speeches from C A's last night's dream, but beginning with "On the ship . . ." C A tries out a soliloquy for *Blue Voyage*, the first draft of which he has begun.
2. Chatham Academy in Savannah, whose football game—not at "waikiki"—was an event of C A's childhood.

stories with the major from palestine, the jew chocolate maker from boston and the welsh rarebit. O the welsh rarebit! with undershot drooling jaw hollow laugh bastioned breast and the whole male population of the ship dancing the whornpipe round her. And o major with exploring hand, and o second stewart ditto, and to chocolate maker of the rabelaisian wit and brutal question, to all propounded, have you been virtuous on this ship? Welsh rarebit, come here! have you been virtuous on this ship, have you lain with any man? scene of scenes." —In london, gaugin and van gogh,[3] in winchelsea the holy family, and a flood of grace's sitwells,[4] whom next week she marries. No work. Never. An inch of snow, and fletcher wants to know why maurice doesnt answer his letters re a book.   selah   C A

52: TO JOHN GOULD FLETCHER[a]   Winchelsea
                                                 December 28, 23

Dear J.G.   Many thanks indeed for the Tyll [Eulenspiegel]—a book I've often intended to get, and that I'm extremely glad to have. It was kind of you.

But your review of Festus in The Freeman [December 19, 1923]! My dear J.G.! —I wouldn't have suspected you of being able to talk so much nonesense in so small a space. The "method" of Festus is "stale?" It is not the method of Punch or Priapus or The House of Dust; it is like Senlin in some respects, but does that make it "stale?" and the technical resemblance is of minor importance when one considers the otherwise tremendous differences. The "attitude" is stale? In what other book have I advanced the Buddhist doctrine that the occupation of the wise is a contemplative exploration of the world through the medium of sensation and thought, an immersion in pure consciousness? Is it a lack of "conclusion about life" to analyze as I have done in Parts IV and V the limits of knowledge, and to select an emotional basis from which to face these limits? And what on earth do you mean, if you really mean anything, by your distinction between "sentimental association" and "intellectual?" Or by a "mentally-fixed conclusion?" Forgive me, but that is mere verbalism. Again, your large loose statement that my interest

3. "go, gin! and *vin,* go!"
4. Grace McDonald, Jessie's sister, married Oswald Sitwell.

in the "play of unconscious psychology within the individual" etc. is my only interest, and (you leave the conclusion to be drawn) the theme of Festus. But that is absurd. Punch, Priapus, House of Dust, Festus are as different as they can be, as regards theme and treatment and tone. And the "play of the unconscious within the individual" has nothing to do with Festus—nothing. The whole poem is an essay, if you like, in epistemology. As for the abuse of minor harmonics—don't you think that instead of picking up this phrase from Untermeyer, Anderson and Co. (their favorite and now widely circulated tag, substituted for the earlier tag of "imitator" and "lack of originality")[1] you might have said something of your own about the verse itself? It is, of course, the best verse I've written: the richest. The most varied. The most highly colored. The subtlest in thought and humor. It is my own opinion, after four years acquaintance with Festus, that parts III, IV and V are the most sustainedly beautiful work I've done. Surely it cannot be that there is so little foundation for this belief that you can dismiss the poem in 150 words as stale and meaningless? And how do you reconcile your present accusation of meaninglessness with your remark a year ago to Linscott that you disliked Part V because it was *too philosophical?*

However, I suppose there's no use discussing it: I merely get the poison out of my bosom. All I can hope to accomplish is to make clear to you that your review is simply a spurious and weak "rationalization" of some obscure emotional "set" towards my work which at the moment you do not understand or wish to confess. I sincerely hope that I am not myself simply "rationalizing" this view out of my discomfort; if so, forgive me; if not, I hope you'll change your mind.   Yrs. C A

53: TO JOHN GOULD FLETCHER[a]   Winchelsea
                                                       Jan 4:24

Dear J.G.:   I'm glad you take my objections friendlily; but you dont begin to convince me that you have thought the thing out with

1. C A blamed Untermeyer's widely used anthology, *Modern American Poetry* (New York, 1921), for the impression that C A wrote mostly "tired but beautiful music" with little intellectual content. C A's debate with Fletcher (Letters 52 and 53) reached Untermeyer who wrote C A (September 6, 1924): "Fletcher, my agency reports, has been so upset by his quarrel with you that he determined to shake the dust of England forever and was about to embark for the happy aisles of the N. Y. Powtray Sasitay."

any care or much perspicacity. Let me briefly take up some of your points.

You say that as our views of "life" differ, a prejudice on your part was inevitable. But let me point out first that I do not anywhere advance in Festus any metaphysical or mythological theory of the nature of life such as you outline: what I do advance is the suggestion that as speculation is all we can manage (as regards the metaphysical constitution of the world) then speculation, plus observation, plus insight, plus experience (since that is implied) is a good end in itself. My view treats simply of the activity of man; yours, of the nature of god; and as they do not occupy the same ground, one cannot say that they are "incompatible," as you claim. Festus could include your theory as one more dream-product, springing out of the nature of thought itself, which it would give him pleasure to meditate upon.—This being so, there is no ground left *here* for prejudice; and if there is, then it ought to be explained *in the review* as operating against a fair view of the poem.

Again, you misquote me and misapprehend my remark that you had perhaps "rationalized *motives* which were obscure to you." You substitute the word "emotions" for motives, and of course are quite right, but quite irrelevant, in your assertion that all art and criticism is a rationalization of "emotions." But the rationalization of a *motive* is another matter: it means that motives which existed in you *a priori,* and which did not concern the book, to some extent dictated your feelings about the book. It means that one is in advance prepared to dislike a thing, and to find *other reasons* for dislike afterwards.

Again, you object to my statement that the possibility of knowledge is limited. But I do not claim that there is a limit to the number or variety of facts man can know: I merely advance here the idealist doctrine that "greater than the world you dream of, rises, immortally beyond, you your own self's wall."

In your review, you said that the poem lacked any mentally fixed conclusion. In your letter, you say it has one, in the repetition of the first section, but that it is a bad one. You seem self contradictory here, and I dont know what you mean in either case.

"The play of unconscious psychology" etc., which you say is the theme of all my work except Punch and House of Dust, is so large a phrase that one could apply it to anything on earth. It is, then, the theme of every one of Shakspere's plays. I assert again that there is

82

a lot of difference between Senlin, House of Dust, Punch, Priapus, Festus, Turns and Movies; that there is a very considerable range, quite as much as in the work of any other. A critic who did his job would point out both resemblances and differences in treating of Festus. In your letter, you refer to F as a technical triumph. But is a technical triumph (supposing you to be right) so common in book length poems that it can be merely sneered at?

I could dig out other errors in your letter—there are several more, all due to loosenesses of thinking. But what's the use. Your real reasons for sneering at Festus were not that it is a bad poem, your phrase "technical triumph" rules that out, nor, as you tacitly admit now, because it is meaningless: for you say now that one trouble is that you don't agree with its doctrines. You are bound to admit, too, that its particular meaning is one not before developed by me; that the treatment is in many respects novel—more highly colored, more metaphysical, and in part five for the first time using dialogue—surely an interesting departure.

Needless to say, I would have no objection to severe criticism which was *reasoned,* or which at least took the poem seriously. What most, and essentially, grieved me in this case was the lack of critical decency which permitted you to dismiss me so cavalierly, and so briefly. Stevens and I have both reached a point where we deserve something better than a few lines in a group review, a review which speaks *kindly* only of Cournos! Hell's bells! Even when I have disliked the work of my contemporaries, I have been decent, analytic, and treated them with the seriousness and length they deserved. If I wallop, I give reasons. I am careful to expose enough of my own personal position so that the reader can make a free choice. And I avoid reviewing books by people towards whom I feel any *a priori* emotional "set"—as I recently refused to review Frost and Untermeyer. As in future I shall refuse to review books by you.

Well, maybe I make a mountain out of a molehill. Perhaps Festus *is* rotten. But feeling as I do about it, I would be hypocritical if I didnt fess up. I'm damned sore, and I think I have a right to be.   Yrs. C A

Letters 54–73: January 1924 to May 1926

Of "the rooms, streets and houses" that were to C A the shaping environments of his conscious life, Jeake's House on Mermaid Street in Rye, Sussex—even more than 228 Oglethorpe Avenue in Savannah and Forty-One Doors on Stony Brook Road in Brewster—was to be crucial: "Just as surely as the great astrologist [Samuel Jeake] had laid his foundations of Caen stone, and built the beautiful house, with the carved serpents under the eaves, he [C A] had himself built the life there, and slowly but surely enriched it. . . . The sorrows, the agonies, the despairs"—of Fletcher, of Freeman, of Monro, of Jessie ("with her sense of betrayal and shame, her grievously wounded pride" at his guilty departure)—"hadn't these, both of family and friends, added most to the enrichment of the spirit which, for all of them, so palpably, so almost visibly, informed the house: even more than the gayety, the laughter, the good times, the mad games of ping-pong, the riotous concerts, the birthday mint-juleps in the terraced garden, or the semi-occasional passade, or flirtation?" [1]

Joan Delano was born in Jeake's House on September 4, 1924.

Recuperating from a series of painful operations for a rectal fistula, C A was taken by Martin Armstrong to Spain for two months in spring, 1926. When C A returned to Rye in May his economic plight seemed desperate; he even—half-heartedly—attempted to sell Jeake's House. "Both Jessie and I have got to the point where we worry all the time about making both ends meet, our expenses increase hourly, and the more anxious I get the less I write, and the less saleably." [2] By fall he had decided to visit once more publishers in Boston and New York.

o   o   o

Bring! Bring! (London: Secker, March 1925; New York: Boni and Liveright, May 1925).

Senlin: A Biography (London: The Hogarth Press, July 1925, first separate edition).

Priapus and the Pool and Other Poems (New York: Boni and Liveright, September 1925).

1. *Ushant,* pp. 250, 260.
2. C A to George B. Wilbur,ʳ May 13, 1926.

Selected Poems of Emily Dickinson, edited by Conrad Aiken (London: Jonathan Cape, 1925).

54: TO ROBERT N. LINSCOTT[w]   Winch
                                                 Jan 13 24

Maybe Maurice has told you the torrific herrendous news, i.e., that we have bought Jeake's House in Rye, in the same block that James, Henry, lived in; for seventeen hundred pounds, e.g., seven thousand dollars; with beams and panels and studios and views and a hotelful of bedrooms. Anyway, it's the struth. Poverty from now on forever will be our lot. We scorn delights and live laborious days. Reviews must be written as by a syndicate, potboiler short stories delivered like bullets from a machine gun, plays turned out once a week, novels elaborated at magniloquent length, poetry alas eschewed world without end amen. I don't know why we did it. Nobody knows. We felt miserable while we were trying to make up our minds: we never did make up our minds: we bought it without minds: we have been miserable to the point of unconsciousness ever since. We feel as if we had bought the Crystal Palace or the Taj Mahal. So vast, so tall the establishment that we are sure that at the end of a year we shall encounter, here and there, rooms unnoticed before, filled with mice and foul with bats, squealing with rats and roped with webs, littered with bones and stinking of ghosts. The plaster is falling off the ceilings. The wallpapers hang in mouldy festoons from the walls. Rodents put ancient grizzled snouts out of holes in the floors. The whole house ticks like a clock factory with the hidden feverish activities of the Death Watch Beetle. The small garden is a haunted wood of black weeds and savage hollyhocks: one leafless tree hangs weeping over the ruin. And creepers have closed all the windows, unopened for three centuries. (A slight exaggeration—the house is dated 1689.)

Weep for us, sundered from our native land. Send us thousands of dollars to deliver us from exile. Send us a cage of orioles and bluebirds, to remind us, and a dead leaf from the Public Gardens, and a drink of water from the Frog Pond. By the waters of Rother we lie down to sleep, yea, we slumber from henceforth forever.

Quae cum ita sint, send me a japanese print: beauty must be domiciled in this wreck. Send them all, save one of the two small snow scenes—take your choice. Of, if you prefer, keep "the thirty famous poets."

Also, as Alyse Gregory invites me to contribute to the Dial once more, send her Strange Moonlight and get from Alice Brown (if she has not already sent you, as I have asked her) a poem, Psychomachia, and send that also to Alyse G.

The Tyger Poet and I have parted. I told him I thought his review of Festus was outrageous: he replied, "What the hell do you expect? Do you want a volume written about you? Even with that you wouldn't be satisfied. I hope if I had your talents (this was magnanimous) I'd put them to better use. How can you hope to write poetry as long as you fail so hopelessly to see the true trueness of the universe: i.e., that life consists in the successive self-crucifixions of the infinite numbers of fragments of the Divine Essence?" How indeed? Our motto: Hic Jeacit.   Conrad

55: TO ROBERT N. LINSCOTT^w   Winchelsea
                                                     3/11/24

Good friend you are, Robert of Lincoln, the way you be selling the miserable poor works of the webbybrained one, and he half starved for the lack of food these frostybright winter days, what with the hard times, and the high prices of castles, and the toughness of prose, and the saintcursed hardgrainedness of the blanketyblank verseline, and may almighty god, inhabiter of clouds and holes, starpolisher and worldlapidary, wombweaver and nervetuner, pour goldfruit at your feet and sweet sounds of music and elfwhispers at your bedhead in the abysms of nighttime, the way you'd be dreaming three pairs of rainbow featherwings for yourself and going up seven whistling lightyears singing glory hallelujah with a halo like a doughnut round your gaunt brow and forgetting forever the sorrow of the flesh, world without end Ahhhhhhhhhhhhhhmen.

And the lord appeared in a dream unto Aiken, and the sound of his coming was as the sound of waters falling from a high rock, and he spake unto Aiken in a dreadful voice, which was like unto the voice of many hungry lions on a desert, in the moonlight, in the month of Boolshat; and the lord said unto Aiken, Write to Linscott, him of Tombstoneham, a fair letter, well carved in the stone with fair letters and a seal of fair curves, and the name of the seal Thuz, that is to say, at the drooping of the first melonslice of the moon, which is to signify, in the beginning of the month of Boolshat; and say to Linscott, in many sweetsmelling words, which is to say words larded with the honeycomb, and the datecoloured hearts of words pierced with cloves, say unto him as I, the lord, worldbooming, bid: and let these be the words of your letter, as I say to you now, to wit, i.e., e.g., viz., Thnks, Bob, yrs recvd, w. Ms enclosed of the twining twain in the twaxi. Then shouted the lord with a strong shout, saying, Sweet hour, and therewith clapped himself with a levinclap into a cloud, and was gone, and swinking swaiken sweating swoke.

And aiken took then the logos in his one hand and the intaxicated twain in the other, and he cried aloud, Lord, Lord, why askest thou me this riddle? And father, he added, weeping damsontears, father, if it be thy will, let this cab pass from me. But no answer did the heavenly father vouchsafe, for he, by this, was well on his way to the paradisal lavatory, wherein, with cloudy steps, and skyey swaying of blue robes, he, stately, worldbending, moved majestic toward the washbasin. And on the washbasin rested a fair sweet small soapcake, round and bright, and the colour of worlds, and aiekn was thereupon smitten and cleft, with a deadly fear, and he opened his tiny sparrowmouth and skreked Lord, lord, washest thou thy hands of the world? And the lord, mellowbellowing, bellknelling answered, I wash, thou washest, he washes, we wash, you wash, they wash,—

And the world ended, and aeikn alone lived, and in his right hand was the logos, and in his left the cab; and he smote the logos three times flashing against the cab, and cried to the cab, Be fruitful, cab, and bring forth male and female after thy kind; and the word was with the cab, and the cab was fruitful, and it waxed, and in its time lo, labouring, ticking and hornsnarling, was delived, in the manner of the podburst, and behold, the twining twain, whose hearts were meters and whose eyes were headlights and whose bowels were pipes, came crying and kicking into the light. And naike wept.
. . .   enaik: Thuz: C A

56: TO G. B. WILBUR[r]   c/o Brown Shipley
                                          123 Pall Mall London
                                          May 5; 24

Dear Jake—   the enclosed I thought might interest or amuse you, according to your present state of mind in re Soviet government.[1] Astonishing to have Pavlov thus turn up again in the flesh after all these centuries of conflict and change. The last I heard of him was about five years ago when it was reported that he was living in a barricaded house in St Petersburg, which he had filled from cellar to attic with potatos. There, behind locked doors, against which freebooters (official and private) knocked from time to time, he pursued a series of experiments. Well done Pavlov.

And I suppose you are doing much the same on quaggy cape cod, observing the sexual habits of the mosquito or the altogether too-domestic fly, Or have you decided to go back to the wild wild west again, and welter among the naive barbarians and subdue your mind and sensibilities to the low lurid level of theirs? god forbid, but I feel it in my bones that that is what you are up to, or shall I say down to. dont, for the love of mud! Move eastward, always, in this evil ignorant world: every step should be eastward. China is the goal. There one rests. But there are many convenient stopping places en route. England would serve you for some time; France; Vienna; India. Come. Join me in a slow methodical pilgrimage round the world, learning much. Beginning with the hospitals of england, and its public schools (impulse almost made me write pubic) we move to the dives of paris, and plumb them all. Thence on foot across france to italy, where we observe the uncaged italian ape and apess at play. The balkans, a wilderness of flowers and pigs. Constantinople, paradise of dogs. India, with varieties of religious experience which even W. J. would have found rich. China, womb-mother of us all. This is to be an intro-uterine pilgrimage, as all good pilgrimages are.

I consider a play, in which my hero (?) is a more or less typical Messiah: god complex, or father complex leading him to suppose himself a god. For the purpose of having, as in greek drama, a chorus, I design splitting him up into six component parts (who will wear suitably designed masks). Six, five, or seven, the precise number does not matter much. Now, the question is, into what six can I split him with the least violation (as of course some violation is inevitable in this kind of over-simplification)? —Father, Mother, Narcissus,—these three come easily to my mind, though the precise

1. Story from the London *Times* (May 5, 1924) reporting that Pavlov condemned new Soviet educational methods allowing children absolute freedom from restraint. He said these innovations would make them unable to resist emotional impulses and "subject to hysteria and other psychoses on the slightest irritation."

nature of the last-named is a little vague to me. Does he correspond to the ego itself, in a measure? —Would a death-complex (I coin the idea on the spot) be out of order? What I have in mind is the notion of Freud in "Beyond the Pleasure Principle": the notion that there is always in any living organism a strong motive towards unconsciousness or death. This strikes me as true, and would be useful to me in my scheme. What, then, for one more or two more such components? Or, in fact, if these dont meet with your psychological approval, for the whole lot of them? —Roughly, for your better guidance in the matter my theme is: The hero is an out and out psychotic (verging on paranoia) who not only has tendencies, very strong, to consider himself a god, or a son of a god, but also has rather extraordinary "healing" (suggestive) powers. But, unlike Christ (on whom in many respects he is founded) he is also intensely conscious of the deterministic nature of things, and, with the help of a psychoanalytic friend, glimpses the harrowing possibility that his belief in himself is of psychotic origin, and not only that, but that his "doctrine" is equally so, and might well retard the progress of man by a thousand or two years. Learning this, he faces a dilemma: to yield to his psychosis, thereby saving himself at the possible expense of man; or to go mad. —I wish you would give this a thought, and let me have a little guidance. I would be profoundly grateful. Needless to say, I dont expect the thing, as producible on the stage, to be absolutely watertight, from a psychological viewpoint; but I want it as nearly so as is consistent with the dramatic. —And please, in any event, keep the idea strictly under your hat, as it is very susceptible of plagiarism. —I should add that I intend to have my "hero" always accompanied by his chorus of component personalities, who will "talk" whenever he is "thinking."

We expect to move the two miles to Rye in about three weeks, god willing. . . .   as ever   Conrad

57: TO T. S. ELIOT[r]   Winchelsea
                                                             May 7: 1924

Dear Tom: Is my evasiveness worse than yours? You say nothing of the Ms of the Dickinson article; so I assume that it has, by this, joined the Thames maidens. Nor, suggesting so movingly (but surely a little pessimistically) that it would be a pity if you or I or

the Criterion should cease—my name not having appeared there—
do you take up my reminder, so tactfully and emphatically put in a
postscript, that this need not occur: you have, and have had for two
years, Psychomachia. Why not print it? It grows old. A year and a
half, to be precise,—the poem itself is not quite two; but able to
walk.

For the article: I really want very much to give you something,
my other ventures having proved so unlucky, and I will make a
serious attempt to do so. I have just come across some old notes on
Dostoevsky which might serve as a starting point. I will let you
know more definitely early next month, when I shall have moved,
and when I shall be once more in possession of my books. It is possible that I shall come to town for a week or two of diversion in
June or July. In that case, I shall be glad to try one of your lunches
at the Cock,—where I had, in 1909, my first dinner in London. I
hope your parties aren't as terrifyingly miscellaneous and self-conscious as those of the Athenaeum in 1920. Good god. But I have
rather a terror, I confess, of intellectuals en masse and at the serious
business of pleasure.

On your return journey to town, you'd better walk, or cycle, or
join a Circular Tour, and come through Winchelsea, stopping for
the night. Your last chance to visit Look Out Cottage.   as ever
Conrad
Do you think there's "enough" of W. C. Williams or M. Moore to
warrant articles in the Criterion?—rhetorical question.

58: TO ROBERT N. LINSCOTTᵂ   Address now:
                                               Jeake's House
                                               Rye, Sussex

                                               May 13:24

Twice of late have I been caught far from my little cottage home in
a violent rain and hail storm, soaked to the skin, blued with cold,
hands numbed, boots bubbling, walking with head down and ears
being torn off by the wind, looking round the dripping edges of wet
spectacles to try and see something of the narrowed world, and
seeing of it, alas, only a drowned road swarming with halfdrowned
red worms, whom it was impossible not to crush. Misery, misery
thought i, and observed the curious fact that a heartshaped stain on

my raincoat, over my heart, remained dry longer than any other part; observed the sheep, with sodden wool, standing miserably with backs turned toward the storm; the lambs, newdropped, fixed in postures of grief by the artilleries of rain and hail. Could anything be drearier, thought I, plodding and bubbling? —Yes, the aiken family grovelling on the bare cold floor after the receipt of linscott's lurid lugubrious letter. Six rainy hours passed, and there lay they still, sobbing; seeing far off the gaunt shape of the publisher, enormous, ravaged and lean, wrestling on the mountain top with the serpent of lightning, the worm of worms. —Yes, truly, what a world, what a wormy world. And as you say, at its seething wormiest in the demonthronged chasm which introspection sounds, cauldron of cruelties, inferno of filth. At the moment when your letter came, retailing sad news of your psychological weather and of my rejected stories, I was on the point of organizing a Society for the Gospel of Propagation; instead I now propose to join you in forming a company for the commemoration of Martyrs to consciousness. For every human consciousness which dies of too much light, we swear to kill one million children, carefully selected as being those whom heredity destines to intelligence. You can be president. I will be secretary. The killing will be done by clergymen, and will be strictly nonsectarian. —I cabled you in a second of panic, when the carpenter's bill had been presented to me. I wanted to know what prospects there were before I took steps to sell a little more of our small capital. I enclose check for onefifty which may cover it. Your reply uplifted us beyond belief. —Did the dial take "the last visit" rather than "bring bring"? that would surprise me. I should have thought the latter was much more their bait, and it's also better, I think. . . .   C A

59: TO ROBERT N. LINSCOTT[w]   Winch
                                                   May 16:24

Jessie, heroically as ever, has devoted two days to typing an extra copy of The Dance of Deth[1]; and here, varlet, it is. Peruse it. I tremble before your appraising eye, remembering your dislike of Punch, and observing the tangential resemblances between that and this. But I shall value your opinion highly, as always; and if there

1. The first version of *John Deth: A Metaphysical Legend.*

are parts that seem to you unsatisfactory, for god's sake say so, that I may consider them in revision. I hardly know, poor moi, what to think of it. There are times when I like it, and think it the best; there are times when it seems flat, as the Spectator says of all my work, and stale, as Fletcher says of it. . . . To be soberly and perfectly and egotistically frank, for your ear alone and in the darkest of secret darkrooms, I have always felt that I had it in me—bold statement—to write great poetry; I say "always," but I mean intermittently; I have at bottom a profound self-distrust and self-disgust, which has grown to voracity in the presence of so widespread an indifference to my labour. The reception of Forslin and House of Dust weakened me: the loss of blood was serious; the reception of Punch and Festus has left me almost propless. The possibility that I have somehow missed my way, and wasted the best of my strength on a series of grandiose failures, is horribly real to me, and I am prepared to be humble and, if possible, to start all over again. Dear dear, how very lugubrious. He wept, he promised a new start. Answer, therefore, WHAT IS WRONG WITH THE POETRY OF AIKEN, AND HOW CAN HE MEND HIS WAYS: Unless you think it impossible for the leper to change his spots.

In the present work, I recognize many of the characteristics which have invited objections to the other poems. First and foremost, the fact that it is in essence a parable, and that the meaning is so deeply hidden and embedded in the poem, and so nihilistic when discovered, that by some it will be disliked for its themelessness and by some for its morbidity. Superficially, the parable can be said to state that a great part of the effort of life is an effort to die; that consciousness is a disease of Matter, an abnormality, and that a part of consciousness knows this, and, like the Sibyl, wishes to die, to return into unconsciousness. A very simple and very comforting idea. In the poem, John Deth and Millicent Piggistaile represent the positive and negative poles of life (the terms should be reversed); and "love," or Venus, is the will or force that moves them. The other figure, Juliana Goatibed, in a sense contains them, is the sum of them, is their consciousness: it is through her that Deth and Millicent know their slavery and misery, and desire, by crucifixion of Venus, to obtain peace. In the allegorizing of this idea, there had to be and are certain imaginative loosenesses; the scheme need not be pressed too hard. What, in short, I have tried to do is to make on the one hand a poem which can be taken simply as a fantastic myth, and, on the other, one which will yield, on scrutiny, a profound meaning. . . .

Are your beans throwing pebbles about? Is your corn a foot high? Swarms the aphis and sings the hyla? Gorge you yet on asparagus? —O miserable world.   Conrad

60: TO ROBERT N. LINSCOTT^w   Jeake's House
                                                    Aug 28:24

. . . Cheered also by your last-ditch waving of the tattered flag and hoarse cry of On to death, boys, I set myself manfully morning after morning to turning out costive pages of novel [*Blue Voyage*]. Two chapters are now done (this after two years) and the third begun. I am beginning to enjoy it a little—I take it that's a fatal sign; it means that nobody else (but you) *will*. My difficulty is to keep it from being too Joycish; I fear I'm not doing so. Still, that's hard to say. I've altered the conception a good deal since I discussed it with you. You recall that there is a narrator, Demarest, young, literary, going to Europe in pursuit of a lady. There are also Smith, an old englishman returning to england after thirty years in a new orleans music store; Faubion a round brisk little strumpet who powerfully attracts both D and S.; the Welsh Rarebit, a hideous and lascivious welsh girl (the whore of the ship); Silberstein a very intelligent massive powerful ruthless bawdy coarse subtle jew who greatly interests and influences D; Hay-Lawrence a monocled englishman with a bad eye and a sea-complex who plays chess with D; the Major, an american officer, rather silly and infatuated with the welsh rarebit; two professional cardsharpers and various minor characters; and then (discovered two days out) Cynthia, in the first cabin. The intention is primarily to present these various people through Demarest's eyes, to present his own particular psychological problem *indirectly* in the course of his musings on these others and meetings with them: i.e., his struggle for balance as between Cynthia and Faubion, the former being a symbol of adolescent sublimation and refusal, the latter a symbol of maturity and acceptance: myth vs blood. A good deal of care will be given to the making of his portrait: it will be as rich and complete as I can make it. His mental stream is, of course, the medium for this as for all the rest of the tale—all the others appear only in so far as he sees them and comprehends them. Having D a psychotic and literary creature has its fine advantages here, for I can permit D to indulge in all sorts of phansies and frenzies and fantastic flights concerning not only himself but all the others. Faubion, for instance, assumes a definite musical key for him (so to speak) and a certain train of cuckoo imagination, highly wrought, is always set off by her. Ditto old Smith, for whom he feels a deep affection and pity and whom he slightly grotesquely (but fondly) conceives. The action, I hear you cry? Almost none, in the accepted sense. One stream of action will flow sluggishly from D's preoccupation (much interrupted) with Cynthia. Another from Smith's old-man lech for Faubion, which D tries to head off, vainly. A third from the progressive losses of the cardsharpers (this always in the background, a low muttering accompaniment) which ends in a theft of gold sovereigns (30 yrs. savings) from Smith. A fourth in the Major-welsh rarebit affair (and the rest of her promiscuous career hinted at) ending in the scene I think I mentioned to you, her cross-examination, drunk, by Silberstein, also drunk, the last night. The end? Cynthia cuts him dead, and he refuses Faubion; he quarrels with Smith over a trifle; and rides from Liverpool to London with Silberstein, swapping lubricious recollections. He is now an adult, but profoundly unhappy. Selah. . . .   C A

61: TO ROBERT N. LINSCOTT[w]   Jeake's House
                                                                 Rye Sussex Sept 4:24

JOAN DELANO AIKEN put in her appearance this morning at 3:25 (Jessie always *will* do these things at night!) with the usual Aiken, or should I say McDonald, speed: so much so that she beat the doctor (whom I, blind with sleep, was sent staggering to summon) by five minutes. Result, Jessie was rather badly torn, necessitating an anaesthetic sewing-up this morning at eleven. She is now flourishing, and so is Joan, who has reddish hair, large flat ears, blue feet, and a scowl hideous beyond belief. Weight: 7¾ lbs. Well-developed instinct for the taking of nourishment. Perfectly quiet— not a chirrup—since her first bath, during which she skritched with skritches of a rabelaisian gusto. John and Jane much intrigued. She was to have been named Ann or Nancy Delano, but Jane was so insistent that the name should begin with a J that the parents gave in! —A nurse is here, doctors rattle in and out, Armstrong (who was visiting) departed hastily this morning while Jessie was hollering lugubriously under chloroform (I always forget what a terrible sound that is.) The new kitten (vagabond, Samuel Jeake, flearidden) went cuckoo during the party and pushed all the pianola rolls off the piano. —Will you be so kind as to insert notices in the Transcript and Herald of this achievement? At Jeake's House, Rye, Sussex England etc. Defray the cost out of the enclosed check? Many many thanks.

I can't tell you how much I was delighted by the fact that you like the new poems and that you have already with such celerity sold one. I dont care *who* you sell them to! —I am delighted also that you think they are a change. They seem so to me, but I can't be a judge of them. Do give me any further lights you can when you have time. Borborigmi is my own favourite, I think—though I like the Old Man Weeping almost as well, and the Hanging Gardens. Armstrong thought the latter still very characteristic of an earlier vein, which surprised me. He liked Cliff Meeting best. (This, and The Road, were direct transcriptions from dreams.) —I'm not sure that any of them go far enough in the new direction, however—I like better what I see they might have been. When I have made some money, I'll try to go on with it perhaps. Or rather to see more clearly where such things might lead. *That* is really the difficulty. Dante is, I think, the grandfather.   yrs   C A

62: TO ROBERT N. LINSCOTT[W]   Jeakes
                                                     Sept 17 24

Southwest gale for the umpteenth day in succession, and I'm going mad, going mad, howling like wolf, cucking like cuckoo, running up and down the draughty stairs to see which stove is smoking now and why isnt the infant being fed and who's in the bathroom now and arent there dammit any stamped envelopes and why the devil why in gods name didn't turner put a stronger spring on that door jesus *CRISTO* the stupidity of the human race etc. etc. etc. A rawnerved suburbanite the Post calls you, with the soul of a poet. Eureka, linscott is described at last, nailed to the cross, moaning, in the southwest gale. Praise god, sang Theophryte, the rawboned rawnerved suburbanite. . . . having eaten a herring, a soft roe, fourteen bones, a pint of ale, a sour baked apple, and pumped john's tires for him (he planning to ride to winchelsea this afternoon) and seen three translucent curds slide out of joan's wideopen

95

tilted mouth, and given jessie K Falk to read, restored to sanity i resume. . . .

. . . You saw that [Joseph] Conrad is dead? speaking of falk.

E. M. Forster: A Room with a View. Howard's End. Celestial Omnibus. A very individual and charming novelist, with a delicious sense of character and humour.

Another short poem written, which will be sent in due course.

> seaholly, a splinter of rock—it was for this,
> this rocklipped facing of brown waves, half sand
> and half water, this tentative hand that slides
> over the breast of rock, and into the hollow
> soft side of muslin rock, and then fiercely
> almost as rock against the hip of rock—
> it was for this in midnight the rocks met,
> and dithered together, cracking and smoking.

and at last I took up the dance of john deth, and regarded it coldly from a great height and saw it to be even worse than you and the other kind critics led me to suspect, and forthwith, suspending my review of Croce for the Nation and abandoning all thought of finishing the novel I savagely seized it and tore it limb from leg and arm from wing and gullet from gizzard. that is to say, I have changed parts two and one from octosyllabics into irregular line-lengths, keeping the rhyme-scheme, and I think it is much improved. part three, I think, will stay as it is, but part four will also be altered, and perhaps part five. this will leave only the bird section as it was, in regular couplets, and that much regularity will, I believe, be endurable; besides, the bird section was the best written, and i wouldnt with such confidence try to change it. —I have also broken the changed parts up into small lengths, numbered, which gives the stifled reader a chance to get his wind from time to time. —I have also now almost finished revising the house of dust, and have reduced it to three-fourths of its original size, lopping out some forty pages or so and making a great number of minor revisions as well. The titles of the episodes will appear in the margins.

o how it has rained this last six weeks o how the wind has howled at all hours and the rain blown in onto my poor head at night and the doors slamming and one door smashing and windows crashing and the cat samuel jeake racing his fleas up and down the halls and john and jane bringing mud on their feet from the garden and the ivy blown down from the schoolhouse wall. death i say to myself and how nice how nice how nice it would be to be dead how good to be safe in tombs and at all times walking or thinking or talking or trying to recall the five tunes i know on the piano, or listening at night to the wind and the wailing of joan and the mewing of a loose chimney cowl or waiting for the next thing or waiting to wait for the next thing or just waiting, and waiting again, waiting empty minded and empty hearted, waiting for the worm to reach the end of the corridor, waiting for the door to open in a flood of light and the bird entering to say PEACE, how nice i think how nice it would be to be safe in a tomb.   C A

63: TO G. B. WILBUR^r

Jeake's House
Rye Sussex
Sept 21:24

. . . Is your book complete?[1] —I was also much amused to learn of your ambiguity of mind in re your new house. *That* touched a responsive chord! I still dream furiously of mixed south yarmouth and winchelsea landscapes, towns which combine boston and london and gatherings of people who mix linscott and wilbur with armstrong and eliot. I wish I could make out why it is that I am so much freer to *write* here (in England) than at home—freer, that is, to write verse or fiction, while not nearly so free for careful or spontaneously vigorous and assured *criticism*. The latter I find extremely painful and difficult; I avoid it in every possible way; I am this very minute writing you rather than finishing the reading of a new Croce book which I'm supposed to be reviewing. To write verse or fiction, on the other hand, is perhaps easier for me than it has been since the delightful years 1916–7 in boston— . . .

Yes I have read Max [Bodenheim] on John [Coffey],[2] with much interest. I think it's deliberately a good deal bowdlerized, and of course tiresomely sentimentalized. I think what surprises me most is to find Max *believing* in the christmotif so extensively, and so little interested in uncovering its particular causes—i.e., giving so little emphasis to John's early history, the sexual influence, the ambivalence of theft and fornication and then the later translation of

1. A projected study of the psychoanalytic movement, never completed.
2. See Letter 31, note 1. C A and Wilbur are discussing Bodenheim's novel *Crazy Man* (New York, 1924), which was based on Coffey.

these two factors, mingled, into the "philosophy" (which called for *"free* wealth," in order that there might be a maximum amount of *"reproduction,"* to wit, sexual indulgence; at any rate, that's the way it always looked to me). Of course, one must remember that Max had his eye on saleability when writing the book, as he had his eye, when following John about, on the réclame which might be his share. So I fancy one cant attach too much credence to his sincerity: John was to begin with and has remained for Max a source of picturesqueness and profit. A case in which the profit was not without honour. Also, I seriously doubt whether Max is very intelligent. Up to a point, yes; but the point is soon reached, and the sooner for the fact that Max is by habit dishonest with himself. He is quite capable of pretending to himself that John is to be taken seriously as a prophet. He did pretend to do so, that fall in S.Y., and was simply berserk when I accused him of not giving a damn about J.'s ideas (this in J.'s presence one night) and of tagging after him solely because it struck him as somewhat romantic and as having a Verlaine-Rimbaud flavour. His anger, and subsequent air of deep injury and scorn, seemed to me very indicative—I may do the coffey story myself one day: with max thrown in for good measure!

Croce (to take up my cross again!) strikes me—more every time I return to him—as a fine case of highclass intellectual fake. I should be glad to know what you think of him. I dont mean that he hasnt his good qualities—he is clever, he is ingenious at logic, he is wellinformed; he even has certain good qualities in applied criticism; but my god what verbalism, vanity, prolixity and above all sophistry. And his attitude toward any scientific threat of his logistic domain! the air of an offended god. He is obviously worried about this, for he never tires of angry references to "these psychophysiologists" who would try to explain aesthetic facts. Query: why exactly did he choose the penname of Blessed Cross? He and Gabriel of the Annunciation are an interesting phenomenon in Italian letters.

It delights me to hear that the dental dream suggests to you a castration motive.[3] That hadnt occurred to me. I should have said rape! but I believe you are right. And I think there is some light here on my difficulty as regards criticism (analysis) here (England), and on the corresponding difficulty as regards my writing of poetry *at*

---

3. C A's teeth were in bad condition when in his dream Jake appeared as a dentist and pulled the wrong tooth. C A had been trying to pull answers from Jake about the "hero-messiah" character in C A's play.

home: I identify you, doubtless, with the far greater degree of self-consciousness and psychological awareness which is current in present american criticism than one discovers over here. Ergo, when in S.Y., you inhibit my normal (?) habit of catharsis by poetry; when I am in england, however, that is resumed, and *I* inhibit the *analysis.* I havent examined this notion, but off hand it looks reasonable. Of course, this mechanism doesnt work perfectly either way: my selfunderstanding goes steadily forward, if slowly, and is finding for the moment a particularly useful field in the novel, where analysis and poiesis can go hand in hand. Whether that will be the last gasp of the poetic, heaven knows. I doubt it, for a new stratum has come to light (as regards verse) this summer; it is itself more analytical, however—it perhaps dates from the enclosed Psychomachia, which was written in June 1922, but conceived vaguely a long time before that. But with this increased analysis also goes an increased amount of *symbolism*—that is what strikes me as odd, and as suggesting that bottom is not yet in sight. I may go deeper, in other words, but my resistance (and its useful poetic handmaiden) go with me. I am finding this process extraordinarily interesting.

The salavation army band has arrived outside (this being sunday) so further throught is impossible. Love to all of you.   Conrad

Salavation: an error.

I used to parody the song "I'd like to be married to the music of a military band" to "I'd like to be married to the music of a salivary gland."

64: TO: T. S. ELIOTʳ   Jeake's House, Rye
                                         Jan. 14:25

Dear Tom: Your suggestion, made via Mr. Fasset,[1] that I should review Miles, Aldington, and Ransom, gives me a sharp attack of schizophrenia, i.e., mixed feelings. Is it as unexciting and mediocre a trio as it sounds? And then I intensely dislike "group" reviews of verse, and avoid it when possible. If you desperately want it done, why then I'll shut my eyes and *take* the mudbath. But I should greatly prefer to miss the opportunity and to wait for some

1. I. P. Fassett frequently wrote reviews for *The Criterion.*

one book a little more enlivening. At the same time,—and again, on the other hand,—and so forth. I leave it to you.

Curse you for printing Read after rejecting my own treatment of that matter.[2] A good article, however, more painstaking than mine, if less comprehensive and perceptive. Perhaps I came a shade too soon. I now have the chagrin of seeing Read, I. A. Richards, et al., playing the parts of pioneers. (The Richards book is extremely interesting[3]—I've been reviewing it for the Nation.)

A nice juicy number of the Criterion—I like what I've read of it (bar Monro!) Your poems are delightful. And speaking of pancakes, can't I sell you a very *very* good short story for your next number? (It would have to be the next number, for my book of stories is about to be set up.) Three for you to choose from: two of five thousand, one of three thousand words. Speak. I will hold my book Ms here until I hear from you, so that I can make copies if you should be interested.   yrs as ever   C A

65: TO ROBERT N. LINSCOTT[w]   Jeake's
                                                May 14 25

Curse Liveright— . . .

I've been ill again, in bed another week, and finally bored with the recurring plague consulted the local doc, who, with a face long as a tombstone, said "periurethral abscess" and threatened me with all sorts of perpetual horrors ensuing on the necessary operation. Before taking me to the hospital, however, he decided to submit me to a specialist in town, and on Wednesday I rose from my bed and went thither, trembling, after putting all my affairs in order: last revisions, financial documents labelled, everything put where J[es-sie] could find it. Mr. Neligan, the specialist, tortured me in every conceivable way—it was astounding. Bicycle pumps stuck out of

---

2. C A comments on the January 1925 *Criterion*, which printed Herbert Read, "Psychoanalysis and the Critic," and a review by Harold Monro of C A's *Selected Poems of Emily Dickinson, Edited with an Introduction*. C A's restraint in "(bar Monro!)" can be measured in light of Monro's: "She was intellectually blind, partially deaf, mostly dumb, to the art of poetry." Though Eliot did not accept a story, Edwin Muir reviewed *Bring! Bring!* in the July 1925 *Criterion*, calling C A's style in the stories "firm, economical, perfectly conscious, and informed with intelligence. These qualities make this volume one of the most remarkable that have appeared for some time."
3. *Principles of Literary Criticism* (London, 1924). C A's reviews in *Nation and Athenaeum* (January 24, 1925) and *New Republic* (March 18, 1925) precipitated a lifelong friendship. See "Preface" by I. A. Richards to Conrad Aiken, *Collected Criticism*.

every orifice of me, bellows were attached to them and pumped, telescopes with lights were thrust into me, I was prodded probed pounded and sounded, and at the end I was gladdened by being told that it was abscess of the rectum instead, which is far less serious. Greatly uplifted I sprang into a train home, buying a paper to read. I felt that I had just been born—a long and joyous and unexpected prospect of life before me. Spring spring. And then and there I saw that my old enemy was dead, Amy [Lowell], noble Amy. How I despised myself then for my facile self-pity and for my failure to die—how she seemed to have worsted me once again. I was surprisingly moved and saddened, and still am. A damned shame. How did it happen? A lot of colour will go out of american letters with Amy; for all her vanities and faults a magnificent creature. My blackmailing review of Keats being on the point of issue, I cabled the Dial (I hope not too late) to temper its strictures or to subjoin a note.[1] I also thought seriously of cabling you to send some flowers on my behalf, but, for a complex of queer reasons, decided not to. Chiefly I was deterred by recollections of my last talk with Amy over the telephone, at ten o'clock on my last night in America, 1923, when she, forgivingly (for I'd never been near her since she had me to dinner the year before) asked me to come out to Brookline at once, bringing my three guests. Impossible, of course, but I neednt have been as cool to her as I was. Last night, therefor, I dreamed that Jessie complimented Amy on a certain poem. "Yes," said Amy, "I like that poem too—it has a lovely golden-yellow sunrise translucence, hasn't it!" And climbing into a monstrous cab, she rolled away down the hill, her round face looking out of the window like the moon. She sang, as she rolled away, and then I realized that I had failed, alas, to take off my hat. Nothing could more accurately symbolize my feeling. . . .

It is heavenly here now—summer weather at last. The cuckoo, the nightingale, and the skylark are all doing their best. Our two little apple trees are blossoming, and one of our laburnums, and two azaleas, and two lilacs; all in a space about the size of your front lawn at Winchester. Clara, the seventeen year old maid, overcome by vernal emotions, has got herself pregnant without benefit of clergy, and has been fired, the departure to take place six weeks

1. See Letter 73; C A's fifteen-page review of Amy Lowell's two-volume *John Keats* was published as written—without comment—in the June *Dial* (C A's *Collected Criticism*, pp. 238–53).

hence. She remarked, when she reported that her family threatened to turn her out, that if they did she'd be the first they ever *had* so treated—her half dozen sisters all went the same road, and the household swarms with little bastards. Well well. I end with a quotation which has pleased me!

> How twas created, how the soul exists,—
> One talkes of motes, the soul was made of motes;
> An other fire, tother light, a third a spark of star-like nature;
> Hippo, water; Anaximenes, ayre,
> Aristoxenus musicke, Critias I know now what.
> A company of odde phreneteci
> Did eate my youth, and when I crept abroad,
> Finding my numness in this nimble age,
> I fell a railing; but now, soft and slow,
> I know I know naught, but I naught do know;
> What shall I doe—what plot, what course, persew?
>
> —Why, turne a temporist, row with the tide,
> Persew the cut, the fashion of the age.

Isn't it delicious? John Marston.[2]   C A

66: TO MAURICE FIRUSKI   Jeake's House, Rye
                                          June 9 25

. . . Armstrong is here, with a boil on the back of his neck; for which reason our tennis party this p.m. with Miss Briggs and snaggletoothed edith is off, thank god. My ancient Cousin Julia Delano, astounding woman, has visited us and gone. My prospective cousin-in-law, Rosalind Parker, of Cambridge Mass, has visited us and gone. Fletcher is coming next week. The Taussigs are coming in the fall. But these tastes of my native land only whet my appetite for the soil itself: the cobblestones of Boston and the sand of South Yarmouth. I should like, for example, to have Bob [Linscott] (learned historian) point out to me where Pudding Lane used to be: in 1719 T. Fleet, as you doubtless know, published The Rhymes of Mother Goose at Pudding Lane, in Boston. Is there no memorial to him? I

---

2. *What You Will*, II, i, in *The Works of John Marston* (London, 1856, "reprinted from the original editions"), vol. I, p. 251. C A had been reading and making notes on all of Marston's works, using this edition.

suggest that on the Common there ought to be a colossal goose erected instead of the civil war memorial. Or do you think it ought to be in front of the Christian Science Church? Or it might be placed at a convenient distance behind Edward Everett Hale, and connected with his hand by a string: the goose, of course, should be about twenty times his size. For isn't that goose Boston's greatest contribution to civilization? —Well, I must put on my shoon and drink some vermouth.   As ever   Conrad

67: TO ROBERT N. LINSCOTT[w]   Jeakes house Rye
                                                june 10 25

eliot is the cruellest poet, breeding
lyrics under the driest dustpan, mixing
memory and desire, stirring
verb-roots with spring brain.
aiken kept him safe, covering
dearth with forgetful verbiage, needing
no notes, no elaborate allusions or explanations,
(for there was nothing to explain).
In the spring I am fond of radishes, tomatoes, and also
the white onion, and the little pot
that is neither red nor yellow, not
planted with mignonette or bergamot.
It is not a carapace for the head
nor a cuirass, nor is it even
the crosse and blackwell pot of marmalade
nor is it the crossed pentacles, nor the three
lilies, nor the wand, by which is foretold
nothing. It is not bone, nor the brain pan
of the friendless and unburied man:
It is the I-know-not-what
on which much chamber music has been played:
it is a simple porcelain pot.

What is this that comes up, in the spring? what
forms on the potter's wheel of el-i-ot?
what is this tubular shape, molto sympatica,
not bloodroot, nor yet hepatica,
mandrake, or forked radish, nor asparagus tip

103

what is this that comes up in the spring, coming
upward, and up again, and again up,
what is it that rhymes with tup,
in spring? there is many a slip
between the cup
and lip

the gypsy woman that lives in salem street
came on mondays to get my washing
bringing always with her a little bag
of blood. It was in this she kept it. It was here
she fed it, grinning, and dropping into the sac
one drop of seawater and two of japalac.
(The sound of the sea, dropping within the bag,
was flat, absurd, the voice of the parakleet,
or of the hooknosed spirochaet.)
Just a little. Just a little bit.
A little while. The pillow subtly placed
The towel ready, the eye chaste or unchaste,
what does it matter? the clothes-wringer
removes all trace, carthago delendum est,
the clothes wringer, or the printer's error
for that flower, which is not blood-red, the syringa.

jug jug twit twit wot twot cuckoo
I know a trick, a trick worth two, worth two

Just a little while, just a little
Pot and jot and tittle
the bed turned down, or here
where shepherd's thumb is sprouting on the moutain
and the little dry red stick
look look is covered with downy hair and leaves
who would have said it was possible, who would have said
the stiff wood would bring roses from this bed
and prick, the thorns that prick?
This is not the scotch
thistle, he said, no no, it is not the scotch
thistle, for that is purple, and has a prick
but come behind that hedge, and I will show you
the thistle that is neither white nor yellow,
I will show you the thistle with the purple prick.

No oh no oh no oh no oh no and that night
she could not sleep, she put it in her bed,
weeping, feeling the dead thing by her, dead
yet living, resurrected, feeling the burning
thorn beside her, or within,
tearing the calamus, or was it the naked skin
io hymen io io

                    a buttocky beauty named bella
                    went out for a ride with a fella
                            she returned from the ride
                            with nothing outside
                  but the knob of the fella's umbrella
          I am a woman in a mackintosh
walking beside the red sea in the morning
          I will wear my rubbers or an old galosh
walking beside the bloodpond in the morning
above the abattoir the chimney smokes,
          or is the smoke the smoke of blood, the slaughter
of mary's lamb, or the ox's little daughter?
          at dusk I walk beside the kadaververwertung
the charnel works are working late tonight
          and the blood flows like water.

Hurry hurry and put me in the ground
hurry before the moon undresses
there, where the putrid brook bears poisoned watercresses
like Hecate's mephitic tresses
dig the grave and let me lie
like a defeated boxer with a purple eye
above my green bones heap
droppings of goats and sheep
say the words quickly
and strew the parsley on me thickly
put the pot beside me, cover me with a sheet
of summer lightning, I, who died of prickly
heat

what next is growing there? what growing? what?
it must have been that canuck, that soda jerker
jerking sodas in my little pot
a fast worker, a fast worker

for in spite of all its technical precisions,
its previsions and illogical divisions,
it is nothing but a series of revisions
such as the aprils and the mays may bring,
or wild oats planted in a windowpot,
to one who reads his eliot in the spring.

C A

I really like it very much, despite its *extraordinary amazing* saturation in T. S. E. But he shouldn't have printed it—should have
waited till he'd got out of the penumbra. It's the most flagrant case
of imitation, the profoundest I ever saw! Nevertheless an astonishing gain in power and maturity, and good reading.[1]

68: TO T. S. ELIOT^r   Jeake's House Rye
                                                          July 9:25

Dear Tom: I'm sorry you can't come at the moment, but glad
to hear from you. I went to town, unexpectedly and unannoun-
cedly, for a day last week, and among other things called at the
Bank of Lloyd; a mere accident saved me from walking into your
office, now labelled Ladies. Aylward informed me that you had
been absent for six months, and I was somewhat alarmed for you.
But I assume from your letter that you are reasonably well. I hope
it doesn't mean that your wife has had a relapse?
    As for the reviewing question. Your very kind suggestions, both
as to the particular reviews and the matter of a book, embarrass me
greatly. As regards the latter (your suggestion of a book of criticism
on contemporary English fiction): even if I were to undertake it I
should probably have to offer it to the Hogarth Press, with whom
I'm at the moment negotiating *re* a book of verse. Woolf wants the
refusal of my prose, and I have granted it. Perhaps it was Woolf
you had in mind? In any case I'm most grateful to you for the proffer of help. —My real trouble is not that, however, but a kind of
paralysis of the critical faculty which is the result of, or is accompanied by, or is the cause of, an intense hatred of reviewing. It's too
complicated for explanation in a letter—I could only make it clear

1. Needless to say, in this note C A parodies a typical "little magazine" critic—reviewing a
poem by C A! In 1917 and 1918 he *had* reviewed in this vein his own books for *The Chicago
News* (*Collected Criticism*, pp. 120–26).

to you by the drooping of an eyelid. I seem to be intellectually bankrupt, and the simplest and shortest review takes me weeks and costs me agonies to do, and then turns out to be worthless. Unfortunate, because it is an important source of revenue. If some really *captivating* book came along (but what it is that might be captivating I don't know!) I might "rise" to it, conceivably; but [David] Garnett and Virginia (though I rather enjoy Virginia) arouse in me, as potential reviewer, nothing but despair. I'm sorry. Perhaps later I'll have recovered my equilibrium, or the pleasant illusion that I have something to say that is worth the saying. In the meantime, I want a few months holiday from reviewing, during which, if I try criticism at all, it will be for American papers, where one can be more irresponsible. Will you, therefor, try me again with something in November or thereabouts? and forgive me?

I hope you've had the time and impulse to write? I've done nothing this year—nothing except one act of a melodrama and a few octosyllabics. —I may be in town for a day or two next week. If so, I'll let you know, and will hope to see you for a minute.   As ever   C A

69: TO MAURICE FIRUSKIᴵ   Fitzroy Square! London [1]
                                           Dec 30 25

Was my pen shaky? It will not be shakier, Maurice—how disgustingly percipient of you to be sure! I was on the verge of Op. 2. I have now performed it, or had it performed; and I might add that the first movement was far, far more excruciating than any that was heard in Brookline. This now seems centuries ago. I came here on Dec. 10th or 11th—and I shall call a taxi to the door tomorrow, and kiss goodbye this Anus Mirabilis—it being the 31st. Pardon the purulent puns. —More soberly: the first operation turned out a failure. As for the second, the surgeon is sanguine, but so was *I*, this morning at 9:51. I give it up. It may be all right. If not, I'll try again; and again, and again. Like the young lady from Spain:

> One night of pleasure
> And nine months of pain.
> Three months of leisure,

1. C A writes from the hospital where he underwent two operations to correct a rectal fistula.

Then at it again:
Such is the life
Of the Queen of Spain.

How did you know that I was dying to read the Greek Anthology?[2] and in fact had begun to do so in Boston at the Harvard Club? —Tom Eliot's new book [*Poems, 1909–1925*] has sold 700 copies already. He is in the firm of Faber and Gwyer—so I'm told. He was here himself the other day, but didn't mention this.

What else? Nothing. The English Nursing Home is singularly primitive—no heat except coal fires. Bath two flights up. Unheated corridors and the temperature down to 30. *Tea* served to unwilling patients at 7 a.m. Hideous gaunt nurses with circus hats on their heads. Porters who come to the bedside with the morning papers. *But*—one is allowed to smoke and drink, and one is fed pheasants, plovers, turkey, and partridge. Yum yum. . . .

. . . I've been reading Wuthering Heights—a french John Webster!

A major chord, please, in your next.   Conrad

70: TO ROBERT N. LINSCOTT[w]   jeakes house
                                                Jan 4 26

Out of hospital five days ago: weak and fat, fatter than ever, unable to button clothes or see feet except in mirrors; a night spent with armstrong and then to rye, where there was no money in the bank, but two weeks food supply and half a bottle of irish whisky. Joan had a sty in the corner of the left eye, the stovepipe in the study had rusted shut, damper immovable, and trying to repair same i removed epidermis from index finger (said finger of vital importance for morning and evening rites relating to rectum; painful now to both rectum and finger). Floods on all marshes, rove the jaded eye where it will, floods in Holland where the Gross Quean rows in a little boat ("down" in the stern) to visit flooded subjects; floods of tears in the glassy eye of the hairless middleaged ex-poet. cui bono? cui bono? says the stray dog, translating it where is a bone? poor devil. Ten, eleven or twelve days on the sea, in rainy weather, with few or no interesting (but what is interesting?) companions, with a

2. Firuski had sent J. W. Mackail's translation of *Select Epigrams from the Greek Anthology* (London and New York, 1906).

disinclination to sit down and a marked inability to stand up, with periodic and dreaded visits from the ship surgeon—alas I am wounded within with a deep wound. On the operating table, half etherized, he laughed heartily, however, and clapping his thigh cried out Ha, that's a good one, that's the best one yet! which much surprised the surgeon's poised knife. Drugged profoundly for a period with morphine, he wrote a letter to T. S. Eliot, who had sent him his new book. Dear Tom: It was kind of you to have your publishers send me your new collection—I am delighted to have it, only regretting that you didn't inscribe it Priapus from Bolo, or something of the sort. An omission which you can repair when you come to Rye for a weekend. It's an appallingly impressive small volume, and surprisingly homogeneous. How the devil did you manage to discover your identity so early? One imagines that you might have sat, "hat in hand, on the doorstep of the Absolute,"[1] at the age of five—your mind and manners already distinct and distinguished. While the rest of us spend our lives trying to find out who we are. I envy you with all my heart. And you must know that there is no contemporary poetry of which the future place seems to me so sure, or which gives me half so much delight. —You see me horizontal, half inarticulate, and somewhat weak—recovering from two small painful undignified operations (on the tail.) If you pass anywhere Fitzroy square, ring the bell and come in to see me. But are you still "out of England"? as ever, Conrad. —The reply to this, after a few days, with a french postmark, was a page torn out of the Midwives Gazette: instructions to those about to take exams for nurseing certificates. At the top, T. S. E. had underlined the words *Model Answers*. Under this was a column descriptive of various forms of vaginal discharge, normal and abnormal. Here the words *blood, mucous,* and *shreds of mucous* had been underlined with a pen, and lower down also the phrase *purulent offensive discharge*. Otherwise, no comment. —The recipient was unable to sleep for mortification and pain. He replied the next day: "Have you tried Kotex for it? Manufactured by the Dupont Powder Co. Absorbent, Deodorant, Antiseptic, *Inflammable*. A boon to women the world over. The problem of disposal—that bugbear to all sensitive women—a thing of the past. LADIES! YOUR ALLURE! *Some* days! Can you wear your lightest frocks, your daintiest silks and satins, with per-

1. Eliot's "Spleen," *The Harvard Advocate* (January 26, 1910), reprinted in *Poems Written in Early Youth* (New York, 1967).

fect security? KOTEX. Used with success by Blue-eyed Claude the Cabin Boy." An asterisk was placed against the word "boy," and at the bottom of the page the letters "P.T.O." And between this and the main body of the letter was the couplet:

"Tut, hang up hieroglyphicks! I'll not feign,
Wresting my humour from his native strain."[2]

There was also an enclosure, a printed slip taken from a cigarette package: "In case of any complaint regarding the contents of this package, please return this slip." (Have you, I wonder, heard of

Blue eyed Claude the cabin boy,
the clever little nipper
who filled his ass with broken glass
and circumcised the skipper?)

Three days later Tom called: a little flustered and embarrassed, a little at a disadvantage, but excessively friendly. There was no reference to his communication to me, and only a passing reference by me to my suggestion of Kotex, a suggestion for which he thanked me. Then to other subjects. —Surely this was the deepest, darkest, subtlest, most malignant and forth-dimensional correspondence yet managed by homo sapiens! I still shudder when I think of it. I was prepared for anything: and expected a permanent rupture; though I hoped I had been sufficiently oblique, savage, and yet unguessably guarded, to make him afraid to take that step. Did I succeed or did I not? Was I the fool or was he? No, we were both fools.

Notes were made en Voyage, and the fifth chapter was begun today.[3]

Last night I dreamt that you were visiting us, and I was taking you to Canterbury. For pete's sake come in the spring.

WHAT was the meaning of the goldfish?

Helen's letter was sherbet in the sahara.

I shant know whether I'm wholly recovered for another month.

What about W Blackstone?[4]   C

2. John Marston, "Scourge of Villanie," Satyre I, in *Works,* vol. III, p. 250.
3. That is, during his hospitalization C A made notes for *Blue Voyage.*
4. With view to a projected poem, C A has asked Linscott to send biographical information on William Blackstone, the "solitary bookish recluse" who was living on Boston Common when the first settlers arrived. He is the prototype of C A's "The Kid."

71: TO T. S. ELIOT^r   Jeake's House
                                                      Jan 21:26

Dear Tom: after a relapse, haemorrhage (purulent offensive discharge) and vivid nightmare of Op. 3, I am now recovering again
and can manage a pub-crawl at moderate speed, thank you. Blue-
eyed claude is himself again.

   Not, however, so overcharged with energy as to take lightly this
matter of reviewing books. A page more of dialogue in my novel,
every second day, about all I can rise to. BUT: if there is no great
hurry, I'd like to try the Wharton primer? I tremble a little at the
thought, for I find that my little intelligence has shrunk, through
long disuse. . . . I know nothing, I feel nothing, and I can neither
see nor think. . . .   as ever   C A

72: TO ROBERT N. LINSCOTT^w   jeake
                                                      may 27 26

physical history since he last wrote: p and o ship from tilbury dock
to gibraltar, that famous rock; dull cold voyage, few passengers, one
pretty girl with whom he did not make acquaintance; she was pursued by an american who looked half dago; a frosty faced english
naval officer, in mufti, with the remains of a shellshock, slightly
cuckoo, became infatuated and having had a drink one night broke
out loudly in the smoking room By god at the dance tonight I'll
warn her against him. She shouldn't, a nice girl like that, be playing
with him. Her brother in the airforce at Quetta. What would he
think of it, eh? Social standing. And by god I never saw such a
hardfaced bugger in my life. Never! —Loud applause. The drama,
alas, was still only in the making when we debarked at gib. We saw
the hardfaced bugger ashore by himself; the girl with the officer.
They were all going all the way to bombay, so there was plenty of
time for murder. —Spain: stinks. Hokusai colouring: red soil, grass-
less, planted for miles with olive orchards and cork trees. Hard slaty
mountains, bare and sharp. Aridity. Buzzards, vultures, eagles, and
orioles. Red goats, red pigs, red sheep, all in one herd, tended by a
boy with a stick. Goats with protracted bifurcated udders which
drag on the ground. White houses with flat roofs, barred windows;
cactus, prickly pear, and aloes. Open drains in the streets fre-

quently. Children wear no drawers and use the streets (preferably adjacent to a wall) for all purposes; nocturnal walking therefor unsafe. Peasants handsome saturnine and somewhat moorish in type; city type more characteristically latin, frivolous and excitable; damned fools fond of noise and chatter. Sleep everywhere impossible, owing to catholic bells which ring all night, cocks that crow up the dawn at midnight, cats that love and dogs that bark, and the spanish themselves who go to bed at three. Patios are charming, open to the sky, crowded with flowers, more flowers dropping scarlet petals from balconies, palm trees in tubs, the center of the life of the house. Food yum yum; but the gap between lunch at twelve and dinner at eighty-thirty was cruel. Hence the national habit of sitting in cafés all the time and drinking coffee, which is good but goaty—goat's milk universal. Goats are driven into the cities and milked at the doors: frequently, if alarmed by a passing Ford, step into the patio or a bedroom. The spanish are fond of clubs; but the main idea of the club is to exhibit its members; hence the front is all glass, and the members sit on view; or even in a row of chairs set on the sidewalk. No privacy aimed at. Café cantantes: you go at night, nine thirty, order a coffee (ten cents) and see the show. Carmen Vargas is in many respects the best and most beautiful dancer I ever saw, the most seductive. Male audience loud in its comments, urging her with shouts to lift her skirts higher, hissing also when she did so if it were not done with sufficient subtlety and grace. Moorish palaces in granada, and mosque in cordova, and cathedral in seville, superb. Wildflowers in prodigious variety. Oranges on the trees. Almonds on the trees. Wines cheap and heavenly. No beautiful women, or few. Respectable women live like prisoners: if they go out at all, with servant. Play no games, never walk, fat at twenty-five, hard eyes, empty brilliant smile full of bright teeth, all alike. No country for fornication. Catholic and pagan combined, they make a tremendous festival of holy week: processions, bearing floats, wearing masks, hoods, carrying red torches, palms, lifesized figures of christ on the ass, christ in his glass and tortoiseshell coffin, christ in jewels and silks, christ in a sheet with blood in frozen stalactites on his waxen cheeks. Trumpeters preceding, centurions marching proudly with spears, mummers bearing the symbols of the crucifixion—the spear, the crown of thorns, the cup of vinegar, the kerchief of veronica. Zealots break out into song, improvising *saetas,* arrows of song, or familiar *coplas.* If applauded, they follow, singing. Climax to all this on easter: the first bullfight of the season. Crowds: everybody goes. Circular stadium jammed with people, as many women as men, balconies with gorgeous shawls, embroidered with roses, flung over parapets. Women in combs ten inches high, black lace mantillas over the combs, carnations under their ears. Trumpet, and the two official horsemen canter in, bow to the president. Trumpet, and the toreadors in procession, crimson and green smallclothes embroidered with gold, tightfitting over the buttocks, buckled at the knee; tricorne hat, white stockings or pink, small neat claspless slippers, flatsoled, tufted with blue or scarlet. Stately bows to the president, the picadors on their lean nags ditto, then the muleteam, bedizened with red plumes and streamers and bells, three mules abreast, they who drag out the conquered bull, gallops round the ring and out. Chulos, servants, in blue linen, remove an orange peel or two. The toreadors take their stations and the two picadors, on their horses, against the barrier. Trumpet, and the doors under the stuffed bull's head are flung open, and the BULL. Gallops in like mad. Sees a matador at the far side, and goes for him like an express train with marvelous terrifying speed and power, the hindquarters nimble and steely, the shoulders and back massive, the horns widebranching and sharp, tail up, head up, till the lunge, headdown. The matador skips over the barrier, the horns crash on the wood, he wheels, sees another crimson and gold cloak, and makes for it. The matador sidesteps at the last minute, leaving the crimson cloak to take the charge, and whisking this away too at the hornspoint, over the upward lunging head. The bull is turned about instantly and charges again, again, again, each charge shorter and at closer quarters, the matador turning the cloak now this way and now that. At a certain moment, how judged I do not know, he perceives that the bull is not again going to charge, and walks off with his back turned, unmolested. A picador now trots his blindfolded horse around the ring till it takes the bull's eye, then brings it to a stand. The bull paws, gives a little shrill stifled bugle, and goes for it, crashes under the stirrups, while the picador bores down with his pike into the bull's shoulder. The horse is lifted, struggles to reach the ground with feeble legs, is borne over against the barrier, falls, the picador flinging himself over the barrier. The bull lunges again, ripping and tearing, till diverted by a flourish of cloaks. The horse staggers up, with yards of tripe hanging, and a red bag or two, gallops round the ring kicking off pieces of his intestines, till caught.

113

Stands submissive while he is remounted (if not too badly torn.) Courage and discipline of horses is astounding. Is again led out before the bull, and stands patiently. Charged again, collapses on the sand, and while the bull is drawn off is despatched with a dagger in the brain, then covered with gunny sack. When the bull has killed two, trumpet, the second stage, the placing of the banderillos. The matador runs out to the middle without cloak, two blue yardlong barbs in his hands, signals at the bull with these till charged, then runs obliquely towards and past the bull, leans over the horns in passing to plant the barbs in the shoulder, assuming for the moment the form of the letter C, and skips away, the bull being as before diverted. The bull is enraged by these, but on the whole slowed down by them, for he tries repeatedly to see them, hears them clacking behind his head, turns his head. He now shows first signs of fatigue, no longer gallops with such abandon, seems bewildered. When six barbs have been planted, trumpet, and the death begins. The matador plays the bull with a small scarlet cloth stretched on a stick, behind which he holds his sword. This is the most stationary part of the drama: the bull makes very short lunges, and the matador remains almost unmoving, mainpulating the bull as a conductor does a symphony, now to this side and now to that, making him leap upwards after the muleta, making him bore downward in pursuit of it, leading the horns across the embroidered chest (a hair's breadth away), enticing him to wheel in a continuous cycle of charge (the radius of action short), till finally he is at a complete standstill. The sword is now bared and pointed from above downward at the neck behind the head: a charge drawn: the matador steps forward to meet it, and thrusts quickly, the sword driving eighteen inches deep. The bull is staggered, stares, takes a tottering step or two, forward then back, walks slowly toward the matador, who lifts his hand for silence, slowly stepping backward; the bull loses control of his forefeet, the hooves trembling give way, he goes down on one knee then up again, then suddenly crashes and rolls over. Trumpet, and the outrageous applause, hats flung into the ring, and the matador circles the barrier bowing, his servant behind him picking up the hats and flinging them back to their owners. The mule team tears in, and hauls out the bull, who is applauded, dragged out by the neck at full speed with cracking whips and jingling bells to the butcher's shop at the entrance; the dead horses similarly hauled out, the heads arching against the pull, and a spout

114

of sand rising from the dragged nostrils. Chulos sweep up sand over the blood, smooth out the signs of struggle; and the show proceeds to the next bull. The audience an important factor—almost more than the bull. Takes sides, goads the bullfighters to take risks, boos and hisses, flings orangepeels, even cushions; the matadors become reckless, agitated, almost hysterical with excitement, particularly if they have been having a bad run of luck, a slip or two, an unexpected turn or two, or perhaps a torpid bull who won't show fight. One bull was stabbed twelve times—like caesar. Another became weary and disheartened and went away and lay down, hoping that he would be forgotten. Another tried to go back through the gates into his pen, but found the doors mysteriously shut. A "good " bull, however, makes the fight far from onesided. We saw a matador caught and flung fifteen feet, luckily getting his hands on the horns and merely receiving a toss. Another fell at a critical moment and *lay still*—the bull charged right over him. A youth jumped into the ring with an old clout in his hands and before he could be ousted drew the bull's charge twice, the second time getting his trousers ripped wide open over the left buttock. The bull was then diverted from him and he was arrested. Five minutes later a drunk jumped in and fought three men, all of them falling to the ground; by the grace of god, the bull bestowed his attention elsewhere. —So, with splitting head, to a café, where I drank several vast whiskies. —Returning to civilized england, we met the strike. Held up two days in plymouth and southampton, finally put ashore at nine in the evening, eight miles from southampton (to avoid trouble) and taken in buses by night to london—got there at five-thirty a.m. Two days later came down to hastings by scab train. Miles of rusty rails, empty signal boxes. Everybody with the miners, but against the strike: it never had a chance. As for me, I'm tory, and would, might, have volunteered had it gone on.   Conrad

73: TO ROBERT N. LINSCOTT^w   Jeake's House
                                                         May 29 26

Alas and alas. My cable to the dial on may 15 was too late to hold up or modify the review [see Letter 65], or even to secure the inclusion of a note explaining the circumstances—so Marianne Moore writes me—so I assume the review has come out in all its cruelty by this time and that my reputation (so unfounded too) as a ghoulish

115

executioner will be revived. Isn't it awful. I feel very badly about it, naturally. But there's nothing to be done except wait for the obloquy which is sure to follow. Damn it, I do seem to be cursed. A malevolent destiny watches over my slightest move. Or so, in my more fletcherian moments, it seems to me. —Louis [Untermeyer] has sent me most appalling details of poor Amy's death. To die in front of a mirror! that seems a refinement of torture more suitable to a Webster or Donne, who would have enjoyed it perhaps. . . . Thank the lord Amy didn't die a week later, with the Dial beside her on the pillow! a possibility suggested to me in a note from Alyse Gregory this morning—she says the Dial ought to have been out on may 15—close enough as it was. . . . I'm resuming, or trying to, the play which I had just conceived and done two pages of when Amy's magnum opus suspended operations for six weeks or so. I've finished act one, and have a one or two-feathered hope that I'll be able to make something out of it. A whooling melodrama, murders, poison, hashish, hypnotism, and buckets of blood. Everything depends on the second act, which, to tell the truth, I can't seem to work out properly; nor, for that matter, have I more than a ghost of an idea of what to do with the third. Still, the first is all right! which is something. Don't by the way, breathe of its existence as I shall very likely, if it is completed, try to launch it over a nom de plume. Make a note of this! Most important. I regard it, au fond, as an experiment in form, from which I hope later, in other things more intrinsically interesting, to reap a little profit. To wit: I am trying to recapture the Elizabethan effect of counterpoint (analogous also to the present movie technique) by rapid and frequent change of scene, always with the same or roughly the same setting. A few expressionist tricks thrown in also. In prose, but I seriously contemplate a little concealed or disguised poetry in act two—it remains to be seen. Intensely interesting to play with a new form, and a great relief to escape from my blasted novel and short stories on the one hand and my despicable verse on the other. Dialogue I find easy; but whether the effect I am getting is a sufficiently lively *stage* commotion is more difficult to decide. Not much characterization—in fact I'm not aiming at it, being for the moment, and the particular purpose, content with the greater lavishness and smaller precision of "type"—I've been desperately homesick this last two months—hating Rye, England, the english, jeakes house, my family,—hating everything, myself included. I wish I could stop "worrying"—the habit has grown alarmingly, and I can't control it; financial, partly, but also health and career and the outlook for the children and "april is the cruellest month, breeding . . . memory and desire, stirring etc." I believe a few months debauch would cure me, or a few months in Boston (singular alternative!) with you and Jake [Wilbur] and Julius [Clark] and Maurice. I am terribly isolated here. There is no one to talk to except mr neeves the pub-keeper who tells me what horse to back and the mad vicar who says that at six a.m. in Peasmarsh place I could hear a nightingale. Why should I walk six miles to hear the nightingale? why shouldnt the nightingale come and listen to me? I could teach her a trick or two—I too can speak of adulterous wrong. (I don't mean by that, either, that J has been unfaithful!) In the morning I work, or try to work, shutting my eyes to unpaid bills, alone; I eat my meals alone, attended by my family; in the afternoon I walk alone, internally weeping; at six thirty I drink rum and read about the races; in the evening I read a little, again and again falling down from the book into a cloaca of despair; at tenthirty I retire to my study and go to bed, lying awake till one, thinking of the revolver, the hatpin thrust through the abdomen, and the muddy water off Winchelsea fore-shore. This is not a playful exaggeration—I wish it were, or that I could somehow pull myself out of it. Imprisoned in myself. Why this is hell, nor am I out of it. Why should I feel like this? I'm damned if I know. I try to think of something I would rather do, or be, hoping to discover a change that would provide escape, but I see nothing. Meanwhile everything I am and do seems poisoned and prepared. I dont want to commit suicide, nor to die, but I should like immensely to be dead! Could anything be more unreasonable? No. —Forgive these fifty-act sobs. I'll probably be king cockatoo of the royal convivial cockatoos tomorrow and forget all about them. A lovely southwest day, blowy and sunny, and aphids swarming on our roses. Well, toodleoo and write me some wild news from boston.   As ever   C

Illustrations

Aug 13 69

CONRAD AIKEN
STONY BROOK RD
W BREWSTER MA
02631

Dear Edmund::Well, I didn't expect you to like it
much,but then,I'd said it to you in private several
time--notably on the occasion when I took Erich Heller up to see you,very funny that was,you may remember,so I xthought no harm. But butterflies in the
stomch,or bats in the belfry!That was a triumph,it
scared the b-jjesus out of me,flew right into my face
where it fluttered affectionately,then went to heel.
Lovely critter,which I will treasure...Wish I cd see
you,but I'mm immobilized with diseases,and can't get
round much.Heller says he'll come in the fall,Maybe
then? ??   as always aff.,   Conrad

Postcard to Edmund Wilson.

Conrad Aiken and T. S. Eliot as fellow editors of the *Harvard Advocate* in 1910.

The author of *Earth Triumphant* in 1914: "Cruel as cinematograph I show life up to you—and smile!"

Conrad Aiken as critic in 1915: "Birds of protean pedigree / Vorticist, Cubist, or Imagist, / Where in a score years will you be, / And the delicate succubae you kissed?"

Grayson P. McCouch, the "Old Bird," about 1911.

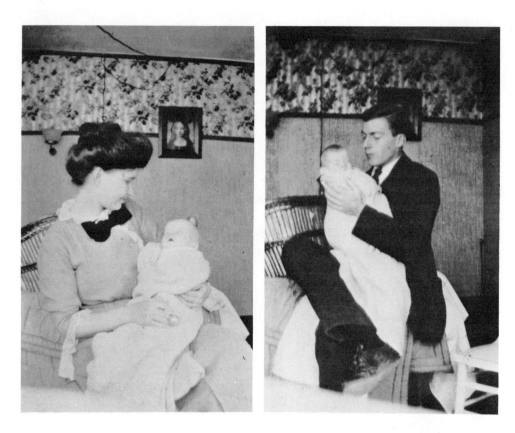

Jessie McDonald Aiken and Conrad Aiken with son John in 1913.

Clarissa Lorenz, 1927.

Edward Burra, Clarissa Aiken, Malcolm Lowry, and Conrad Aiken breakfasting at the Pension Carmona in Granada, in May 1933. (See *Ushant*, pp. 358–60.)

George B. (Jake) Wilbur, Cape Cod, 1927.
Oil painting by Waldo Peirce.

John Gould Fletcher, Robert Linscott, and
Conrad Aiken in Rye, 1931.

Conrad Aiken and Malcolm Lowry in the gardens of the Alhambra, May 1933.

Malcolm Lowry in his garden at 62 Calle Humboldt in Cuernavaca, taken by Mary Hoover a few days before her wedding to Conrad Aiken in July 1937.

Maurice Firuski, about 1934.

Robert Linscott, about 1940.

Henry A. Murray, about 1933.

Malcolm Cowley, about 1954.

Conrad Aiken on the beach at Brewster, 1948.

Conrad and Mary Aiken in Jeake's House, Rye, 1938.

Conrad and Mary Aiken with Mary's portrait of
T. S. Eliot in the "slumlet," 1955.

Mary Aiken in the backyard of the "slumlet" (332 East 33rd Street, New York City), 1955.

Mary Aiken and Edward Burra at Rock Harbor, Orleans, Cape Cod, 1955.

(Above) Conrad and Mary Aiken with Edward Burra and Mary's portrait of Gordon Bassett in "41 Doors," Brewster, Cape Cod, 1955.

(Right) Edward Burra in his home at Playden, Rye, in 1976.

"41 Doors," Brewster, 1955.

Aiken at his desk in the Library of Congress, 1951.

Aiken at 230 Oglethorpe Avenue, Savannah, 1965. The portrait behind him was painted by his aunt, Edith Potter, when he was twenty-five.

Mary Aiken's map of Rye, 1938.

Jeake's House, built in 1689, on Mermaid Street, Rye.

Aiken's two homes on Oglethorpe Avenue: number 228, at left, where he spent his first eleven years, and number 230, at right, where he lived for his last twelve years. He stands at the entrance to 228, while Mary stands at the adjoining entrance to 230.

"41 Doors" and Aiken's study.

Mary Aiken's portrait of Aiken in his Jeake's House study overlooking Romney Marsh, Winchelsea, and the Channel, 1939.

Mary Aiken's portrait of Aiken with "Nipperty" in the Red Top Graveyard, Brewster, 1944.

Aiken mowing the terraces at "41 Doors," 1955.

Part II: 1926–1935

Not until he had been moored safely at Saltinge, and had lost it and refound it, with Lorelei Two and Hambo, in that miraculous return when he had discovered the beautiful house empty and forlorn . . . not until then was the consistent view at last to receive his consistent attention, and to find at last its own expression in the two volumes of parerga, *the serial essays towards attitude and definition. The preoccupation had been prolonged and deep: and perhaps it had only needed the shattering disequilibration which followed the fatal interview with Lorelei Two at Aunt Sibyl's house in Fayerweather Street, and the resultant wrenching of himself away from the three little D.'s, and Saltinge, to bring it up, into full and clear consciousness, as now discoverably the very heart of such conviction as, in his moment of greatest distress, he could hug to his self-inflicted wound.*

. . . And the abandonment—hadn't that too been a compulsory repetition of the family pattern? . . . Must one dare the lightning, invite it to strike one's heart? and thus deal it oneself, at the same time, to others? If he had been thus abandoned, flung overboard, should not they?—

. . . It was as if he had needed to test the reality of his feeling for the little D.'s, or could only test it, by losing them. Was this perhaps true of everything, and everywhere—and was it perhaps only in the profoundest experience of annihilation, and of the dissolution of all hope and pride and identity, in the great glare of cosmic consciousness, that one could regain one's power to value? It certainly looked very like it. And as the dreadful feeling of personal exposure, of being lost at sea, corresponded quite preposterously with the feeling of intellectual exposure with which now for years that "consistent view" of his had been confronting him, but of which he had heretofore never quite accepted the true consequences, the effect on him was revolutionary. What had been merely an idea till now, or a system of ideas, which he could contemplate, or disregard, with complete detachment, had now become a terrible and tangible and wonderful world again, like that of which he had learned the first vast and shocking syllables at Savannah; and what, in the realm of personal relationships, in the nexus of society, had been easy and light and habitual, had now, just as suddenly, become fearfully and brilliantly alive, an end-

119

less profusion and confusion of every shape and shade of the progressions of love and hate. Values! —The values began a Heraclitean pour such as he hadn't know since he first crawled on his hands and knees. . . .

But if it was good, what at first blindly he began to see of it, it was also difficult: for a world so new, a new language would have to be discovered, or rediscovered, and for this, one's own muscles readapted and reeducated. . . . But it was difficult; and the prolonged, if shadowy, difficulties with dear Lorelei Two—for their steps, their gaits, after that first magical moment when their every most random movement was that of the dance, had gradually ceased to be parallel—these had added to the burden, already pressing, of consciousness; and to the need, for rest or insulation, of alcohol. . . .

. . . Despite these libations to the god of forgetfulness, the moment had at last supervened when such temporary rests from the vision seemed not enough, and when a more famous sleep had suddenly appeared, one evening, as the ultimate, the only desideratum. If one had learned, all dangerously, to live, should not one also learn, as dangerously, and of one's own purest volition, to die?

[*Ushant*, pp. 221–26]

Letters 74–102: November 1926 to November 1929

C A's visit to Boston in the fall of 1926 produced no certain prospect for income, but the company of Jake Wilbur, Maurice Firuski, Bob Linscott, and a new friend, Harry Murray, greatly improved C A's spirits. At the beginning of November he met Clarissa Lorenz when she interviewed him at his Aunt Edith Potter's house for the Boston *Transcript. A secretary to Murray and Morton Prince in the Harvard Psychological Clinic, she wrote feature stories on the side. In the next week before he sailed for England with Linscott, C A saw her five times.*

In January 1927 C A returned to Boston and Clarissa (Clarice, or Jerry, or Joan he called her). In September C A became for one year a tutor at Harvard. At last, in November 1928, C A visited London to conclude a divorce agreement with Jessie, who had informed him she intended to marry Martin Armstrong. Malcolm Lowry arrived in Cambridge to visit C A in August 1929. C A and Jerry were married in February 1930 at William Carlos Williams's house in Rutherford, New Jersey.

o   o   o

Blue Voyage (London: Gerald Howe, May 1927; New York: Scribner's, July 1927).

Costumes by Eros (New York: Scribner's, September 1928; London: Jonathan Cape, September 1929).

Selected Poems (New York: Scribner's, November 1929).

74: TO CLARISSA LORENZ[r]   [Harvard Club, Boston
November 7, 1926]

Joan dear: . . . When I got back to the club at 1:10, there also rolling in was Waldo Peirce, drunk as a lord, and when I had successfully avoided him (what a horror that would have been!) and was in the elevator, I discovered that my key was at the desk—where Peirce was. However, I outwitted destiny—I rose to an incredible height of intelligence and strategy and sent the elevator man for my key. Now I ask you! Wasn't that beautiful? And it saved me. And then in my room, as I took my toothbrush out of my typewriter, I was positively almost gay. I sang like a dead lark. And

I began observing all sorts of little details in a way that I had not done for eight years. There was only one thin blanket on my bed, and I thought "what fun to find another blanket in the bureau and spread it out on the bed, and then afterwards to tell Joan about it!" And so it was: and so it is. I found the other blanket, and I fished out my blue-striped pajamas, and opened the window quite wide, and got into bed. And then chaos. But I slept after a while—I think at about two. Not a dream—oh yes, there was—it was about the refusal of my novel. (Suddenly I feel certain that I have written all this to you before!) Then, at five, I awoke. And after an hour I again slept and again plunged up from the unconscious for the joy of seeing you at 6:30. And then—when I thought of your astonishment at my not having cried since I was five, and of how with such a divine gesture of compassion you took me into your heart, I put an end to that thirty-three year drought. In other words, I took a bath! Lachrymal, however, not lacteal! Then another *little* one! Then a shave and a cold tub and here I am.

My dear: don't forget that I adore you, and that I simply go to pieces when I think of you. You have genius—Genius—GENIUS—and I love you.   Conrad

75: TO CLARISSA LORENZ[r]   [S. S. Cedric
                                            November 9–14, 1926]

Dearest Joan: Tuesday: Here it is, ten o'clock Tuesday morning—four bells have just struck—but by my watch which I have refrained from setting forward—so that I can tell by looking at it where you are—it's now 6:27, and you are just this minute setting out for Emerson Hall. How extraordinary that seems. Being on a ship has a very peculiar effect on one—one cannot concentrate, one's consciousness is dissipated, and neither one's past nor one's future have any reality. Boston and Cambridge and Cape Cod and New York and Philadelphia, which I walked in only the other day, have become far-off, unreal, tiny and soundless, as a little dream. Have I really been in those places? Did I really see you! Yesterday, last night particularly, you almost escaped me, and an extraordinary panic assailed me. I ran to and fro in my mind, which had become vast and empty as Mammoth cave, and found scarcely a clue, till I remembered the exact intonation with which you said,

"I'm nettled. I'm very much nettled," and then, "You are the eternal lover," and then "Do you know what I did to that? . . . I left out all the viscera!" My dear, dear Joan: you have no idea what you have done for me, and what you are still doing, and what I hope you will always do. I have come alive again, when I thought I was dead. I am Lazarus coming up out of his tomb, still with the cobwebs on him! But *alive* again, thank God, as long as you care to keep me alive. I was like a compass which had no function, because there was no longer any magnetic pole to which it could respond; but now I point to you. Hell's delight! I must stop this Narcissistic self-indulgence in images and try to talk a little sense. It's impossible to express feelings—I begin and end, as one must, with the simple assertion that I love you, I love you, and when I rested my head on your shoulder and you touched my hair with your hand it seemed to me that this was what I had been waiting for all my life. An illusion? Then everything is illusion, then let my life be all compact of illusion, world without end. . . . My dear: my dear Joan: I am having a horrible time trying to remember what you look like. I wonder why this is? Is it a sort of defense-mechanism, do you suppose—to protect me from the awful wave of hysterical grief which engulfs me when I see, in my mind's eye, your face? Or is it because, our meeting being so brief, our memories lack body? It is inevitable, I suppose, in the circumstances, that our feelings should have outrun our impressions; and perhaps to some extent, also, the intensity of our feelings precisely prevented a clear registration of impressions. If you knew how I have stared and stared at the two photographs in the hope of really finding you there! I take off my spectacles and look at them, I hold them close to the light and stare at them, I turn them over and read the spidery inscriptions on the backs, and still I only succeed in half apprehending you—Good God, how frightful this is—to be in love, but to be able to evoke only a ghost! I comfort myself, however, with the knowledge that this is only temporary: all of a sudden you will again jump into my mind. And even when I cannot wholly grasp you, visually, I know just the same that I love you with an unbearable intensity. What on earth are we going to do about it? My darling Joan, what are we going to do? . . . Fragments of verse which have occurred to me and have amused B[ob Linscott] and myself in our weaker moments:

123

And spent his leisure, since he had no wife,
Embracing *opportunities* all his life!

Also, for the last line of a mockromantic sonnet—

The long lugubrious laughter of the loon!

Or, again, for a sonnet à la E. A. Robinson:

And so laid down, under the surgeon's knife,
His foolish and expensive little life.

It was decided that the first line of this sonnet should be

When William Smith first came to man's estate—

but no further progress was made. You will gather from this how
frivolously we spend our days on the Cedric. . . .   Conrad

76: TO CLARISSA LORENZ[r]   [Jeake's House, Rye
                                          November 1926]

My dear—my beloved—my dearest   —After a black rainy day,
pouring on my study roof and tall windows, a lovely rich orange
sunset has burst out under the clouds in the west, over Winchelsea
and Fairlight hills, and the raindrops sparkle on my panes, and the
chimney pots have all turned into marmalade pots and honey pots,
and a flock of starlings has just flown in a dense mass right across
the glory, and ME, I sit here and look hard into the west, where
you are, and the whole thing seems to be you.

I have worked all day at a review of Palimpsest by H. D., a lovely
thing, which you must read. I found myself identifying, in the third
section, the heroine with you—just why, I can't say. Anyway, there
you were, and there was I (reading about you) and after reading
about you all evening I crawled up to my remote monastic little
frozen bedroom positively on my hands and knees, like a dilapi-
dated cat, or a very old and tired and motheaten dog, trying to
prevent myself from tears by the caustic thought that tears were
only the result of narcissism. But are they?

Now it's raining again, golden rain falling softly like golden
harpstrings (how very paradisal) across this golden soft sunset,
and—yes—I have been to the window, and there is, as there ought
to be, a tall rainbow.

You with your vegetable cart, and your old coat (for rain),—but I can't finish the sentence. All I want to do is BEGIN sentences like that. And end them with a kiss, complete surrender, complete abdication. Such a pity, too, when you are so damned intelligent! I feel that I'm not taking proper advantage of you. But there is all the time in the world for intelligence, and what I want, passionately, in the meantime, is your love, the assurance that you love me. Do tell me, in a fugitive whisper, that you love me?

I discovered a new chord on the piano before lunch, and made a new tune, four bars long, and absolutely for you. You have no idea what a perfect idiot I am. Or perhaps, alas, you have! The sunset is turning to pink and mauve and I must go down to tea with Miss Violet Eustis (bad cess to her). My dear adorable Joan, here's all of me in a hieroglyph—   C

77: TO CLARISSA LORENZ[r]   [Jeake's House, Rye
                                   November 24–25, 1926]

Darling, I don't complain, protest, murmur, object, cavil, whine, moan, plead, nor do I tear my teeth, gnash my hair, bite the chair-rungs, shake my fist at the heavens-deaf-to-my-imprecations, nor do I grovel like a whipped cur, nor cry in my secret heart of hearts, nor shut my lips with stoic fortitude: none of these things; but if I had you here, WENCH, HUSSY, STRUMPET, by godfry I'd wring your neck. Swelp me bob I would. Do you really think it's humane? No, by god, I don't. You really think she ought to have written you sooner? You know bloody well she should have. There, there, little boy, don't cry. Besides, think of the nice little accumulation of letters there'll be *tomorrow* morning: maybe *three* all at once. Tomorrow and tomorrow and tomorrow. Dyrad, come out of your oak-tree—rise from your pool, blue nymph. And now I go out in search of a nice dark wet sewer.

> Here lies one whose heart was fract-
> ured (otatatòi) by a world of fact.
> Jackinthepulpit prays above him:
> only the weeds and sewerworms love him.
>
> Rats will nibble his ears and fingers;
> His eyes are shut; but near him lingers

Whimpering little his tethered ghost
and mourns for the one he loved the most.

Where is she, who should be sitting
Here on the sewerlid with her knitting?
Gone with the rosebud, gone forever,
While *he* waits here in Pluto's river.

Will she come back, and will she find him?
Kiss him, or with her fair arms bind him?
No, she forgets him, she is fickle
(Alas, alas) as the new moon's sickle.

The sparrow brings him a withered leaf,
The mole with blind eyes weeps for grief;
Jackinthepulpit tolls his bell;
The ghost is released and flies to hell.

Who shall we pray for, him or her?
Pray for the one who remembers, sir.
And let that other be cursed forever
With the sight and sound of Pluto's river.

And let her constant comrade be
The cry from the cross, Sabacthani.
This be her curse, until she come
To find her lover and bring him home.

So, now.   C

And now, by gosh, I do feel betrayed. Here's Thursday morning—THANKSGIVING, if you please—and after dreaming all night about letters that didn't come, and waiting till nine to go out, so as to give the mail time to arrive, THEN I go down and find—   C.

78: TO MAURICE FIRUSKI[h]   Jeake's House
dec 31 26 last day of this bloody
year thank god

permit, Maurice seraph, this lunatic to rage before you for ten minutes by the clock, and to say a vain thing or two, and to tear out his four remaining hairs. but before I do this, before I deliver myself to my evil passions, let me, with a last effort at sanity and regard for

126

the decencies of human intercourse, tell you how much I enjoy having the Sappho, and how nice you are, and what a keen delight your
letter gave me. why should this monster of selfishness (my own and
Jessie's phrase) be the recipient of gifts and friendship? one of the
mysteries of this impenetrable world. the snails have fallen from my
eyes, and I perceive alas too clearly that I do nothing to deserve—
anything. bad egg, bad egg, say I to myself two hundred times a
day, and four hundred times a night; bad egg, bad egg, and you
know the queer thing is that I can't very genuinely *despise* myself
for being a bad egg. why shouldn't there be a place in the world for
bad eggs? make the world safe for bad eggs! poor little bad egg, is
there not room in the world for thee and me? etcetera, tra la la.
after all, what is a bad egg but a good egg grown old? perhaps also
a little touched by the sun? and I further reflect that this paragon of
civilization, the chink, actually *likes* bad eggs. so perhaps I am
merely a *china* egg.

sour prelude to a sour letter: flourish of trumpets, and the villain
enters, made up in the guise of a lesion incarnate.

I had hopes, this morning, to have another letter from you which
might shed a light on two letters from Clarice: two letters which
have caused me indescribable pain. Into their nature, I will not go;
but in the second of them she refers to an interview with you, cryp-
tically, and I gather that the *occasion* of the interview, which is of
course known to you, is the occasion of the subtle poison that has
worked on my adored Clarice, and that now works on me. I implore you, Maurice, if you haven't already by this time written me
of all this, to tell me *fully* of everything that has occurred: I cannot
endure this being in the dark and at the mercy of the unknown: I
am in an agony: I know that something has gone frightfully wrong,
but I cannot attack it, for I don't know where it is. Clarice has
cabled me that she is writing an "explanation," and asks me to disregard the contents of these letters. But I also want to know from
you what has happened, what is happening, how things are, above
all how Clarice is. Is she ill? has something happened to her? have I
done something that has hurt her? My dear Maurice, I hope you
will waive any promise you may have made (of secrecy) to Clarice,
and mercifully tell me. Will you? and at once? and without mentioning any of this to her? I don't want her to know the extent of
my misery about this—she has quite enough misery of her own.
And I am only too afraid that my own last two letters to her (writ-

ten out of my bewilderment) will add intolerably to her burden. At this point, words fail me.

I am hoping desperately to start for B[oston] in mid-January. Of this, too, say nothing, for it may prove impossible. If I can get an advance on my novel—if the Dial and New Republic send me checks enough—if the New Year's avalanche of bills isn't too vast—und so weiter. It hangs by a hair. I have given Jessie a bad time of it—for me, too, the affair has not been innocuous. In fact, the whole thing has been infernal and still is. Tout de meme, barring that sort of drastic news from Cambridge which I now live in constant dread of, I shall make the attempt. If the drastic news does come, I may start anyway; it's little use my staying here. (In this Jessie agrees with me.)

Forgive me for launching this flight of poisoned darts at you. This is one of those occasions—when a monster of selfishness is a super-monster. . . .

And think of it! in the midst of all this I am solemnly engaged in the writing of a *farce*. Vox humana, stopped horns, arpeggios of the plangent grief of the harp, for the dying clown! Tut tut. This everlasting narcissistic smirk.

If I arrive, I may arrive penniless. Could you in that case give me a job cleaning furnaces? polishing boots? sprinkling salt on the tails of bookworms?   frenetically— C.

This is really a *revolting* letter and I'm sorry.

79: TO MAURICE FIRUSKI[h]   [Jeake's House, Rye]
                                   jan 4 27

Maurice   —your letter this morning—and the check—and I cabled yes to your question whether I would accept such a job—and what CAN I say that would begin to express my feelings? Nothing. I am no good at expressing feelings. Rebecca West to the contrary, who says that it's the one thing amurricans *are* good at. She's crazy.

Your letter was tonic—I *did* show it to Jessie, who shared my view. Our cards *are* on the table. What will happen, God knows. Between you and me and the nearest star, I want to marry Clarice; but I don't know whether it will be possible. You will naturally say *nothing* of that to her. The complications are, of course, chiefly the children,—one, can I give them up; two, what about their future (economically); three, if I'm providing for the children, how on

128

earth am I going to be able to marry? But it's no good trying to see too far into the future. I'm at present not holding out too much hope of marriage to Clarice: it wouldn't be fair to anyone. Just the same, I repeat: it's what I want, from the bottom of my heart, to do. And I hope to God I can.

What you say of her is manna to me. *Isn't* she positively an angel? Isn't it a horrible, unbelievably horrible, trick of fate that should have confounded her destiny with mine? When I think of that I become wordless.

As for the job and the check—really, Maurice, your goodness of heart is too much. The job frightens me, but beggars can't be pernicketty, and if you should succeed in landing it for me I shall be immeasurably grateful forever. If there's no lecturing or classroom work, I don't see why even *I* couldn't swing it. Anyway, I've got motive enough to take on *anything*. I'd even dust third rails. . . . There's a line which periodically turns up in the Times agony column—Tout passe, l'amitié reste.   Conrad

80: TO G. B. WILBUR[r]   Jeake's House Rye
                                          jan 5 27

Hell's Bells, Jake   —I'm sailing a week from Saturday—the fifteenth—alone—and am horrified to hear that I won't have you to fall back on. Any chance of seeing you before then? I suppose not. Yes, I plan to spend the whole winter there. Am deserting the family. Getting, or trying to get, a job. Probably will remain in America forever. May possibly come back to Rye in June—but then again I may not. I might import the family, if I got a *good* enough job— then again I might not. There is more in this, I'm sorry to say, than meets the eye. Tragedies, comedies, melodramas, everything. Lots happened after I left you in N.Y., between that and my sailing a week later. I.e., I fell in love. This under your hat—I'd rather you didn't inform Joy as yet. Bob and Maurice know about it, but no one else in America, and until the thing takes more definite form, I'm not anxious to have it broadcasted. Suffice it to say that hell is popping, that I've told J[essie] my whole past history, all the cards are on the table, and divorce is not impossible. I now know what hysteria is—one definite addition to my fund of misinformation about the world. The lady is a miracle: let it go at that. The only person I've met since reaching the age of adultery that I've wanted,

129

and wanted desperately, to marry. Very strange—there is lots in it that baffles me utterly.

Yes—Boston. Address Harvard Club.

How long are you staying here? Will you come and see Jessie and the kids sometime?

The children are of course the crux of the problem. If it comes to divorce, I shall give up my income entire; even so it comes hard. How the hell can one give up one's children? Insoluble problem— misery either way.

But here I am going back, which is in itself an indicative fact. . . . best of love Conrad

81: TO ROBERT N. LINSCOTTᵂ   Jeake's house
                                              jan 9 27

Linsk—   . . . So now you're in boston. And you've seen Clarice. And no doubt given her lots of advice, confound you. For the love of pete, don't! Your wisdom surpasses mine infinitely, in these and all matters; but one essential in such a relationship as mine and C's is that we should be able to trust each other as acting each on his and her own initiative entirely—without outside influence. Don't you admit it? Yes, you do. Otherwise, mutual trust would be and must be poisoned. —Now if you *haven't* been giving her advice, don't be angry with me. I'm in a state of mind in which I suspect everyone ferociously, wolfishly: as you already know. Write me down a worm (*worm! worm!*—your greeting will live in my memory forever) and forgive me if you can. I'm more profoundly grateful than I can possibly say for all that you've done for Jessie and me, through this nightmare; and as deeply apologetic for having so horribly embroiled you in it. You've been a saint. —I sail on the fifteenth, barring the unknown: will turn up in Boston eight or nine days thereafter to lunch with you. I feel as if at last the cord had been cut: the arrow loosed: the bowl broken: any simile you like. Jessie is calmer, more resigned, but still (I fear) a little too hopeful as to my return. She's been extraordinarily fine. And I feel the more that I am indeed the chief, the lowest, the slimiest, the dirtiest of   worms

Dear Jacob: . . . I suppose that you aren't surprised doesn't much surprise *me.*

I'm off tomorrow: in a state of paralysis. To put the lid on things, the inconceivable has happened—in some extraordinary way the news has *already* reached Rye, although only two people in America know about it. What to make of that, I don't know. Anyway, there it is, and Jessie is in an indescribable agony and funk about it. As for me, I've been up and down the gamut of feelings and sensations and emotions and thoughts so much that I'm no longer even sure that I shall be in love with Clarice when I see her—*that* aspect of things doesn't help much either. Though it's psychologically interesting.

Jessie has suggested among other things that now would be a good time for me to be analyzed. What do you think? I'd be damned glad of your view about that—right away. I suppose it would remove this new passion root and branch? And how would it leave me feeling toward Jessie? Or isn't there any saying? Let me have your view, c/o Harvard Club. Of course, I'm not at all sure that I'd have the courage to take it on: for I have a conviction (for what it's worth) that I shall be happier with Clarice than I've ever thought it possible to be. It's the real thing—not a shadow of a doubt about that. Can I afford to throw that away for the sake of the children? Answer, O God! Answer, O Freud! For years I've been sure, and happy in being sure, that I would never fall in love again. And now Clarice and I look at each other for ten minutes and the whole bloody world is blown to smithereens. And nevertheless, my feeling for the children is so intense, and my compassion and fondness for Jessie, that I wonder incessantly if *that* will not present a very real and permanent obstacle to happiness.

Well, have a good laugh at my expense: don't for heaven's sake let this depress or worry you—I merely spill it out because there's nobody here to whom I *can* unreservedly spill, with any chance whatever of an atom of sympathy.

Damned glad to hear you're nearly through. You sound much—what shall I say?—"better-toned." Integrated, perhaps. Calm. Felicitate Rank for me. And the same to you.   as ever, affectionately
Conrad

83: TO T. S. ELIOT^r

83: TO T. S. ELIOT[r]   Jeake's House
                                                Jan. 13 27

Dear Tom: I'm sorry—but not, to tell the truth, greatly surprised. For I have no illusions about the book's [*Blue Voyage*]
saleability. Very many thanks, however, for your efforts.

I'd like to do the book on James: but I fear the moment is not
propitious. I shall have to leave all my books (and notes) behind
me; and in any event I shall be rather unsettled for some months,
and quite incapable, I fear, of doing anything like concentrated justice to Henry. *If* I find a lucid interval, may I then let you know and
proceed? . . .

. . . Plans: the vaguest. I'm looking for a job. It may be a tutorial one at Harvard(!); it may be in a publishing house. I even
consider the Hearn lectureship in Tokio, which has been offered to
me: but I don't consider it very seriously. Anyway, it looks as if I
would remain in America for some years, perhaps returning here for
a month in the summer to dispose somehow of my family.

If I can find a minute or two tomorrow (Friday) afternoon, I'll
drop in on you or ring you up.   as ever   Conrad

84: TO JOHN, JANE, AND JOAN AIKEN[r]
                              Hampden Hall Plympton Street
                              Cambridge March 18 27

Dear John, and Jane, and also Joan
(Or Fidzy, called for *long*)
I meant to start a letter to you,
But find I burst in song!
Apologize, and start again:
But find, alas, the words
Will rhyme—as now again and Jane—
As if the words were birds,
Alack—gadzooks—fie fie—confound—
To be thus led by the nose,
To be enslaved by a mere sound,
And follow where it goes!
I'll start again, and plainly say,
In flat unrhyming prose,
That March this year's as warm as May,
And blossoms like a rose;

Just think! the crocuses are up;
The geese are flying north;
And many a tiny snowdrop cup
Is bravely coming forth;
The lilac buds are swelling green,
Old men have shed their coats,
And where of late thick ice was seen
Small boys are out in boats!
Dear dear—I see I'm rhyming still.
It must be spring that does it.
The spring, you know, makes poets ill.
It must be just because it
Is such an easy thing to do
When birds all day are singing
To rhyme and chime a word or two
While typewriter bells are ringing.
(You have to read that line quite fast,
Or else it won't fit in.
Now Conrad! let that be your last,
And let the prose begin!)

So be it. I will write in prose, the flattest ever seen, and scorn the muse, and tell the news, and *drive* this old machine: compel it to my every whim, and disregard its jingle, forswear (upon the seraphim) to use of rhymes a single. You see how well I do it now! Prose positively *pours:* from this forevermore, I vow, all verse is *hors concours.* (Pardon the French. It's incorrect, as also is my spelling; but better that *this* should be suspect than the method of the telling.) And as you see, so plainly see, these lines are all dispersed,—and how can I a poet be, since I am all unversed? Was that a pun? Why heaven forbid: no no no no no no. For you might pinch me if I did, and I should *hate* that so! I will not rhyme, I will not pun, but calmly will proceed to say today there is no sun: there is no sun indeed. And why, you'll ask? The answer's plain. It is because today there's rain. That sounds like Wordsworth—true—I know: but it's not *verse* because *that's* so. For he, like many another poet, wrote prose in verse and did not know it.

Mercy! I do declare the thing's
Been rhyming all this while!
Will no one tell me why he sings
In plaintive numbers vile?

Cuckoo jug jug pu wee to wit
A woo: the nightingale
Says that, when spring enlivens it,
And gone is winter's hail;
So why not I? Why can't I sing?
Who dares to say I mayn't?
So let us frankly hey ding ding
And rival the bird's complaint.
Twixt bird and bard there is small dif-
Ference: one letter only.
So let me sing, especially if
I'm feeling lorn and lonely.
So John, and Jane, and Fidzy too,
I'll loudly loudly sing;
Like that mad lass in Xanadu
I'll sing like anything.
I have, alas, no dulcimer,
I have no tambourine,
My hair is not like gossamer,
My eyes don't flash, I ween,
But I can sing as never crow
Was heard to sing on earth:
And make the plaintive numbers flow
For all that they are worth:
And rhyme and rhyme time after time
Till all is blue, my dears;
Until the highest tree you climb
And try to shed your ears—
Well now, good bye; you've heard the news;
I hope you all approve;
So farewell, Kids, and farewell, Muse,
And here is all my love.

Cahoun

85: TO G. B. WILBUR (IN PARIS)[r]

Hampden Hall, Plympton Street
Cambridge April 7 27

Delighted to get your excellent letter, Jacob, and to hear you're all
over, and well over. Also that you're coming back soon—if you still

adhere to that notion. Do you? —If you do, I'd like to make a bold and unconventional proposal to you: to wit: would you consider renting to me or Jerry (Lorenz—my lady) at a more or less nominal rent your small house opposite the church for the summer? Jerry had arranged to spend the summer with a girl who has now suddenly decided to get married—so Jerry is left high and dry and poor; needs a rest in the country; and it occurred to me that if you could see it that way it would be heavenly for *us* to put in the summer, or a good part of it, near you. If she could have the house, and I could visit you, or vice versa, or something of the sort which would sufficiently meet the conventions—you get the idea? —However, don't be embarrassed if you feel it wouldn't do, or would be inconvenient, or anything like that: say no. Jessie writes that she is going to Montreal in August and thinks it better if I don't come to Rye. So, ceteris paribus, I'll stick around here somewhere. Meanwhile, Jerry and I have decided that sooner or later we'll separate, if we can muster the courage to do so—but in the meantime get what little happiness we can out of these few months that fate allows us. So it stands. It remains to be seen what we actually will do. It's one thing to decide, another thing to act. And as I've got a job as tutor at Harvard for next winter, there is that complication. She insists that if I remain here she will go away. And my present idea, whether or not she stays, is to keep the family in Rye; anyway; not here. —I think you might as well, now, tell Joy how the wind lies.

I had dinner the other night with Harry Murray, who's working in the Harvard Psych Lab with . . . [Morton] Prince. He's a great guy—the real stuff. You'll like him. He's conducting a lot of fascinating experiments in conditioning of dreams, etc, and also writing a psychological study of Melville which sounds like hot stuff. Also on the side doing a lot of analysis. I mentioned my predicament to him—couldn't very well help it, as it was he who sent Jerry to me, and she works in his office—and he's all for our making it a "permanent" affair. . . . Murray may be helpful to us in our efforts to straighten things out—but I wish to god *you* were here. I should like to lean hard on you, if I may, for guidance. No one else has been any use to me. And I'm in a baddish hole. I've played feebly with the idea of suicide, but when it came to a showdown, pistol in hand, I discovered that I didn't have the nerve. Evidently I don't want to die, much as I sometimes think so. But I find the business of living pretty painful—divided—and can't see my way. At the same time I wonder if it isn't the sort of thing that I've got to decide for myself—passionately as I desire to have fate decide it for me. Forgive me once more for dumping all this on you. . . . as ev Conrad

86: TO MAXWELL PERKINS[P]   Hampden Hall Plympton Street
Cambridge April 9 27

Dear Mr. Perkins: I'm more delighted than I can say that you like the second half—for I've been rather anxious about it ever since I heard of the manuscript misadventure.[1] As for the whale-ship episode: I dropped that out very largely because [Gerald] Howe wanted the book cut down; and if you really like it, and want it restored, I'm not only willing but glad to have it put in again. It undoubtedly makes the psychological picture more complete, and also, as you say, adds a cheerful note which is not elsewhere conspicuous.

I am having trouble with Howe. I've just had a note from him—or rather from Bullett—saying that some thirty emendations or omissions have been made by him (in the reading of proofs—which I gave him permission to do) in the interests of the public morals. I've cabled him that I cannot consent to publication till I've seen his alterations. I wonder whether you would be so kind as to let me look through your page-proofs, so that I can see just what liberties have been taken? Among other things, I shouldn't want you to set up the book from a defective copy. If the alterations are extensive I'd rather have you set up from the Ms.

I'm sorry to give you this trouble—if you'll send me the page-proofs I'll let you have them back again *quam celerrime.*   Yours sincerely, Conrad Aiken

1. When Scribner's decided to publish C A's *Blue Voyage* in the U.S., Maxwell Perkins became his editor. Perkins later wrote to Mrs. Malcolm Lowry: "When *Blue Voyage* came here I was greatly excited. . . . By phone I told him how great was our interest, but that it seemed to me unfinished. From his response I saw that he thought I meant that the ship ought to get to port, or something like that. He said he didn't see how anything could be more completely finished, and asked if we wanted it. I quickly thought even if it is a fragment, to my way of thinking, it is amazing, and we'll take it at that, and I said so . . . a few days later his agent brought in the last third. . . . They had mislaid [it]" (*Selected Letters of Malcolm Lowry* [Philadelphia and New York, 1965], p. 436).

Hampden Hall Plympton Street
Cambridge April 14 27

Dear Mr. Perkins: Many thanks for your awfully nice and damned sensible letter about the matter of the deletions. . . .

In general, I agree with you, wholly, about the moral aspect. I'd prefer to publish the book mutilated, rather than have it attract the *wrong* kind of attention. But, other things being equal, of course I want the psychological portrait to be as true and as "morally unedited" as may be possible. . . .

I can't begin to tell you how much it means to me to have you like Blue Voyage. I'd really begun to despair, not only about its ever being published in this country, but about its quality as well. It gives me really extraordinary pleasure to have it liked by you, and liked as I *wanted* it to be liked. I feel, in consequence, a very comforting trickle of returning confidence. I'm afraid it may end by my having my head turned.   Yours sincerely, Conrad Aiken

88: TO JOHN, JANE, AND JOAN AIKEN^r   South Dennis Mass
Sept 11 27

Dear John and Jane And Fidzy: I was hoping so much that I would see you before you went back to Rye—you don't know how disappointed I was to find, when I heard from you, that you were already, by the time I got the letter, on the sea! And here was I, half hoping that John and Jane might suddenly turn up here, or on the other hand that I might myself pack a knapsack and make a dash to Montreal. . . . —Well, and now you are in Jeaky again. Give my love to the Grandfather clock, and to my study window, and to my books, and to the Chinese painting in the drawing-room (especially to the old man with the smiling face who is holding the baby in his arms) and to my blue stove, and to the rug with the run colours in the front hall, and to the crack in the wash-bowl in the bathroom, and to the big Hamida Bowl on the Queen Anne table, and to the flowering quince, and the Budleia, and the old chimney pot that stands in the corner of the lower terrace by the house; and throw a kiss for me into every one of the rooms; and tell the front door that I haven't forgotten how it squeaks when it shuts; and tell the lamp outside that I still know *exactly* how, at eleven o'clock at night, the steps of the lamp-unlighter sound as they come down the cobbles of Mermaid street, and cross from the Old Hospital, growing softer, and how then the walls of my room grow dark; and remind the Quarter-Boys that I can still hear them, when there is an east wind, striking their bells with a slow TING-tang: TING-tang—For isn't it wonderful how, if one has the kind of memory that man has, one can be in two places at the same time? Here I sit in South Dennis on a grey rainy day, with sea-gulls mewing, and wind moaning through the flyscreens, and my typewriter clacking, and I look out of the window through pine-boughs at the lagoon of the Bass River, and see the low marshes; and at the same minute, by turning on my memory, I am also in Rye. I remember every stone, it seems to me. I walk every walk: by the shipyard, by the playing-fields, by the tennis-courts, up New England past those knotted roots of trees, where the winter heliotrope grows; past that long buttressed wall; and so to the top of the hill and down across the cemetery to the view of the Rye from the field, and thence to the steps and down to the Tillingham and its lime-trees. —Well—and now in ten days I'm off to Cambridge, where I shall begin being a teacher. I shall have the same flat I had last winter—in Hampden Hall, on Plympton Street: you can address me there, after this. And I shall have my office in a building called Holyoke House, where I shall have office-hours every day; and the young men will come and talk to me about English literature there, and smoke my cigarettes. And I shall get all my meals at restaurants—till I get sick and tired of the very smell of a restaurant. . . .

Now I must stop and go for the morning-paper, to find out whether France or United States won the Davis Cup. Good-bye, Implings, and give my love to Mamma, and here is lots and lots for you—   Old Cahoun

89: TO MAXWELL PERKINS[P]   South Dennis Mass
                                             Sept 12 27

Dear Mr. Perkins: Linscott writes me this morning that Blue Voyage has been "quietly" suppressed in Boston—rumour to this effect having reached him, he attempted, and in vain, to buy a copy. Pressing the point, he was informed that the booksellers had decided that they would rather not risk possible police action, and had therefor withdrawn the book from their counters.

I don't know whether you will want to do anything about this, or give it publicity; but anyway I mention the fact to you in case you shouldn't have heard of it yourself. If you want to make capital of it, I'm willing to stand the gaff if you are![1]   Yours sincerely, Conrad Aiken

90: TO CLARISSA LORENZ[r]   [8 Plympton Street, Cambridge late 1927]

Preliminary list of books[1]: in Russian, the works of Chekhov, Turgenev, Dostoevsky, Tolstoi's Anna Karenina, short stories of Andreiev and Sollogub, Nekrasov's "Who Can Be Happy and Free in Russia?" In French, Stendhal's Rouge et Le Noir and Chartreuse de Parme, Flaubert's "Madame Bovary" and "Trois Contes," and the works of Anatole France; perhaps Rousseau's Confessions, and the prose of Remy de Gourmont. Maybe de Musset's and Mallarmé's poetry, and Verlaine's and Rimbaud's, and Paul Valery's, and Laforgue's. But I am pretty weak on French literature myself, and can't properly guide you. Italian: Dante's Divine Comedy, Leopardi's poems, possibly d'Annunzio's *Il Fuoco* (translated—Modern Library—under the title of Flame of Life: Henry James dismissed him as merely vulgar, and there is truth in it, but he's also magnificently eloquent) and Croce's "Aesthetic," largely to disagree with it—the most complete absolutist aesthetic. Oh, I forgot, in French, Rolland's "Jean Christophe." German: Goethe's Faust.

Of the ancients: as many of Plato's dialogues as you can stomach, and ditto plays of Aeschylus, Euripides and Sophocles. Likewise the Greek Anthology. (All the books I mention can be got in fair translations!) Chapman's translation of the Odyssey, for example. Apuleius: The Golden Ass. Suetonius: Lives of the Caesars (a thing to read *at,* a superbly disillusioning thing).

English: Chaucer ad lib. The Elizabethans I take it you know, but you may not have tried Webster's fine plays, or Tourneur's, or Day's Parliament of Bees, or the masques of Ben Jonson (a few of them exquisite). The poetry of Donne, Marvell, Herrick, Sidney's "Defense of Poesy." The romantics you of course know—Words-

1. Perkins replied drily that the sale of a good novel was not much injured by "suppression in Boston," the Boston public preferring the "manufactured sort" of novel to the real thing (Perkins to C A, September 13, 1927[p]).
1. C A sent this list of books to read "for your education."

worth, Keats, Coleridge, Shelley, Blake. Francis Thompson, Arnold's essays, a dash of Browning, Meredith's "Modern Love" and a few other poems, and perhaps a little Swinburne (I don't like him much myself). Of modern poets, Davies, de la Mare, Brooke, Masefield (a lot of rubbish, but Reynard and Dauber have fine stuff in them) and of the Americans Eliot, Stevens, Frost, Robinson, H.D. and Fletcher.

Fielding's Tom Jones, Richardson's Clarissa Harlowe, all of Jane Austen, Borrow's Lavengro, Meredith's Egoist (ouch), Peacock's Crotchet Castle, Reade's Cloister and the Hearth (thriller) and Trollope's Barchester series. Of modern fiction, Joyce's Portrait of the Artist as a Young Man and Ulysses (you'll have to borrow it, and it will horrify you), Virginia Woolf's Jacob's Room and Clarissa (!) Dalloway, some of Dorothy Richardson's endless series of novels all about the same young girl (some excellent stuff), Katherine Mansfield's stories (beautiful). Melville and Henry James—read the latter chronologically, beginning at the beginning of his last period with The Spoils of Poynton. He's difficult but rewarding.

91: TO T. S. ELIOT   8 Plympton Street Cambridge
                            Jan 3 28

Dear Tom: I am grieved to hear that I missed a meeting of two such distinguished societies [see Letter 93]. I had somehow supposed, ever since that day, some years ago, when I recommended a diet of Götterdämmaroids for the King, that Bolo was gone to his reward. Perhaps he had merely enlisted, incog, in the tank corps. Anyway, I rejoice to hear that he still lives. And I will do him homage at the earliest opportunity.

When will this be—? Don't esk. Is the gin here plentiful and good? The gin here is plentiful, but not good. My bootlegger (and in this I claim distinction) is a nephew of Dean Briggs. I expect him this evening at 7:30.

This business of being a Harvard Don! Cristo et Ecclesiae.

I have no brains—I am but six days old. I am ceasing to be interesting even to myself. I would run away to London, if I could or if jobs were to be found there. My favorite job is dusting third rails in subways or undergrounds. If you hear of a vacancy, let me know.

Thanks for the guinea, thanks like hell for the review of Blue

Voyage.[1] A piece of critical blindness so fantastic that it positively uplifts me. The faults of the book I know with nauseous intimacy. Its virtues I am also aware of. Your reviewer discusses neither. I suspect him to be a gentleman (or lady) of very elementary understanding; or else an aesthetic bigot who comes to a doubtful or difficult book as the auto da fe to one suspected of heresy. Serene in this comforting conviction, I kick his pants. So that's all right.

In New York, I saw the Three Sisters, and reflected on your dictum that you "preferred your Ibsen straight."[2] And I was astonished, and am still astonished.

Etcetera? I write bad reviews on a bad typewriter for the N.Y. Post, the Dial, the New Republic. My family is in Rye, my heart is in my mouth. My office is in Holyoke House; and there, with my feet on the desk, I tell my young men to read Harmonium and The Golden Bowl. I fill out innumerable blanks, sign my name innumerable times, petition, re-petition, file exceptions, and make reports.

But I hope to float over to London in June. Do write me.   As ever   C A

92: TO JOHN, JANE, AND JOAN AIKEN^r

hampden hall cambridge
feb 14 28

Dear Kids, all and some: here it is Valentine's Day, and by George I entirely forgot to send off valentines to you. My sorrow, and here I apologize on my bended knees, nose to the floor. It's hard to know about these things in advance—how was I to know two weeks ago that Valentine's Day was two weeks off? If I were the prince of whales, no doubt I'd have an equerry or some such dignitary whose duty it was to tell me in the morning, when he brought me my matutinal tea and my shaving-brush, "Your 'Ighness, beggin' your pardon, but a fortnit hence is Wallingtime's Day: remember to send floral tokens to your mother the Queen and your father, his royal 'ighness, the Kink." But not being the prince of whales, nor even of minnows, there's nothing I can do but devote

---

1. In *Criterion* (July 1927), p. 565. C A suspected that Eliot himself inspired or wrote the anonymous notice, which said that Alec Brown's *The Honest Bounder* was "immeasurably superior" to *Blue Voyage* and that *Blue Voyage* was prompted by Joyce and exhibited a "deliberate indulgence in the prolix and fragmentary."
2. Eliot's comment when C A praised Chekhov's plays.

my whole life to writing apologies for these unfortunate oversights. —Last night I dreamt I was in London, and I discovered a perfectly beautiful new square in the East End. It was all in tudor style, heavily beamed and very tumbledown, but entrancing; and its name, I found, was Godowin Park. I explored all over it, and looked around everywhere for a nice house in which we might all live. I also discovered a *lovely* BAR. But when I got in, it was shut. There was a great VAT full of gin-and-italian, and a small boy scooping and mixing it, and dropping into it great cakes of ice; but alas, there was nothing to drink. It was sad. . . . So goodbye, and my love to the whole fambly, from   Cahoun

93: TO T. S. ELIOT^r   8 plympton street cambridge
                                                 march 31 28

I believe wuxxianity might be a great help in time of trouble. Perhaps you will not like me to take so utilitarian a view of the credo?

As for the united Bolovian and Royal Coprophilic Associations, Ltd. I hereby apply for honorary membership. My illegitimate children are in Nashville, Tenn., Birmingham, Ala., and on the shores of Lake Tahoe. They may be seen on application. Male and female created he them.

I grieve for you over The Criterion. For myself as well. Vrai dire, I always thought there would be just this outcome. Which same will not console you. I'm damned sorry about it, and hope you'll find a millionaire or two without arriere pensees, or axes to grind, or arriviste ideas, to back you in a new venture.

As for me, I've been fired for moral turpitude: politely fired: which is to say, "there is no vacancy in the tutorial department next year." I was offered some lectures in the summer school, and refused. Next? I don't know. I may go to New York. I was planning to return to my abandoned family in Rye, in June; but [Martin] Armstrong has beaten me to it. He is going to marry Jessie. Sir Charles Russell undertook the case for Jessie, but died of it. I may come to London anyway, to arrange the *dot* for Armstrong. —

It appears that four Graduates called at the Office in University Hall to protest that the author of Blue Voyage was not a fit teacher of the young. . . .

I have learned to compose verses on the typewriter. Portable verses. My seven-dollar-a-gallon-gin starts it off with a rush. Can you buy cheaper gin in London? No, you can't; nor better either. Just the same, I want some whisky, and will come for it.

News please.   Aff. Conrad

94: TO HOUSTON PETERSON[r]   8 Plympton Street Cambridge
June 8 28

Dear Peterson: Yes, it was a swell party; and I heard from Linscott that it got even sweller after I left; that your taxi bill was enormous; and that in fact it was a gala night. It shames me to have to admit middle age, but the time is passing when I can do as well as that. But next time we have an evening, I'll try to do a little better by you.

Far from having any misgivings about the book,[1] I am being eaten up by a raging curiosity. And Scribners, to whom I mentioned the thing as still in a projective stage, were as excited as myself. I like extremely the way you are attacking the thing: I mean, the way you *see* it. After being told for fifteen years by almost all the reviewers, from Phelps [Putnam] to Untermeyer, that my work lacks intellectual content, it's a godsent relief to have some one detect an idea or two in it.

With which prefatory remarks, I'll try to take up your questionnaire.

(1) Orginally, the idea of writing verbal symphonies occurred to me in connection with a passing passion for [Richard] Strauss, about 1912–14; under which influence (crossed with Masefield!) I wrote the three parts of Earth Triumphant: i.e., that poem itself, and then the two similar things 'This Dance of Life' and 'Dust in Starlight.' As you will see, the development here was crude and pretty simple, with obvious repetitions of leit-motifs, and a good deal of monotony; and the theme was itself slight, the problem of disillusionment and repetition in love. The first step toward a freer and more flexible form was in Disenchantment, which, if I am not mistaken, was written in 1914—though it may have been a year later. Anyway, it was in this that I first tried a shifting and broken-up approach as a better medium for the flux of mood and idea. In 1915, then, I began the first out-and-out symphony, on the theme of nympholepsy: The Charnel Rose. And it was as I was bringing

1. Peterson's projected book on C A, published as *The Melody of Chaos* (New York and Toronto, 1931).

this to a close, in November of that year, that I first thought of a series of symphonies which might project a kind of rough and ready "general view." I think Santayana's preface to Three Philosophical Poets, and the book itself, were deeply influencing me at this time: especially his view that philosophical poetry best affords a first-rate opportunity for the poet. Anyway, I began The Jig of Forslin on the same day that I finished the Charnel Rose, and had it done early in 1916. And here again the new poem led on to the next one: I saw the House of Dust as I was finishing Forslin, saw it as a corollary. The House of Dust was written then in the following winter—1916–17. At the end of '17, I began Punch, and did the first half of it, roughly. Then, early in '18, came Senlin, as another of the symphonic group; after which Punch was finished. And in the following fall, I began Festus, which took me (with intermissions) two years. —This gives you the actual order; it will also perhaps make clear to you that the idea of a general symphonic view was of gradual genesis, and a cross-fertilization of form and idea. I was attracted, on the one hand, by the notion of achieving a kind of absolute music in verse: paralleling, for this purpose, a kind of musical structure; and on the other, by the notion of embodying in this absolute music my own complete (?) "view of the world." The actual form these experiments took only cleared itself as I went along. Freud had been influencing me since my last two years in college; his shadow (and Ellis's, too, whose six volumes of sex studies I had read) was on the Charnel Rose; and it furnished the starting-point and main theme of Forslin. Rumours of Le Bon[2] and crowd psychology crossed me while I was in the midst of Forslin, and the House of Dust took off from that. Specific influences on Senlin and Festus I can't recall. I don't think there *were* any. They were logical enough developments of single items in the earlier things.

As for my circumstances, mental and physical, during this period of gestation: all I can say is that I experienced during those four years a tremendous feeling of fecundity, excitement (the war here played its part) and well-being. Two of my best friends at this time were M.D.s: one of them in process of becoming a psychiatrist G. B. Wilbur, the other a neuro-physiologist Grayson McCouch. The whole problem of the nature of mind fascinated me and was the constant subject of our talks. Politically, I was by way of being a

2. Gustave Le Bon (1841–1931), *The Crowd: A Study of the Popular Mind* (1897) (a translation of *Psychologie des foules*, 1895) is the book C A had seen in 1915.

sceptical radical: opposed America's entrance into the war. Religion, I had none; my parents were renegade unitarians; my maternal grandfather was a somewhat radical unitarian minister in New Bedford, and his freedom of thought was in the air in my childhood. So everything was ripe at this period for my own perfect freedom for intellectual and emotional adventure into chaos. I attacked the thing with gusto, had the time of my life, felt an extraordinary energy and sureness of insight, and only began to distrust the latter when the books, one after another, fell dead. Each one fell deader than the last; but with Festus I felt that anyway I had come to the end of that particular course, and so I simply resigned myself.

(2) Literary influences: Masefield, as noted above, at the very outset, and lasting part way through Turns and Movies; Masters influenced me briefly in the vaudeville sketches in that volume; Eliot influenced me a great deal at this time also, his influence becoming shamelessly apparent in the horrible volume called Nocturne of Remembered Spring, where it got itself out of my system; Fletcher influenced me somewhat in the Channel Rose period: he was living next door to me at this time (1915–16, at 11 Walnut Street, Boston) and eating his meals at the boarding house in which we lived: we saw a great deal of each other, and fought over the whole free verse and imagist question, to mutual advantage; the "Others" crowd, under the leadership of Kreymborg and W. C. Williams, also drew me somewhat at this moment: the general effect of all this being to teach me flexibility, new colors and tones, a new recklessness with form. These purely literary influences were being crossed by

(3) the psychological: Freud, Ferenczi, Adler, [Ernest] Jones, Jung; in philosophy, William James and Santayana; Bradley I never read; Bergson I did; and Kostyleff, Le Mécanisme Cérébrale de la Pensée, gave me a lot.[3] There was also, as above, Ellis, who contributed a lot to the Charnel Rose.

(4) Donne I came to rather late: not thoroughly in fact until about three years ago; so I think he can be ruled out. There is a kinship here I think: just as there is between Eliot and Donne. (Incidentally, I have known Eliot ever since my second year at Harvard, intimately, and the extent of cross-influence here is incalculable; Eliot and I have always in a curious sense kept our eyes on each other: anyway, I've always kept my eyes on him, and I

3. For C A's review of this book see Collected Criticism, pp. 34–41.

fancy he has increasingly kept his eyes on me; though I may flatter myself. Just between ourselves, there has been something very queer in this: something analogous to the curious relationship between Melville and Hawthorne; I believe I was the first to see Eliot's genius: I was the first to try to get Prufrock published, taking it to London with me in 1914, and offering it in vain to English publishers. Eliot, on the other hand, has never especially liked my poetry: has been very guarded about it. This used to make me rather miserable, for I greatly respected his judgement. Now, I can see why he *does* distrust my work. His work, if you like, to use your term, is a chaos from which he tries to escape, or in which he tries to find a principle, an absolute; mine is a mere revelling in chaos for its own sake? Something of the kind. Anyway, he has always moved toward Rome and Aristotle, while I have if anything gone the other way. Again incidentally, I have always wondered whether the shape and design and color of Forslin and House of Dust had not influenced a little the texture and direction of the Waste Land. There are some interesting parallels.)

(5) Greek I had at school, but have read little of since, except for the New Testament and the Anthology.

(6) Medical influence: my father was an eye and ear specialist; my brother Kempton Taylor is a surgeon; and from 1913 to the present time I have associated intimately with the two M.D.s noted above: G. B. Wilbur, who is now an analyst, and G. P. McCouch, who has specialized in neurophysiology. While Wilbur was at Medical school, I was with him constantly, and met any number of docs, talked medical talk day in and day out. When I was nine, my father took me to see him operate for the removal of an eye! I have since seen several major operations at the Massachusetts General. In other words, there is plenty of medical background. My friend McCouch used me as corpus vile for some experiments in neurological research at the Maudsley Hospital in London in 1920.

Enough? Far too much, I guess; if I've bored you, forgive.

What about A Poet of Chaos, as more modest? But any of these titles are o.k.

I think your idea of a series of short chapters is excellent: and your idea of avoiding the setting up of an artificial system.

I've just had proof of John Deth, by the way. . . . It's the last of my long poems (if you except the much shorter Changing Mind, in the Am. Miscellany) and very likely to remain the last. An experi-

146

ment in pure parable, fairy-story, for the purpose of putting over an idea somewhat comparable to Freud's in Beyond the Pleasure Principle (but I hadn't read Freud's book when I wrote it.) In short, a mythos.

Well, here's wishing you an azure voyage; and I hope we'll encounter in London. And if not there, in New York next fall. Best of luck, and drop me a line any time you want more dope.   Yrs.
Conrad Aiken

95: TO JOHN AND JANE AIKEN[r]   july 21 28 8 plympton street
                                    lower case cambridge

Dear John and Jane: I'm ashamed at my dilatoriness—here it is almost two weeks since I last wrote to you; and I've had two ever so nice notes from Jane, and only written her a poem in exchange; and I've not told you any news for ever so long; though to tell the sad truth there's not much news to tell. . . .

Anyway, here I still are. And Maurice has come back to town for a few days, which is very nice for me; though on the other hand Bob Linscott has gone away to Maine for two weeks, which is not so nice. Because it's pretty lonely here nowadays; and I'm terribly homesick for Rye. I dreamt a long dream about Jeaky the other night. I arrived as usual on a night train and went into Jeake's House. But everything was changed. There was a big room at the left of the door, and in it were several fat English cooks and a coachman and a blacksmith, and they looked at me as if I had no right to be there. I saw Mamma and asked her who these extraordinary people were, and then I told them to get out; and they did. Then I went upstairs and there was an English governess who ORDERED me to pick up the toys and blocks from the sitting room floor; and I was short with her and refused; and she was angry and went and complained to Mamma. And then I went out on to a porch at the back of the house, and there was a large tea-party of English people there, none of whom I knew; and they all looked askance at me when I came out. Nobody got up, Mamma didn't introduce me to any of them, a dismal silence fell, it was apparent that I was not wanted. But I wouldn't be so easily got rid of. I marched out and again said "Well, who on earth are all *these* remarkable people?" And there being no answer, I seized a deck-chair, with the idea of sitting beside a lady whom I saw, but the

deck-chair came to pieces and I flung it over the railing. And in falling, it broke one of the supports of the porch; the porch began to sag. Everyone looked uncomfortable: they all thought it was my fault for behaving so badly: me, an interloper, who had no right to be there. And thereupon, one by one, they all began to go. They got up and said good-bye to Mamma and Aunt Marian,[1] shaking hands, but didn't look at me at all; and after a while they were gone. —And then the dream faded out. . . .   Much love—
Cahoun

96: TO ROBERT N. LINSCOTT[w]

1 Brunswick Square London W.C. 1
Dec 7 28

Hail, Linsk, hornament of Boston, stone of stoneham, spark of park street: thrice hail. Your dozen letters received and read with gusto. So I hasten to reply, giving you all the heartrending news from this frore (I always disliked that word frore) fringe of the Pole. My beard is hung with icicles, my eyes are as hard as stones, and thank god I don't feel my feet any longer at all. Nor my heart? but you never were a believer in that organ, so I pass it by. —I have met the enemy and I am theirs. I surrendered on every point. Gave them additional evidence of my domicile. Signed on the dotted line. Threw to the winds my chances of saving a god-damned cent. Trusted my soul to bloodhounds, who are all of them as hard as basalt, who won't offer a single guarantee that I won't be ruined, and are all of them frankly determined to see me walk the plank as publicly as possible, and Jerry with me. Was anything ever so monstrous? I went to Rye, called on the family, and found the Game in command: she has wrapped herself around Jessie's mind like an adder, tells her just what to do, just what to think of Conrad, pours poison into her ear night and day, and, in short, has been as responsible as I thought in the shaping of events.[1] Jessie refused to talk with me: wouldn't listen to me: turned a blank ear on my request for fifteen minutes' discussion of ways and means, with the notion of coming to a sort of amicable agreement as to the financial and other ar-

1. Jessie's sister.
1. C A attributed some of Jessie's attitude to the influence of her friend, Margaret Game. Needless to say, Jessie and others felt she required no outside prompting for her reaction to C A's abandonment of his family.

rangements. Then she jumped on her bike and rode proudly away into the distance, leaving me vis-à-vis with the Maggot. I had lunch with the kids and the Maggot: intended to spend the day there, even perhaps the night (at a hotel, of course) but on finding that Jessie thought she would have to stay away as long as I was there, I thought it no use, and rushed back to town. So that was that: a heavy defeat. Next day, weary and ill, (pathos: tremolo, vox humana, distant bells, cry of a lost soul, etc.) I decided the best thing to do was to instruct my solicitor not to defend, simply to get the bloody thing over with. So I handed out further proof, for the assistance of the enemy, arranged to have the petition served upon me, had it served, and there I am. Selah—My husband in law keeps discreetly out of my way, and out of London. His book is making him pots of money,[2] and he's got himself a house in the country, which he's fixing up and furnishing for the family. I am arranging to have it bombed. For the rest, I've seen Tom, Fletch, Monro, [Herbert] Read, Freeman, Radclyffe. . . . I attended the Criterion Christmas dinner, and got tight as a tick. Fletch is minus an eye-tooth, and looks more John Ghoulish than ever. Tom is a lost man. He's unsure of himself, more dependent than he used to be, wary, and now faced with a growing opposition and a shrinking following: so I read the situation, anyway. They are all of them on the defensive, I think, a little bit weary and frightened, a little shrunk in size, feeling the frost. A lusty young fellow like me, hardboiled and Yankee and accustomed to chaos, feels among them like a great coarse Samson. —And by god, Linsk, what do you think? Is there something rotten about me? am I even worse as a poet than my secretest fears? is there in me a foul germ of popularity? an easy rank plausibility? a glycerine glibness? that rich and yeasty pus on which the stinking public battens? for lo, I leave one biographer behind me in America and find another one in England. Here's a Bergsonian poet and critic hight George Rostrevor Hamilton who wants to do a book on Haiken, with a preface (mind you) by T. S. Eliot. Now by god this is too much, and I'm off to the Sahara tomorrow by submarine. And think of poor Tomeliot being asked to write the preface! *There's* a poetic justice for you: how he must have squirmed, what visceral doubts must for a moment have cramped him. Or do I do him wrong? —Anyway, I shall tell Hamil-

2. Martin Armstrong's novel, *St. Christopher's Day* (in America, *All in a Day*) (London and New York, 1928).

ton of Peterson, and see what happens. —And day before yesterday I bought a chinese painting of colossal size, a great pair of pines clutching the scarred edge of an abyss, with a straight waterfall falling straight from Heaven, and a sound of wind and ruin in it, and a tea-pavilion on a rock, where sit two Taoists drinking tea and perpending chaos. Chaoists, among which sect I count myself. And on the strength of this, I coughed a poem and began a novel: Book of the Dead. And there I hang.

And that's all for this year. Happy yooltide: there won't be any card from me. Prepare to weep when my review of Archie comes out, and tell me what he says about it, if it's repeatable.[3] Tom agrees with me about it. The voyage was terrible: we were all of us continuously drunk, gambled like mad at twenty-one and bridge, and strange to say my total loss for eight days was only one dollar and twenty-five cents. I lived in the smoke-room. And there was the best raconteur, bar Silberstein [in *Blue Voyage*], I've ever met. My regards to them that wants them.   C A

97: TO THEODORE SPENCER[u]   1 Brunswick Sq.W.C.1
                                              Dec. 13 28

My dear Ted—!   what a letter, by god; it fills me with glooms, nostalgias, aches and neuroses; not to say psychoses; have you lost a leg? I have lost a head; without you and Harry [Murray] I feel absolument non compos mentis; without Jerry, minus a heart. . . . I stare into the fog of a December afternoon and my tears fall like ricegrains. The chinese association is exaggerated by the fact that I've got a Ming painting on the wall opposite me, as I write, and a Tang figurine on the mantel behind me. —And I'm so cold that I have to keep drunk to keep warm: which is as good an excuse as any.

At this moment, I'm supposed to be tea-ing with Lady Ottoline Morrell, whose portrait by your friend [Augustus] John you may have seen; at the last minute I funked it, and telegraphed that I would not be there. To "meet Mr. James Stephens." Odd that you should cough up John this morning of all mornings, when my first association with him was that portrait, displayed to me in 1920 by a niece of Sargent [Reine Ormond].

3. C A's review of *The Hamlet of A. MacLeish*, in *The Bookman* (January 1929). See Collected Criticism, pp. 280–83.

Well: self-searchings are good; healthy; don't go back on them. Why *not* kick out for a year or two? Here rather than New York, I should think, despite the physical misery. A profound, wonderful, and horrible place; rich inferno; death and transfiguration if it isn't plain suicide. You aren't sterile—how could you be? You have a damned good mind *and* imagination, if only you won't let them be swallowed up in heres and nows. Make the experiment, anyway; you won't regret it. If you want, at the end of two years, to declare yourself insolvent, it won't kill you! and you'll be so much the wiser, and so much the better a critic, to put no better complexion upon it. —All this other affair, the transition from adolescent fluidity to the "something stiffer," isn't that the mere business of growing old and hardening one's harteries? I think so. It takes care of itself. And it's never done with, either. I have often envied you, Ted: I've many times coveted things of yours. Your bat had first-rate things in it: really first-rate. You needn't cry it down, though I know from my own experience how one feels about those "stations" in one's progress; when you grow only a little beyond them, they make you ill; when you grow still farther beyond them, you smile upon them as you do on your children. All of which you know already. Only, knowing with the guts is different from knowing with the mind: it's slower. You can't rush it. The time just comes when you begin, naturally, without foresight, speaking your own language: telling the world who the hell you are. Isn't that it? Before that happens, one often has times of panic. In fact, one goes on having these times of panic, if my own adventures have any general validity. Tout de meme, I go back to the fact that I've often envied you, felt in you a kind of power that I've never had myself. Am I wrong? are we both wrong? God knows. But isn't it worth gambling on? —It all comes down to the elementary question of what it is that makes one happy. If this makes you happy—voila tout. —As for this matter of "being conscious before the fact" (with regard to writing poetry), My Heavens. Yes and No. No and Yes. But better No than Yes. If you can tuck the Yes in at the last minute, tant mieux; it will ram down the charge, but will hardly alter its first nature. But if you *begin* with the notion of ramming down a charge, the result is likely to be a flash in the pan. Am I too drunk to be talking sense? But there is no sense to be talked about these things: we are discussing the control of the auricle. Qui, d'ailleurs, n'existe pas. —No, I think one shouldn't beat away the "hypnosis":

it's the only proper way of getting at the thing; but by degrees one's "guts," "unconscious," "integrity," "whole character," or whatever you want to call it, assume control of the mechanism. You surrender to the hypnosis, but with a grinning kind of arriere pensee. *Without* the hypnosis, you're nowhere. It's not a thing to be afraid of: I suspect it's god, but not in tomeliot's sense.

Et al? I had Xmas dinner with the Criterion, and heer je, what a paltry party. I dropped asafoetida bombs all over the table, made myself very objectionable, but have none the less also been invited to the Epiphany party. MY god.

My divorce goes forward ventre a terre: what a hell of a lot of bad french I seem to be talking. So presently, I shall marry Jerry, d.v. I wish you and Nancy could like her.

Forgive this drunken loose epistle—   as ev   C A

98: TO MAURICE FIRUSKI[h]   [8 Plympton Street, Cambridge
                                     July 18, 1929]

Why go all the way to these Saguenays or Rimouskis,
When if you want to have a swell time all you've got to do is go to
     the Firuskis?
We went last week for a visit, and the weather was hot but fine,
And we picked peas and drank cold purple drinks and had a fine
     time.
The house is situated very picturesquely among the Taconic Hills,
Which is plentifully wooded and waterd (as usual) with many rills.
There are also ponds, very numerous, in which you can bathe or
     fish,
These have cottages beside them, and you can do as you wish.
The house is of honeycolored brick, with a dash of pomegranate,
The fruit is so plentiful that the Firuskis both eat and can it,
Fourleafed clovers abound on the perfectly neat lawns,
And in the wood behind the house there are deers and fawns.
In short, it is no exaggeration to say that the house is a Persian
Hanging garden of delights, and this with no animadversion:
The meals are wonderful, full of surprises for the jaded city tongue,
By both Mr. and Mrs. Firuski many delightful songs are sung,
They have two cars, both of which can actually go,
And it should perhaps be mentioned that Mr. Firuski's driving is
     neither amateur nor slow.

152

But why prolong this list of praises to the length of a panegyric,
What is really required is a typical skylark sort of a lyric:
Or something in the style of the Lakeville Times,
Which makes up for weakness of meter with pronounced strength
    in the rhymes.
If your taste is for reading—and most of us don't read half
    enough—
You will find an excellent library, full of interesting stuff.
An oil burner keeps the water always hot, the water in the well is
    cold as ice,
And in fact everything, including the Firuskis, is just as nice as nice.
With which warm sentiments, and thankfulness to host and hostess,
    I will end my ditty,
Deeply regretting the harsh change from Taghconic to the city.

                                      Mournfully, C A

99: TO JOHN AND JANE AIKEN[r]   8 plympton street
                                      cambridge the lesser
                                      july 22, 29

Dear John and Jane: . . . It's villainously hot here today—my
pink candles are bending over in their candlesticks—and that's
pretty much the way I feel too. I couldn't sleep last night—it was
hot and noisy, and then in the early morning a hard rain beat on the
roof, sounding like Niagara, or coal going down a chute; and I
dreamt and dreamt and dreamt. —This is one I dreamed two weeks
ago: I heard two voices talking, and the first one said to the other—
"After years of research I've found a remarkable language, a language in which meaning is so dispersed in a multitude of words,
and so little a fraction of meaning left in each word, that it takes
1,800 years to amass a sufficient number of words to constitute, in
one sentence, one completed MEANING." The other voice then answered: "Why that's nothing. *I've* discoverd a language in which
meaning is so *concentrated* that ONE WORD is the equivalent of
1,800 years." And that was all. Now I'd like to know what the psy-
choanalysts would do with that! —My young Englishman [Mal-
colm Lowry] will be here at the end of the week to be taught how
to write novels—I look forward to his arrival with great curiosity.
He's coming from the Barbadoes, having gone there from Liverpool; at this moment he's on the sea somewhere between the Bar-

badoes and Halifax; from there he takes a third boat and comes to Boston. As you see, I'm sending some stamps which his letters brought me, or rather which brought his letters. . . .   Cahoun

100: TO THEODORE SPENCER[u]

8 Plympton
July 24 [1929]

. . . We've visited the Firuskis in Taconic, Conn., where they live in manorial splendour—or should I have said manurial, for it's very bucolic. . . . My young genius arrives this week. Last weekend, on the Cape with Edmund Wilson, Burton Rascoe, Wilbur, and Linscott: and damned entertaining it was, too. Wilson, drunk, is like the March Hare: sober, like the dormouse. In either state a remarkable object, full of marvellous states of abstraction. Rascoe has the same trick of going off into a remote stargazing kind of mag: which he can do even while looking you dead in the eye. Between them, they gave us a conversation which was full of surprises. —And voila tout. I've written two little prelewds, two or three drunken little reviews, dreamt a series of staggering dreams, drunk long and deep, held hands with a gypsy, played one set of tennis, quarrelled with half a dozen analysts, composed a jazz tune which has started an insurrection in Hampden, seen three prize fights and two ball games, and that's my life. Ay mother mother, what is this man, thy darling kissed and cuffed, thou lustingly engenders? etc. —Wilson and I held solemn wake over the sacred relics of tomeliot; prayed for him, wept over him, and cursed him for a quitter. And now I'm reading Lady Chatterley, my eyes popping at the quaint four-syllabled words. Wilson thought it good. Pour moi, not so sure. Goodish—. . . .   Conrad

101: TO MAURICE FIRUSKI[h]

8 plymp
aug 8 29

Dear M—   you bet, I'll do them things with gusto some time next week, d.v. I say d.v., advisedly: for lo, you'll scarcely credit it, but I have a fractured skull. Now isn't that spectacular? and no more spectacular than true. Last Thursday there was a wildish party, in celebration of young Lowry's arrival: Rob[1] and L[owry]

1. Robert Potter Aiken Taylor, C A's youngest brother, then living in Boston (see Cast of Correspondents).

and I. A wrestling match between L[owry] and me, at one in the morning, for possession of the porcelain lid on a w.c. tank, (!) ended with me in possession, but unconscious on my hearth, having slipped, fallen, cracked my head on hearth-and-shattered-porcelain simultaneous-like; I bled for 48 hours. I've got a Christopher cross of some size on my brow, am dizzy as a fool, my nose has also changed its shape, and in general things are not too good. I shall have a scar, I fear, and am waiting for enough strength and stability to go and have an x-ray: Harry thinks it advisable. There is an off chance that I have a piece of porcelain in my grey matter. In any case, it's as well, apparently, to know just where the fracture is. I tried to keep it dark and at a minimum for Jerry, but she smelt blood and galloped up here three days later, and stayed long enough to organize a greater comfort for me. Now I'm on the up grade, thank goodness, and as you see can sit up long enough to write a kind of letter.

. . . Like the grasshopper, I sing cheerily right into the frosty weather: lie on my bloody pillow and secrete little preludes—even have started a novel. Is this courage, obtuseness, or lunacy? All three, I think, says he with modestly downcast eye. —Meanwhile, no news from abroad, and as last year the children forgot August fifth.

Lowry is a nice chap, but incredibly dirty and sloppy and helpless. Writes exceedingly well, and undoubtedly should do something. Very companionable, too, and awfully nice in the present situation; though as I say a trifle vague. —I'm reading [Melville's] *Pierre* with fascination. Also K[atherine] M[ansfield]'s letters.
. . .   C A

102: TO EDMUND WILSON[y]   8 Plympton Street
                                            Nov. 19 29

Dear Edmund: . . . I'm glad you find something to like in my selected poems—but my god how I wish it had been anything but Music I Heard with you, dear heart. That blasted poem has made life a burden to me. I hate it. I put it in in deference to its ungodly anthological popularity. Now Edmund, you aren't pulling my leg, when you pick out this of all things? For the love of god let me recommend in its stead Tetelestai, or King Borborigmi, or Sea Holly, or Psychomachia, or Poverty Grass, or Sound of Breaking, or

155

The Room; or if you can stomach a long symbolico-epistemological affair, Festus; or even Senlin. But not Music I Heard with You! Your letter upset me so, that I drank a quart of gin without breathing once.

I liked exceedingly your remarks on Tomeliot. Though I thought you were perhaps just a shade too guarded about the poems which come after Waste Land and the essays which come after John Dryden: e.g., the Eliot of the Great Retreat. With its smell of mummy and exhaustion. Just the same, a damned good article.   as ever Conrad Aiken.

I now remember that I've never told you how much I enjoyed Daisy.[1] Awfully good—the only thing I didn't like was the visit to the professor, which didn't seem to me to shed its theme backwards and forwards enough in the rest of the book—didn't seem to me to grow "out of" and "into" with enough persuasiveness and pervasiveness. The Rita part of it, too, I thought a little sketchy. But as a whole, a first-rate piece of honesty.

1. Wilson's novel *I Thought of Daisy* (New York, 1929).

Letters 103–129: August 1930 to January 1933

Heartened by the Pulitzer Prize for his Selected Poems, *and "as if he were a hermit crab returned from an almost disastrous foray over the sea-floor," C A returned to Rye in August 1930—with Clarissa (Jerry) and Malcolm Lowry—and "miraculously" found Jeake's House unoccupied (see* Ushant, *pp. 221, 224). Then opened for C A five years of unprecedented creative outpouring in his search for "the consistent view." They were also to become years of bitter hurt for C A and for Jerry.*

Ushant *(pp. 234–39) describes C A's attempts to save the broken John Gould Fletcher in 1932; in October, after a suicide attempt, Fletcher was committed to "Bedlam" (Bethlehem Hospital). C A, on receiving a long despairing letter of farewell from Fletcher, set in motion a train of events to rescue him "from what was virtually a burial alive," and succeeded in early 1933. But from February to September 1932, C A too was arriving at his nadir of discouragement: "he had now had perhaps as much of the vision as he could bear, and more than—obviously—he could find any adequate expression for." His suicide failed, but the past "had been, in some uncanny fashion, finished" (*Ushant, *pp. 225–28).*

Begun in 1927 and completed in the summer of 1931 were sixty-three preludes, first called by C A Preludes to Attitude, *in a series, C A said, which "still shows signs in its clinging to the shards of former beliefs, but with ironies underlying them, of a bewilderment, if not quite a despair, in the face of the new order." This series was published as* Preludes for Memnon. *A new series was begun at once to be called* Preludes to Definition *"which goes farther, I think, into the heart and mind of the matter, becomes more analytical and more abstract . . . in its discussion, above all, of the relationship between* being *and* speaking: *of the world and the word. And it ends with an* acceptance, *but on a new level." The second series was eventually published as* Time in the Rock.[1]

o   o   o

John Deth: A Metaphysical Legend, and Other Poems (New York and London: Scribner's, September 1930).

1. "Preface" to *Preludes* (New York, 1966), p. vi (written in 1965).

The Coming Forth by Day of Osiris Jones (New York: Scribner's, September
   1931).
Preludes for Memnon (New York: Scribner's, October 1931).

103: TO ROBERT P. A. TAYLOR^r   Jeake's House, Rye, Sussex
                                            Aug. 30 30

Dear Rob: . . . As you see by the address, the impossible has
come about. We ventured to Rye, to look for houses; looked at one
in Winchelsea; saw a notice "to let, unfurnished," in Jeake: applied;
found that it was only five hundred dollars a year; that a lady almost had it, with a bid of four-fifty; made a bid of a hundred, and
got it, for seven years. Jessie has taken every bloody thing out of it,
except my books and most of the pictures. It's in a deplorable state,
with plaster off the ceilings and paper off the walls, and no paint;
but we moved in last Tuesday, with Malcolm Lowry, and have
made ourselves at home. The trustees will slowly put it in shape.
Meanwhile, I've found a little of my own furniture in the shops of
Rye,—a rug, a chair, a clock,—and am beginning to make the place
look as it used to look. We've been here for five days, with Malcolm, and hope to have John and Jane here next week.
   More later. For the moment, exhausted and confused.   as ever
Conrad

104: TO G. B. WILBUR^r   Jeake's House, Rye, Sussex
                                    Sept 30 30

Dear Jacob: Delighted to get your characteristically laconic indecipherable cryptic and allusive letter, with its golden hints of
news, unfinished beginnings, additions and divagations. . . . —Yes,
my idle remark to the idle reporter certainly got me into—not exactly hot—but lukewarm water: endless comment. As usual, the idle
remark was incorrectly quoted. I think I merely said that I found
England a pleasanter place to live in and work in, nothing, naturally, about that old dodo inspiration. Nevertheless, by gosh, something like it seems to be true. I already feel dark underground rivers
at work, blind fishes frolicking in my little mammoth caves, and am
eager for Malcolm (much as I like and enjoy him) to be gone, so
that I can find out what it's all about. He goes in a day or two now,
so we shall know all too soon. And then I shall miss him. —Jessie's

friends have made it clear that we are to be "cut": not very cheerful, and for a week or so I feared I should accept the communal
guilt, and wince at the idea of walking these small narrow streets
where everyone knows everyone else. But now I find myself in the
best of spirits, and increasingly, if not relievedly, indifferent. Robert
Nichols lives in Winchelsea, and Paul Nash (the artist) has signalled
his welcome, so I shall as a matter of fact be better off for company
than ever before. —Pour le reste, it's grand here, and the quiet and
solitude, at first frightening, now seem positively a boon. I caress
my books (meant to look up your line from Bailey's Festus—is that
what it was?) admire my pictures, carry coal and wood, go for
walks, drink beer and wine instead of gin (and a little whisky) and
already feel younger and harder. We plan to go to London to a
series of ten symphony concerts, and for occasional weekends with
Gertrude Freeman [1] and Harold and Laura Knight. . . .

Well, when shall we meet again at the shore of Swan Lake, and
find wet dollar bills? Will it be on Mars, or in the fifth dimension?
For fear it may be so, send me the news. Anything that comes into
your mind of a frosty evening, or a rainy afternoon, will be received
with such applause as that with which the long dead greet the newly
arrived.   Aff. Conrad

105: TO MAURICE FIRUSKI[h]   Jeake's House, Rye
                                              Oct 3 30

. . . We feed mayflies to the spiders, a wolfish lot, in the garden.
My almond tree lies prone across the court, blown down by a gale.
The old sailor who sells shrimps comes once more and sells me a
pint of shrimps for sixpence. Miss Beadell—alas alas—died of
cancer two years ago, and the New Inn has been hopelessly and
brightly transmogrified: the old bar gone, and a horrible varnished
room in its place, with a dapper young cockney gent in charge.
Winchelsea beach is a suburb of little villas and tea-rooms. Camber
Castle has been shut off from the public, and a golf links is being
built round it. The Findlaters are the latest to cut me in the street.
Shall I say "Emily Dickinson" as I pass, or, merely, whoso that is
without human nature amongst you? The Mermaid is going to
present us with a kitten: Jerry has just been to inspect it, and pro-

1. The wife of John Freeman, who had died in September 1929.

nounces it to be "a pet." A bowl of tigerish nasturtiums is on the refractory table as I write. Recently, when John and Jane were here, and we all tried the sortes Shakesperianae, in three ventures at the Oxford one-volume Shakspere, I twice (TWICE) put my finger on the line "May you be happy in your wish, my lord." The second time after patting and turning the book several times, closing my eyes, and saying "Now William, be good to me." What do you make of that, Watson? The movie in Rye has been talkied, and we see two good films a week, and usually a Mickey Mouse as well, sublime fellow. The Camber tram still runs, or is it walks. Day before yesterday we all three went to Canterbury for the day, by bus: ate Whitstable oysters in a nice little oyster bar. Jerry surreptitiously took a photo of the pulpit in the cathedral. —Malcolm and I have had some good tennis, thanks to which my pot belly is fading away, and also some good ping pong, on the aforesaid refractory table. The Salivation Army still salivates on Sundays, and Lady Maud Warrender still, I believe, bends a bow on Leasam Hill, where it is hardly safe to walk for the arrows. The hop pickers are departed, the rat is still in our kitchen cupboard, despite two traps and a poisoned heel of a loaf, and yesterday we had a baked rabbit (prepared by Mrs. Neeves, at the Ship) for lunch. Yum yum. And that, by god, is all. I hope you wont really be waiting till 1932 to come to England? Come and stay with us for six months, and play bridge, and go to town from time to time to buy books, or even bring your book business with you.   —And our love to you both—C A

106: TO THEODORE SPENCER[11]   Jeake's House Rye
                                                 oct 31 [1930]

. . . SIR I resent the suggestion that I am a maggot in a dead lion. Out of the dead cometh forth sweetness. But what the hell are we talking about anyway? There is no sense in this. England is alive for anyone alive, or who can be alive, in England: ditto America. Pour moi, America is a weariness of the flesh and spirit; I do no work there; I merely kill time and myself; drink bad gin, poverty preventing good wine; rot my body, stupefy my mind. Here, I actually feel like working, and actually have begun to work: partly, it is true, because there is so little else to do; but one needn't complain of the causes. Not that I don't like America. I like it if anything too much.

I could do nothing but like it from hour to hour and place to place and person to person. Which is pretty much what I did when there, especially in these last three years. I could cheerfully have stayed there forever, but a pricking of conscience said why not go to England, where you'll die of melancholy and nostalgia and do some work before you die, bad or good? A little enforced misery to heaven knows what end. —And on the whole I think this is a better life. Serener. Simpler. More real. Harder. Clearer. Perhaps even, when one thinks of the landscape and the speech and the tempo, more beautiful. This day I have swept the coal-yard, the kitchen, the dining-room; mopped out the fireplace, in the diningroom; answered the door, admitting a gallon of paraffin and three dead pigeons; cleaned out the fire in the drawingroom and laid and made a new fire; carried coals and ashes. I like sweeping and mopping floors and sifting ashes. I hate it also. But in either case it's better than one's taken-care-of existence in cambridge, and one does somehow through such humble agencies get down to—what? that sort of searching of the soul which produces another half dozen preludes. And god help us that this should be so or half so or not so at all: that we must have recourse to such means for so ambiguous an end. —Nero, the grey kitten, who has just been banished to the garden for laying a warm waffle on the hearthrug, is hurling himself claws and all at the dining room door, and mewing like hell to be let in; a margin call from my broker, two weeks old, lies before me, cold dead and glaring; bills? they still come from cambridge mass, the ass. gas, and such; and I see that Harvard was beaten by the Army. . . . —And what to say about John Deth? I'm glad you can like it at all. An interim book, if not a terminal one; full of odds and ends and warmedover leftovers. I was resolved, if ever again I should have enough verse for a book, to have cleared the way for an entirely new sort of show. So, these relics and derelics had to be assembled together, with what help they could get from the sonnets and Changing Mind and a few lyrics, and do what sort of mob-dance they could. The title poem—well, it ought to have been printed seven years ago, but nobody would do it; it's now at *least* seven years old. Medusa? Thirteen years old, but in some ways younger than Deth. Good things in both, I think,—skill, verbal ingenuity, perhaps more than a touch of the lingual vascular; a few passages in each I can still roll on the tongue; but I confess I can't read Deth and wish I'd put the short things first. —The new preludes are so-so. If I'd written you three days ago I'd have said very good, but my return from a holiday in town finds them not quite so radiant as I thought. However, I'm in the mood, and there will be more. —We had a good time in London, and come back exhausted. I saw my kids—went to Hayes and dug out my daughter Jane, took son John to a Queen's Hall concert and Bitter Sweet; even encountered by accident my husband-in-law, and smiled at him with christ-like hatred. I tea-ed with Monro and his wife—he is at a vegetarian newthought nonalcoholic nursinghome in Watford, where he has had a fistula carved out of his tail. He looked ill and old. His wife has four Sealyhams, three white and one brown. —I lunched with Eliot, and Gordon George. Vivian, said Tom, had been much disappointed at being unable to join us, but as she was having a massage at four thought it easier to stay in bed. Gordon George was a kind of high church or catholic fairy who had written an article on T and was submitting it to him: Tom said that when revised he would himself send it to the Bookman. —After the first course Vivian appeared, shivering, shuddering, a scarecrow of a woman with legs like jackstraws, sallow as to face. She examined me with furtive intensity through the whole meal: flung gobs of food here and there on the floor: eyed me to see if I had seen this: picked them up: stacked the dishes, scraping the food off each in turn; and during everything constantly directed at T a cold stream of hatred, as he did (so it seemed to me) toward her. George said something about pure intellect. Tom, giving his best pontifical frown, said there was no such thing. Vivian at this looked at me, then at Tom, and gave a peacock's laugh. Why what do you mean, she said. You argue with me every night in your life about pure intellect, don't you. —I don't know what you mean, says Tom. —Why don't be absurd—you know perfectly well that *every* night you tell me that there *is* such a thing: and what's more, that *you* have it, and that nobody *else* has it. —To which Tom's lame reply was You don't know what you're saying. —And thereupon I banged with my fists on the table and said Hear hear and more more, and the hate subsided. —Now isn't this a dainty dish? —We had a very nice pair of dinners with Harold and Laura Knight (whose new show we visited) and spent a night with them. . . . Fletcher and I are plotting a plot—but that's later. Ohoo bay-bee—! Why let us change the world.   as ever aff., Conrad

107: TO HENRY A. MURRAY^r   jeake's house
                                                nov 29 30

mad bad glad sad Swinburne Melville Harry—   . . . Life here is
so deep, so still, that one falls or rises a couple of worlds without
hearing a sound. At an old church in the Marsh, while we listened
from the churchyard to the forlorn congregation singing hymns
within, and ourselves gazed at human bones on the greensward—
without, (put in for rhetorical balance)—a white owl detached itself
silently from the church-eaves, circled the yew-tree, and vanished.
Even the broadcast of the harvard yale game came in such a whisper that only Redvers Opie (Taussig soninlaw) claimed to have
heard the amazing score. —For the rest, if you don't mind, a poem,
this moment secreted, which associated itself with you, and led to
this note. One of the 45 preludes from the doldrums—or roaring
forties?

> When you have done your murder, and the word
> lies bleeding, and the hangman's noose
> coils like a snake and hisses against your neck—
> when the beloved, the adored, the word
> brought from the sunrise at the rainbow's foot
> lies dead, the first of all things now the last—
>
> rejoice, gay fool, laugh at the pit's edge, now
> heaven is come again, you are yourself
> as once you were, the sunrise word has gone
> into the heart once more, all's well with you,
> now for an instant's rapture you are only
> the sunrise word, naught else, and you have wings
> lost from your second day.
>   Wisdom of wings,
> angelic power, divinity, destruction
> perfect in itself—the sword is heartshaped,
> the word is bloodshaped, the flower is a coffin,
> the world is everlasting—
>   but for a moment only:
> the sunrise sunset moment at the pit's edge,
> the night in day, timeless for a time:
> childhood is old age, youth is maturity,
> simplicity is power, the single heart

cries like a Memnon for the sun, his giant hand
lifting the sun from the eastern hill, and then
handing it to the west—
                    and in that moment
all known, all good, all beautiful, the child
ruling the god, as god intends he should.

Marginal comment on what? analysis, conversion, recapitulation,
the necessity for divine stupidity, resurrection, regression—or is it
only a synapse gone wrong somewhere between Rolando's fissure
and the Island of Reil? (I looked the other day at a map of the
brain, and felt like Livingstone in Africa, or Andree at White Island,
or on the floes.) . . .   Conrad

108: TO THEODORE SPENCER[u]

jeakes house; in rye; sussex; 1930 [November]
house being painted, and the weather dirty.

Dear Theodore: our letters must have crossed;
or if yours fails tomorrow, it is lost.
Which is a kindly way of saying, sir,
that—in this 'change of letters—you defer.
Have you no news of cambridge mass to
    send, sir!   influen-zir?
Has Chau, cir, laid you low, or influenza?   (possible variation)
Lectures too many, and tutees too frequent,   cf. Tennyson,
with chills and fever (and debility) sequent! ⟶ Locksley Hall
These Johns and Nancies, true, encroach on   No. 2
    time; ——————————————————
retard the letter and delay the rhyme.
What with the cheerful far-from-able C-man
and also—ah!—the cheerless P. H. Demon,—
him whom the muses flout, but whom the lowell
adorns with mortarboard and gilded trowell,—
and also, too, those meetings of the bards,
charioted by bacchus, *and* his "pards";——cf. Keats (was it?),
well, all these things considered, I condone   Nightingale
that you should pipe me letters of NO tone.——cf. Keats (was it?),
                                                Grecian Chamber
Abuse enough! Exordium too hateful.   pot.
All with the implication that I'm grateful
for news of nothing, almost nothing at all.

Send me a postcard of memorial hall!
Send me a subway transfer, or the stub
torn from a theatre ticket in the Hub;
and I will weep such tears as flood the Nile
and pay the extras of the crocodile.
Here, all is hushed; November strips the leaves;
the bat, despite his mouse-fur, hugs the eaves;
save for his *haws,* the hawthorne tree is bare: — stet/
rank smoke and fog combine to foul the air.
The snail has homeward gone to underground,—
his shell by frost and mildew whitely bound.
Winter has come again. Sole sign of spring,
in the bare tree, the young thrush learns to
    sing.   /This is quite true.

And we, too, learn! Why, in the heart's despite,
we put our nose to ink, and learn to write—;   And this.
oh christ that we should write the things we do,
and have to write them, and be glad to, too!
When we have gone to heaven, as we will,
hoisted by cancer, murder, or a chill,
old age or penury, in nineteen blank,
and seek amongst defrauded hosts our rank;
and climb the hill to God, and see his face,
and tell him what we think, and take our place—
then we will find that heav'nly Sat.Eve.Post
which takes the effusions of the UNholy ghost;
prints what we write, and prints it gold-embossed,
with deckle edge, regardless of the cost.

Enough, of which, and that, and thus, and so.
Are we downhearted? the reply is no.
Profundities are always on the tongue:
even when snoring, we are not unsung.
A kiss for Nancy, and my godson John,
my love to you; and for the world a NON.

with which I take my leave, and sneak away
under a withered privet leaf; c a.
And high time too.
For now, of sich * & such,   * I think this is good Anglo-Saxon
Going & coming,   or low german or is it Danish?
We have drunk too much.   Anyway, see Grimm's Law.

165

Dear Jake—   Your literary style is certainly developing—this last letter is a treat, and I've been over it several times; so packed with ideas however that I don't hope to reply to it in detail, nor to understand all of it either—especially when you voyage into terminology new to me, hence undefined save by guesswork. You sound serene enough, anyway, and that's the main thing. To do or be? That was one of the first rows I had with Jessie—I defended the to be, and on the whole I still think it's a more satisfactory and rewarding pursuit, and doesn't at any rate give out on you when your energies give out. If the doing can be made ancillary to it, it's a good team to drive. Jessie could never understand that a person could be of importance—i.e., influential in a creative sense— without doing important things. As I look back on it now, I can see that this led quite easily to her increasing resentment of the fact that I didn't make money for the children, and instead created a good life for them by my wits—viz., by taking them to the Cape and then to England, where it was possible to live on very little. I think she felt this was immoral. —Ingenious but improper. . . .

The novel hasn't been touched since October, when I merely made a sort of note-outline of the characters and certain scenes.[1] It had me excited for a week or two, and then the poems got me by the throat and have never released me. Result, a new book is finished and will go soon to New York. The preludes, as you supposed. Did I say they were an ending? a beginning? they are both, of course. They represent, *partly* intentionally, a process of adjustment to a new "reality"; the first of them was done at a time when suicide was never long out of my mind; the first third of the book during a period when I was never sober for very long, and many of them written moreover when actually tight; the rest of the book with increasing sobriety and—sanity?—or at least with an increased awareness of the process of reorganization and the necessity for it. Anyway, the book makes a kind of spiritual diary, a history of my reflections and backings and fillings on a good many planes—varying from the intensely and immediately personal to the purely speculative and analytic. Incidentally you will find here and there in it

---

1. What was to become *Great Circle*.

psychoanalytic doctrines quite nakedly (in so far as poetic symbolization permits) expressed. Usually when such a phrasing of an idea was really an incorporation of a new item in *experience*. Knocking softly on wood, I believe it's my best book, and in my rasher moments I believe it's a knockout. But then I've had those delusions before, so I shall wait and see, and my heart is too old and elastic to be broken. —As concerns their place in my career, they are again both an ending and a beginning, for they move out into new ground, and only partially bring it into the kingdom. Or do I mean they move *in* into new ground? for they are more directly my own voice and mind, in many senses, than anything done before. They make the rest of my poetry look as if I had always been dodging the essential "What" of aiken. Perhaps ten years from now I'll be saying the same thing of these. Here we go round the mulberry bush. The self-remembering self-devouring self-forgetting continuum, new and old at every point. —I find in my own case that poetry increasingly is of use to me in the recognition of what I have been and am going to be; and therefor is itself a process of becoming. Hence my (abandoned) title "Preludes to Attitude and Definition." But this would be too stiff for the Gen. Reader, so it will probably be Preludes for Memnon. . . .

John Deth? The title poem is not a success, despite good detail; but the theme—the necessity to die—the desire to die—oddly paralleled F's Beyond the Pleasure Principle, which I hadn't read when I wrote. Changing Mind might interest you, however—built on a series of dreams, with simply the notion of portraying the mind in a moment of affective transition—an adjustment, symbolically, to a highly painful group of memories and recognitions. And the poem itself projected in pure symbolism, until you get to the final statement in the lyric at the end, where the major theme—death of father and mother and one's at-last-acknowledged-connection with them—comes out into the open. . . .   aff   Conrad

110: TO HENRY A. MURRAYʳ   Jeake's House Rye Sussex
                                   Jan. 26. 31.

well Harry your dionysian paean uplifted me for days and exalted me for nights, but I'm recovering now, and won't look again at your letter for fear of again becoming drunk. As you were saying, isn't it a funny delicious tragic farce of a world, the nicest thing about it being that there's so much more in the wings than on the stage? By god if only we could approach via the stage door and see what actually goes on there. And maybe we will. The clinic is one stage door and made poetry is another and one of these days we'll "meet guiltily on a tilted corner of time-space," you holding hands with a chorus angel of the Follies of Eternity, and myself in the embrace of the Long Arm of Coincidence. But be that as it will. — Meanwhile, anyway, what a good time we're having in the continuous act of resistance which for all I know might be another way of saying consciousness. Or agreeably controlled alternations of resistance and acquiescence? Anger and peace. —Acquiescence is pleasant, if only one could be sure that it didn't mean old age, merely. But I increasingly like to acquiesce: I think I'll become a professional yes-man. I'm already a gifted amateur. I can say yes to the primrose and the sea and Arcturus and death, but not yet successfully to the subtler and nearer poisons. One's own little meannesses—particularly when seen abroad—these aren't so easy. To accept back from the world one's vanities and envies, for example? I'm simple-minded, and find it hard. —You say nice things about J Deth, for which I like it better. I daresay the thing has more virtues than I credit it with, just as one may have a more agreeable voice than one supposes. I'm glad you liked the xmas prelude—which I wrote a year and a half ago, the day after I broke my head. A tour de force, as it were. But the new preludes, some thirty-odd, are much better. The book is done, and I whole-heartedly like it. I'm trying to peddle the items to magazines—and hope to get the whole thing out in the fall. And I've pretty nearly completed a book of stories, not awfully good, but I hope a sop to Cerberus. What I'll do when my little brain-sponge has again filled itself, I don't know. Perhaps I'll have the courage to have another shot at Cambridge Mass., but I kind of doubt it. —For the moment, I'm drained. . . .

We're conquering Rye, slowly but surely—the Christians rage and say a vain thing, but the heathen come to call. Nichols is a nice fellow—mad as a hatter, and writing a very promising Don Juan.[1] Paul Nash has now settled in Rye, so I shall see more of him—a nice creature. Fletcher comes down periodically with mephistophelian fomentations against the St. Eliots. Jerry and I remain serene, and listen to Ravel and Beethoven on the radio. And the cat

1. Robert Nichols, "Edward" in *Ushant* (see pp. 261–62), poet and dramatist, whom C A had met in Chicago in the twenties (see C A's *Scepticisms* [New York, 1919], pp. 175–77).

is a cat of genius. Presently he will be playing chess.   and so.
Conrad

111: TO R. P. BLACKMUR^p   jeake's house rye
                                                     feb 14 31

Dear Dick: Delighted to get your excellent letter, with its variety of news and comment on the times. Some of the news is legen-
dary: as, that I am writing a novel. In September, or October, I did
make a dozen pages of notes for a novel—Cambridge Mass.—but
discovered in myself no burning impulse to write it, and stopped
where I was, which was nowhere. But that report, starting from a
letter or two written in the middle of my little week of enthusiasm,
has spread apparently from Hudsons Bay to Popocatapetl. —It was
largely a fever for writing verse which brought the poor thing to an
end. I had an outburst of preludes which was as bad as spotted
fever itself; and have completed, in fact, the *book* of preludes, and
sent it off. . . . Since completing that book, I've also all but finished a book of stories (series of paltry gunshots at the siberian wolf
who howls nightlong outside jeake's house door) in which two or
three might well be worse. —And since that, I've written also a
short-long poem, with a marathon title, The Coming Forth by Day
of Osiris Jones. This jeu d'esprit gave itself birth in a few days, and
what to make of it I frankly don't know. It's a kind of scenario,
partly in prose and partly in verse, very choppy and bleak and
episodic and oblique; length, about 1200 lines. I know of nothing
like it since Noah built the ark; it's a freak; it may, when published,
kill me as dead as cock robin; on the other hand I see it as not impossible that it might achieve a sort of side-show cat-with-three-
heads notoriety. Anyway, I read and reread it with a Good God
where did this come from feeling. —Result of all this activity, I am
exhausted and brainless and listless; I am kept awake only by the
very curious and surprising success of John Deth in England—it is
better reviewed than any other of my books here (odd contrast with
the American fate of the book, which I gather was unfortunate,
though I've seen only three reviews there) and I rub my eyes at
hearing myself with some persistence being called, for the first time
in my life, a major poet. Christ what a breeze! Where are the values
gone? What are our weights and measures? who said peacock pie?
This is disturbing. —Enough of this prime ego. I congratulate you

on writing, and finishing, a play—something I want to do and simply can't. . . . As for Stevens—I don't know what to suggest. You can link him up, of course, with the Rimbaud-symbolist business—even with Valery, and "pure" poetry—in the latter connection I once, in a drunken moment, called him the playboy of the western *word,* which again suggests a corner to be discussed: the mere delight in verbal legerdemain etc. for its own sake. But again, and I think this is important, and I haven't ever seen it suggested in any discussion of Stevens, he's perhaps the most remarkable *humorist* in poetry: I mean, he carries humor farther into terms of poetry than has perhaps ever been done. This is something to shout about. Even his titles are like those changeable signs one used to see: they are funny and/or beautiful. Then, finally, there is of course the extremely keen critical awareness knocking about everywhere under all this brilliant and delicious meringue of surface. Crispin is fuller of things than The Waste Land, and then some! Hamlet married and put to bed and the father of daughters and a good indigenous tiller of soils and all with a laconic bright precarious la-la for the lost world. (This among other things?) Ideas all over the place: but presented with such fastidious and indifferent nonchalance, such absurd inflations or deflations, with rings in their noses and cockatoos on their wrists. An aesthetic, and a pretty complete one, presented polychromatically piecemeal: now in terms of music now in colour. And of course, often enough if not too often the colour-buffoonery for its own sake, with (at least as far as I can see) no hidden complexities of moral anagram. —But I'm rambling, I'm rambling. All I can add to this I've said to you before—that I think him as sure of a permanent place of importance as Eliot, if not surer. Eliot will go *down,* somewhat, (keeping however a marked historical importance, in addition to his pure merit) and Stevens will, I feel sure, come up. — Incidentally, you ought to look up his three or four verse or prose-verse plays, in Poetry, etc., if you don't already know them. Carlos Among the Candles, Three Travellers at Sunrise, and one or two more. If you can't find them, why not write him: I suppose Knopf would reach him? Or you might find him in a Hartford telephone book. Our best to you both. I still regret that I didn't drink punch at your wedding.   vascularly   Conrad

112: TO ROBERT N. LINSCOTTᵂ   jeake's
                                               march 12 [1931]

well, linsk, or hell, linsk, I couldn't have got your disapproval of
osiris jones at a worse moment—for two weeks I've done no work,
waiting for your and Pete's [Houston Peterson's] report on it, and for
pete's report on the complete preludes, and—and—and—for
Creighton[Hill]'s report on the market. The latter has not come,
despite his cable Feb. 24 saying he was writing. In this cable he said
my balance was 2000. What *does* come today is Moors & Cabot's
monthly statement, to the effect that my balance is—not 2000 but
1290. So much for C's accuracy. . . . Now to turn to those trivial
matters which are the breath of my being. Osiris? I am in a quan-
dary about it. Since I sent it, I've had inclinations to expand the
trial scene, to cut slightly the inscription section, perhaps to introduce another section. In short, I've felt uneasy myself about the
whole thing, but with that sort of uneasiness which invites, and
would approve, approval from another source. I still think the thing
is good. Better than that! You object to its stenographic nature—
but that, my dear fellow, is what was aimed at. This is a behav-
iourist drama. Everything, almost, is reported scientifically and in
brief notes from outside. Character or identity is reduced to nothing
but a series of reflected items. Jones becomes the statements of
various people, the rooms he lived in, the signs he read, a moment
of awareness when facing a mirror, bemused reflection of the face
(mother), physiological report of a medical student, occupant of
various costumes; in the trial scene, is merely a memory of various
books; in the final scene, only a shape seen by trees and hills. A
story? My god. What do I want with a story? That, Linsk, is the
voice of the publisher, I'm afraid. The very essence of the thing is
that there should be no story. It's a nothing. It's a mere congerie.
It's a bitterly ironic comment on the fact that the human is nothing
but a series of reactions to his environment. I could go on like this
for a long while, praising my idea, or praising the *verse* which em-
bodies it (and *it,* the verse, is good, though you don't say so) but
why? To give myself courage. God knows I need it! I could crawl
under a toothpick. Or I could echo your own statement that you
have frequently disliked my things at the time of writing and only
found them likeable later: viz., Tetelestai, Punch, etc. Why is this?

171

Let us take the discussion into the other field. Is it because you don't really understand them at the outset, and await explanation? Is it because you crave a more merely sensational thing than I ever give you? You want something more outré, either in matter or in manner? something with the rot conspicuously on it, greenmould of the soul's corruption, combined with a kind of outrageousness of expression? If I read you aright (and who in hell am I to read you aright) is it not possible that you are one of those people who can recognize the good only when it comes to you in terms of the "novel" or strange but not when it comes to you in terms of the simple or (I blush at this suggestion) classically restrained? This is why you didn't like John Deth, for example? —If I am not mistaken, that poem is going to wear well; it is tough; I begin to feel longevity in its fibre. I think it will outlast many more obviously complicated and shocking things: Crane-bridges, MacHamlets, etc. Why? dunt esk. —The indispensable of literary criticism is perspective. Judging the contemporary, one should look both forwards and backwards. As one understands the remote past in the act of becoming the present, so one should foresee the future as a selecter of the present. What has the past selected? what will the future select? etc. To be a good judge of this, one has to be able to *go abroad* from oneself, aesthetically; in a work of art, one must look not merely for oneself, a reflection of one's own likes and dislikes, but for a reflection of what is likely to be a reflection of what is permanently human. On the first plane, one must discount the element of *linguistic* shock; one must try to be aware of what elements, in the contemporary (slang, tropes, references, idiom, topical notes, or subservience to a literary school or manner) will survive. Now and then a fellow of terrific genius can embody the most outrageously contemporary of language and material in his work, and survive: viz, Rabelais, Burton, and in parts the Elizabethan dramatists; viz., again, Joyce, on whom I would bet; but viz., also, in the opposite sense, [Dunne's] Dooley, O. Henry, Huxley (A.), Lardner, Fitzgerald, Milt Gross (you liked him once), and so on, who will all fade away slowly but surely. These are striking cases, but one might also cite (on another level) G. Stein, Hemingway, the Tate-Winters-[H. Phelps] Putnam school of poetry, perhaps A. MacLeish, perhaps even the greater part of Pound. All this is too contemporary. It lacks for all its brilliance (which I grant) a sufficient reference to the continuum of the racial spinal fluid: relies too much on shock, too

172

little on depth of thought or feeling, or real exploration of these: wants too much to be new, is too much afraid of being old: and finally, is afraid of form, or of all form which is not at the moment fashionable. Even Eliot (despite his avowed admiration for Dante) does not achieve form. The truth is that at the moment formlessness is regarded as a kind of esoteric form—and this is all right so long as genius informs the formlessness. Qui d'ailleurs n'existe pas. —The third plane gives us the shock of the morbid: i.e., anything abnormal in experience. This again can be used by a genius (Webster, Shakespeare, Joyce, Proust, Dostoevsky) and in that case will be so caught into a larger pattern as to acquire value and meaning. In smaller hands, it becomes a Faulkner's "As I Lay Dying." —But I'm tired of this foolish essay, and will drop it. It was of course intended to prove that I am myself endowed with insight as to what is or is not classic, and that you are not. And, equally of course, it proves nothing at all, except its writer's vanity. —And now, why the hell do you suggest that the earlier preludes should be excluded from the book? Which do you mean, arrogant fellow, if you mean specifically? I think you're (when you dictate your letters) a little too much of a strong-arm guy, for the benefit of ulrich? a shade too loose and large? Meanwhile Pete suggests that I'd better omit some of the later ones, which he thinks are echoes of the earlier. Which of you shall I believe? Neither. I will print the whole damned book as it stands, and the devil take you both and butter your pitiful bottoms. The truth is, you haven't read the early preludes—now come, not really read them, you don't know them, you merely refer to a vague half-memory—and are just for the time being feeling powerful. Nicht wahr? I am being nasty. I want to be nasty. —Believe it or not, I hadn't read the Nymph-Yew passage in Joyce for five years, and didn't remember it. On reference to it, I don't find enough correspondence [with *Osiris*] to matter. My own use of that method is more concentrated and poetic than his. Suits my purpose. And is mine. Why not accuse me of burking Maeterlinck's Blue Bird? or the middle-english debate of the carpenter's tools? Jesus, Linsk. —But I give up, I give up, And as I'm slightly illumine, make allowance for the growl.

march 13

This sour letter must have a postscript—christ what a bad temper I was in when I wrote it—I might better tear it up, but then, for all its bile, it lays the ground as it were for an exchange. So smile at its angers. —Meanwhile, this morning, a note from Pete, who likes Osiris enormously and tells me that Scribners are getting it out in June. So I shall let it go more or less as it is, and then later on, when it goes into a larger book, with other stuff, I can revise or enlarge it. —And still not a word from Creighton. I begin to wonder whether my letters angered him. —And what will we do when another winter comes?

I feel surer and surer that I shall never write another novel.   C A

113: TO WALTER PISTON[r]   jeakes house rye
                                            avril 25 31

Pawn to king four? H'wahyah. Nice day. Trifle windy, what? or christ what a breeze. And so on and so on. . . . And here am I, dreaming night before last that your latest work, a string quartette, was about to be produced in every town in Germany. What more could you ask? I ask you. Now what the hell have I got to say to you, except that I miss you, and miss our parties, whether for chess or the gin bottle or beer bottle or the Greek's or the Italian place whose name I don't remember,—I mean the one where Alice was sick and Virginia wasn't? —Nothing. You can't expect me to have any news. . . . Malcolm Lowry has just been here for five weeks and gone back to Cambridge [University], where he at once indulged in a motor accident—overturned at 55 m.p.h. Nobody hurt. He still plays the uke with passion. As for us, we live, but just how, I can't make out. On the whole, too, we have a good time—there are long gaps when we see no one, and work; so much the better; and then see a few people, have visitors; and then again the quiet descends. Paul Nash, artist, is nice, and ditto his wife, and another wild young artist, [Edward] Burra, is amusing . . . and Nichols the mad poet drops in now and then; and Radclyffe Hall passes our house with her flock of lousy caterpillars; and my kids have been here for two weeks, . . . and we have with us a rather charming Austrian girl, au pair, who departs this week, after two months— but that's a long story; her left hand is deformed, and looks like a minor collection of pink sausages; and then, Walter, then, then, there is the SHIP INN, paragon of inns, pinnacle of blisses, helicon of delight, and only fifty yards away, hard by the river. Did you say hard? Yes I said hard. So hard, that one day three weeks ago I fell at midnight into the river, balls and all,—I mean highballs. Malcolm pulled me out. I survived, with a very nasty cut on my right little hand. But I had had a good time—among other things having pushed a white wheelbarrow through the streets of Rye, with splendid eclatter. That's the kind of simple life we lead. . . . COME. I mean this. Why not? And for gods sake drop me a dirty postcard. Best to both of you   as ever   Conrad

114: TO HENRY A. MURRAY^r   Jeake's House
                                                      May 15 31

Well, Harry, we were seated together on a lawn, in the spring, and opened on your knee was a volume in old Greek, and at a little distance were four spheres of lapis, about the size of toy balloons, rolling of their own accord on the grass. You looked up at these with mild amusement and curiosity, and I informed you (imagine my informing you of anything) that they were "————" (name forgotten) a creature so rare that only five remained in the world, and of such a profound conceit that they conceived themselves to be gods, and all the universe subservient to them. As I spoke, a dozen servants ran out and made obeisance to those blue spheres, and spread napkins on the lawn before them, and announced to them that the ship was waiting,—the ship which would shortly bear them to Africa. And tolerantly the spheres allowed themselves to be folded in the napkins and borne to the ships, which we could see in the distance; without in the least changing their shape or their colour, they managed to convey the impression that all this was precisely what they expected, and indeed that it was the result of their perfectly sure magic. And so they departed for Africa, surrounded by serfs whose serfdom was purely voluntary, serfs who saw through the whole fraud, and were cynically entertained by it. —At this point you lost interest, however, and asked me for the Greek word for love. I replied, "apothanein." —And as if this absurd dream were itself magic, your letter and E[leanor Jones]'s poem (which I've seen before) came this morning; and with a cheque from the Mercury for a poem ten years old. Strange collocation. And as if this weren't enough,—nothing is enough,—this afternoon, sorting out old magazines to arrange them on my top shelf,—old Dials, Mercuries, English Reviews, Chapbooks, etc.,—suddenly I came upon a coverless Atlantic, and opening it found No Margin, and clasped in its pages one hair of Jessie's head. So I read No Margin again, again struck dumb by it, and then went on and read the hanging gardens, which is in the same number,[1] and marvelled at the warped and woofed wonder of the world. —I refer to that sort of queer "correspondence" which everywhere seems to beset one, the weaving of coincidence out of which our lives take pattern. You, the Mercury, the Atlantic, Eleanor, Harry Wehle, Jake—but I give it up. How has it all come about? —I'm glad you like the landscapes at all— sorry you don't like them more—I wondered if you perhaps underestimated the amount of "direction" in them—for there was meant to be a good deal—perhaps I'm needlessly obscure and "affective" about it. Anyway, the theme (among other things) is precisely (as you put it) that in a disappointing world a ham sandwich is better than nothing, and that one must therefor perforce educate oneself into acceptance of the ham sandwich. And, in the upshot, that this acceptance is tantamount to one's coming of age as a god, one's discovery of freedom and power. In short I would only perhaps differ from you in not being able to sing quite so noble a paean to the sandwich, or so completely give myself up to all-embracing all-exhausting love and enthusiasm. And that may possibly come down to a mere question of energy: I ain't got much. Is there something to be said for not having too much? The other night I woke up thinking (alas I seem only to think in my sleep) "an artist usually, at last, achieves perfect economy of art, or classic form, when his material has just begun to give out, or when the natural exigencies of the material (as with the halfcut block of marble from which Michelangelo had to carve his David) impose in an artificial way limitations which are similar. And similarly may one perhaps guess that one finally reaches clearness of thought, or vision, when one's energies have passed their apogee and turned downward?" A transparent little half-dream, all too pitifully plain to you,—you see me whistling to keep away from the dark. . . . As for me, I'm so rooted here that I could go on forever without seeing a soul or riding a bus through London: I haven't spent a night away from Jeake's House since November, and would now be I think really frightened if I had to do so. Not that I don't at times frantically long for the cheerful promiscuity of my life in Cambridge, or a little solid and concentrated dissipation. —But I have an entirely unwar-

1. Eleanor Jones's poem "No Margin" and C A's "And in the Hanging Gardens" both appeared in the *Atlantic Monthly* (December 1924).

rantable Micawberish feeling that good luck will somehow befall us, and that presently we'll achieve a little freedom. —I've begun a novel—or think I have—viz., I've done 8000 words of the first section—but I find my prose has gone to the devil. Why? I haven't given it up, and am determined to push through the first part; but thus far it's sorry stuff I fear, and my "touch" with dialogue seems to have deserted me in toto. A mystery. The truth is I want to go on writing verse and have a chronically "verse" state of mind—whatever that is. A highly impractical state, and most illtimed. And I suppose this conflict, this absence of any real desire to write prose, does the trick. I seem to have plenty to say in the lightning shorthand of poetry, plenty I *want* to say, and nothing at all, or nothing that doesn't bore me, in the cumbersome dishevelments of prose. Perhaps, after all, as I've often thought, I have only one novel in me. —In this connection, could you possibly lend me any books which contain complete histories of analyses, all the questions and answers, etc., and preferably of an adult oedipus complex? I don't know whether such books exist; if they do, they would be of great help to me. I'm too poor to buy such, but if I could borrow them I'd be careful of them and return them punctually. —A dreary cold spring here—not much sun—but our garden looks well. . . .
Conrad

115: TO THEODORE SPENCER[11]   [Jeake's House, Rye]
                                  may 20 31

Dear Ted—   Forgive my long too long delay—my wits and energies have been to seek. . . . I've become increasingly indrawn and sullen and uncommunicative—I sit and sit and sit—I don't quite know how the days go by—but go they do, and leave me none the better. Birds pass my window from time to time and shit on the panes in long white-and-black streaks, like hasty sketches by A. John—rain falls perpetually—washes them off again—more birds, more rain—and such is my life. I no longer seem capable of thought or even desirous of it. Why think? I have no sex, I am but two days old. I bark at poor Jerry, complain about the food, kick the cat, curse the stoves, moan at the mud on my shoes, not to mention the sheepdung, slaughter slugs in the garden and dream about them afterwards, pay bills, dodge bills, dream about bills, have nightmares about dirty socks, and in short I feel like the grievous waste of dead grass and horsebuns left by last year's circus. And why is all this you ask? I wish I knew. Has a final disaster begun in this all too yuman brain? It may be. I forget the simplest things, and have to say to myself—Don't worry old fellow, the spilt water will dry off the windowsill, a cloth will wipe up the milk, the wrinkles in your coat will straighten out if you'll only remember to hang it up for a week, holes in sleeves can be mended, the scratches in your shoes will disappear with polishing, the polish is upstairs on the watertank, your bedroom is on the third floor—but it's no use. I have to say these things over again each time in order to be sure of them. When people talk to me (not that they often do) I don't listen, say yes yes yes or no no no, smile foolishly, offer them a cigarette to find that they're already smoking, tell them an inopportune story which, half way through, I remember having told them a few hours before, am puzzled by the simple statements they make, can't focus on them, and finally give it up and turn on the radio. What on earth are ideas? I seem to have forgotten. I recall that there were such things, and that now and then I had one; as one might have a flea; but now, when I meet an idea in a book, or someone hands me one in a stole of silken phrases, I can't get at it—it defeats me—I find myself indulging in circumlocutions, evasions, temporizing until I can retreat, or even flatly lying. This is bad, Ted, this is bad—gor blymy it is. Is it just boredom? Impotence? the sense of wearisome repetition? Must I begin all over again and educate myself, learn that things fall when dropped, that there are two sexes, male and female, both repellent, and that one is only really happy as long as one is comfortably vain? Well then, and must one be happy, or is there an alternative state? What? Action? That may be the answer. Perhaps I have too little action. Maybe I need a love affair. But what fool of a female would take on a middleaged potbellied feeble shortwinded unsocial smallpeckered sentimentalist whose orgasms are a mere fly-twinkle? Otatatoi. No, it will have to be something else. —But enough of this—it has begun to rain again, and the latest birdsketch is being washed away from the tall window which looks toward France—the cat is in the garden getting wet—Jerry is downstairs writing a fairystory—it's cold as the balls of god—but I have a bottle of whisky left, between me and the dark, and down to it I shall go in a few moments, and thus fortified I shall read [Oskar] Pfister on Expressionism in Art, striving once more to understand the nature of an idea. In the grammar of thought, may one say that

178

a concept is a noun, and an idea a verb? Is that an idea? . . . My son John comes day after tomorrow for the Whitsuntide, and I look forward to his playing of Haydn and chess. He does both remarkably. But now I *must* go and see about that whisky, which may be all this time evaporating, so forgive me. I'm really in the pink, and only a little depressed because I can't get on with my just-begun novel—but this will take care of itself. Have you done any verse lately? to send me? Do. —Give Nancy my love—I hope she's well? —and the same to you.   as ev   Conrad

116: TO G. B. WILBUR[r]   jeakes house rye
                                           july 2 31

Dear Jacob—   . . . I feel very keenly the need to talk to someone,—not for any special reason,—just to talk, for a half dozen days, without design. And who better than you? You could give me—as you so often generously have—just what I need. What that is you know as well as I do. A mere juicy swap, as Mark Twain put it, and the muscular-mental exertion which that would mean for me in talk with anyone so intelligent and so trained as yourself. One of the greatest pleasures in life is bluffing one's way with someone more informed and armed than oneself. Nicht wahr? —And with relation, particularly, to a new novel which I've begun, and done a little of at last—a mere 15000 words—a novel which seems to be "going psychological," but a little aimlessly. I need to be sharpened. Just the same, as far as it's gone it amuses me; not to say disturbs me. Odd, how these damned things get to digging into one's unconscious on their own hook. I thought I'd pretty well analyzed myself with B[lue] V[oyage], but now I begin to see that I'd only scratched the surface by way of a little exhibitionism. The new thing has taken the bit in its teeth, and rides me blind. It has come to an end, pro tem, largely because it has uncovered so many infantile blocks and such that it has momentarily paralyzed me. And very curious too to observe how my dreams have gone back many stages. Night after night I've revisited my father and mother; alternately replaced my father and accepted him; death and birth inseparably interlocked; and the latest is a visit to the tomb of my grandmother, tout complet,—she wept tears through the sockets of three superimposed skull-masks, and asked me when I would come. I assured her that it would be soon. Whereupon she begged me to

179

have a long life, to take my time, and be in no hurry—there was no reason, she said, why I should come before I was 79. I kissed the uppermost skullface and promised to have a good time, and to arrive in the tomb in due course. Now I ask you. Must these things go on? Must one get down, or back, to this sort of poison in order to write a bad novel? It seems a little hard. And certainly it spoils one's sleep. I've had so continuous a diet of skeletons and bones lately that I begin to get thin (relatively) myself. —Just the same, it's fun, discovering these forgotten things. Renews one's wonder. I'd forgotten my hatred of my Aunt Grace [Tillinghast] for concealing from me the fact that my brothers and sister were being adopted—a neat dream brought this back to me. All this is very simple, no doubt, but it amazes me none the less to see how persistently the dealing with one's central problems, even in the dilute or projected form of a novel, re-immerses one in infancy. I'm learning a lot, but will I remember it, or re-emerge? Or will I get stuck fast in yesterday, like poor Jim Jay. Not that it much matters. —Anyway, I'm certainly stuck, and have got to a point at which I seem incapable of any work or reading, in fact of anything but a continuous flabby autistic thinking, a drift, a vagueness, a profound laziness. I welcome the newspapers, for I can read of the tennis at Wimbledon, or the stock market (the devil fly away with it), or Wiley Post, or the Harvard Yale race, and ignore myself for an hour. The garden too I enjoy, where I can take a mild inactive unpractical interest in a new poppy or the capture of a woodlouse by a spider. Whisky too I enjoy, for it makes me sleep dreamlessly. I wake with a sense of torment, but the torment is shapeless. —More and more I see that I have no will-power, in the nice accepted sense of that word: what I do, or have done, is by accident, precipitated by unanalyzed desire, hurriedly, wantonly, regardless of any will or direction or forethought: I am a shuttlecock with a memory, and with (be it said) a keen sense of regret. Perhaps this is the highest state of consciousness which one can reach? But it doesn't make one exactly happy. To be happy, one needs to be a little simpler, a little narrower, I suspect—one needs blinkers. Perhaps I ought to go to work. I mean, in a practical sense. But at what? I'm too timid, too old and timid, to do much—the only thing that suggests itself is analysis. This, as you know, attracts me. Why don't I go into it? The thought of so drastic a reorganization of my already so altered and broken life is appalling to me. The mere financial problem would be too great. And au fond, also, there is this still not-quite-dead literary vanity, which whispers, Keep on old fool, and you may do something yet. —But this is drivel, and I leave it. I now remember that you gave me information about the mammary line, for which many thanks. The queer booklet [*The Coming Forth by Day of Osiris Jones*] in which I make use of the term will reach you not long after this. If you detect any other misused medical terms, let me know, so that they can be altered in subsequent (if any) editions. . . . John Aiken and I get on famously now—what a crash occurs, what extraordinary readjustments, when a father begins telling his son smutty stories! We've now become boon companions, old cronies, and I believe the effects to be deep-reaching and admirable. But we shall see. I shall keep my good ear to the ground. Enough for this grey day.   Conrad

117: TO G. B. WILBUR^r   rye

oct 17 31

Dear Jacob—   at the risk of being somewhat stupid, for I've written six letters today (an unusual effort for me), I take my pen in hand. And as the other letters were all of the difficult sort (for example, a note of condolence to [brother] Rob for the death of his fatherinlaw) I shall now, if you don't mind, just relax, and speak as the spirit wills. Or not at all, if it doesn't. Above all, I won't try to answer your own last letter in detail—that would kill me. You wax more and more abstruse and involved—I never saw the beat of you for getting conversational knots down on paper, all the quirks of the turning mind, the mind that turns as the voice speaks, the voice that hesitates as the mind turns—and to attempt to follow your every veering would make me even more than the weathercock I usually am. Suffice it to say that it was a grand letter and that your letters are in general the best I get. —I liked your incidental comments on Osiris, at the end—your comparison, I mean, of the commands with the Freud idea—and so on. Yes. But you are right in your second guess, viz., that when I state them, as moulding in a sense the shape of the man, I do not imply a rebellion against them? no. If anything, I like them—they please me—I like the notion of our shape being given to us thus automatically—there is something definitely pleasing in it—and the passage to which you refer (inscriptions in sundry places) was one which I greatly enjoyed writing and feeling. There is something very healthy or healthgiving in looking as far as possible from outside at the matrix from which one came—nicht wahr? All the don'ts and do's that made us what we are today—all the signposts and warnings and enticements—one sees oneself genetically for a change, in the process of becoming; and personally, I flatter myself that not only do I do that without rebellion, but positively with joy. I react quite muscularly to that—I get back a renewed and defined sense of identity, oddly enough, just from seeing how random and miscellaneous were the forces from outside that gave me the shape I have—I can realize my shape from looking at the catalogue of odds and ends—just as one can only properly realize a week by naming the days of it. —As for your further speculations, viz., that reality is only the outward representative of man's ego, and so on, that is the ground I muddied in Festus, of course—forcing the question, but not trying to force a solution. I don't think one can. The world creates the ego, the ego then creates the world—it's the hen and egg. Both ends against the excluded middle! I doubt if it matters much which you assume to be the first agent—does it? Anyway, in Osiris, I'm interested in stating chiefly that Osiris was, (as) Ezra Pound once put it in a different meaning, a broken bundle of mirrors. He is presented (as) quite (as) much a helpless victim of fate (as) Oedipus was seen to be by Sophocles (what a hell of a lot of as's.) Even in so far (as) he can be considered to have reshaped the world, nearer to his heart's desire (an impulse mentioned on p. 13, (as) coming from his pride) this could logically be thrown back to a cause in external forces. This is therefor the *world* trying to reshape itself. Or do you prefer to consider (if one wants a monism) everything   ego? It doesn't seem to me to matter, on the whole. And I suspect the dualism is more apparent than real. —*Is* this all nonsense—and am I (as Eliot once said to [George] Boas at the Greek restaurant in Kneeland street, in 1912) using words of which I don't know the meaning? I daresay. —To go back a moment—to your mention of tools as the first instance of man's projection of purpose—we might dispose of that too as influenced from outside? behaviouristically—animal drive and the learning process! The ego as the sum of accidents. The "world" as the sum of the ego,—I mean, man's view of the world. And then a new series of accidents made possible by the first, and so on; but no matter on what level the ego—I prefer the word consciousness, as being the container—is still merely a sum of accidents over which it had no control. Hooray. —But enough of this nonsense. I was thrilled by your suggestion that you might come to england—now's the time—with the pound where it is—there are lots of cheap houses and cottages to be had, whether for sale or rent. . . . Your remarks about my continuity are grand—perfectly true—I needed only to be told. Thanks! I feel much better. (Just the same, I'm not sure we're talking about the same thing.) —I hope by this time you've got the preludes, and will like them—the book is as near as I'll ever come to a statement of beliefs—not that it goes very near—but I doubt if I'll ever go as near again, or want to go,—well, not in terms so comparatively explicit, anyway! But I'm becoming dull and confused, and had better stop.   love   Conrad

118: TO SELDEN RODMAN[ca]   [Jeake's House, Rye]
                                 November 8, 1931

I liked Max Eastman's article: 22-carat commonsense: I believe he is absolutely right in his analysis of the current vogue for pretentious unintelligibility.[1] Mind you, I believe in the use of pure *aff*ect, or the more purely *aff*ective sorts of speech, for certain purposes, and that nothing whatever can take their place; but one must be wise in their use, not blindly and conceitedly idiosyncratic (as I think Crane often is, if not always—which is not to say that I don't like his phrases, sometimes very fine, his rhythms ditto—). —But the best poet is—isn't he?—the one who has learnt how to make his idiosyncrasies intelligible to others—he will calculate the precise weight of his idiosyncrasy and mix it properly with more assimilable elements. The mad phrase—inspired nonsense—nonsense with an overtone of meaning—will here fall into its place; will not usurp the major role. There will be reference to variety (of kinds of consciousness), not merely to one. In Shakespeare's gamut, Crane might have been little more than Ophelia. —As for Joyce—Ulysses was a landmark in my life; and if I feel the seeds of ruin in the new book, the fragments I've seen ["Work in Progress," to become *Finnegans Wake*], nevertheless I reserve judgment till I've seen the whole, which might conceivably shift the schizophrenic fragments into a comprehensible pattern, something with a universal meaning.

1. "Poets Talking to Themselves," *Harper's* (October 1931), which followed "The Cult of Unintelligibility," *Harper's* (April 1929).

Perhaps not. Even so, there is verbal genius, even in this (as it so far appears) spendthrift broadcast of dementia praecox— Conrad Aiken

[Jeake's House, Rye]
                                        March 6 32

Dear Jacob—   . . . The novel is still stuck where it was, for the foregiven reasons. As always, I've been writing verse when the pot ought to be boiled—though I did, also, get a story done, one that pleases me—a little symbolic study of dementia praecox, of with-drawal—Silent Snow, Secret Snow. I began it in hopes of getting some cash—now, alas, I fear it's not too saleable. It became too bloody poetic. . . .

I'm experimenting with nonsense poetry—now don't rise and say, with Cammaerts, that all poetry is, or should be, nonsense! It's lots of fun. What I'm trying to find is a nice compromise between the two sorts of nonsense—the kind that amuses, and the kind that strikes deeper, and thrills. To manage the passage from one sort to the other. To go from the vulgar to the profound, and back again. It's too soon to say how it will come off, but I have in mind a book of it—possibly with some such title as Blues for Ruby Matrix. If only it weren't for that goddamned novel!—under its shadow I hardly feel free. But I think I see great possibilities in it, a new form, something which might permit of a wider spread of percep-tions,—as, of course, of language also. Mind you, when I say non-sense, I don't mean quite what the lay reader means! I mean *pure affect*. Insofar as one can get it in words. What about a mixture of Rimbaud and Lewis Carroll?

Have you read any Kafka? he would interest you. I'm reading his allegory, The Castle,—fascinating. Get hold of it if you can. . . .   As ever, aff.—Conrad

Rye
                                        March 24, 1932

My dear Ted—   . . . Sorry to hear that Nancy has had to be deprived of an ovarian cyst. (One of the few operations which aiken has witnessed, and a very good one too, after which he went to see a performance of Carmen.) . . . I still wish you'd sometime or other give up teaching, live in a cottage, and do nothing but write for a few years; give yourself a thorough tryout: or are you, like Eliot, one of these fellows who can do best when *prevented?* who make a welcome of adversity, or is it indifference? inditing odes on the backs of bills of lading, or bank of england notes. No, I haven't seen Tom for a devil of a time. In fact, I've not been to town, except twice for lunch, in almost a year. Seen only such people as could be dragooned into coming to Rye. And in that connection,— i.e., my inertia-plus-poverty—I shall for the rest of my short life nourish a guilty conscience at not having gone to see poor old Harold Monro—I suppose you have seen that he is dead?—while he was at a nursing home in Broadstairs. We'd been corresponding about it for six weeks—he and I—I suggested his coming here to convalesce—had no idea he was fatally ill—nor had he, I think— and then suddenly, six days after my last letter to him, an obituary in the Times. A perfect example of the will to die. A miserably unhappy and under-rewarded fellow, of whom I'd become extremely fond. In point of fact, I liked him more than anyone else in England.[1] —Fletcher is my sole remaining male friend, of any intimacy,—and he too in a process of break-up: so my world here closes in. I shall be driven back to Tom, I suppose. And in fact quite deliberately plan to "pick him up" again, faute de mieux. I'm interested to hear of his new poems,—are they the ones which have been coming out in the Ariel booklets? which are quite nice, I think. Though I should hesitate to call them intelligible to schoolchildren. But then, I don't think Tom's poetry is unintelligible because it's complex, or overconceptual, or abstruse, but because it's so increasingly empty of everything but pure *af*fect! and more and more idiosyncratic *af*fect, at that. But the skill in the use of time and sound increasingly impresses me, in the later things—Ash Wednesday, for example—there was never a more beautiful gibberish of language, surely? the whole, or detailed, meaning almost nil, but the *effect* lovely. Pure *skill* has never gone farther. And in the light of this, I begin to wonder whether his remark to me (years ago, after the publication of the Waste Land, when I said to him that I'd called my review of it "An Anatomy of Melancholy") "There's nothing melancholy about it—it's nothing but pure calculation of effect"—

1. C A describes his growing attachment to the ailing Monro in *Ushant,* pp. 258–60.

185

might not have something in it. *Something,* by no means everything! For there is undoubtedly an element of selfdeception in it. The Waste Land is his Inferno, Ash Wednesday his Purgatorio—they parallel the stages of his own emotional development too strikingly to be put down as mere calculations. . . . and thas all   Aff. Conrad

121: TO JOHN GOULD FLETCHER[a]   Rye
                                                       May 3 32

Dear J. G.:   I'm relieved enormously that the money has actually at last got there—and that in addition you've been able to raise some from U.S. Good. That ought to do something to take the edge off the panic. Now for heavens sake take things as calmly and slowly as you can: don't let the situation rush you. If you decide to go back, I wish very much that you would go first of all to Boston, stay there for two or three weeks and get into touch right away with Murray: first letting me know so that I can write him about you. I *urge* you to do this. If anyone alive can give you the very thing you need, I am sure it is he. So I *beg* you to do this. . . . I suggest that you take a boat direct to Boston, get yourself a room on Beacon Hill, and settle there for long enough to see him daily for a period of three weeks or so. I am absolutely positive that you would never regret it. He's a great man—a genius—the ideal fellow for a genius in psychic trouble. Let me know, anyway, what and when you decide.   aff., Conrad

122: TO HENRY A. MURRAY[r]   [Jeake's House, Rye]
                                                       May 9 32

Harry, old ruffian angel—here's, if you will, a job for you which might be to your liking—a chance to save a queer kind of genius from madness or suicide—old John Gould Fletcher. He's possibly going to New York this week, and has promised me to go to Boston to see you and talk with you. Will you forgive me for urging him to do this—I believe if anyone alive can save him it's you—I know it comes at a bad time for you—when you're already overburdened externally and internally—but if you *can* lay a hand on him I shall be impossibly grateful. He fell in love with a married woman last autumn. . . . He left his wife Daisy and lived unhappily with her, her husband permitting, for a couple of months. He hadn't a tough enough skin to carry it off, particularly as his wife dogged him with threats of suicide and breakdown, etc., and as also at the same time he encountered pecuniary misfortunes, the exact nature of which I haven't been able to understand; as he is not badly off, I believe, having about five or six thousand dollars a year. The situation further complicated by his lady's unwillingness to divorce her husband and marry him, and Daisy's refusal to grant a divorce to him. And further again, by the fact that the lady belongs to some cuckoo religious sect which frowns on fornication, whether with one's lawful spouse or anyone else. Result, that Old Fletch has pretty nearly passed in his checks: has lost all direction, all will, has become a mere embodied, or almost disembodied, vacillation. I've worked hard over him myself, merely trying to pour courage into him, but to little effect: I found him a hell of a drain and at last my strength failed me. He's difficult, I warn you; closes himself up in some remote blue lagoon of misery from which he has to be hauled back to the diurnal by mainforce; then yields readily to persuasion, but changes his mind the minute you turn off the current. And so on. He's still in love with the lady, and she with him, but she has left him, and refuses to come back. From mere fright at being out in the open, with no home, he frequently flies back to Daisy for a few nights, then again runs away in horror. America may do him good, and I think it would be excellent if he could be persuaded to do some regular work, perhaps reviewing, to keep him occupied. His own work he can't do at the moment, not unnaturally: he's lost all pride, appetite, feels himself a failure. (I got Jerry to "interview" him for the Transcript in the hope of feeding his amour propre a little, but I'm afraid he saw through it.) In short, as you'll see, a second Van Wyck Brooks, but not yet *quite* as far collapsed, and I think salvable. Do be an angel and try to help him? As soon as I know definitely when he's going and what his address will be I'll drop you a line, and you could perhaps then write him in New York and urge him to Boston: I'm a little afraid that when he gets to N.Y. he'll just go inert and fear to impose himself on you. So if you could yourself then make a gesture—? And make a gesture of forgiveness to me. . . .

. . . Yesterday I read for the third or fourth time E[leanor]'s "No Margin"—a lovely lovely thing. Praise her for me. Gosh, how much *love* she spends!   miserably   Conrad

123: TO ROBERT P. A. TAYLOR[r]   Rye
                                                  June 3 32

Dear Rob: . . . I take it things aren't too good with you—you've certainly had a lot of rotten luck in the last few years. Along with a good deal to be thankful for. But everything is relative, and I put forward my own sad little case as infinitely worse. And I'm about to put forward to you also a suggestion which you may think absolutely insane unsound ridiculous mad and idiotic, and which in any case will make you groan louder than ever, or tear your hair out by the roots. Here it is in a bombshell: would it be in any way possible for you and Kemp to form a private corporation known as the c. aiken co. ltd., the aim of which would be to pay to c. aiken annually the sum of (say) $2000, which would enable him to remain in Rye, where he can work in return for which c.aiken would assign to said company all royalties from his published books, including those not yet published? To which might be added also receipts from articles, stories, poems, etc., sold to magazines, in fact all sources of revenue whatever. You might come out on the debit side for several years running: impossible to judge. My total receipts for the past two years, as reported by my agents, Brandt & Brandt, were just under two thousand for 1930, just over two thousand for 1931. This year, my guess is that they will drop to about a thousand. What they will be for the next two years will depend largely on what the new novel does. If it does as well as Blue Voyage, it should net $3750 in a year and a half from date of publication; of which I've already drawn a thousand in advance. It might do better—a second novel tends to do so as a rule—but it also might do worse, for it's going to be a hellish highbrow affair. If it does better, it would automatically start all the other books selling. In any case, total annual sales ought slowly and steadily to show an annual increase. As far as analyzable at the moment, my average income from all *books* is about seven to nine hundred a year; to this must then be added receipts from sales to periodicals, fees for reprints in anthologies, and all such things, which vary enormously from year to year. . . .

Will you despite its wildness give it a thought—and if you think it could *possibly* be arranged, would you then *cable* me? My decisions have got to be made *fast* in the next few weeks. . . . And whether yes or no, no bones broken: I shall perfectly understand all the problems and necessities which must go into your decision. . . .   as ever   Conrad

124: TO KEMPTON P. A. TAYLOR[h]   Rye
July 7 32

Dear Kemp: Many thanks for your cable and letter—disappointing as they were! I hadn't really hoped for much, for I know only too well that things are bad for everyone. And I'm grateful to you for even considering the idea. . . . It's pretty frightening to have nothing whatever to fall back on, not even a prospect of a job; I think you fellows with a fixed income don't realize what that means. You say the publishing business hasn't suffered as much as other things—I don't know about that, but I do know that I can't sell enough stuff at the moment to make a living. I've got, for example, a whole book of short stories on hand which I haven't been able to sell: and at least three of them as good stories as I ever wrote. Last January I took three weeks off from my novel to do a story—Silent Snow—which I deliberately aimed at Harpers, and made a swell job of, and which, had it sold, would have made a whale of a difference. But no luck. Last week I learned that it had finally been taken by the West Virginia Quarterly for $75, instead of the $375 I'd expected. The sales of my books have dropped sickeningly also. About half the royalties of Preludes that I'd expected. New poems don't sell to magazines—in short, a battalion of disappointments all round. The result is that the end of our resources is in sight, and not a prospect of anything coming in from anywhere. To live by one's wits as I've been doing since January 1927 is amusing enough at the beginning, and when things go well, but it takes it out of you, and takes it out of your work. I'm apparently not the sort who can turn out masterpieces and hand them out of the window to the waiting sheriff, even if the sheriff would accept them as payment for roof and potatoes, which he wouldn't. To work without either response or reward can't go on forever,— it's like dropping things into a void. I've now reached a point where unless I can get help for the next few years I'll have to give up my

189

career and enter the lists with the other 10,000,000 unemployed, and with no qualifications or training for any sort of job. . . . The whole thing makes me sick with anxiety. I don't mind saying that it makes me all the sicker to look about me at a family of well-to-do if not wealthy people who are all safe as churches, and whose worries are of the sort that turn poor men into bolshevists! There's a lot of difference between being relatively poor and absolutely penniless: if I were to pay my rent and taxes today, it would leave us without a cent in the bank, and that's not a nice feeling. —It isn't as if I were a useless creature, either, or as if I weren't doing something. I've worked damned hard in the last two years: an output of three books of verse, one of short stories, and two thirds of a novel, in that period, is nothing to be ashamed of, especially as I believe it to be my best work. . . .   Conrad

125: TO G. B. WILBUR[r]   Rye
August 25, 32, 20th anniversary
of Wedding No. 1

Dear Jacob: . . . —Your letter I won't take up in detail—it's too complicated, and at the moment I ain't got no brains and not much of a heart. Much of what you say is sound enough. But here and there I felt that you *over*-complicate the issue—it's true enough of course that into any situation whatever one must inevitably project a great deal of one's own past—one perhaps feels it more acutely than one might if one were someone else or if one's conditioning had been different—but the fact remains nevertheless unaltered that there must be also a definite objective reality in any such situation. To take a simple unrelated example: if one of two people is an incurable pathological liar the other will quite naturally resent the fact, or at any rate find it a *real* difficulty: and it's not much good just telling him that he shouldn't mind it or find it difficult. He has not himself manufactured the problem—the problem is there, and is real. I think you tend a little in your subtle analysis of actions and reactions projections and counter-projections to lose sight of the fact that in such a situation the right of way lies with the normal rather than the abnormal, and that the solution of the problem must not involve any sacrifice of the normal to the abnormal, but vice versa: in short, one must be guided by simple reality. Of course one can persuade the normal one to be patient and to relax any too-

190

private tensions he may have: in my own case I'm quite aware of my honest-complex (an old friend, like Holt's,[1] based on adolescent dishonesties, and the relations between my father and mother, also my own relations to my father in this very matter) and know only too well that I'm often somewhat too fierce about it. (If one can be!) . . .   as ever   Conrad

126: TO G. B. WILBUR[r]   Rye
                                                         Sept 21 32

Dear Jake: . . . The Old Bird was in very good form, on his way to Oxford, to work for several months with Sherrington. His visit here gave me a lot of much needed help, a breath of sanity and reality; not at least, material help to the tune of a loan of $500 to be repaid when our ship comes in, which will enable us perhaps to stick it out here. His divinations are as acute as ever. He had apparently *felt* that I needed help—psychologically speaking—and hurried here from Antwerp on a hunch. As it happens, I very much did. Last week I reached my peak or neap or nadir of discouragement and attempted suicide. Waited till Jerry had gone out to the theatre and gassed myself. And succeeded, too—or would have, if Jerry hadn't come back sooner than expected. Passed out very cheerfully and without a qualm, not a bloody qualm. The return to life wasn't so pleasant. The whole thing was an admirable experience, and has had a profound effect on me: difficult to define, but I feel myself permanently changed—hardened and detached. Jerry took it like a brick, and I think here too the effect will be all to the good. To have made such a decision calmly and to have acted on it effectively—for to all intents I was dead—gives me an altered focus. Not least interesting however was the fact that Jerry found me lying against the door, where I had fallen or crawled: and as my last memory is of sitting at the table and reading an article by Wyndham Lewis I must have made this abortive attempt to save myself unconsciously: amusing to think of. Good old animal instinct, it takes a lot to beat it—John comes tomorrow for a few days before he starts in at London University. As soon as he has gone, back I go to the novel—And if four or five weeks can possibly be fortunate and finish it, I may come over with it—or I may come anyway—

1. C A refers to the theory of Edwin B. Holt in *The Freudian Wish and Its Place in Ethics* (New York, 1915).

The suicide under your hat. I've told Bob [Linscott] and the Old Bird and I shall probably tell Harry Murray, but beyond that I don't want it to go.   as ever   Conrad

127: TO HENRY A. MURRAY^r   Jeake's House
                                              Oct. 24 32

Harry, old fellow—   . . . I was seriously worried as to what had become of you. Letter after letter I had despatched into the blue, where they vanished as soundlessly as leaves in limbo—and while I had concluded that it meant merely that you had gone into a hermetic retreat, nevertheless I feared vaguely that your analysis might have done you some mischief. I am enormously relieved that things are no worse with you. . . . —Well, as you may have gathered from my earlier letters, I've been pretty neatly trussed up myself—half paralyzed, frightened, sick, tired, bored, everything—marking time in a miserable and almost hopeless sort of way—all kinds of Worms which can't be detailed in a letter—the disintegration reaching its climax a week before your cable came, when I attempted to kill himself with gas—ignoring your remark of a few months ago that suicide was now so common as to be vulgar. The effort was completely successful, and very satisfactory—but Jerry got home a quarter of an hour too soon and managed to revive me. I report this to you not to make play of it, nor boastfully, nor with an atom of self-pity—but the thing is now an important fact which simply must be mentioned to you, that's all. I'm not sorry I did it—it has given me something quite new and useful—among other things a comforting contempt of death—and it has brought J and myself much closer together, and in a better way than before—everything is more real. It was hard on poor Jerry—but she took it marvellously. So now, you see, I am living a posthumous life. —In spite of all these permutations and combinations I've done a good deal of work—a lot of new preludes, some of them pretty good, I think—and the Novel, my faithful old nightmare, actually marches steadily forward now, though with increasing agony for me. . . . —I've just been to London for four days on the grim errand of trying to get poor Fletcher out of Bedlam, to which his . . . wife has had him secretly committed, and transferred to a decent nursing-home. I fear it will be a difficult and unpleasant business—appalling. If he hadn't, three weeks ago, written to me himself from the hospital no one would have known where he was—we had all lost sight of him. Whether he will recover I don't know. His former doctor, a psychiatrist named Crookshank, seems to be hopeful, but only on condition that Fletcher can be got out of Bedlam and away from his wife; but as his wife holds the legal strings it will not be easy. Monro dead—Freeman dead—Eliot estranged—and Fletcher mad. What next? London has become a city of ghosts for me, and I find myself almost, but not quite, too weary to set about the sad labour of making new friends, contacts, which will presumably suffer the same fate. I *have* the impulse, however, and more so now that I'm posthumous, and have begun to reach out here and there, and to find that it warms and wakes me to do so. —One never changes without an Act? but words are acts, ideas are acts, feelings are acts, attitudes are acts? . . .

and that's all for this cold grey day—   Conrad

128: TO ALFRED CLAGHORN POTTER[u]   Rye
                                                    Nov 12 32

Dear Uncle Alfred: I've been shockingly remiss about letters—written none to anyone for weeks and weeks—partly because no one has written to me—but more because there has been nothing but the dismalest of news to send. . . . I'm now dead tired, not to say mentally exhausted, but beginning to feel the enormous relief of having a long piece of work practically finished. How bad or good the thing is I have now no idea—I know it will be distasteful to many—it will shock some people—those who know much of my own private life of the past few years will undoubtedly think it in bad taste, and too revelatory—but that is the sort of thing that can't be helped. The public at large will know nothing of that, and will accept the book for what it is meant to be—a novel, and will like it or dislike it on that ground alone. I have a feeling, or shall I say a fear, that you may dislike it yourself, as too intimate—I hope not—for I want very much to dedicate it to you, feeling that it is high time that I gave you something in exchange for the great deal in life that you have given me. How about it? does the fact that the scene is Cambridge, and that it contains may caustic comments on Harvard and the Cantabrigians, make you uneasy, or doubtful of the compliment? I hope not. But if you feel in the least dubious about the expediency of it, from your point of view, as an official of Harvard, say the word, and no bones will be broken. (The book is in no sense an attack on Harvard, or Cambridge—the references are only incidental, and chiefly as regards the smugness and hypocrisy of both institutions—there are no personal references whatever, none that are invidious, and I feel sure myself that the book is in this sense quite harmless; but I'm bound to admit that it is pretty likely to be eagerly read and commented on by Cambridge and Harvard readers, and might in such quarters occasion some small stir!). . .   aff., Conrad

129: TO JOHN GOULD FLETCHER[a]   Rye
                                                           Jan. 5 33

Dear old J. G.:   It was good to hear from you, and to learn that you feel so much better—that's splendid. I do hope you'll soon be out [of Bethlehem Hospital]. It's been a long pull for you, but personally I never doubted that you would recover. As for your suggestion, or I should say fear, that we'd forget you—good heavens, old fellow, what do you think we all are! I shall be tickled pink when we can get you down here for a weekend again. And I hope it will be soon. Meanwhile I'm relieved to hear that you are allowed to read in the evenings, and I'm sending you a bundle of papers,—not very exciting ones I fear, but as you mention not having got the Times Lit I thought you might like to have some of the recent copies. I wish it were possible for me to come and see you—but as I was refused permission to see you before I feel some embarrassment about trying again—and furthermore I'm at the moment so appallingly hard up that I couldn't afford to come up to town anyway. Can't even pay the rent. Our affairs have once more taken a downward plunge into the abyss, and heaven only knows what is going to happen to us. God may look after the sparrows, but he doesn't seem to do much for the Aikens! —On the subject of poverty, since you speak of being hard up yourself, it may relieve you a little to know that when I saw Amphlett a couple of months ago he informed me that you had really nothing to worry about, that your affairs were o.k. and that your funds would be quite ample for your needs. So do put that worry out of your mind.

We've had a quiet Christmas—my own was rendered particularly quiet by a fiendish attack of sciatica which practically paralyzed me for a week. That's better now, thanks to my giving up cold baths, which I suspect were at the root of it. And John and Jane have now been here for a week, which has cheered us up. Needless to say, during this period I've done no work—but during the autumn I've got through quite a lot. I finally finished my novel, Great Circle, and sent it off to America, where, alas, it doesn't seem to have aroused much enthusiasm in the Scribner bosom. . . . You speak of your reputation being almost nil—but that seems to be the lot of almost our whole generation—my own is smaller than it's been for twelve years—it's increasingly difficult for me to sell anything. I think one factor in it is the arising of a new generation of poets and critics, or poetasters and criticasters, in America, an exceedingly self-sufficient and conceited and bigoted lot of young people, without sufficient historical sense to give us our due. They regard us as old-fashioned and vieux jeu, the Objectivists, for instance! played out, they are themselves too intent on their own little foolish experiments, and too filled with their own sense of importance, to regard our work with anything but an unsympathetic eye. I've been very seriously tempted, in the last few months, to re-enter the critical arena in America, if only to torpedo some of the arrogant and pedantic nonsense that is being talked about poetry in these days. Have you considered that? After all, J. G., we could give most of these fellows cards and spades in the field of criticism—there isn't a really sound critic among them. Not one. And the worst of it is that this crowd of earnest and narrow secondraters—in the New Republic, Hound and Horn, Poetry, the Nation, not to mention the Tribune and other papers, or the radical sheets—have got complete control of the situation. And we old-timers—yourself, Frost, Stevens, Marianne Moore, Ransom, and I—since we belong to no groups and write for no particular audience and are no longer actively on the scene, well—we're simply forgotten. Voila tout. Not very nice, at our age, to fall again into limbo: but it may have its compensations. I think it gives one a freedom that the very successful writer—Eliot, for instance?—doesn't so much have. One is freer to grow and change, since one is not under a spotlight on a stage—one ceases to care so very much what people will think—thinks more personally and feels more personally precisely because one is alone. At any rate I find that true of myself—I would certainly like to have had more success than I've had, or shall I say more recognition by those whom I consider my peers—but just as certainly I'd distrust too much recognition as unhealthy. And moreover, if we go

into an eclipse now, it may be that we shall have some sort of recognition later on, when it will be most pleasant to have it—when
we are getting old. Better to have that—and I hope to god we will—
than to be the darling of fortune and fashion in one's early life, and
then to be shelved. If Eliot lives to be eighty,—? and we? our
chances will be as good as his, I think. His stature is bound to
shrink—because it is now so overestimated; our own is underestimated and is therefor—I knock on wood—bound to grow.

This gets boring I fear. Do write me again soon. Have you given
up your notion of a series of hospital sketches? you ought at least to
keep careful notes. It might make a remarkable book.   as ever,
affectionately   Conrad

Letters 130–136: January 1933 to June 1935

In April 1933, C A sailed to Spain with Jerry and Malcolm Lowry for six weeks. In the same month Great Circle *was published in New York. Reading it, H.D. and her friend Bryher (see Cast of Correspondents) saw at once that C A was steeped in "the insights of psychoanalysis," and sent the book to Freud in Vienna and to his colleague Hanns Sachs in Boston, suggesting that Freud analyze C A. H.D. reported that Sachs "found the volume a 'tour de force' and brilliant"; Anna Freud wrote H.D. that Freud had been "seriously considering Mr. Aiken." H.D. commented to C A: "He evidently smelt a rat, funny old Wizard, though you say you had not written him of your early life. . . . But he* knew *something . . . why not risk it, Vienna way?? I have £100 for you to draw on at once. It is not a loan or 'charity,' it is hardboiled speculation." When Freud became ill, H.D. and Bryher arranged for C A to see Sachs in Boston before going to Vienna. In September 1933 C A sailed for Boston, and on board met Erich Fromm, who discouraged him from undergoing analysis "as long as you're a going concern" as a writer. In addition, C A found he disliked Sachs. H.D. continued to insist that "Vienna is indicated." In November 1934 she said "I find* Great Circle *in the Master's waiting room." But C A never met Freud.*

With Jerry, C A returned to Rye from Boston in May 1934 with several journalistic jobs, including "The London Letter" for The New Yorker.

o   o   o

Great Circle (New York: Scribner's, April 1933; London: Wishart, October 1933).
Among the Lost People (New York: Scribner's, March 1934).
Landscape West of Eden (London: Dent, October 1934; New York: Scribner's, 1935).
King Coffin (New York: Scribner's, September 1935; London: Dent, October 1935).

Dear Max: I've been a little worried by the absence of news about Great Circle, and hope it doesn't mean that the poor thing has been received with disappointment or concern. It's certainly not an "easy" book, nor a pretty one, but I think it's effective, myself, and a profounder thing than Blue Voyage. Psychologically it's deeper and sharper, the problem more clearly set and more precisely solved, and formally too I think it is an advance on the earlier book. The parallel to symphonic form is very carefully worked out, and indeed as you know I'd thought of giving the four sections musical subtitles; but on second thought I rejected this as a shade too obvious. I hope it's coming out soon, and that you're giving it a good ballyhoo? . . . For a simple description, aimed at the man in the street, it's of course simply an exhaustive analysis of jealousy, with which is involved the hero's search for, and discovery of, a richer and more all-accepting plane of reality than the one to which the experiences of his childhood and early maturity had conditioned him. The hero moves out of his enclosed and selfishly adolescent world to a deeper understanding of himself and therefor of the objective world—in short, he learns, as a result of his betrayal, to accept the actual. As [D.H.] Lawrence remarked, "It is the hour of the stranger—let the stranger now enter the soul." . . .

I've just sent to Bernice[1] the mss. of a poem, Landscape West of Eden, about the length of Osiris Jones—I'd originally thought of including it in the new volume of preludes, later on, but now I see that it wouldn't fit, and must go by itself. Paul Nash, the English artist, wants to do some drawings for it, four or five pages, as well as page-end decorations, and personally I'd like that very much—he does most beautiful work. It would have the effect of thickening a slimmish book, and if done in a limited edition, solely, might pay for itself, I should think. Anyway, I hope you'll consider the idea. If Landscape could be got out this year, that would give me another year or two to finish the new book of preludes, which gives signs of becoming a longer book than Memnon, and a better one. . . . Best wishes, as ever—Conrad Aiken

1. Bernice Baumgarten, C A's agent with Brandt and Brandt.

131: TO ROBERT CHILDREY^{ch}   Rye Sussex
                                                         Jan 27 33

Dear Mr. Childrey: Thank you for your letter—it was nice of you to take so much trouble with it. But I suppose it was your teacher who suggested your writing it—and I wonder if you will be so kind as to ask your teacher if she realizes what a burden is put upon American writers by this practice, which is now very common in American schools? Schoolchildren all over America are told to write to authors—often to authors whom they have never before heard of, whose work they are too young to understand in the least, and often in letters which are almost illiterate. If children are to be taught to respect the work of American poets I think some better way might be found to do so—some way which would not make such an inconsiderate demand on the author's time.   Yours sincerely   Conrad Aiken

132: TO HENRY A. MURRAY^r   Rye
                                                        August 24 33

Daimon Harry—   . . . Things continue to look brighter for Great Circle here—Mrs. Aldington [H.D.] had shown it to Freud (who has not yet commented, sphinxlike) and Sachs, who pronounced it brilliant, and is in fact making a breeze about it in continental psa circles—is also eager to stir up things in London when she comes here next month—so there seems a reasonable chance the book might at least get a good hearing chez the highbrow critics. I only hope, of course, I don't expect—and I also hope the book will come out before I actually leave, so that I can see how it starts off. . . .   my love as ever   Conrad

133: TO KEMPTON P. A. TAYLOR^h   8 Plympton St. Cambridge
                                                      Dec 6 33

Dear Kemp: Thanks for your note and the article. The article doesn't much convince me. Any fool knows that the psychoses don't yield to analysis, and that all analysts refuse them, so why they should be included here in the percentage tabulation (where of course they inevitably add to the number of failures) *god* alone knows. Nor can any such general conclusions be drawn anyway

199

from so small an observed field It's quite true that many analysts prefer not to take patients over 40, but on the other hand there are innumerable instances of very successful analysis above that age. In my own case, the situation is somewhat different anyway, as I shall go into it (if I do) at least partly with the idea of myself becoming an analyst: that would have to depend on how the thing goes. The whole thing is still pretty indefinite. An Englishwoman has offered to pay my fees, which leaves me with the problem of how to live in Vienna for the necessary time. I shall simply wait and see what luck I have. There is also the possibility of a European bust-up, and with that and the other factors in mind and on the advice of a psychoanalyst friend of mine, Erich Fromm, who lives in Geneva, I have postponed the date of my analysis till October, with of course the further possibility that I may ultimately decide against it altogether. Meanwhile last week I cabled to Jerry to come here and I plan to stay here till March, trying to get together enough cash to return to Rye for six months work on a new novel.

I wish to hell you would stop talking nonsense about our getting "hard work." I very much doubt whether there is any other work as exhausting as literary creation, nor any other career as fraught with anxiety and as poorly paid. What diversions I can get in the way of games of chess or tennis (I played tennis about a dozen times last summer, and chess perhaps as many evenings) I deserve, damn you, and if I can break the monotony of an isolated life in the country, as well as renew contact with the world for a moment, by having a friend visit me for a weekend, it's a great deal less than you or most people have. As for vacations, I haven't had any for three years. My trip to Spain, if that's what you're thinking of, wasn't a holiday by a damned sight—I was in charge of a dipsomaniac, and was paid for it. In the past three years, I haven't had more than seven or eight days in all in London—I've been too poor, couldn't afford either the money or the time. Your attitude towards the whole thing makes me increasingly sick—I dislike to have to say it, but it seems to me you are showing a streak of *meanness* and smallness which I hate to think is in the family. My god, to begrudge me a game of chess or tennis! I never heard anything like it in my life. Smug and envious and anal-erotic all in one. And so goddamned sure of yourself, so conceited. A little insight might make you more modest and less eager to disapprove where you don't understand.

But what saddens me most of all is to have the classic old situation of the philistine towards art crop up so close at hand—to have my own brother telling me that my work isn't work and that I'd better give it up and find *real* work, never for a moment considering that my work may be important and necessary, never for a moment giving me credit for a very hard and anxious and sometimes desperate struggle, and usually ill rewarded: I've been loyal to my job as I see it, have made little or no compromise, and if you can't honor me for that, thank god at least the rest of the world can. It's a beautiful irony, and one that I shan't soon forget, and it makes me wonder whether we have much further to say to each other. That you were once very generous to me I shall always remember: but please in future keep you stupid advice and gratuitous insults to yourself. It's a waste of time and soul.   Conrad

134: TO WINIFRED BRYHER[r]   Jeake's House, Rye, Sussex
                                          June 4 34

Dear Bryher: . . . As you see, here we are in Rye, again, we've been here for a month, pretty busy with the routine detail of picking up dropped threads and broken dishes and windowpanes—what a business an old house is, so many things collapse or go wrong! Which is also half the fun, being the natural food of one's affection for "places." We've enjoyed it, and *are* enjoying it, our cat survived the lonely winter very well, the little garden is doing its best for us despite the drought, and now we've both got down to work again. The unbroken sunshine is a novelty and a temptation—the countryside is lovely, much too inviting, it's not so easy to keep a studious eye turned down on the page when to lift it shows a mile of green Romney Marsh and the blue edge of the channel—but the temptation is being resisted, and I'm making progress with a scandalously potboilerish little horror of a novel, which I hope to be able to finish before autumn. That is, if it "comes out," which it's a little too soon to say. If it doesn't, I shall groan and go to work on the one I had really *intended* to write, but which I've postponed partly because of its difficulty and partly because of its obvious predestined unsaleability.[1] . . .   Conrad Aiken

1. *King Coffin* was to be the title of this "little horror" (this is *not* C A's opinion of the finished novel). *Reading a Book* was the tentative title of the postponed novel, which eventually became *Ushant*.

Dear Max: Delighted to hear from you after all this time, I was
beginning to think you'd maybe dropped me! . . . The novel, King
Coffin, is half done. . . . I hesitate to say much about it—entre
nous my heart isn't really in it. I don't feel very close to it, and it's
difficult for me to judge of its interest or success. The two people
who have read the existing 30,000 words like it better than Great
Circle, and think it "queer and exciting": that's as it may be. I
don't know, myself. I don't know whether I told you the theme? A
Nietzschean young man, who begins as an anarchist and ends as a
monomaniac individualist, a complete egocentric, conceives the notion of committing a pure or abstract murder just by way of expressing in a final action or gesture his complete hatred and contempt
for mankind. The subsidiary characters are few and lightly sket-
ched: the novel deals almost exclusively with Jasper Ammen's state
of mind, the background which brought him to this state of mind,
the semi-philosophic working out of his idea, his discovery that to
be a pure and motiveless murder the victim must of course be a
complete stranger, the discovery of the right stranger, a study by
him of his victim's life and habits, and then, just when he has everything ready for the actual murder the *self*-discovery that he can't go
through with it. Very simple, as you see: the precise turn of the ending I haven't quite decided yet. What he finds, of course, is that it's
really himself he's all the while been wanting to kill, not poor little
Jones, whom at last he realizes is someone he really likes: his hate
of humanity turns out to be a fraud. The chief secondary character
is a woman, Gerta, with whom he is unconsciously in love: I think
there will be just enough of her to act as the necessary foil and as
mere sex-interest. Violá tout. The lord only knows whether it will
come off or not, or whether it's the kind of thing which will catch
the Great Public Eye. I hope so. Anyway, it's an oddity. —The
method, very straightforward and simple—a direct line in time—
short chapters—no or few artificial devices for complication—a
mere accumulation of suspense. The difficulty is to find enough episode in a story so essentially plain and with an unchanging point-of-
view: it means that the current of Ammen's thought must itself be
exciting, he must appear as a rather mad and horrible and terrifying
person whose purpose isn't really as clear to him as he thinks, so

that the reader won't quite know *what* he will do, or when. In this, and in the natural feeling of sympathy for little Jones, and of course fear for him, is the real "story," such as it is. But of course, things may develop in it which I don't foresee: I make no guarantees. . . .   very best to you as always   Conrad Aiken

136: TO G. B. WILBUR[r]   Rye
                                                           June 23 35

Well, Jacob, if I were any longer capable of feeling guilt no doubt I'd feel guilty, but I don't, and if I write to you even less than I do to the one or two I ever write to at all, it's at least in part because you call for so much more of an effort, damn you! In short, I've become lazy as hell, but that's not all of it either—indifference, boredom, isolation/insulation, a general clotting and hardening of the affections and sensibilities, a general *rotting* I'm afraid, a cessation of life in any very useful sense, a terminal dropping off and decaying—a large wide vague feeling that america is my home and what I need and want, but unfocused—a progressive shedding of all my friends and relatives—*all*—so that at times I wonder if I'm beginning the inward journey of the praecox from which no traveller returns—increasing difficulties with John and Jane, perhaps just the inevitable marking off of generation from generation, but I think more than that, complicated of course by Jessie and Martin, by England, by money or the want of it—increasing distance from Jerry, on the whole amiably traversed, but just the same with its violences and its ultimate loneliness—and increasing dislike of myself. The latter nothing new, of course, but this time it's without *curiosity*—a deep difference—and in consequence I often wonder why I'm alive at all, though, I hasten to add, it isn't that I especially want to *stop* living; not even that I don't, just as often, consider the career of aiken as a thing quite apart from his life and a thing for which I still have, goddammit, a kind of responsibility, though fading. I think—"perhaps if I can get somehow through another ten years there might again for a while be something worth trying to put down," or "confound it I'm only 46," or simply "after all it's fun changing, and we might change." And at moments I indulge in actual notions of projects, though alas most of these are in part dictated by the wolf at the door, and therefor dropped at once, until such time as they become necessities. Then taken up reluctantly and

dealt with half-heartedly. . . . My own plans are necessarily vague. My journalistic job with the New Yorker will continue through the winter, but as it doesn't bring enough to live on by half, but at the same time swallows up so much time and energy that I can't do anything else, it's a nice metaphysical problem which as yet I haven't solved. I may come back and beg to be allowed to hibernate in your cottage? and dig roots around your pond. I may up and do something really rash—just clear out to god knows where—at times a "fugue" feeling comes very attractively over me, like a fragrant wind from the well-known island of Nostalgia—in short I'm in a queer in-between state, with feelings of latent fertility mixed up with the blankest of despairs, so the lord only knows. . . .
as always   Conrad

Part III: 1936–1973

And if Saltinge might once more be lost, there was now a new and astonishing virtue to turn to: the house in Charlestown. A vision, like so many others that joyous winter . . . and from Charlestown to Mexico City and Cuernavaca, with Lorelei Three and Nicholas, and the fantastic visit with Hambo, beside his cloacal barranca; and thus to Saltinge (once again with a new wife) and into the war, and out of it; and so, at last, to the new house on Cape Cod, the "new old" house and the new life? The "new old" life, too–for the Bass River still flowed there, past the house of Cousin Abiel, the Quaker. . . . The house at Brewster had cast a spell upon them. . . .

And then at last Savannah, the incredible city, the city lifting out of the southern sky its landmarks, of one spire or steeple after another, which were still as familiar to him as his own blood in his own hands. . . . Yes–it had been like moving, by some extraordinary sort of magic, rightly and profoundly into one's own heart, this homecoming. Everything had waited for him, everything had stood still. . . . the conversion [to America] was clearly, as one could realize after the event, a resolution of feelings and attitudes of long standing, perhaps lifelong: perhaps it was now possible to say that it was only by obeying the ghostly summons of the poet of White Horse Vale, and going to Ariel's Island, and accepting it and being accepted by it, that he had been able to accomplish what essentially and profoundly all this time he had most wanted and needed to accomplish, the retention of that nursery floor, that room, that house at Savannah, that house and the vivid life in it–father and mother, and the tremendous parties downstairs, which D. could watch through the banisters of the curved staircase, and the deeply satisfying sense of belonging to it all, whether there, or at New Bedford, or Cambridge. Hadn't he, ever since, every time he set sail for England, actually been setting sail for that carpeted floor, on which the copy of Tom Brown's School Days still lay open at the luminous fragment of verse? Hadn't time stood still, ever since, at that echo of a moment, that phrase of incantation? . . . Because of it, he had had to try to become a writer, and a liberal one. . . . In one's devotion to this singular necessity, one would find oneself over and over again unfaithful to pretty much everything else in life–one's wives,

205

one's children, one's friends, one's lives—even, at times, one's practical interests; and just the same, all this astonishingly intricate come-and-go, which seemed to be perpetually leading him farther and farther afield, and in ever-widening circles, whether outer or inner; all this was really the quite incredible equivalent of one very simple little thing: it had been the stratagem by which he could remain forever on that floor in the room at Savannah, reading, for the first time, a passage of verse; a passage, which, like Paul's sheathed arches of eternity, unfolding and receding endlessly away, was indeed a passage, a passage to everywhere; but from which he would return, at last, to find that he had never in effect gone anywhere at all, and was still, exactly, there.

The wheel had come full circle: but without a vengeance.

[*Ushant*, pp. 331, 338–40, 300–01]

Death is a toy upon the nursery floor
broken we know that it can hurt no more
and birth, much farther back, begins to seem
like that recurring and delicious dream
of middle age, the twin isles blest
in the Atlantic, where we paused to rest
and saw the sacred people of the west.
Ourselves? But in another time to be?
No, no such luck for such as we.
Angelic beings through and through
heart and mind and stature equal grew
all that they did and said was crystal true
a distant chime
from worlds invisible and unspeakable
in human prose or rhyme.
Dream, or a vision, we could not stay
and it is lost.
How can old age receive such Pentecost?
And yet, not so.
For no,
we heard the mystics, saw the mysteries,
it is to these
with clouded sight we turn once more
to look at death upon the nursery floor.

[C A's last poem, unrevised, written on
Oglethorpe Avenue in Savannah
four months before his death]

Letters 137–160: August 1936 to September 1939

His second marriage dissolving, his attitude toward writing "become negative, sterile, valedictory," C A made his way, in August 1936, to New York, where he saw Malcolm Lowry. He revisited Savannah for the first time since 1901 and returned to Boston. There he met a young artist, Mary Hoover. C A's mood that winter became joyously transformed in Mary's Charlestown house: Ed Burra arrived and painted in the dining room, Mary painted in an upstairs bedroom, and C A wrote in the "salon-cellar." He asked Clarissa for a divorce, without success. By the summer of 1937 he was advised to seek a Mexican divorce and marriage. C A and Mary, with Ed Burra, traveled in May to Mexico City and then to Cuernavaca and Malcolm Lowry. Married on July 7, C A and Mary returned to Charlestown, sailed to England on July 17, and settled into Jeake's House in early August. While Mary painted, C A wrote A Heart for the Gods of Mexico. *Poverty suggested they offer in 1938 a summer school in writing and painting, and by January they were distributing among American friends brochures to attract applicants. The school went well, but left C A and Mary exhausted and no richer. In the spring of 1939, Mary accepted a commission to do portraits in Oxford and left C A in Rye on April 22. The seven weeks of separation drew from C A the first poetry since his marriage to Mary, a series of sonnets to her, eventually linked to* Time in the Rock *as* And in the Human Heart. *Twenty-two of these made part of C A's almost daily letters to Mary. By June 1, when she returned, C A had completed, and sent to Maxwell Perkins,* The Conversation. *War clouds had reduced school applicants for summer 1939 to one. The prospect for making ends meet, especially as impoverished aliens in war-time England who might not be allowed to live in coastal Rye, decided C A and Mary to sail—reluctantly—on September 29 for New York and the cheaper living of Cape Cod.*

o   o   o

Time in the Rock (New York and London: Scribner's, October 1936).
A Heart for the Gods of Mexico(London: Secker, January 1939).

Boston, Mass
Aug 22 [1936]

Dear Ed—   . . . Speaking of royal Simps, and the crowned
heads of Holland, give the enclosed an eye-rub. Merry doings in
Salzburg, and as for the king leaving the launch, poor terrified
wretch, soothed by the maternal Simpson, I never in my life saw
anything so funny. I suppose they wouldn't print these in England.
—Well, you'll never believe it but I found the old Malc [Lowry],
living in a dreary cellar in 72nd Street West, off Central Park. I'd
first found Mrs. Malc[1] living two blocks away, but she kept the
door almost closed between us, eyeing me suspiciously the while,
denied that Malc lived there, just gave me the other address. At
72nd street a slattern in dirty white silk pyjamas opened the door,
and when I said what I wanted howled down the dark stairs Mal!
O Mal! And there sure enough was Mal, just finishing a short story.
Such a basement scene, too, with laundry, negresses, cats, Mrs.
Taussig and a Stranger whom I wasn't introduced to. Subsequently
I met Malc downtown several times, including a supper with Mrs.
Malc. Malc himself in very good form indeed—looks remarkably
well, much thinner, cleaner, spotlessly dressed, punctual, much easier to talk to, less self-absorbed etc. Harper have taken his novel,
comes out in Jan., and Story is featuring a novelette a month
hence—which same is all about his visit to Bellevue Hospital for the
Insane.[2] O boy oy Boy. Such conversations with blacks—I read a
few pages which were superb. Jan is working at nights on the Mirror, just for experience, and her quondam sweetheart was following
her round the night I dined with her: Malc saw him snooping past,
twice, and the second time challenged him to a glass of beer. This
was in Times Square. Said the fellow: It's time we met, for we have
something in common! Which struck me as setting an all-time low
in tactless truthfulness. But the old maestro was feeling full of lov-
ingkindness, and took the cheap skate all martyr-like to his bosom,
and the three of us sat and drank beers for a long while. I gave up,
and the two of them then went to call on Jan, both drunk I gather,
and she threw them out. . . . The trip over wasn't bad—Harry

1. Jan Gabrial, Lowry's wife, had met him and C A in Spain in 1933.
2. Lowry's novel *Ultramarine* had already been published in London by Jonathan Cape in
1933; when C A saw him, Lowry had completed a first draft of *Lunar Caustic,* which made
use of his ten weeks in Bellevue in 1935.

Wehle and K. upstairs, and I came to the conclusion I detested K., a spoiled brat if there ever was one, such gigglings and poutings and making of charming moues and so archly sure that he was the center of attention—jesus. Or as they say in America now, Christ bite me. In New York I went to Minsky's and also another strip-tease theatre in 42nd Street, and very fine they were, and leaving I may say remarkably little to the enfeebled imagination. On the ship coming over by the way there was a Shirltye Temple film, title re-translated from the german as The Smallest Instigator.[3] Which I thought was pleasing. Yesterday, my god Ed but isn't it a small world, in the University theatre Harvard Square you'd never believe it the long-sought Paramount news reel of the Surrealist monstros-ities, including Revolver Dream, suddenly swam before my tear-filled eyes. Yes, there were all the old favorites, Objects Found by Nashes on Beaches, tree-trunks at sea, cannons looking out of bathroom windows, syphilitic seaweeds, and so on. It made me that homesick! The Cambridge audience I may say was quite interested. Creighton [Hill] has a job in Washington, but I found him by chance last week in the front room, with a lady, as usual—a little awkward, but we passed it off lightly. I may drive down to Savan-nah with him. Tom Eliot is due here next week, Ted Spencer sends his regards, and as for me I fear my days at Rye are numbered, though it looks possible I may have one last winter there. Not much money to be squoze out of the publishers, alas. . . . But I expect I'll be back in old Sussex about Sept. 20. So I'll be seeing you soon.   love   Conrad

138: TO EDWARD BURRA[r]   Charlestown, Mass.
                                           Oct 18 36

Dear Ed—   As you see from the above I've moved again, since I got back from Savannah, and am now living in a wonderful slum a stone's throw from the harbour, on the other side from Boston, with a view of the Custom House tower from the back windows, also of the Savannah Line steamers, which are literally only two hundred yards away. It's a very nice old georgian (sort of) brick house, circa 1780, occupied by a very gifted and charming artist named Mary Hoover, who lets me have a room at what you might

3. Presumably "The Littlest Rebel."

209

call a nominal rent. Lots of fun. She's done portraits of Creighton Hill and Catherine Huntington which fairly make your hair curl, and is now in spare moments doing one of me which threatens to lay bare my very soul, or super-ego, or something. She studied with a painter named Quintanilla in Spain for a year, mostly in Madrid, where she helped him to do some frescos. While there she also learned to make spanish rice in a fashion just too unbearably beautiful to think of—Walter and Catherine Piston came here night before last to help eat one, and such a dream of shrimps, calamares (we found we could buy them fresh at an Italian market just across the river) scallops, clams, mushrooms, chorizos, and red peppers I never did see. As Walter observed, it was the real Elephant's Breath. —My affairs get more terribly mixed with the passing of every hour. . . . I shall probably stay here for at least half the winter—I even foresee that I may stay forever. Sad as it makes me feel, for I genuinely and dreadfully miss Rye. But there it is. —Savannah was the loveliest thing I've ever seen, and as I think I mentioned on a p.c. I wouldn't in the least mind living there. You simply *must* come over and make a trip down there. I was interested to hear that your mother was now beginning to consider Canada. Opinion is pretty general here now that wars and revolutions are absolutely inevitable in dear old europe, and that europe is an anachronism anyway, and will just have to destroy itself to make way for something a little more up-to-date. United States of Europe, soviet model. But I don't know, it looks just about as likely to me that germany and italy might turn the whole thing fascist. . . . My new book [*Time in the Rock*] has just come out and is being given the royal purple raspberry. One paper describes me as having joined that clique of poets "who with subtle fingers pass the day dismembering their own intellectual corpses, proudly extracting here a mental maggot, there a neurotic slug." Lovely. Are you thinking at all of coming over. I wish you would.   Conrad

139: TO EDWARD BURRA[r]   17 Elwood St.
                                           Charlestown Mass.
                                           Nov 24 36

Dear Ed—   Yrs received and with glee—especially the news that you're coming to the land of the free and the home of the brave. Everybody is tickled to death to hear it—especially Gordon Bassett, who was here last night singing And cruelly he broke her tambourine, etc. . . .

. . . You may have gathered from Sundry Signs and Portents that things weren't any too merry between Jerry and myself lately—in fact, they've become so bad that I'm asking for a divorce. I think she'll probably give me one—but I don't yet know. I'm afraid it's one of those deep disagreements which there's no mitigating, and that we'll just go on making each other unhappy. . . . I shall miss Rye and Jeake's House like the very devil. Maybe I'll struggle back to it somehow—I'm due for a little good luck, god knows. It would be fun to reappear a few years hence complete with the third Mrs. Aiken, by gosh—and perhaps a child or two. *That* would give them something to talk about, the cats. —So. And meanwhile I continue to live in this very charming slum, where there are the cutest waterfront cafes you ever saw in your life, with such names as the Morning Glory, the Rainbow, Jack's, Charlie's, Jimmie's, Rocco's, and O'Neill's. Jack's is the toughest—and how! O'Neill's is my favorite. Brother Rob and I picked up a wonderful sailor in the U.S. navy, who said the fleet would someday soon just sail over to Leningrad and join the russians. (This is where the navy yard is, hence large quantities of gobs, or what you would call jolly tars.) . . . And now the Malc is in Mexico City, with Jan, staying there long enough so as to renew his permit to stay in the U.S. He went out via Hollywood, where he made life miserable for John and Clement Davenport[1] for a month, drinking whiskey at the rate of one bottle per day, or damned unpleasant when they *couldn't* have the bottle, which John said came expensive in the end. They were glad when the Lowrys went away, I gather, reading between the lines. John says Malc's new novel is no good, but that some of the short stories are swell. —John himself is having a grand time in Hollywood, which apparently comes up to expectations. He's trying to get King Coffin done, so far no nibbles, but much interest. —Yeah, what you say about going left is sadly to the point. I ought to have called my book Poetry in the Red. . . . I went and saw Kermesse Heroique the very day your letter about it came—wonderfully funny I thought, and beautifully acted.[2] I hope to see it again. Otherwise, I haven't seen anything much good. Except old Nazimova, eighty if a

1. John Davenport, English journalist, man-of-letters, script writer, was an old friend of C A and Malcolm Lowry.
2. Jacques Feyder's 1935 film comedy.

211

day, in Hedda Gabler—*the* most marvelous thing I ever saw. She was doing it when I was seventeen, and she's better now than she was then. The most extraordinary face, miraculously corrupt and fin de siecle, and such voice control as your ears couldn't believe— little birdlike sounds, flutings and trills and chirrups, so attenuated as hardly to be audible, but still so charged with meaning that they made your hair stand on end. Baby. —Well, Ed, I hope we'll be seeing you soon in our prosperous country. Everybody's getting rich again, the dirty dogs. Except me.   Conrad

140: TO MARGARET AND ROBERT MACKECHNIE[h]

Charlestown Mass.
Dec 6 36

Dear Margaret and Bobby—   Well, it's a melancholy business, this writing to Rye from three thousand miles away, instead, dammit, of being there—and more melancholy still to think that in all likelihood my Rye days are over. Gosh, the way life or circumstance or fate or folly just grab us up and fling us to the edge of nowhere—! And the way we hurt each other when it happens. I suppose you must have heard by this time, either from Jerry herself or someone else, that the Aikens are in trouble—to tell the truth we've *been* in trouble for a long time, and what is happening now was probably inevitable. No need to go into painful detail, which you wouldn't want to hear anyway, but the word divorce has been bandied between us since last spring, and then things got acute after I crossed the Atlantic—*really* acute, so that divorce seemed to me the only way out—and while I was in that state of anger and despair I had to go and meet just the kind of woman I could fall in love with, and proceeded, quite unaware of what I was doing, to do so. And there I am, and there we are, blown to smithereens. . . . I wanted the divorce anyway, and this subsequent development merely added weight and speed to a decision already made. So I've asked Jerry to divorce me, and am now awaiting developments. It's all very sad, and I feel terribly unhappy about Jerry of whom it's impossible for me even now to be anything but very very fond, and I only wish she could meet someone with whom she could be really happy, and reasonably secure. Perhaps she will.

Meanwhile, everything is naturally in the greatest confusion, and a government publicity job, in connection with the Federal Art Project, which I had practically been promised, has failed to materialize, so that I'm broke, and I don't know whether Jerry is coming back to America or not, and so on and so forth. It's all, as they say in America, just good clean fun. If Jerry *doesn't* come here, I may borrow the money to come there—to talk things over and get them shipshape, which seems to me absolutely indispensable. In which case I shall probably spend a bachelor Christmas at Rye. Will you be there? or gone to Edinburgh. And one advantage of that would be that I could attend to the sad business of emptying Jeake's House of its chattels and locking the door on a chapter of life which, in spite of everything, had much to commend it. It makes me miserable to think of it, for I loved the life there despite the fact that Jerry so hated it; and to feel that I shall probably never be able to live there again just cores my solar plexus as if it were an apple. I wonder. Maybe after four or five or six years—but I dunno. To bring back a *third* Mrs. Aiken to the same house, even such a delightful and gifted one—she's a painter, and a very good one—would perhaps be inviting disaster. Do you think it could *possibly* be done? I wish with all my heart it could, and hope with all my heart it can. And Mary herself is *determined* to. Though I tell her that she doesn't know Rye, and hasn't, like the vicar, heard it's little heart beating. . . . My chief adventure since I got here—apart from Mary—was the trip to Savannah—which must really be one of the most beautiful cities in the world. I wouldn't in the least mind living there, though I think there might be a starvation diet, intellectually speaking. So mellow, so decrepit, so leaf-and-flower-filled, and so *friendly*—old ladies who knew my father and mother called me "my child" and took me to their bosoms—it was perfectly delightful.

And so, dear creatures, a merry Christmas, or Hogmanay, and presently I'll be sending you a book, the second batch of preludes.
. . .   Conrad

141: TO MARGARET AND ROBERT MACKECHNIE[h]
Charlestown Mass.
Feb. 11.37

Dear Bobby and Margaret: . . . Ed Burra, who arrived here Jan. 11th, got off the ship looking a remarkable green colour, and at once came down with some peculiar marine variety of flu—the fake silver ring which he bought in Tetuan turned jet black on his finger, strange to relate, and subsequently, when he recovered, resumed its Tetuan brightness. Odd! —He seems to have settled down with Mary and myself for an indefinite stay, as a p.g.: the latter a very great help to us, in our divorce-straitened circumstances. And is lots of fun to have round. He brought 25 of his latest works with him—crazy magnificent things—and we've got fifteen of them up in our queer cellar-salon, and thanks to a judicious gossip-campaign, and the grapevine system of social news-mongering, quite a lot of People of Importance have been coming to see them. We hope to sell some of them, and also to move the whole lot into Boston presently for a real show at a real gallery. Meanwhile, it's lots of fun, and the fright of the conservatives is exceedingly entertaining. "But don't you think they're morbid?" Etc. Mary and Ed seem to get on wonderfully well, thank goodness—Mary likes Ed's work extravagantly, Ed is non-committal about Mary's (as indeed about everything) and they spend their days in separate rooms toiling away at very different works, while I sit in the cellar toiling away at a thousand page manuscript of a novel, by a Creole aged 18, which I am hired to reduce by three hundred pages. —It was so nice and reassuring of you to extend a long-distance welcome to us, if and when we get to Rye—as we desperately hope to do. I wanted to be sure of *some* support before I even *thought* of trying such a thing. But with yourselves and Ed I have no doubt we could weather the social blizzard. The thing is, how to raise the money to get there, how to manage to stay there *when* we get there. . . . Ed brings home raucous records, very jazz and negroid, for the gramophone— he's put one on this minute—and mostly we just sit at home, except when we sally into Boston for a littleneck clam or oyster, or to O'Neill's—the best bar in Charlestown—for a glass of beer. You'd like it. . . .   as ever   Conrad

142: TO MARGARET AND ROBERT MACKECHNIE[h]

Charlestown Mass
May 7 37

Dear Bobby and Margaret—   What a wonderful thing! We've been compelled to take things into our own hands, are going to Mexico City for a divorce and to marry there amongst the Aztecs and Incas and Tlaclopetls and things, and are then sailing, with a paltry handful of silver, to Havana, New York, and London. Unless we can let Jeake's House at an immense profit, therefor, we shall spend the summer there. . . . Ed is coming with us, at least as far as Mexico—but he threatens darkly to stay there, and I kind of suspect he will. (We *might* ourselves!) . . . I expect by midwinter we'll be on the town, in Rye, buying and selling rabbit-skins—will you give us a crust now and then? O well, it's an immense relief to regain freedom of action after a winter of paralysis, and we're beginning to feel happy again, and a little more confident that our recklessness will at least lead to fun, so maybe it's all for the best. Anyway, here we—probably—come!   much love   Conrad

143: TO WILLIAM CARLOS WILLIAMS⁵   Mexico D.F. Mexico
May 16, 1937

Dear Bill Williams,   No doubt you will think this is a comedy or a lunacy or an irony, and an irony it is, for here am I asking the fellow who helped me to get married seven years ago to help me to get *un*married. I am kind of ashamed to have to bother you with it, but alas now, as then, you seem to be in the unenviable position of being the one person who *can* help me. The facts are simple. In order to get a divorce in Mexico it seems I must have a wedding certificate and as my hostile wife has possession of same far away in Boston what I need is a duly authentic copy. Could you therefore ask the Rutherford Town fathers to give you one, and will you then send it to me by air mail care of Wells Fargo Express, Avenue Madero 14, Mexico D.F. Mexico? And when you send it will you also be angelic and let me kow what it all has cost you? —It's all very sad and complicated and it's a pity our contacts should be so seldom and so odd. The present one however is really an emergency, the element of time is of the utmost importance, and if you can manage to do this it will make me very happy and very grateful.   Yours as ever, Conrad Aiken
P.S. The date of the marriage was February 27th or 28th, 1930.

144: TO HENRY A. MURRAY⁵   c/o Lowry, Calle Humboldt 62
Cuernavaca, Morelos, Mexico.
May 27, 37

Well my golden Harry, you see us here in your Cuernavaca, which turns out to be much nicer than you gave me the impression it was: Malcolm Lowry, you remember? my sometime protege, the english

215

lad, now married, had by some divine accident decided to take a house in C.; and so now we're installed there with him and his Jan as Paying Guests, with a bottle of habanero always on the table and scorpions falling from the ceilings and Black Widows darting out of drainpipes and the Tropic Rain roaring through the pantiles. Jesus, what a climate, what a country, what a people. We arrived more dead than alive—no sleep for three days—constant midnight and early morning changes at godawful little way stations—but O the Mississipp and St Louis, the diningcar on the banks of the Mississipp in the twilight and My Lord as you would yourself say the *wonderful* northern deserts and enchanted mesas of Mexico—never shall I forget the early morning landscape seen from the train, the stunted date-palms standing motionless as hooded men, the dreary little mudwalled pueblas, the prairie dogs, the one wolf, the Indians leaning timelessly on dead or dying walls. Gosh, the train ride was alone worth the agony. But Mexico City too was marvellous—except that the climate, the altitude I suppose, killed me—my heart began to achieve a *hum* rather than anything so discrete as a beat, and my insides came out of me in a steady and portentous stream, both ends, and I couldn't move for a week. Terribly enervating, I still feel weak, though here in C. we all feel a *shade* better. And the divorce, dammit, has proved more troublesome and expensive than we guessed, will take a month, and we must stay in Cuernavaca for it, since here it is quickest and cheapest: for which reason of course the Lowry development is a godsend. We'll almost save the extra cost of the legal fees in the cutting of living expenses. —In Mexico City about all I saw was one bullfight, in which a boy was killed— so quickly that one hardly realized it—and perhaps a dozen assorted churches, all very fine. It's as full of churches as Venice, and they're quite as exciting. The bleeding Jesuses, of carved wood, dressed in lace panties, are miracles, I think, and the madonnas too, in their glass cases—incredibly beautiful, both Mary and I, not to mention Ed, have gone into a permanent dither about them, and I'm trying to get Mary to put some of them down—I think she will. (Also, she's hoping to get some watercolors done here in C., which I think will be grand—loads of stuff on every side just begging for it!) And here too in C. the churches are first class—with a wooden Pieta that makes Michelangelo's suavity in St Peter's look like so much shaving cream. O god it's all superb, if it weren't so exhausting, and Popocatapetl leans in from time to time over our verandah,

216

and there's a small swimming pool as blue as a Hokusai sky, and *what* do you think Harry, in the market in C. the other day I saw amongst laces and Oaxaca pottery on a stall something that looked unmistakably like neat yaller little human faeces, beautifully curled and coiled and spiralled, and sure enough that's exactly what they were, made of baked clay, done with a miracle of loving care, and complete in details down to a few embedded lentils and a bean or two. So I bought the entire supply, viz., three, and it occurred to me that no Psychological Clinic could possibly be complete without one—good heavens, what it would do for your anal erotics! So if you want one or two, say the word. Getting them through the Customs will be fun. . . .   Conrad

145: TO HENRY A. MURRAY[r]   c/o Lowry, Calle Humboldt 62
Cuernavaca, Morelos, Mexico
June 12 37

Well my beloved Harry here we still sit waiting for the interminable processes of the law to wind and then unwind themselves about us: it's wonderful how these lawyer fellows just keep on busily doing absolutely nothing. So god only knows when we shall escape. . . . Meanwhile we've all been ill, dammit, with more of the same, and poor Ed Burra so eviscerated that we had to get a doctor in last night—today he's better. Mary and I find that by dint of getting a morning swim, before breakfast, we can *just* keep the metabolic wheels turning over, and no more. Lethargic, comatose, drugged with heat, but nevertheless enjoying ourselves in a queer primordial ophidian fashion, like a couple of amiable old snakes. My god the jungle feeling here is wonderful—I could go on sitting in the garden and watching the ants and lizards and butterflies and birds forever: it's a continuous riot. You feel as if were you to sit *too* still, for more than five minutes, you'd be covered with mistletoe, inhabited by wasps, and hung all over with magnificently phallic fruits, becoming in the twinkling of an eye a miniature jungle. And with a queer sort of lizard-god in the middle of it. —Yes, one does feel that one has known this before, been in this slime, and it's enormously enriching—but tout de meme I find my appetites run all the other way. Now, at any rate. But it's queer, I remember ten years ago having a dream, and telling it to you, of a journey to Mexico City, and there finding that all the houses were built in the water, with transparent floors—in the light of which it's disconcerting to find—and of course I never knew it?— that actually Mexico City was built on the site of a lake, drained off by the Aztecs. Tres rum. —Cuernavaca improves I think on further inspection—the back streets, the cafes, the country round it, the terrifying barranca which divides the town in two, a miniature of the tajo at Ronda, and in its way as impressive—all these are good. What we miss is a further range of the countryside, but that economy forbids. I think we shall try to go to Taxco, and be content with that. I want to see that monstrous eighteenth century church, which sounds like a masterpiece of the baroque. But if we don't manage I shall be quite satisfied with this, and I think it wouldn't at all be a bad place to come back to. . . . Ed's slaughtered Jesus makes progress. Me, I'm doing a little private delving, and beginning to feel the presence of something, god knows what, and also to feel a little suppler—I suppose I'm shedding the harsh skin of two years' journalism. And also I'm reading Malcolm's really remarkable new novel, unpublished, very queer, very profound, very twisted, wonderfully rich—In Ballast to the White Sea. Gosh, the fellow's got genius—such a brilliant egocentric nonstop selfanalysis, and such a magnificent fountain, inexhaustible, of projected self-love I never did see. Wonderful. Too much of it, and directionless, but for sheer tactile richness and beauty of prose texture a joy to swim in. Well, our deep loves to you fellows. . . .   Conrad

146: TO ROBERT P. A. TAYLOR[r]

c/o Lowry, Calle Humboldt 62
Cuernavaca, Morelos, Mexico
June 23, 1937

Dear Rob—   . . . Delays have been terrible—one thing after another—and us ill into the bargain. Ed has gone back to Charlestown, poor fellow. . . . He was fearfully sick, couldn't shake it, and thought the only hope was to get back to sea-level and clean food. Wish I could do the same, I must have lost fifteen pounds, feel weak as a prawn, have little interest in life. But slowly getting better, now, I think. —Mary is okay, and reasonably cheerful considering—but it's of course a great trial all round, and I daresay even for the Lowrys! Malc is on a bender at the moment, while Jan is away—he's been drunk for about a week with little variation in the density, so to speak, and at times troublesome. We don't know whether to be glad Jan is about to get back or not. . . .   Conrad

147: TO ROBERT P. A. TAYLOR[r]   Cuernavaca
                                                  June 29 1937

Dear Rob: Just a hasty line to say that affairs took a sudden turn for the better this morning, the divorce will be through in two or three days, we shall be married probably on the 4th of July (Independence Day!) and on our way north a day later. . . . We go straight to N.Y., then after a couple of days I shall come up to Charlestown . . . where Mary will join me and we shall sail. . . .   Conrad

148: TO HENRY A. MURRAY[r]   Jeake's House, Rye
                                              Aug. 22 1937

Harry, old Leviathan—   . . . The Inner Coils are magnificent—everything here is a huge success—Mary, wonderful great gal that she is, simply loves the place, the house, the life, the smells, the landscape, everything—even John and Jane and Joan, who are all here at the moment. No ghosts hover over us, as I somewhat feared—nary a ghost, it's all serene and good, and if there's any work left in me, as in darker moments I doubt, I feel I can here get down to at least an attempt at it. . . . The trip over was pretty terrible—really bad third class, and poor Ed had a hellish time of it, and is still only very slowly convalescing. He came down to dinner last night, looking somewhat better—not so green, and a *shade* better fleshed. He has to have shots of iron in his tail. As for my Mary, I increasingly think things will open like a flower for her here— Laura Knight is all agog to see her work, and Paul Nash ditto, and the local fellows in my own art gallery—Jeake's Gallery—are on the qui vive about her, so it really looks promising. What I try to dare to foresee for us is a life in which we could stay here for six or eight months at a time, and then raid Boston, so that Mary could take on a handful of commissions, at the same time arranging for a show of her latest work. Meanwhile, I'm trying to line up a few celebrities for her—Tom Eliot has half consented to come down and sit, and if we can get half a dozen more it would make the nucleus of a show

219

in London. Anyway, as the novelist said we go forward with caution reverence and hope. And o baby it's so good to be here and to be so happy. Now come and see us, and our Ship Inn, do. Till then our devoted loves.   Conrad

149: TO HENRY A. MURRAY[r]   Rye
                                              Nov. 14 37

. . . Tom Eliot came for the weekend, last week, played pingpong, went to church, drank his beer like a man, was in fact very good company, and promised to come down again to sit for Mary—was much impressed. And it looks as if we'd be able to get Julian Huxley and one or two other literary celebrities through May Sarton. Which is all to the good. —I've taken the liberty of asking H.D.—Mrs. Richard Aldington (she's divorcing him)—to look you up—she will be staying with papa Sachs sometime during the next two or three months. A fascinating byproduct of psychoanalysis, if not indeed one of its disasters—do have a look at her. I've also suggested that she look up Christiana [Morgan]. She's a very muffled and involved and self-nursing creature, and may not feel able to make the first move—but I think she would really interest you, at any rate to see *once!* . . .   Conrad

150: TO HENRY A. MURRAY[r]   Rye
                                              July 25 38

Harry my angel,   . . . The school is a huge success, a continuous revel of good nature and good juices, a wonderfully homogeneous lot, who mix well and clash well, so that the harmonics and discords that arise from it are a joy to us. Kathryn White Ryan is the star—a remarkable little warm, sharp, woman-prism, fiftyish or more, full of gentle wisdoms and fresh rediscoveries, alive, sensitive, humourous, witty, tender, full of a directed and discriminating love, and writing a novel and a rambling book on rural New England (New Hamp) which are full of things you would delight in. (I seem to be full of "full ofs.") And she fits in admirably with the young fry, affectionately checks and guides and prods—reveals too—so that she's really a wonderful help. Paints pretty well too—altogether a godsend. Your worcestrian Charles [Hamilton]—what a marvellous thumbnail you did of him—is a darling too, and we all love him—a blunderer from the honest soles up—cautious, but learning quickly to let go and meet, reaching in his awkward short stories for a maturity which he can't quite grasp, but already pretty richly foresees—altogether a godsend too, and amusing even in his stubbornesses and *paul-pryisms*. A queer hysterical giggle, and hysterical thing, which shows signs of diminishing, a compulsion of some sort—a father-rivalry . . .—a medicine-taker and infection-preventer, a long-range worrier—but all these things are already yielding to Rye, and he seems a year older than when he arrived. Dunstan Thompson, who wants to talk with you in the fall (Junior at Harvard, president of the Monthly) is the cleverest, a great rattler and improviser, looks like one of those fish-parasites that are towed sinuously by sharks, a real gift of the gab, raconteur, mimic, clown, somewhat in a hurry but shrewd too, adaptable and imitative, still a good deal of a fashion-follower, but honest and psychologically alert. (Wants to take some courses in psych. at H., and to discuss this with you, something about skipping an elementary and taking an advanced course—and might be encouraged I think.) Pamela Richards, Bennington gal, very nice, calm, assured, unselfconscious, with a lovely Egyptian-semitic head, paints *pretty* well, steers a sure and easy course between the two lads, and adds just the right touch of young Glamour to the cluster at the table—knits, drawls, wears bright colours, plays Beethoven to herself while we go to the pub of an evening. . . . Voila tout. I have morning conferences with them, individually, as often as they need, recreate their creations for them, an exhausting job, but fun. In the evenings, four or five times a week, we read their works and discuss, over beer, and this has proved an enormous success—I try to keep still, and let *them* do it, but now and then take a hand, and any visitors are pressed into service as well. Mary, of course, when she does say something, hits the nail on its head, and is wonderful as always—besides running the house, cooking gargantuan meals, and keeping an eye on Pamela's painting. But alas her own work (and of course mine) has had to go by the board—pro tem, to be sure, but it's a pity. —Today our Gallery's water-colour show is having its private view, and once more Mary steals it all, lock stock and barrel. . . . —We're both perpetually tired, and financially we won't clear even as much as we hoped, but we're enjoying it hugely, learning a lot, and at least feel that we have a future! Which is something. Our loves to both of you.   Conrad

Jeake's House
Rye Feb 2 39

Dear Tom: Many thanks for the grandfather's sermons, which I was indeed beginning to think might have gone the way of all books. (I still have a copy of Browning's poems which belongs to the Signet, gift of Pierre du Chaignon La Rose.) Just the same, I'm sorry it troubled you—your conscience must be tenderer than mine. I'm pretty tough, myself. —I'm grieved, sort of, to hear of the death of the Criterion—I never wholly subscribed, as you know (double entendre), but it was good, and that good things come to an end is sad. What a relief to you, though—I should think you'd feel like a cork. I take it you won't be in a hurry to start another. Now what about coming down to Rye again, and amongst other things allowing yourself to be impaled on Mary's brush. How would sometime between the 18th Feb. and 7th March do—? Weekend or midweek, makes no odds to us, but make it two or three days, or else *two* weekends, so that Mary can get you well fixed, if you can. (Mary has just gone grand, been canonized into the Metropolitan Museum, N.Y.) . . . Yes, Tinck was quite a chatterbox.[1] Me, I'm saving up the really juicy bits for your seventieth, and not letting any cats out of bags prematurely. I give you warning. . . .   as ever
Conrad

Rye
Feb 8 39

Dear Jacob—   . . . My new novelette [*A Heart for the Gods of Mexico*]—which someday I'll send you—has had a bad but extensive press—*more* extensive than any ever had here by me, but very bitter from the highbrow and leftwing quarters—and I fear wont make any money. Nothing surprising in that, of course, but the sheer malice which has been spat upon it has taken me aback—odd the way my books time after time have the faculty of making so many people *angry*. How would you explain it? *I* don't know. I think I must be suffering from a kind of spiritual B.O.! However, the new book may really be bad. —Stung by the viciousness of the

---

1. William G. Tinckom-Fernandez, classmate at Harvard, had written a memoir for the 1938 T. S. Eliot issue of the *Harvard Advocate*.

attacks, I've begun a new one [*Conversation*], with S. Yarmouth and John Coffee for background—a domestic symphony as it were—too soon to say if it will jell. Better keep this under your hat—no use getting people worked up, and fearful of possible libel! —Mary has had a picture bought by the Metropolitan Mesuem— bad luck in a way, as it didn't belong to Mary (previously sold) but good of course otherwise, as it will be a useful sales point. She's done some magnificent work this winter—boy what fun I have, with a genius at work under my own eyes! Life has certainly been good to me. . . .   Our loves to all of you   Conrad

153: TO MARY HOOVER AIKEN[h]   Rye
                                     Wednesday [April 1939]

Well, my raven-haired beloved beauty, . . . Yesterday I did nothing beyond writing three—count 'em—three pages of the new chapter, being suddenly seized with same—much to my surprise Buzzer decided to take a hand, and so the new section opens with a repetition of the opening theme of the book—Buzzer taking a bath again. I'm kind of pleased with the idea, as (1) it throws a sort of symphonic bridge back to the beginning and (2) the actual talk links it immediately with the previous section *and* fills in the time-gap with dialogue narrative, so that there won't have been any time unaccounted for all day. A stroke of luck, that was—by god it occurred to me when it happened how *much* there is in luck of that kind, and how easily, if I'd forced matters, begun sooner, begun when I didn't feel much like it, or at any one of a dozen moments when I *almost* began, but didn't, I could have missed this particular solution. And it *does* solve things pretty completely, I think—it's a present, in fact, of five pages or so, which comes in very handy. The actual dialogue is okay, I think, without being anything sensational—it moves, which is the main thing. Today I shall knock off—it's a lovely sunny day, the first since you left, my pet, so I shall go to Hastings for lunch, hoping to find Vernon [Nash], and try to bring him back for dinner. Molly[1] has got a leg of lamb, so if Ed [Burra] should appear too there will be plenty for all hands. —How lovely that you've started sketching, and done one of those ruined heads, which I've always liked. . . .   Pinkie

1. Molly Mills (later Southerden) helped Mary to clean and cook.

. . . I do, to be frank, feel wretched. I'm afraid the visit to Vernon
was responsible—I wasn't feeling too lively anyway, sort of weak
and fuzzy, if you know what I mean, when I went, but I was afraid
he'd vanish. So I went. And at the house I found no Vernon, only
two workmen taking out the phone. Then in the alley I saw his
car—or thought it was—went to peer into it, to make sure—and as
I did so heard a sound behind me, in one of the garages, and on
looking round the half-swung door saw Vernon, with his back
turned, crying, and beyond him, on the dirty floor of the garage,
[his dog] Gretel, lying dead. A bit of kindling wood lay over her
eyes—to keep them closed, as he explained later. Well. There was
the usual scene, of course, hysterics, weepings, protestations, a torrent of explanations—but I'm afraid it was really a murder. Everything had been going wrong, poor fellow—a last minute chance of
selling the business for twentyfive pounds fell through only that
morning—Deirdre [Nash, his wife] phoned, and upset him—he had
to move in 24 hours, found he had only six pounds left in the
bank—and then, the door being left open for a moment, Gretel escaped into the streets, it took him twenty minutes to catch her, and
he abruptly made up his mind to have her destroyed. Took her
straight to the vet's, held her in his arms while she was given a hypo
to put her to asleep, then waited outside till she had been chloro-
formed. On his way back, stopped at a catholic church and went in,
there crossing himself. When I arrived, had apparently been standing there looking at her and crying for an hour. Twice later in the
day he mentioned his often repeated desire to kill Deirdre. So Gretel, poor creature, was in a sense perhaps just a substitute, and of
course the wretched Vernon was desperately unhappy and guilty
about it, and passionately looking for extenuations. A dreadful
business altogether. I decided I'd better do all I could for him, so
succeeded in dragging him to the Queen for lunch, and blew him to
a good one, with fat steaks and saute potatos and all the fixings—
and to my surprise he cheered up with really extraordinary speed!
After which we went to the Gaiety to see quite a nice picture (I
couldn't prevent his treating me—two shillings out of his six
pounds) and then he saw me off at the station, before going back to
bury Gretel in the garden and pack his things for departure in the

morning. I urged him to come over for the night, either last night or this—he didn't appear, and I doubt if he will—but I got Molly to make the bed, in case. He says he'll go to Brighton first—good lord what a forlorn business! —Extraordinary, you know—I didn't realize till I got back here how much of a shock I'd had—guess I was too weak to take it.[1] . . .   oodles of love, my lamb—Pinkie

Pa Burra appeared just looking for Ed—viz., at 10:30 a.m.! Ed vanished last night, it seems. So Pa is now on his way to the Pertinezes. Seems, too, Ed has asked the P's and others to lunch tomorrow in the midst of Spring Cleaning, so Pa Burra is un-inviting them. Sort of looks like a family row! Ho ho.

155: TO MARY HOOVER AIKEN[h]   Rye
                                      Sunday [April 1939]

Well, my poor frozen darling, here's *your* poor frozen darling sitting in the diningroom of a sunday morning with cold hands and feet. . . . I went to Hastings (as no doubt you discovered from the postmark) and saw Pygmalion again—it's if anything better seen a second time, very funny. Then when I got back, of course Ed turned up, me being engaged to the Mck's [Mackecknies] for dinner—but he had a drink and we arranged for the following night. (He was much entertained by his papa's antics, derisive, said the business of his asking the P's to lunch during spring cleaning was a fantasy, so god only knows what the true situation was!) The dinner with the Mcks was pleasant—fish, chicken (the smallest bird I ever did see—size of a sparrow) and I got what seemed quite a lot to eat, till I woke up hungry as hell next morning. —Bobby was more attentive with the second helps than usual, ditto beer—quite a reform. They informed me that the Mayoress has a new son. . . . Well, it being then only ten thirty, and me relieved to be home, and to hear from Henry [Murray], and missing my sweety pide like anything. I sat down and wrote two feeblish sonnets, viz.,—

> This body must my only altar make,
> there will I burn the miracle, and there
> the bread and wine of strict communion take,
> beating my heart as a deliberate prayer.

1. For the story of the Nashes (as "Gloria" and "Julian") and Gretel see *Ushant*, pp. 263–74.

225

There the pure knowledge, and the only, hymns
of the divine and only Known-Unknown.
O altitudo in the bloodstream swims,
the god of love sings in the very bone.
Here is your praise, and all of it! What more
has this sacrarium of flesh to offer—?
a whisper in the brain, yet, like a shore,
wide as the sea, with all the sea can proffer.
A mystery, confined in little space:
the whole world's wonder in a sleeping face.

And search the senses—ah, but not too well:
to search the senses is like searching roots,
and the dark-loving knowledge needs its Hell
to send the simple bough its simple fruits.
Not search them, no—but let them windows be
for the unsifted and untroubled light,
the great choir flooded by infinity,
the holy body like a church made bright.
In such a light our knowledges will meet
quicklier than light itself, cunning as air,
our worlds, conjoined, filled with the same wing-beat,
and that divine vibration everywhere;
the body, cruciform, by godhead stilled,
like a poor church by golden rumour filled.

Yeah. And by then it was twelve-thirty, and I went to bed, and then damnation I couldn't sleep—had a real all-night insomnia, and got up in the morning feeling like a ghost. So felt all day, lay down the whole afternoon (with a fire—wasn't I virtuous), but the butcher boy woke me just as I was going off, and the cat came up with muddy feet and had to be barricaded out of the drawingroom with a chair, and howled on the landing, so the rest wasn't a success, and I got a headache, and found we were down to one aspirin, and went to Boots in the rain and got some more, and read Night Flight feeling like hell. (And wishing Ed wasnt coming to dinner.) But the Ship revived me somewhat, the Mcks were there, and Tony [Bertram], and the party with Ed was unusually nice—Molly came all dressed to the nines, with a short tight skirt, and perfume, looking very giddy. When she left she said she was going out to look for the boys—at a pub, if necessary! And rolled a terrific eye. —Ed was much impressed with the Wyndham Lewis portraits (his wife and Ezra) in Picture Post—we chewed the fat on the usual round of topics, art, poetry, america, Boston, Gordon [Bassett], Jane, Portugal, Mexico, Malcolm, Svanna, New Orleans, Cuba, and back to Rye in time for him to leave at 11:30. And so to bed, and the cat again naughty in Jane's room this morning—crying outside the door and waking me at seven—I was too far down to get up, and so he disgraced himself. . . .   a whacking big kiss, from Pinkie

156: TO MARY HOOVER AIKEN[h]   Rye

Monday morning [May 1939]

Hello my sweet—and it's a lovely day here, if only you were here too—really the best this year—bright and really *warm*. And I am again better, really now beginning to enjoy life—hooray! The ears show signs of unplugging, making strange womping noises, opening and closing, like ice breaking up in rivers in spring—so I guess the woist is over—But it would be nice if you *were* here—Molly again coyly inquired at breakfast—so I told her I'd probably know her and my fates later today. She's quite prepared for anything, I think, so it's all right—What I really hope is that you'll finish say Saturday and come back here—I still don't really feel ambitious about travelling and visiting and sich—and have a sort of stay-puttishness. Yesterday I had a lovely long lazy loaf all by myself—read Chekhov in the garden four hours, listened to the Beethoven concert on the wireless, read some more Chekhov and some Delmore Schwartz, wrote Bob Linscott at great length, wrote Jennings [Rice] at less length, pulled up five dandelions, and then, lo, it was 7, and time for the Ship—Where Tony all beaming and bristling had a piece of gossip ready for me, ABOUT US. It *seems,* my pretty pet, that the whisper is creeping from house to house along Trader's Passage, and up into Watchbell Street, and up also into Mermaid Street—can't you just *see* it—?—that Mrs. Aiken the third has left Mr. Aiken,—what do you think of that, my dears?—and now WHO will the *fourth* Mrs. Aiken be. And isn't it poetic justice, doesn't it serve him right, that this time *he* should be left alone in that old house—etc. etc. etc. etc! Boy, isn't it wonderful? I'm afraid I really screamed with delight, and Tony had actually been rather afraid to tell me. It seems, par exemple, that Mrs. Rood's bringing of the rhododendrons was a piece of scouting, pure and simple—for on her way back she darted into the Moreton's kitchen, hissed quickly to Mabel "It's *all right!* She's coming back next week!" and darted out again. Only by degrees did Mabel and Tony [Moreton] figure out what she had meant. And Mr. Perugini, also, inquired obliquely and insinuatingly of Tony as to your whereabouts—"Where's Mrs. Aiken? We haven't seen her lately?" *And* on hearing that you were doing portraits in Oxford said "O, I see" with manifest disappointment! O baby, I haven't enjoyed anything so much for years—And now my darling your magnificent four decker lady baltimore strawberry shortcake angelfood chocolate fudge nut sundae of a letter has arrived, and I'm left quite speechless. Gosh. What an inexhaustible gold-mine of wisdom goodness love perception power and delight you are. . . . And I'm so often secretly afraid of cramping or deflecting you, darling—both as a person and as a painter—that devils me a lot—. I've occasionally thought that perhaps you'd lost a little of your boldness and imaginative speed out of a mistaken deference to me—which would be a calamity of more than hideous hue. I do hope not—and on sober thought when I look at the thing I don't really believe it—yet it's something to remember as possible. It *oughtn't* to happen—we ought to cross-fertilize each other—and good lord you certainly do me, witness this winter's work, which so clearly reflects the *tone* of our love and happiness. —But what a wonderful letter, darling—so much better and truer than any sonnets can ever be—a *real* poem, by god, and beautiful, and true— bless your good heart. —Well—I shall hope for a wire today—and I kind of hope it will mean your coming back here say Saturday. . . . Last night: I was having a dreadful time in a dream trying to call you to come and see the blackbird who had lost his mate, and was shivering his wings and mourning—but a teaparty was going on, people got in my way, voices drowned me out, I never succeeded in telling you about it, until after the blackbird had gone- —see? Yes. But anyway I adore you, pinky, eyebrows, toenails, moles, stuffed ears, blotched face and all. And you're *beautiful.*   Pinky

157: TO HENRY A. MURRAY[r]   [Jeake's House, Rye]
                                              May 30 39

. . . And now it begins to look as if Mary's seven weeks work on the two child portraits is wasted—or may be—the parents have suddenly become undecided about it. That's the sort of thing that happens. —If the european thing would only show some signs—reliable ones—of settling down, it might be best to hang on for another winter, and try the school once again—it's a good idea, there's no doubt about that, and workable, as we've proved. But how to tell—? So we may decide on Boston, or rent Jake's cottage on Cape Cod, and see what we can do at potboiling between us—portraits and book reviews and short stories and another novel and another show for Mary—this time in N. Y.—and so on. With the idea of coming back to Rye in the spring. Something may depend on what I hear from my english agents about the new novel [*Conversation*], which I've just delivered to them. If they appear at all hopeful—well, I dunno. —I quite agree with you about "Mexico." I've just in fact re-read it, and with some dismay. . . . I don't quite know, however, what you mean by the lack of "will." Perhaps "will" is something unknown to me. I don't see life as that—or as profitably that—so much as understanding. Therefor there are no heroics, as you say, in the novels, no great enterprises, no conquests, no mighty decisions—nothing in fact but the flowering of reflexes, the knotting and unknotting of neuroses, circumstance and sensorium marrying and unmarrying—the flowing intermixture of more or less uncontrollable undirectable life—such small heroism as there is being simply in the individual's working out, half conscious and half not, of his situation, himself, or not. I suppose basically the problems have been "to accept or not to accept"—to accept with full awareness or not—to *live* (fully) or die. (I'm thinking of G Circle and K coffin.) There is even, in the latter, a social problem—viz., to what extremes *can* individualism be pressed—or at what sort of point will the social responsibility intervene? But I grant that there is no neat arrangement of Hero vs. World or Hero vs. Hero. The battle front, I think, is farther on. —I'm still ill, I regret to say, with plugged eustacheans, and very one-cylindered, but enjoying life like the devil— I've missed Mary terribly, but my god what letters the gal can write—it's been worth having her go away to find that out. And pari passu with finishing the novel I've reopened a poetic vein, and bled myself of 22 sonnets, which has been good for me in more ways than one—though I'd be put to it to try to tell you why. —Oh well, Harry, this is just thanks, and our loves—and maybe by gosh we'll be seeing you—   Conrad

Jeake's House, Rye
June 29 39

Dear Max: I had hoped to have word from you or Bernice [Baumgarten] before this as to the goings on *re* The Conversation, but maybe no news is good news? I hope so, and fire this off to you anyway, by air mail, just to save a little time. First, I very much hope that you liked the book, and second, that you'll be able to get it out in the fall. . . .

I wonder if you'll agree with me that whatever else its merits or demerits The Conversation is much the most saleable book so far???? I really think so—and I can't help feeling that with the right sort of build-up we can actually make something out of it. May I make a suggestion—viz., that on the jacket, and in all advertising, there should be no mention of me as a poet whatever, but a strict concentration on the prose—in short, a careful emphasis on aiken the novelist and short story writer, with plenty of hearty tub-thumping, too. "With this, Conrad Aiken's fifth novel, his eighth volume of fiction," etc. is the idea. (Fifth, counting Mexico, which we might as well—!) Perhaps use quotations from the Graham Greene (Spectator) review of Great Circle, and Edwin Muir (Listener) of ditto, which were particularly juicy. (The Spectator mentioned Great Circle again the other day as one of the best novels of the past ten years—oddly enough coupling it with The Great Gatsby! Which is one of my favorite books, incidentally.) In all of which I don't mean simply to indulge in idle bragging, Max, but simply to point out that we've really got now a very nice little line of hard-wearing fiction which an astute campaign might start selling. Worth trying, anyway?

In line with which, I'd kind of like it if you'd list the whole lot of fiction—including the early Bring! Bring!, now out of print—on the page opposite title-page, perhaps separating the novels (and here again include A Heart for the Gods of Mexico, if you don't mind) from the short stories.

Also, I've got a new book of verse nearly ready—I could deliver it really whenever you felt the moment was most propitious for it. Probable title—Ave Maria: Blues for Ruby Matrix: and Other Poems. The great part of it—and it's a shortish book—is a sonnet series. . . .   Conrad

Jeake's House, Rye
                                                July 6 39

Dear Max: I'm awful sorry to hear from Bernice that it was
thumbs down on The Conversation. Which makes my air-mail letter seem a little foolish, doesn't it? Just the same, perhaps it's all for
the best, all round. I can't help feeling, you know, that ever since
Blue Voyage you've had a kind of queer *idée fixe* as to what was to
be expected of me—some remote and grandiose notion as to the
sort and shape of novel you wanted me to do—and I've felt, with
every book since, that your *idée fixe* simply prevented you from
seeing anything else. The result was that you were disappointed in
Great Circle, and went about publishing it sadly and reluctantly,
and you did the same thing only moreso with King Coffin—and of
course the short stories, as well. I didn't feel, to be candid, with any
of these books, that they were really *published*—rather, that they
were merely *allowed* out. . . . I knew that Great Circle and King
Coffin were not only good books—better than anything else you
were publishing—but were perhaps by way of being classics: I feel
pretty damned sure now that The Conversation is another: and it
has amazed and saddened me that you should be so blind, so ad-
dicted to other and it seems to me shallower ideals, that you were
not only unable to see this but actually convinced that the books
were really inferior. In England, Great Circle and King Coffin are
slowly but surely getting the kind of position I suggest above—it is
being discovered that they have depth as well as form, a kind of
permanent significance. . . . I must admit that I'm rather relieved
at the prospect of at least hoping for a publisher who will see The
Conversation as it *is,* a classic domestic symphony, and do it justice
as such, instead of dismissing it because it's short or because it's
"about a small domestic situation"! Good heavens, of course it is!
That is its precise virtue—that the small domestic situation is turned
into a symphonic poem on married life, which, in small compass,
nevertheless says so much, reaches so far. It *is* made into a poem,
that is the point: it *does* achieve beauty: it *is* significant, profoundly
so: and if you don't see it, well then I'm glad I have to take it elsewhere, even though it disappoints me and saddens me—more than I
can possibly tell you—to have to end this long and friendly collabo-
ration. You've been wonderfully generous to me, despite these dis-

agreements, and our growing inability to see eye to eye, and I don't want you to think I'm not. And I hope too we can go on in that key of good feeling, even if now less actively.   as always   Conrad Aiken

160: TO HENRY A. MURRAY^r   Jeake's House Rye Sussex
                                                      Sept 20 39

Well Harry, we're a-coming, and if the SS Washington, star-spangled and floodlit, can whisk us past the mines and torpedoes we'll be in New York about Oct. 6th. Sailing the 29th, or there-abouts. The film job looked too uncertain, and we feared that if it *didn't* materialize we'd by that time again be too broke to sail, so off we go, taking with us a small boy of three, on behalf of our friends the Noxons.[1] . . . Gosh, what a world, what a world. How fascinating, how terrible, how everything. England is astonishing—The simplicity, absence of rancour, calm, and stoical *indifference* with which they're going about it is something to have witnessed: a great people. We hate to leave them. . . .   Conrad

1. Nicholas, the son of Betty and Gerald Noxon, a writer and a friend of Lowry's.

Letters 161–187: October 1939 to September 1945

Suddenly, in October 1939, C A received from Malcolm Lowry an appeal "to save my life." Lowry had followed his wife Jan to Los Angeles and spent a depressed year in bars until he met Margerie Bonner. In July 1939, B. S. Parks, a lawyer acting for Lowry's father, had hustled him away to Vancouver and the care of a Sgt. Maurice Carey. To C A, Lowry now said he had written "at least one book since seeing you which is I feel mature . . . The Lighthouse Invites the Storm, but I do not want to have it published without consulting you." He begged for money to return to the States and to come to C A. In response to C A's letter of Oct 29, 1939, Lowry then wrote a long scenario beginning "Mein lieber alter Senlin Forslin Malcolm Coffin Aiken" (pp. 18–25, Selected Letters of Malcolm Lowry, with deletions), suggesting "the hook, line and sinker" which C A should use with "the Old Man." He also mentioned sending C A's agent The Last Address, "about a man's hysterical identification with Melville." Lowry admitted about The Last Address: "this still has many echoes of Blue Voyage—not to say a design-governing posture in one long chapter of it from Great Circle—but why the hell not? The influence is more fructifying than it ever was." Within a month Lowry wrote three more long letters, describing further his entrapment, new strategies for escape, and his desire to see C A: "a psychological necessity apart from a pleasure, because I feel the obstructions and dishonesties and Judas thinkings in our relationship—caused by myself— have been removed, and I am on–by a hell of a route but still on—the right path." On December 16 Lowry's father, through Parks, in a long wire requested C A to answer "immediately whether willing accept responsibility management Malcolm personally and his affairs if allowed join you in accordance his request." C A agreed at once. A long grateful letter from Malcolm's father to C A emphasized his anguish and exhausted patience, but his willingness to follow C A's suggestions, among them that Malcolm see Dr. Henry A. Murray. Eight pages from Malcolm, "bewildered and hurt," argued with C A's unwillingness (Jan 19, 1940) to conceal Margerie from his father, and retorted: "if drinking rots the honesty it is a curious thing to say I have yet to meet the teetotaler

whom I can wholly trust. So much then, for alc." But Lowry wrote
on February 23 that "the axe has fallen . . . I am refused and can-
not get back to the States. . . . Meantime I have work to finish, and
now, when everything seems lost, it seems all the more important to
finish it." At last, in August, the Lowrys were able to move from
Vancouver to Dollarton, B.C., where they lived until 1944.

o   o   o

Conversation: Or Pilgrims' Progress (New York: Duell, Sloan and Pearce, March
    1940; London: Rodney, Phillips and Green, May 1948).
And in the Human Heart (New York: Duell, Sloan and Pearce, November 1940;
    London: Staples Press, October 1949).
Brownstone Eclogues and Other Poems (New York: Duell, Sloan and Pearce,
    November 1942).
The Soldier: A Poem (Norfolk, Connecticut: New Directions, November 1944;
    London: Nicholson and Watson, October 1946).

161: TO MALCOLM LOWRY[ch]   Belmont, Mass.
                                             Oct. 29 39

My beloved Judas-Malc—it was good to hear from you, not so
good in all respects (but in some) to hear your bagful of queer news.
But what can I do to help you—? Damn all. I'm a bit knocked-oop
meself, we're broke to the wide, on borrowed money (and little at
that) and about to live in one of Jake's cottages, which we get for
nothing, on the Cape. Cash, nil. Prospects, dim. Nor can I find anyone who would lend me more, at the moment. All I can immediately suggest is this: I talked of your plight with my agent, Bernice
Baumgarten, Brandt & Brandt, 101 Park Avenue, N.Y., and of your
work, and she said that if you would have your mss—all you can
get hold of—sent to her, as per above, she would see what could be
done. If some publisher—and there of course I'd myself add my
say-so—would take an interest, something might then be done in
the way of getting some money to you, and thereafter arranging to
summon you to New York as it were for "business"—which would
perhaps carry weight with the authorities? Anyway, let me know
quam cel about this, and Bernice too, and we'll go on trying to
improvise *something*. What about the Old Man. Would it be any
use my writing to him, and if so to what effect—viz., what line
would most profitably take—if any—? But anyway, don't be down-
hearted—we'll maybe think of a way out. Or in. —Ourselves, worn

234

out and ill with ours and the world's troubles, but of good heart. A new novel (and a new publisher) a new book of sonnets [*And in the Human Heart*] and a new dealer for Mary's pictures in New York—so we at any rate feel that we are *building* something. . . . Ed's pictures are in the British pavilion at the Fair—he may come over in January—why not keep your eye on Boston? A good place. Avoid the army my dear fellow—nothing in it. As for Jan et cet, and the new Gal, blessings and congratulations. And Mary joins me in sending love—lots of it—   Conrad.

If you prefer, have the mss. sent first to me, and I'll confer with Linscott about the next steps. Just as you like. Have you finished Ballast—?

162: TO EDWARD BURRA^r   South Dennis Mass.
                                            Nov 6 39

Well Ed it's a long time ain't it, but goddlemighty what a whirl these chickens have been through, you'd never believe it. We're both of us practically dead. Worn out, worn to the bone. What 13 days and nights on the ship didn't accomplish, N York finished off, and Boston is burying. You can imagine. We didn't sail for 30 hours after embarking, Gerald and Betty [Noxon] weren't allowed on board at all, Gerald in fact we never saw, so we were just swept aboard ourselves with Child, and how we did enjoy it. Late the next day we actually sailed, and late the day after that, much to our surprise found ourselves in France, viz., Bordeaux. All very nice, but there too we were not of course allowed ashore, but stared at it from the docks for three and a half days, too bored for words. The food was pretty good, my god what a crowd however, the lounges were turned into dormitories, rows of little cots, there was no room anywhere to sit down, Mary shared a cabin with three dames and the child, I mine with three other gents, all very *intime*. Under one of the bunks in my room was a suitcase labelled John Rothenstein,[1] a name which seemed familiar—a small world dearie, and you can imagine how the gossip flew—his wife Elizabeth roomed with Mary, we arranged to have a table together after that, and had really a very good time, regardless. (Regardless of crowds and the Blessed Child.) We liked them both very much, took them to dinner

---

1. John Rothenstein was director of the Tate Gallery, London, from 1936 to 1964.

with the Wehles, saw John again here when he came to Boston to lecture, and got him drunk on two cocktails at Chris Morgan's, so that he fell down the front stairs—he hasn't been seen since, but went away leaving one shoe behind—I hope he got to Washington all right. Very nice I thought. A great admirer of yours, but very down on Paul [Nash], whom he considers inferior to John N[ash]. Odd. We hope to get them both back to Cape Cod for a visit later. . . . Conrad

163: TO MALCOLM LOWRY^{ch} South Dennis Mass.
Nov 15 39

My beloved misguided misfortunate chaos-loving Malc— as you see from the reverse of this, I started to write the Old Man and then thought perhaps I'd better write you first, for even MORE information. Firstly and most importantly, this: do you know of the difficulties, not to say practical impossibility, of exporting money from England, and do you know for a fact that the Old Man *could* so send it to you were you to cross into the US? Is this possibly the reason why he wants you to stay in Canada? Anyway, it's necessary for me to know about all this, and whether *you* know and the Old Man knows. If you don't know, maybe you could find out from the authorities there in Vancouver? And then I'll let fly at the Old Man in the most ingenious manner I can. But first that is essential. As for the rest, of course I'll do everything I can. . . . As for acting once more in loco parentis, of course I'll do it if it will help you, though our own circumstances are precarious in the extreme, and we don't know where we'll be or what doing two months in advance. We may stay here: but on the other hand, Mary now it appears has chances of doing some society portraits in Boston, so we may go up again in Jan. But Boston would be all right for you, you and Margie could find a corner for yourselves and I could as it were (from the O M's viewpoint at all events) keep a Benevolent Eye glowing upon you from a distance, i.e., from S Dennis or wherever, why not??? I think you could work in Boston (your own work, I mean—there are no jobs I fear) and you would know people, so it might really be the best thing. (In this connection, by all means send Margie in advance if you think best. But certainly with funds, for our own are nil, and we could do nothing for her. Sad, damnit, but true.) Meanwhile, the Mss will I hope have arrived, and will if so perhaps have

begun something. I'll do my bursting best. Be sure to write to Bernice Baumgarten, Brandt & Brandt, 101 Park Avenue, telling her who you are and that it is at my suggestion you send In Ballast: it's a big office, and in the machinery it might be forgotten that you were the chap I'd spoken to her about. —As for your general Saga, jeez, Malc, it's a horror, it is, and I partly understand it, but not all: more light, more light, if you can and will. Are you drinking 'eavy-like? are you confused, or is all now lucid? Us, we're trying to be good, drink less (but still too much) and are really striving towards a Better Thing. High time too, for I'm far from well, weak in the knees, toothless, and must this winter probably lose the rest of my teeth in exchange for a porcelain mouthtrap, once I've acquired the stamina to undergo it. No, the new novel is The Conversation, a sinfonia domestica, a little poem of marital love (?????) in four movements, setting Cape Cod, a very ordinary 36-hour quarrel between a normal male and female, about nothing to speak of, and ending in holy bedlock. I'm pleased with it—I think it's a multum in parvo, and if I do say so as should, I believe it's got some, at least, of the classic virtues: form, delicacy, restraint, poetry, perhaps even a little wisdom. Reading a Book maybe will be next—if this winter I feel well enough and settled enough to get my fumbling paws down into it. —Margie I must say sounds like a brick. We both send you and her our loves, and do count on us, we aim to do all we really can. I only wish to god I actually had some money, for that would so simply and quickly solve everything for you. But gosh if we even paid one tenth of what we owe—but let's not go into that. —Our devotions, old fellow, and keep up the chins—
  Conrad

164: TO HENRY A. MURRAY[r]   South Dennis Mass.
                                          Nov 15 39

Well Harry we're here, but as yet hardly know it—the landscape flatter and less interesting than I'd remembered it, but with its gradually emerging vitues none the less, though forlorn too and humanly speaking very empty. Also when we got here very cold—20, and a fierce wind, and Joy Wilbur as cold too in her different way—a very comic reception, to which Jake was an abashed and helpless witness. However, we are dealing I think successfully with the Joy part of it, Rounds One and Two were definitely ours, so we hope to keep things under control. . . . The church clock across the street kept me remorselessly reminded of the time all the first night, but quite softly and pleasantly—and so on. We're nearly a mile from the p.o. and store and papers, so goodness knows whether we'll even bother about news. But altogether we begin to like it, if we can stick the bleakness and keep the house warm. . . . We've organized order out of the chaos, removed the offensive pictures and vases, placed our own patron Buddha on the mantelpiece, where he serenely takes possession, along with our two little Dog Fohs, our netsukes, and a fine peeled and twisted stick picked up on the beach this very morning, and so now we feel that it's ours. And our own candlesticks on the dinner table, our own knives and forks, help us to bridge the gulf from Rye to Dennis, too—we celebrated last night with a fine salvo of dry martinis, sans ice, and went to bed happy. When will you come down? . . . I hope to get into the Melville in a day or two, unless I feel impelled to do first an article on poetry which T Weeks has commissioned for the Atlantic—but I think not: poetry looks skinny and unattractive to me at the moment. And speaking of Melville, I've just had a huge and dreadfully despairing letter from Malcolm Lowry, in Vancouver, an incredible chaos of complications, at the end of which, apropos of his work, he says he is sending me a thing called The Last Address, which is "about a man's hysterical identification of himself with Melville, I think it might interest Harry Murray." Strange   our devoted loves   Conrad

165: TO MALCOLM LOWRY^{ch}   South Dennis Mass.
                                          Dec 15 39

Abracadam. The enclosed wire came yesterday, Malc—but as you will see, the end is not yet, and we must wait and see what comes of it. Maybe nothing; but at least my letter appears to have had the desired mollifying effect. What your own predicament—viz., as to being allowed to cross the border—will amount to, I can't myself imagine. IF the O M is in favour of the whole idea, *and* cash is put up for you, I don't see why not. I should think you could wangle something? Worst coming to worst, there might however be advantages in your idea of moving at least to the eastern end of Canada— Montreal?—there to be under my Eye as now you're under Park's— Anyway, I'll be keeping in touch, and you do the same, and we'll hope for the best—Ballast has just come—it will I fear be some time before I can get down to it, for I've got some work on my hands. Baumgarten reports that she couldn't make head nor tail of it, and alas that also she thought it not a commercial prospect. Mind you, B & B are pretty hardboiled anti-highbrow agents, who regard even me only with tolerance because I'm a friend of the family—so I wouldn't attach too much value to *their* judgment. As an offhand quick opinion, from just flipping it over, I'd myself say that it looks too confusedly elaborate, too circumambulatingly metaphysical and ego-freighted, to be effective. My own influence again has been bad, as in the chapter of unwritten, partly written, letters—elsewhere too. I think it's time you cut yourself adrift from all these here ghostly doppelgangers and projections and identifications and let loose some of your natural joy in swiftness and goodness and love and simplicity—put your complexity into reverse—and celebrate the sun. Some of the latter poems go that way—though your metrics *is* queer, blimey yes. Here again I think the influence of the Complex Boys, these adolescent audens spenders with all their pretty little dexterities, their negative safety, their indoor marxmanship, has been not too good for you—something with a little more gusto is wanted, guts, juices, blood, love, sunsets and sunrises, moons, stars, roses,—for god's sake let's let in the whole romantic shebang again, it's high time—I agree with old Ed [Burra] about this. (What ever became of *Volcano,* by the way?) Ed writes that he may be coming over to Boston next month—if he can get here—so maybe we'll all be having a reunion. You knew, I suppose, that Jane [Aiken] is in Cambridge, working on Melville for Harry Murray? Everything comes round and back, the eternal return. . . . my novel comes out March 22, and on the whole life is damned good. It is, I assure you. So keep a-comin', old fellow, and we'll be seeing you. Meantime, our loves to you both—   Conrad

166: TO BENJAMIN S. PARKS^{ch}   South Dennis
                                          December 16, 1939

Quite willing assume responsibility for supervising Malcolm personally and his affairs if decided to let him join me here stop would appreciate having full report of past year by letter and if decision is favorable approximate probable date arrival Boston.   Conrad Aiken

S Dennis Mass.
Dec 17 39

Now, my dear undependable confused exacting but well-meaning Malc, comes the moment for plain speaking, nicht wahr? I had yesterday a long wire from Parks, asking me if I would undertake full responsibility for supervising you, and your affairs—"Malcolm personally, and his affairs"—and adding that your trouble was "irresponsibility as to money," and "continuous heavy drinking unless closely watched." Well, I've wired back that I will *take* this responsibility; but with natural misgivings, my dear fellow, which you should be the first to understand. It's no idle barroom jest, undertaking a thing like this: it means we give up our privacy, independence, quiet, everything, and with grave risks of accomplishing as little for you as for ourselves: we have our own work to do, our own lives to live, and you should think of this, think of it *now*. I don't want again to be accused, as in 1933, of being indifferent to your welfare, and only putting up with you for the Old Man's money. To hell with that. So right here and now I'll say this: I don't even know what the O M or Parks or whoever proposes to pay me for the job, and haven't *inquired*, even. I'm doing this, in short, (and there are few I'd do it for) because I've always as you know been damned fond of you and because you've come to me for help at a crisis. So now: I hope you'll give me your word before coming that you're really going to make a damned fine and convincing effort to *behave well*, and to be as considerate of us as we shall be of you. No secret drinkings round the corner, eh? No disgracings of us with our friends, no scenes: and above all no continuous argument as to the amount of drink allowed: I'm to be the boss about that, or it's no go. An amiable boss, a loving boss, a good brother: that's all: but let's have that agreed. Mind you, too, in all this, there is my beloved Mary to be considered. It means more work and less fun for her, it means worry for her as well—bear *that* in mind. She agrees with me, just the same, in thinking that this is something that has to be done, in *wanting* to do it—I think she'd be a little ashamed of me if I didn't take it on. So there. Now put all that together, please, and think it over, and if Parks and Co. permit the move, and you yourself want to come, still, come with good intentions: clean fingernails, a pure heart, a clear head, and prepared to be helpful and to work.   Conrad

S Dennis Mass.
Jan 19 40

My dear Malc— a short one today, time presses, snow falls, millions of letters wait to be writ, but just a line to wave you on— yours and M[arjerie]'s received and enjoyed, appreciated too— deeply. We've written, or Mary has, to a friend of hers in Washington, just on the chance she might know someone in the Labour Dep't and expedite or charm your application—an *outside* chance, but we thought worth trying. So now we wait. If all blows up, if you *can't* get in—well, then we must try to think of something else. Maybe the Montreal idea, or some such. But let's wait and see.

Meanwhile, I'm glad you see my point about toeing the line. This now becomes, I think, all the more important, for I've had my first letter from the O M, and I'm afraid I must tell you that the whole situation is very serious: he says flatly that unless *I* can report in due course that I find you trustworthy and reformed and working—and for this too he wants you to live *with* me at the outset—he's made up his mind to cast you off, and never again to come to your rescue, no matter *what* happens. So, my dear fellow, it's up to you. *And* it's up to me to play absolutely fairly with him, too, you can see that. No cutting of corners: we must do it right. Frankly, the Margie thing worries me on that score, as it ought, I think, to worry you. It puts me, at the outset, in the awkward position of having to conceal something, which I don't dammit, much like. Would it perhaps be better if you were to write the O M yourself telling him about her, and asking whether you might bring her East for, as it were, an Official Inspection by Mary and myself—subject of course to my agreeing then to the idea. I think this might be wise. I'd suggest you do it right away, so that by the time you get here we might have a cable from him okaying the notion: or at any rate leaving it to me. You can tell him, if you like, that you've *just now* informed me of the situation, and that I've agreed in advance to M's coming along later for a visit. That would put things on a squarer footing????? Think it over, anyway? And believe me Malc I don't bring it all up just to make difficulties—good god no. It's simply that I feel we *must* be honest. And the other isn't, quite. But if *steps* have been taken to regularize it, before Margie comes, I shan't mind so much: I'll then be in a position to say that you'd told me you'd written, asked *my* permission, and I'd taken it upon myself to consent. See? Yeah.

Also, and this is sort of hard to say, my poor Malc, but I think I'd better say it now—viz., you know, prolonged drinking *does* rot one's honesties, kind of—if you'll forgive my saying so you'd already become somewhat oblique when I saw you in Mexico—I gather from Parks you've since got worse, though of course I take it you're now very much better again: but the point is, I shall want to be shown. I'm going to trust you, of course, that goes without saying: BUT, I warn you fairly, if you *should* let me down I won't lie to the Old Man. Let's have that understood, eh? It puts me in the invidious position of having the final responsibility of getting you cut off without a penny, which isn't much fun for me, any more than it is for you: it gives *you* a damned heavy responsibility to *me:* don't ignore that, and if it comes to pass, remember that I warned you, and try now in advance to absolve me, as you must!

Well, hell's bells, I didn't mean to get off on all this, it's merely that it's been on my mind. For the rest, we look forward to seeing you, and I hope it's soon. Mary goes up Monday to look at a house in Charlestown, which we think of taking—she really *needs* to be in town, so that her portrait painting can go forward properly. And if you and M come it will give us all I think a better place to live in, with more scope and freedom. Incidentally it's entirely surrounded by cheap bars and dens of vice, hard by the Navy Yard etc., so Temptation is going to be your middle name! Steel yourself — Otherwise, we'll stay here. In fact, we may have to anyway. —We'll see. —Mary will be answering Margie's good letter—she joins me now however in sending much love to you both, and best wishes for speedy solutions—   SIEG HEIL   Conrad

169: TO MALCOLM LOWRY[ch]   S Dennis Mass
                                              Feb 1 40

My poor old bewildered explanatory protestant Malc—! What a deluge of Kafka-like elucidation, explanation, analysis, qualification, apology, reproach, everything! Every man his own Laocoon group, complete with the serpent. But my dear fellow there was no need for it, surely—it's all been settled, long since, I thought, that you were coming—you don't need to tell me in advance anything about yourself, since I shall be a-seeing of you with my own eyes, and a-hearing of you with my own ears, and knowing for myself what has become of you, and what truth or lies constituted the now quite alarmingly hypertrophied Legend of the Lowry which has been built up by alternate touches from yourself, the O M, Parks, Margerie, and not forgetting Maurice Carey. Seen in its queer total, I can assure you, it doesn't make sense: it's the goddamndest farrago of inconsistencies I ever did see, and as hollow as a cream puff. No, let's let go of all that, and just sit tight till you get here. As for my suggestion that it would be wisest and best and most honest to tell the O M now something of the Margie thing, I still think so; but, I'll agree to waiving that for the time being, with the understanding that maybe we'll do it a little later. So, come along now, as soon as you get your walking papers, and then we'll begin to shape our future as we think best. Whether here or in Boston. . . . Conrad

Will you thank M. Carey for his letter, on my behalf—and tell him I *much* appreciated it—? It was very nice of him.

170: TO MALCOLM LOWRY[ch]   S Dennis Mass
                                                                Feb 21 40

Just a line, or a between the lines, Malc, to signal our continuing presence here, with faces westward turned hopefully, not to say prayerfully, for your wellbeings. What news—if any? I trust the novel goes forward ventre a terre, and if the Labour board would only come to bat and beckon you in—! But anyway, let me have a card or something. Here, we go from winter to winter—day after day of snow and freezing winds housebound, shivering marooned—if it weren't for the cocktail hour our courages would have given out. No end to it. But I suppose really another two weeks should see the winter's bloody back bloody broken: I can only say if it isn't, ours will be. I re-read most of the Lighthouse, and with much increased interest, respect, and delight. If you could haul out the audenesques, which are obvious and usually detachable by the unit. I think a small book might be put together, and *good*. Perhaps first sending some to Poetry. But I'd like to go over them with you when you come. Meanwhile, I've sent the whole shebang, Ballast, Lighthouse and Address, up to Bob Linscott for a general report and suggestions. His first brief note, before he'd gone far, merely says he finds Address "tainted with genius" but unpublishable, wishing you'd expended your talents on a more useful theme etc., and adds that he's now reading the pomes with enjoyment. I'll doubtless hear more from him quite soon. I thought his hardboiled practical eye might be useful to us. . . . Mary's off shopping at Hyannis in a blinding blizzard, with Ruth Whitman, while I type at the window, facing a white and whirling world—I think it's Lapland, and I'm a witch. . . .   Conrad

171: TO MALCOLM LOWRY^{ch}   S Dennis
                                                      Feb 29 40

My dear Malcs—   just a swift line to try and catch the air mail—yrs just received, and already out of date, old fellow, for I cabled the O M last Tuesday, the 27th, urging him to transfer you to Montreal immediately on the ground that I believed Vancouver environment most unsuitable, and offering to assume responsibility for you on any arrangement he wished. I've also written to an old friend of mine a painter Kenneth Forbes in Toronto, to ask if he'd sort of sponsor you if you came to T., or recommend someone if to Montreal. So now we wait for the O M's next move—and I done all I could swelp me. This must go off now to wunst, so chin chin, cheery ho and all our loves—   Conrad

172: TO MALCOLM LOWRY^{ch}   South Dennis Mass.
                                                      March 7 40

My dear defrauded longsuffering Malc—   I've delayed writing chiefly because I had hoped by now to have heard from Parks, or some fragment of good news from anywhere—but no, not a word. I didn't like to report *only* the melancholy cable from the O M with its sad dismissal of all hopes for six months, nor *raise* your hopes with report of my letter to Parks till there was perhaps some chance of a chance. But no. Nothing. The O M simply said that you must stay in Vancouver, at the same address, till six months were up, and then reapply for entry at the same place as before: no possible chance of a removal east. This seemed, and seems, ridiculous to me: but then, of course, I know nothing of these regulations. However, on the strength of my feelings, I wrote to Parks and asked for a complete report as to the reasons given, names of persons who gave them, and so on, with a view to then trying to find someone in Washington who might at least *attempt* a reopening of the case. . . . I said to P[arks] that *I* saw no reason why you should not come to Montreal pro tem, at least—and then perhaps return to Van for the reentry. I've written to the O M to the same effect, and informed him of my intention to try to wangle things in Washington, on my own responsibility—repeating the statement of my cable that I believed your circumstances in Van most unsuitable, together with reassurances about your work, Linscott, pomes, novels, and so on. In short, my dear old Malc, I've done all I could think of. And of course if there proves to be any chance whatever, or so small whatsumever, I'll go on trying. But it looks bad, I admit, and so I suppose you will be wise to decide now that you must somehow manage to stick it, AND above all try to get the Volcano done quam cel. [*Under the Volcano*] That will or should comfort you to do, that and whatever you decide to do as well—some more pomes???—and more to the point, it will be a help all round if you can get the Mss to me for Linscott while he is still freshly interested. Try to do it, now, and do it well, too—really I think we might get somewhere with it. For you sound in good form, and I find myself believing from the tone of your recent letters that the work you are doing must be good. But above all, don't permit yourselves to be depressed: no use now in that: you'll only risk a hurt to everything. Think, if it will help you at all, that we're keeping our eyes on you, and waiting to see you, and will be here for you when you come: and how good that will be. Not so damned long, either. And then we can expect at least six months of genial juice-swapping in Boston, if we get our house, or here, if we don't. . . . So keep the chin up. And get on with the work. . . . I've just had the 1st copy of my new book—they've made a nice job of it, I think,—and now we wait for its fate with fingers crossed. I think it has a good chance—not too highbrow (if at all), a perfectly normal and simple and *good* theme, simple, straightforward, vivid—and tender, I think—so that while it's a good job of work, qua form etc., it's also perhaps near enough the l.c.d. to catch on. Good god, I can't tell you how much we pray for that, nor what a difference it would make to *these* two lives. If it should sell, you never know, we might even come out to call on you! So add your prayers to ours if you still pray. —And now all our loves and devotions, on a grey day in March—   Conrad

173: TO MALCOLM LOWRY^{ch}

s dennis Mass
May 21 40

Dear Old Malc: yrs. received, and contents noted with relief: viz., that you've moved into better quarters, and are more independent and prosperous. Good. You don't say how you managed it—it must have taken some doing??? And of course if you could manage to get *east* that would be swell. And we've believe it or not acquired a ROOF of our own, this very day acquired it, five miles from here, at West Brewster, on the north side of the cape, high up, and with distant view of the sea, which is a couple of miles away: a fine wreck of a house, (the other one was snatched away from us by the lowest of chicaneries), and already the delight of our hearts. Rats pop in and out of a fresh deep stinking shit-shotten hole in a mattress in the attic, all the windows are broken, the floors bend under the foot, the rooms stink, the chimneys are falling, the rotten bulkhead door is shored up with seaweed, and the old W.C., outdoors, practically blows you off your feet: BUT the whole thing is going to be wonderfully rich and beautiful when we've scoured it and painted it and hung Mary's pictures on the walls, and there are lovely trees round about, and apples, and a peach, and grapes, and wild currants, and seven acres of pines, and a cranberry bog, twenty feet below, which in spring becomes a pond. The house sits there among the spruces as if it had been there a thousand years, upstairs there are umpteen unfinished cubicles which can become rudimentary bedrooms, so we are ready for the refugees when they begin coming—Knights, Nashes, Aikens, Armstrongs, the Royal Family, Lowries, or whoever. Bear us in mind! We are now in process of bespeaking a water-system, lighting, reorganization and repairs, but hope to move in within a month. Then, perhaps a fragment of a summer school. . . . while we scrape walls and paint them, dig the sand and plant beans, or sit idly among the hollyhocks reading of the sunset of the western world. Let us not, however, mention that: you surely, I feel, won't be dragged in: nor need you be? I hope to god not. I'm so glad Burnett is keen on Volc. Had he seen the new version, or was he speaking of the old? And I thought you meant to send it to Linscott? But of course as you think best. My own poor book is now dead: I saw the publishers in N Y and they were very hangdog about it. What boots it? or wrexall, for that matter. I feel a bit fed up, but nevertheless am girding myself slowly and rheumatically for another go, probably this time at a sort of fictionalized haughtybiography, Rooms, Streets, and Houses: it somehow seems to be essential that no year be allowed to pass without another book sent spiralling down the drain. . . . Ed is still in Rye, and wisecracking bitterly through the combfalls. Ourselves, we pick off the woodticks, and pour another gin and french, and count out the last dollars as they pass, but are as determined as ever to shape things well while we can, and with love. Nevertheless, I still believe, axe in hand I still believe! And we will build our house foursquare. Come and see.   love to you both   Conrad

174: TO EDWARD BURRA[r]   w brewster mass
                                           sept 7 40

Dear Ed: . . . We moved in a month ago, viz. Aug. 4 . . . after a simultaneous struggle to get that cottage clean for incoming tenants and this one habitable, where the carpenters and plumbers etc. were still working. It was chaos and no mistake. . . . And so it went, with Mary trying to get meals and make beds and lighten a little the darker corners of unswept rooms, and myself weeding the vegetable garden, mowing lawns, cutting down trees, shooting at woodchucks and squirrels, attacking poison ivy with a squirt-gun; and both of us wrestling with the problems of building and paying for the building. The workmen became so devoted they wouldn't leave, and actually worked two and a half weeks without pay, or in the hopes of deferred pay: we then had to shoo them off, lest our whole future be mortgaged. Result of everything, a three-quarters finished house, with wrecked purlieus and bad gaps, but pretty damned nice. It is really a lovely place. The country is as simpatico as any I've seen—rolling, wooded, with cleared patches, and far views to the sea, marshy as it approaches sea level, then fine broad sand beaches. Fishing weirs far out, far glimpses of Provincetown. Pines, oaks, deer, and wild life of every sort—quite alarming. You meet giant wasps in the garden, dragging giant caterpillars by the throat—six foot blacksnakes—woodchucks eating the lettuce— swarms of maggots an inch long trying like salmon to swim up out of the garbage pit—there are times when it seems better to stay indoors! But the whole thing is good. And we both thrive on hard physical work, and feel extremely well. Mary is at the moment scrubbing the kitchen—I spent the morning scything tall grass and

247

weeds and poison ivy, taking an occasional shot at a red squirrel who is trying to nest in the outhouse. Summer folk have largely gone—our road is very quiet—life is simple. (If it weren't for the daily paper and the wireless, dammit.) (The wireless this minute reports that Princess Martha of Norge is arriving this p.m. at Hyannis for a month on the Cape.) On Saturday we had a house-warming for the builders and masons, with a sprinkling of others—everyone got tight as ticks, and we ended by having dinner at a quarter to eleven, quite spanish dearie, and much fun was had. If ever there was a time when drinking served a useful purpose by gosh it's now. We heard last week that the [Henry] James house was gone—I hope it's not true. And what else? I suppose we shall never know, despite your ingenious use of hippogriffs etc. I had only just had a letter from Kitty Buchanan when your news about James came—I don't dare write to her. Poor creatures. She told of spending a week's holiday in Wales with him, he on leave, in July—I suppose she must have known only too well it couldn't last. I'm glad you see something of the McK's—I really must write to them. Trouble is, we get the most awful feeling here that a letter will never get to you fellows, or that England will suddenly disappear. Papers most depressing. We pray for an early and dark winter. Thank goodness for the destroyer exchange, which I believe conceals more than meets the eye—I think papa R has slipped something over—practically an alliance with Canada, and with these new bases ditto with England—predictions here are now heard that we'll be at war in 3 months. . . .   meanwhile our loves—
    Conrad

175: TO EDWARD BURRA[r]   Brewster, Mass.
                                           Jan 11 41

. . . Life here I may say is damned good—we enjoy every minute of it. The landscape is lovely—changes all the time—the old ford takes us here and there very efficiently, if noisily, she farts furiously whenever we try to slow down—we get to a movie about once a week, and once a week M has her art class, with Ruth Whitman and W. Robinson, which is fun—and for the rest it's read a little work a little walk a little, through woodpaths or to the beach, and at six the trampling and splashing of the buffalos going down to the old gin-hole for a souse, and then dinner at an indeterminate hour with

248

everyone a little tight, and so to bed. We had a fantastic time trying to get poor Uncle Alfred [Potter] buried—first, the Uncle's ashes got lost, and we had to go to New Bedford to find 'em—then we were told we couldn't bury him because no permit had come from California—unless, someone suggested, the permit was inside the box. We unwrapped and pried open the little cedar box, in the ford, and finding another cardboard box (very like a bonbon box) inside the cedar, dared go no further. But in the offices of the Cemetery Board we tried again, opening even the bonbon box, which to our dismay turned out just to be the Uncle himself, spilling a few pink ashes on the mahogany desk: these I blew on to the floor unobtrusively at a suitable opportunity. Everyone was a trifle shocked by all this—but there was nothing for it, we had to take him back to Brewster and wait for the permit. John Hay was I think a bit upset at the notion of our carrying the poor uncle round thus casually,[1] and also at our having him in the house for a week, till the permit came. But the second trip to New Bedford was more successful. The permit had come, the little grave had been dug, we saw the cedar box into the ground, and then repaired to a good lunch and some drinks. (Time before, we went to our own former little cafe—just the same.) . . . For goodness sake do take out your pics before they glue themselves to the glass. I wish somebody would take the place [Jeake's House]—I can't pay either rent or rates, and god knows what will become of it and of my treasures. I wish too you people wd move from Rye, which I have an awful feeling is going to be in the path of something pretty dreadful sometime soon. Most here are sanguine about the repelling of an invasion, but a few think the germans will succeed before we can get sufficient planes and guns etc. across. There is now no longer any question of our doing all we can—simply a question of *time*. Which little adolf knows. Dammit. I loved the review of Pearsall Smith on milton, with Ezry's pants taken off—I look forward to that book. [*Milton and His Modern Critics*]. I've just been reading the latest cantos, a few quite fine, but sawdust for the most part, say what you will . . . I'm thinking of writing a novel all about dear little Rye—but dont breathe a word of it sweetheart. We'll be sending you a lot of mags in a few days— some pearls of great price believe me.   Much love from us both, Ed— Conrad

1. John Hay, a young poet and naturalist, had come to study with C A before entering the army. He later built a house in Brewster and was one of the Aikens's closest friends.

Brewster Mass
                                                                        feb 8 41

Dear Malcolm: How curious. Three days ago I wrote Bob Linscott and asked him if he would use his good offices to appease Edmund Wilson, whom I feared I had offended, or with whom I
thought I had disgraced myself. Viz., last December, writing to Wilson a propos of a delayed review (delay due to a very bad case of
ivy poisoning, complicated by potassium burns), I asked him point
blank, but with apologies, whether it wasn't time the New Republic
gave Aiken a careful and considerate review, for a change—pointing
out that the NR had never, in the twenty odd years of Aiken's loyal
service, been too bloody generous to him. (Neither they have.) I got
no answer from Edmund, and instead heard indirectly that he had
complained, around New York, of my dilatoriness, etc. So, the letter to Bob, in which I repeated my sentiments about the NR's treatment of Aiken, sentiments which he now writes me that he shares.
—This the prelude, Malcolm, to my mixed feelings on reading your
own letter this morning. Of course, I'm delighted that you like the
sonnets, and that you want to say so. My only fear is, that if I'm to
be used as a kind of *corpus vile* for the attack on the Jarrells, Tates,
Winters, et al., me and the sonnets will come out at the small end of
the horn: this would naturally depend entirely on how much actual
space or emphasis you planned to give them and me, and whether I
was to be merely incidental. It makes me a little sad that after all
this time I still can't be given to a critic who is both intelligent and
not wholly unsympathetic; the fellow [Vincent McHugh] who reviewed King Coffin for NR wrote me that his phrase of it, "a little
masterpiece," had been deleted; of the reviews all the way from
John Deth and Blue Voyage through Osiris Jones, Preludes for
Memnon, Landscape West of Eden, Great Circle, and the books of
short stories to Conversation(?), not one but was tepid and pejora-
tive, not one that admitted or suggested that my work as a whole
was of any importance, or added up to anything. Frankly, this has
been a poisoned thorn in my side: read over the reviews of me some
time, and consider it! It makes a melancholy history, and not a brief
one, and compares oddly with the views of Graham Greene, for example, who thought Great Circle and King Coffin amongst the best
novels of their decade, with a kind of Elizabethan poetic power, or

Freud, who said G C was a masterpiece, or the Times Literary Supplement, which two years ago devoted half a leading article to Festus, Senlin and Punch, under the title Virtues of Abundance. ("The essential quality of Mr A's work is missed unless we realize that the pictures we see, and the plangent music we hear, are pictures and music inside the mind, with the border of the subconscious for background. Even the subjective poet shares, as a rule, the common habit of reverting continually to the world outside. And yet it is a glory of the mind to be full of images, and injustice is done if the images are always projected outwards and viewed in space. The inner world to which they belong demands exploration, even though, in order to turn inward on itself, the consciousness must do violence to its natural bent. In the extreme kind of introspection Mr A is a pioneer, his imagery recalling at times that of Thompson" etc.) —Well, if I thus labor the point a little too much, it's, as I say, because the whole thing has been just now on my mind, and your letter comes so luckily a propos. The sonnets have had a very bad press—that is, they have had *no* press. No reviews in Sunday Times or Tribune, nor indeed in any of the better spots—Time, etc. One nasty one by Bogan in NYorker, that's about all. So, my real worry is simply whether they, and I, in a falling Aiken market, can survive one more such slaughter as you outline. And as I remarked above, it all depends on how much you plan to emphasize, in your rebuttal, *my* plight. If considerably, then I suppose I might even profit somewhat by it. But as I see it, it's up to you anyway,—I'm perfectly willing to have you go ahead on the lines you indicate, and I think your *precis* is very good. (The sonnets *were* written to Mary when she was away, and when I was ill—how could you guess, or did I tell you?) And this I'd like to add: that I myself think the sonnets are amongst my best things, *much* richer and subtler than they appear to be. I find some people are fooled, by the conventionalisms and formalisms, into thinking them mere rhetoric, or empty: most such people are those with axes to grind. But I also, thank god, find that such folk as *love poetry* see them and like them at once. And I will back them, b'god, to become in due course a kind of classic. —As for the poet-critics: yes indeed. Did you see my assault on them in the Atlantic [August 1940] last summer? I agree with you whole-heartedly that they are a scandal and an outrage: they are in fact downright dishonest, they simply dont tell the truth!

—So there. . . . Well let me know what happens, and I'll keep my eyes averted and my heart full of gin.   our loves to you both—as ever   Conrad

177: TO MALCOLM COWLEY[n]   brewster mass
                                             feb 17 41

Dear Malcolm: Thanks thanks thanks thanks—your letter was balm manna panacea and goulash, all in one—and it came in the nick of time, too, as I was still staggering under the first-round pounding of mr. jarrell. (Baby, but he packs a mean wallop!) Seriously, it is a great comfort to me to have you say what you do about the book, for under the repeated sneers and snipings I had begun to wonder whether it indeed wasn't as they maintained a piece of unmitigated tripe: you know how one's confidence begins to ooze away, at such moments, and the profound self-doubts begin to take their place, in this world of fluid relativities. One ends by being ready to agree with anyone, anything. It's really all very odd—you wouldn't think 43 sonnets could so enrage so many people—what is it they're so mad about, what is it they are so afraid of—? And yet in 20 years I haven't had a book get so few reviews or such venomous ones. If I could believe the critics, then obviously it would be time for me to dig a hole and crawl into it, pulling my shirttail after me. Happily for me, a handful of plain ordinary citizens, with no pretensions to omniscience or an exclusive understanding of the Last Word, sustained me in my own stubborn belief that AITHH was good and would survive the belabouring. And your own very kind words, together with your admirable analysis of the sequence, puts the seal upon it. I guess I owe you a lot of drinks!

   You know, I have a lot of respect for Jarrell, as a matter of fact—I think he's damned intelligent and he writes extremely well. One of the few new people of the past two years whom I always go out of my way to read, as it happens, and for that reason I'm all the more troubled by his—shall I put it mildly—disapproval. Obviously he was annoyed by my Atlantic article, and my living in England, and my coming back from England, and my plea for romanticism —but why should this add up to such a monstrous hate? I confess I don't see it all, the ramifications of the party-lines in the present battle of the books becomes too complex and changes too often for any careful or exact scrutiny. But fun, just the same. I think the Tate-to-Blackmur-to-Winters-to-Brooks (Cleanth)-to Ransom roundelay is becoming a menace, and with widening rings, and ought to be dealt with, but they're tough babies. And that O-so-private language of theirs! Jesus.

Well—I look forward to the article. But I'm already feeling a hell of a lot better, for which I'm grateful to you.

When it gets to warmer weather, we meditate spurting down through Conn. in your direction, in our beautiful 1931 Ford, to pay a round of calls,—if pressed we'd spend a night with you.   as ever   Conrad

178: TO MALCOLM COWLEY[n]   brewster mass
                                                    Feb 23 41

Well Malcolm I think you did a swell job of it,[1] very well balanced in itself, with malice towards none and justice towards all—you were more than kind to me, and justly kind to Jarrell—and I can only hope that it will do us both a lot of good! And the critics, the other critics, as well. Thanks a lot. I was quite shocked to learn the book had had only 17 reviews—I suppose you got the fact from Pearce?[2] I don't subscribe to a clipping bureau, so the full enormity of the book's failure was happily unknown to me. Jesus! I mean, jesus. I hope this will be a lesson to us all, but just what it should teach us I hesitate to think. Something pretty bad—something like Play the Game, you dumb cluck, or take the consequences. Well, let's take the consequences—but thanks again Malcolm, it was extraordinarily nice of you.   as always   Conrad

179: TO EDWARD BURRA[r]   stony brook rd, brewster mass
                                              feb 23 41

Dear Ed: . . . Have you heard that the renegade english poet mr. W H Whoreden is living with a beyootiful boy in Brooklyn Heights, along with other gifted people who have all taken a house together? Carson McCullers, latest southern phenomenon, with two novels of faulknerian horrors, lives with them, writing about nymphomania-

1. In the *New Republic* (February 24, 1941) Cowley answered Jarrell's attack on C A.
2. Cap Pearce, of Duell, Sloan and Pearce, C A's publisher.

cal horses, ladies who cut off their nipples with scissors, half wits and such, and who do you think also lives with them dearie—who but Gipsy Rose Lee? I suppose she drops in for a five o'clock teas. All very odd, *I* think—and is occasioning Talk. Dunstan Thompson is planning to go to see them in their little perfumed menagerie, and I long to have his report. What things do go on, to be sure.

The above mentioned carson mccullers is a gal of 22, who lives on whisky, has a permanent fever of 101, plays all of bach by heart, and is given only two years to live. Linscott says she is the most obvious genius he ever met. I think I must get the new book, and send it on to you—I think she can write, if only she'd let go of the horrors. (In Faulkner's last, I'm told, the hero is in the act of buggering a cow when the cow defoecates. Pretty!) I think that is about all for today. Malc sends me a photo of Margie in which she looks both pretty and jolly—what a relief! . . .   love from us both   Conrad

180: TO MALCOLM LOWRY[b]   brewster mass
                                        feb 23 41

Bless you Malc, and bless Margie too for all the glowing words and numbers and phine phlattering phrases about my little dead sonnets—how good of you both, thanks thanks and thanks again! I rushed to re-read the ones you liked, to see if they were ones *I* liked—it's always such fun to read one's own things through somebody else's eyes, don't you think?—a kind of twice reflected narcissism. And agreed in many cases, though occasionally with a preference for others—which is only natural. Very comforting altogether, for such reviews as this book has *had* have been *private* reviews, like yours, viz., in letters—the press reviews have been few. This culminated in an attack by Jarrell in the N Republic two weeks ago, and a reply, attacking Jarrell and poet-critics by Cowley, the week after. Whether his generous remarks can resuscitate the book, at this late date, I incline to doubt. All very sad. The galilean note I hadnt noticed—in fact I'd have said if anything that *that,* if at all, might be more prominent in Time in the Rock than here, where the weltanschaung is more lucretian, more pagan—but then one never knows! And interesting anyway. As for the portrait of the husband and father, the kids, the cats, the kitchen—well, I dunno, that seems to me not so adapted to my purpose, which was a celebration of joy-in-love, and in defiance of fate, zero, death, time, space, terror, god, and everything—namely, in defiance of *knowledge*. This in turn called for the grand manner, sort of—and your suggested gemütlichkeit would hardly accord, I think? Perhaps Conversation contains the portrait you want. —How nice to have your pictures, and how lovely, may I say, Margie is—as everyone here delightedly agrees. Jane [Aiken] was delighted also with the cat! —Gerald [Noxon] reports you have got your passport straightened out—do you think of coming east? . . .   love to you both   Conrad

181: TO MALCOLM COWLEY[n]   brewster
                                                       march 1 41

Dear Malcolm: yrs received and read at breakfast with intense delight and amusement. Good god what a shindy. You must feel as if you were in the front line. I'm glad however it is starting something—it was badly needed not only by me but by everyone who gives an honest damn about the State of Poetry.

[Louise] Bogan is very funny—that about Conversation especially tickles me—I had always thought she might have very odd feelings about being half in and half out of that book—I turned her into a pianist (a BAD pianist!) who plays the piano offstage for a whole chapter but never otherwise appears! Of course I never consulted any lawyer—but it's amusing to know that she thinks so! and revelatory. (John Coffey incidentally wrote me a very nice letter about the book, apparently much pleased with his own apotheosis.) . . .

Mme. Gregory's [Marya Zaturenska] line about my facility and overproductiveness is interesting as a twenty-year holdover from the reign of Untermeyer—just shows how those notions will hang on. Fact is, between Priapus and the Pool—1924 or 25, and AITHH three months ago, there were only John Deth, 1930, Memnon and Osiris Jones, 1931, Landscape West of Eden, 1934, and Time in the Rock, 1936—viz., five books in 15 years—surely not so bloody overproductive. Another interesting item in her comment is that to the effect that *only recently* have my books been badly treated— tacit assumption being that the earlier ones weren't. *That* line might be described as the theme-song of my literary career. Each new book is panned—but in the background is the implication that all the previous ones were good. I have never been able to figure out just how I have acquired a reputation on a succession of books all of which were, as they appeared, either ignored or very tepidly noticed. Odd. Extremely odd. There were a few exceptions, of course—Time gave a lead review to Osiris—Marianne Moore did that and Memnon handsomely in Horn and Hound—but that's about all. Landscape got about five reviews, I think—few people ever read it. Etc. etc. etc. It would in fact make a very entertaining study in the dynamics of a reputation—and how unlike Tom Eliot's. Dynamics of reputation would be a good research theme, incidentally. Taking, I mean, a span of twenty or thirty years. Has anyone ever done it?

Well, here's hoping the Dirty Deal in poetry is over, and the Raw Deal too, and the New Deal on. Though heaven knows we can't keep *all* the poets and *all* the critics happy *all* the time. And thank god I live in the country, and so far from the Broadway millstream. Really, the amount of back-scratching and mutual softsoaping, not to mention of backyard cliquery and claquery, makes one a little sick. The Waltons and Deutschs and such should be somehow poisoned once and for all.

Very fine snowstorm here today, the landscape at her best—looks like more winter—but after that we may be coming down your way. Towards the end of the month perhaps.

Meanwhile, do keep me informed of all the dirt—as always   Conrad

182: TO EDWARD BURRA^r   Brewster Mass.
                                                  May 10 41

Dear Ed: your last two much enjoyed, your scabrous elizabethan style in its best form, and a relief to us too to find you feeling moderately gay in spite of everything—toujours gai, as Mehitabel the cat said, toujours gai dearie, and there's life in the old bones yet. Your hell's muster of hounds I would give my eyeteeth to say—did I say eyeteeth? A mere facon de parler, for I have no eyeteeth, nor indeed any teeth at all—in seven protracted sessions of novocaine and misery, with copious and painful and all-night hemorrhages afterwards, I have laid down my whole equipment of teeth for good and all—they're all out, and down the drain, and I now mumble a bit of sopped bread like a two-year-old. I go without dentures for two months, and then acquire a fine set of du Pont falsies, the very latest thing in plastic and cultured pearl—dazzling I shall be, and perhaps once more able to whistle. I wish I could see your pics—I'll bet they are something truly horrendous. I suppose with sinkings so frequent it wd be madness to try to send them over. . . . Boston was quite nice what I could see of it—we had a furnished flat for ten days in the very Heart, or should I say Twat, of the Brothel district, and such sights as we saw—a hardfaced pink pyjamaed whore, flatten'em blond, who had an obscure passion for a bicycle, which she sat beside, on the doorstep to her Lair, or else rode up and down the block—some very special form of perversion I'm sure! It seems the drains are always getting blocked up with little dismembered foeti—as Walter [Piston] remarked, "Little foeti didn't want!" (Can't you hear him drawl it—little feet I didn't want.) W's Incredible Fluteplayer was being played on the opening night of the Pop Concerts (Proms) and he appears to have had a very good year. . . . Rain here, east wind off the sea, and cold—everything growing greener before our eyes. And the Invasion moon once again filling at the end of the road.   both our loves   Conrad

183: TO JOAN AIKEN^r   brewster mass
                                          july 14 41

My beloved Fiddles—   . . . Jane's wedding was of course an agony for us, we not being used to that kind of wholesale sociability, and it was vastly expensive too, but I think it went off quite brilliantly, and that many people, including the principals, had a good time. It poured with rain, and sixty very miscellaneous folk buzzed and chattered in our four small reception rooms, and drank five gallons of very powerful gin-and-rum punch, and ate every scrap of food, and all but one slice of wedding-cake, that same being mine, which I had hidden; and photographers from the Press unexpectedly appeared, with flashlights, and took pictures of us all in a variety of poses—some of them are very peculiar; and Jane looked very pretty; and her new portrait, done by Mary as a present to them, hung in the diningroom, with a spray of Bridal Wreath, alias spiraea, hung over it by her papa; and the wedding itself went off nicely, Angus [Smart] frightened and inaudible, Jane clear and determined; and they escaped into the rain without rice or old shoes, leaving behind them their camera and other oddments, but taking with them my one and only raincoat. . . . A dozen of the more intimates stayed on, four of them for the night, and that part of it was fun. But the poor house next morning! You can't possibly imagine the state it was in. I even found scrambled egg in one of the fireplaces—and only day before yesterday, when the grass at the road's edge was mowed, a stray punch-cup came to light, abandoned there by some unknown strayed reveller. It was, in fact, a Party. Well, that's over, and I hope they'll be happy, and we've just had the first report from Saskatoon, of their safe arrival—Saskatoon—goodgod! I'm glad *I* don't have to live there—it sounds pretty awful. But perhaps in a few years they'll wangle their way back to civilization. Here, it is lovely, summery, green, and peaceful—our new rose-bed does wonders—catbirds and robins nest in our trees, and orioles too—the quail whistles us awake in the morning, or the whip-poor-will, the poison ivy embraces us tenderly, the wood-ticks burrow into our legs—we have pink yarrow growing at the edge of the lawn (which is now, ceaselessly mowed by aiken, really becoming a lawn, and extending its bounds into the wilderness) and wild roses everywhere; bouncing bet just blooming (a sort of bladder campion); blueberries to be picked everywhere now by the roadsides, and our own cherries; the vegetable patch lavished beans, peas, lettuce, and cress upon us, to be followed soon by limas, okras, oyster plant and tomatos; we have an improvised badminton court, and are learning to play; and the new herbaceous border on the Sunset Terrace is doing itself proud. There are more terraces to this house than there are to a Henry James novel—we have the north terrace, overlooking the cranberry bog; the Cow House Terrace, which includes the badminton court and rose garden; the Upper Terrace which is above the Cow House Terrace, i.e., further east, and itself on two levels, with locust and hornbeam trees; and the sunset terrace, to the west. Every night at the cocktail hour, we all parade around them all, glass in hand—or run, if the mosquitos are too thick (which they usually are.) In short, life here is GOOD. You must come and see. Though I must admit that last night, like many nights before, I dreamt I was taking a taxi to Russell Square, and stopping just long enough at Peter's Grill for a nice deep whisky and soda. My nights I spend in England, my days in Brewster. I'm glad you're taking up the pianner. Good. and still doing some pomes. As for me, I'm starting out as a new pote, with a new name, just for fun—I'm now (secretly) Mr. J. D. Cahoon, a young pote who writes very urban and slightly formal pomes about the Urban Scene—I've just sent out the first batch, and await the result with excitement! We shall see. If it succeeds, I shall continue, and gradually build up a new reputation, if it can be done. Fun, I think—and what a mean trick on the critics. Well, there we are, thassall, and we both send our devoted loves—   Cahoon

184: TO MALCOLM LOWRY[b]   Brewster Mass.
                                                                          Feb 12 42

Our best beloved Malc—   . . . I have been trying to finish a new book of pomes, and trying to sell them, for we have been broke, and in Dec and Jan a long article for the Atlantic had to be done, and read for, and sat over me like the belly of a cloud, preventing me from thinking freely or happily of anything else. (Jesus how I hate writing criticism.) Now that *that* is done, and the proofs dispatched today, I can look round me at the sinister world again, and begin to imagine—or try to imagine further devices for keeping us out of instant bankruptcy. . . . Rye, they do say, is spoiled. Gone tough, full of rape and violence, even murder; Canadian soldiers kicked to death by midlanders; chiefly because they get all the girls. The son of the Bryan who runs the Ship Inn was stabbed to death by his swiss wife the other day, and so on and so on. Blimey. Ed writes more and more gloomily, so do the Mackechnies. . . . You and Margie were damned nice about Conversation, and very flatteringly perceptive. Yes, it all comes down to a heavy defeat for the poor old male animal, a great victory for the élan vital and the more deadly female; also of society over the artist. Is he, you say, really in love with his wife? Blimey if I know—I'd guess not, what with that there other gal from whom he thinks he is parting. Wasn't he fooling himself? I dunno. But I think so. I wish the publishers had left my own title—THE conversation—it points a little more the form, as of one continuous argument on a given theme, reaching its inevitable conclusion, but embracing other oddments en route. That conversation is the theme. The deadly female thing working itself into the superior position, and dragging the male to bed, even persuading him that *he* was the one who thought of it by gosh. Holy cats. As for the Chorus characters, I would have left them out entirely, if I could—but feared I must supply just a scumble of background folk, for visual support; hence the slightness. They exist only for the sake of plausibility; furniture, scene. I'm delighted you liked it, however—that's *good*. How goes the poetry? and what else? and how the merry hell do you get money out of england, or is

259

it that you finally collared the funds in Los Ang? I'm delighted that you prosper, however, whatever the source. As for me, I've finished the new book of perms, Brownstone Eclogues, an urban series, —too soon for me to judge them. They are more objective/reportorial, than anything previous, I think, strict in form (pretty—mostly heroic couplet or quatrain, and formal in flavour) and with jazz and quotidian ingredients, not to say humour. What it all adds up to is beyond my own adding machine, but I kind of like 'em. Now I'm attempting a pseudo-autobiography, or attempting it again, with a new title: The Lives and Adventures of Merrymount Nipmuk. But no great progress yet. . . . And now I feel sure it's time for the glass of california sherry, in fact; so pop goes the weasel.   love to you both   Conrad

185: TO MALCOLM LOWRY[ch]   brewster mass
                                             aug 22 44

Dear Malc: it was fine talking to you in the middle of a dream walking, sandwiched between fragments of a Nyorker short story—but so brief, so brief, and I couldn't make out more than 50% of things said, especially by you—your telephone voice my lad leaves something to be desired. But it's wonderful that you're relatively in the east, even if alas driven hither by fire. How did it happen. Tell all. Did you fall asleep smoking, or what. Or was it spontaneous combustion of a hot manuscript? or dirty work by the japs? My conscience has been bad these many months, ever since you so kindly and carefully and skilfully advised me about the aiken poems for the anthology: I combined your suggestions with some of Bob Linscott's and a whim or two of my own for what I think is a pretty good, if somewhat too long, parade. Thanks be to god the two books are done, proofread and all, and come out I hope this autumn.[1] They are both greatly improved I think—especially the twentieth century one, which is really changed in toto and almost twice the original size. I have hopes that the two together will end by supplying us with a consistent and modest living: both have begun to sell in the last three years, each royalty statement doubling the last, until now they bring us pretty nigh a thousand a year, and

1. C A's Modern Library (Random House) anthologies: Twentieth Century American Poetry, edited and with a preface by Conrad Aiken; A Comprehensive Anthology of American Poetry, edited by Conrad Aiken.

rising. So I was glad when I finally persuaded the Boys to let me modernize them, as they were both summat dated, particularly the Mod Am one. We can now settle down to look carefully the other way, while we wait and see. —What other news? That Jane is here, white, thin, not too well, and preparing a separation from Angus pro tem, in New York, while she and he meditate on divorce: he remains in Washington. Sad to see the successors coming after us with the same sad missteps into traps and pitfalls, and suffering, and having to find out for themselves the hard way, and oneself unable to help in a durn thing. . . . Meanwhile Ed writes sardonic splenetic hilariously misspelled and diverting letters from Rye, with the buzzbombs splitting houses and people round him, and Bobby Mackechnie is back in Rye looking haggard and old, and Laura Knight as usual dominates the Academy with bigger and blousier and brighter coloured gypsies. Jeake's House still stands, somewhat battered, and serving now as a rest home for weary firemen, but it may cop one any moment of course—shall we ever again gather by the river? where old clubfooted Bill, the car-park demon, fell in, in the blackout, and went to sea? The Mermaid is gone, and the soda bottling works, and the Methodist Church behind Ypres Tower, and the graveyard behind our school next door was unearthed by a bomb and distributed seriatim far and wide, and the cinema flattened out, and the Bodega in Hastings together with the Plaza cinema, my favorite bob's worth, dammit—I fear many another gap as well. Maybe we'd better sell out, maybe it's all over, and if the house does survive I suppose we'd get quite a penny for it, dear dear. Or shall we try another part of england entirely?? a cottage in Westmoreland, a flat in London? a sooty house in mortuary Glasgow? or just stay here amongst the mussels and poison ivory?—and what about you?? —Our manic depressive arrives on Friday, and we await that with some apprehension: her husband says she used to throw eggs at people. But it's only for three weeks, at $85 per, so we figure we can stand it. Our social life seems to be odd. Alleviated a little lately by two fine parties with Konrad Heiden and his plump little blonde hausfrau mistress and George Grosz mit frau. Heiden and Grosz are enormous fun—Heiden very sly and subtle, Grosz a brilliant talker and humourist, and wonderful at kidding himself, and a fine drinker: all very gay and good, in a cottage overlooking miles of inland salt water: we all got drunk, and talked about oysters and food and german beer and the idea of giving germany to the jews and exporting the germans, and Goethe's elective affinities. And what else? Mary is doing a nasty job of handcolouring 100 olde huntynge printes, while I await proofs of a new long poem, the soldier, which new directions brings out this fall, and which will probably get me into a great deal of trouble. And I ponder that three levels of reality novel which I dreamt of on the voyage back from spain eleven bright years ago. And that my fine fellow is all, and it's time for a little noonday beer, the sun being over the yard-arm. Our best to all of you, and Mary will write to Betty as soon as the end-of-summer rush is over—she has a portrait to do, as well as this Thing to finish, and the egg-thrower to keep at bay. But then—. And give us a line yourself.   Conrad

186: TO JOHN GOULD FLETCHER[a]   Brewster Mass
                                                July 31 45

Dear John: Thanks for your letter—it's good to hear from you again after all this time. Shades of Great Ormond Street, Winchelsea, Rye, and Queen's Hall, god rest its ashes. I do wish our paths crossed oftener—I remember being awake at midnight in the Little Rock station, when Mary and I and Ed Burra were on our way to Mexico in 1937, and thinking of you as somewhere not far off, but alas not to be seen. . . . I've just learned from Burra that Jeake's House is intact, or rather has been completely repaired (from bomb blast) by the firemen who used it as a rest-home during the blitz, so we are very seriously casting our eyes in that direction. To sell it or not? to go or not? and what would life be like there now? and how to make a living there? . . .

    As for the anthology, there are no changes in the Fletcher section, and few elsewhere, save for the addition of a lot of younger poets to bring it down to the present . . . I'm thoroughly disgusted with Random House myself—they forced me into this shotgun alliance with Benet much against my will, are paying me the ridiculous royalty of one percent on the first 25,000 and two percent afterwards, and as if that weren't enough or too much have taken it upon themselves to refuse to print Pound. Think of it—fascism all over again! When I objected to political interference (Saxe [Commins] had referred to Pound as a fascist and traitor) they said that it really wasn't because he was a fascist or for any political reasons, but simply that he was a "dreadful person" that they were throwing him out. Complete hypocrisy. On my threatening to withdraw my name from the anthology, they offered to print a note, where Pound's poems would have been, explaining that I had wanted the poems and the publishers had refused to "print a single line of Ezra Pound." And this ridiculous thing is actually being done. I hope, when the book comes out in the fall, we can get a few people to write letters here and there so as to make them appear as they are—utter fools. I think the whole thing is quite shocking—as I hope you'll agree with me. . . .   Conrad

187: TO MALCOLM LOWRY[ch]   Brewster Mass
                                                    sept 14 45

Dear old Malc—   Months and more months I've been thinking of writing you a nice long dull leisurely letter, with all the gossip and juices in it, and now it seems to be that I must instead fling a few hasty sentences at you over my eastward turning shoulder—for away we go to Rye, Nov 1st or so, to spend a dark, cold, hungry winter in Jeake's House. Seems if we don't the dear Pile will be seized, and thus any chance of selling or renting it prevented, so the move is a forced one, and we most certainly don't proceed with unreluctant tread, and hardly rose-crowned. Grim, I calls it. Yet it will have its compensations—Mary will have a chance to paint, and I(d.v.) to write, with so much less manual, nay corporeal, labour to perform every day and all day long; and that Mary is ripe for a new development is vitally plain from a really astonishing portrait she achieved this summer, of our cromagnon gal patient; and as for old aiken, a play [Fear No More], based on Arcularis, and writ by an english lass named [Diana] Hamilton, has been contracted for and will go on tour in the provinces this winter. I'd like to be there to see it before its probably brief career comes to an unapplauded end. Also, the Soldier is coming out in London, and the sonnets [And in the Human Heart], so we shall at least feel that we are living, even if numb with the cold, hungry as wolves. Like to come?? Ed will be there of course, and the Mackechnies, and Tony Moreton is back, and still managing somehow to keep tight, and Joan is married and living in Ormonde Mansions, Southampton Row, and John seeking a divorce even as my first grandchild is gestating. Life, life, life. Gerald [Noxon] wrote me at great length in praise of your book— why not let it come out, my dear fellow? cut the unbilical cord? I'd love to see it. Send it to Bernice Baumgarten, Brandt & Brandt, 101 Park Ave., NYC??? And have you started a new one? I was grateful for your letter about my tin soldier. He had a poor press, on the whole, and a stupid one, I thought—so few saw that the real theme was the evolution of consciousness, with the soldier as incidental to it, and the socratic gnothi seauton as its core. Does one have to print an explanatory note with every book? I hope at any rate that my little book for the kiddies, A Little Who's Zoo of Mild Animals,[1] which has just been taken by the Creative Age Press, won't need such—a collection of nonsense verses, for which Mary is doing the drawings, nineteen imaginary animiles, and very silly indeed, but fun to do. As for life here, it has been the usual struggle against the ever encroaching wilderness, mowing and then scything and then sickling and then mowing again, and feeding the hens and capons, and burying the offal of fowls and shooting woodchucks and so forth. Useful as it takes off the ten pounds I invariably attach to myself in the winter months, and besides I damned well enjoy a really first rate sweat. And you—how does the new house go and grow? has the phoenix clapped its wings? are the saddleboards on and tight? tell all. . . . With which, well, bless you Malc, and our loves as always to Margie and your self—   Conrad

1. Published for the first time by Jonathan Cape in May 1977.

Letters 188–204: December 1945 to August 1950

C A *and Mary sailed from Halifax to Liverpool in November 1945 "to rescue Jeake's House," a voyage that was to provide the opening scene of* Ushant. *But poverty and the postwar English scene decided* C A *by March 1947 to sell Jeake's House. No buyer appearing,* C A *felt forced in June "to cut and run by self, leaving poor Mary to sell Jeake's House and wind up Rye affairs while I rush back to '41 Doors' in Brewster to cope with the rising Jungle!"*

In his ancient farmhouse on Cape Cod he had written Skylight One, *including "Mayflower," "Crepe Myrtle," and "Hallowe'en."* The Kid *was written in Rye. All were fruit of "that powerful seed of conversion" to his New England heritage, lodged in him by his discovery of William Blackstone in 1925 and again, while working on the* Massachusetts Guide, *in 1937. His five early long narrative poems, substantially revised, and with* Changing Mind *added, were published together for the first time as* C A *wished them to be understood, in* The Divine Pilgrim.

In 1947 he was elected a Fellow in American Letters of the Library of Congress and in 1950 accepted the Chair of Poetry with title of Poetry Consultant at the Library, which took him and Mary in September 1950 to Washington.

o   o   o

The Kid (New York: Duell, Sloan and Pearce, August 1947; London: John Lehmann, December 1947).

Skylight One: Fifteen Poems (New York: Oxford University Press, September 1949; London: John Lehmann, September 1951).

The Divine Pilgrim (Athens: University of Georgia Press, October 1949).

188: TO GORDON BASSETT[r]   Jeake's House,
                                             Dec. 30th. 1945

Dear G— Your wire received and relished, and it warmed our hearts, but at the same time saddened us, for it brought to mind o lasso that this was the first Christmas in so many years that we had not shared, and HOW, with what liberal and byootiful potions,

265

what ginerous libations, with your much loved self. Funny sentence, but the meaning I trust is transparent. Yes, we miss you and Boston and Brewster, and have both of us taken to dreaming of the little house very vividly and often—it had a way of stirring a conscience where seemingly none lived. Is it all right, we wonder? knee deep in snow with icicles over its eyes? and the drifts up to its chin? and are there still a few last sad peanuts for the chickadees to come to, dropping their litter of peanut skins on the snow beneath, o dear o dear? Perhaps I'll send a dollar to Charlie [Ellis] and ask him to buy some more and replenish it, lest the poor things become discouraged and lose their faith and habit. And meanwhile, as for us, well, here we somehow are, and Ed was here last night, as many before, till half past one, and we had visited the Mackechnies at six for a tot of rum and another of Scotch, and then had one with Tony Moreton at the Pipemakers' Arms, their last drop it turned out, (for the supply is sporadic and scarce) and then returned hither, where Ed had brought in his Little Satchel a half dottle of Merry Sunshine Rum into which we darted a squiert or two of bitters filled up with water, and had three fine glasses each, while my darling Mary gat us a dinner of cold chicken, galumptious bread sauce, gravy, boiled potatoes, and brussels sprouts. What more could you ask? except the many quarts of light ale which we quaffed out of the pewter mugs all evening? The house is dreadfully shabby and run down, dreadfully defaced by the Philistine firefighters—nails driven in everywhere, into panels, doors, walls, ceilings, windowsills, mantels—everything detachable has been mercilessly looted, even ripped bodily from their metal roots—no scrap of paint is left on stairs or floors, where hobnailed feet kicked and trampled—two wall partitions which were blown half out of place have only roughly been pushed back into position—sheets of wallpaper and ceiling paper are gone, or hang by one corner—floorboards flop up loosely under foot as you pass—leaks go bang bang bang all night when the southwester howls over us—a temporary ceiling of asbestos paper showers the kitchen floor with Little Nell snow whenever the wind blows—panes of milky untransparent glass baffle the eye in many windows, wartime substitute for the truly transparent—and leaded windows have been replaced with ordinary, or with bits of board—and yet, by god, with all this, and with only three pieces of furniture of our own, and of course our own pictures and rugs, the old place still contrives to stir our hearts. It has a tenacious dignity and serenity which apparently nothing can alter, not even the layers and layers of grime, soot, plaster, dust, grease, and plain dirt. It's a good house, and it knows it. . . . Explored the ruins in London on foot, again less than expected, and mostly where they don't matter too much. All around Piccadilly Circus and Regent Street for instance looks practically untouched, and Whitehall and Westminster,—only the Tate Gallery is flattened. Not of course that there aren't acres of cellar holes— as round Gray's Inn and St. Paul's and the Temple. . . . So. Psychologically we are better received than ever—taken to everyone's bosom, and on every social level, from tradespeople to the top. Frankly delighted to see us back. And the food and fuel are copious, cheap, and good. Only the egg eludes us save for a few that Ed steals from his hens. But butter, milk, bacon, lamb chops, rabbits, Dover sole, skate, corned beef; and until last night, more gin than we could really afford to buy, but did. . . .

. . . Laura Knight has been heard from at Malvern, and we hope to see her next month; Paul Nash has been having a nervous jag in a nursing home at Oxford, but is better and cheerful, and we saw two magnificent new paintings of his in London. May go up to visit later. . . . We had amongst other things a fine day in Hastings with [Ed], prowling into antique shops, buying chests and chairs, lunching at the Queen's Hotel, and in the afternoon regaling ourselves with the old deMille classic, The Sign of the Cross—marvellous. —This week, with constant violent gales, mines have been washing up all along the coast and exploding— gentle reminder of what might have happened to us. But today, a lovely still sunny Sunday, and the thrushes have already begun to practice their spring-song, we heard them tother day when we walked up to call on Ed, and smelled the winter heliotrope too. Spring is round the corner we hope. If only Brewster were too! Or you fellows—but our loves to you all and some, and let us have a page of news. . . .   Conrad

189: TO MALCOLM COWLEY[ch]   Rye, Sussex
                                                      Jan 22 46

Dear Malcolm: . . . It's queer but true, that I've managed to slide through 32 years of publishing, and into about as many books, and into what you might I suppose call a Position, without ever at any point being treated to a full-dress consideration as This or That; or by any of the more important of my literary contemporaries.[1] . . . What I get, of this sort, was almost wholly private: from my English pupil Malcolm Lowry, and through him from a long and still continuing line of Cambridge (Eng.) University young writers,—John Davenport, Gerald Noxon, Julian Symons, Nicholas Moore, *et al.*; a sort of "acceptance," in this country, and an influence, which if neither official nor explicit has been for me real and sustaining. . . . As for a preface, I may try to do a short one: Reader, here it all is, or most of it; no chaste little winnowing this, of desperate jewels, but the whole sprawling and awful example; and perhaps the more instructive for being so. Here you can see a young man who fondly thought he was seeking a kind of absolute music in word and verse, when in reality he was embarking, unknown to himself, on a psychoanalytic celebration of the consciousness of modern man, a celebration which took the form of five overlapping symphonies; Changing Mind; Landscape West of Eden; The Soldier, and two volumes of so-called preludes; not to mention sundry other false starts, dead ends, and intercalary experiments. You may not like him, but he is at least a little history of his time, and if he offers you no moral or social beliefs, and not even much belief in personality or character, preferring series to name and number to identity, he seems anyway to imply that there might be a kind of tragic virtue in this, and is for the most part consistent in his self-unwinding—etc. etc. —And I think it all stinks, myself! —Missed seeing Tom [Eliot] in town last week, regrettably, as I did a sosostris and had a bad cold; but I did meet little Dylan Thomas, a delightful gnome, and had a glimpse of Empson too.   Our loves to you all   Conrad

190: TO MALCOLM COWLEY[n]   Jeake's House Rye Sussex
                                 Jan 23 46

Dear Malcolm: . . . I like your notion of an aiken number of something, but fear I can't help you or myself in the very least. Four or five critics who have dealt with my work with under-

---

1. Cowley had suggested that an "Aiken number" of some periodical might be an occasion for gathering critical appraisals. In answer, C A wrote this letter, but did not send it. He sent instead Letter 190.

standing, say you? My dear Malcolm what are you dreaming of? No sich animals. Amy Lowell on Punch in the N Republic, 1921, or was it 1920, Marianne Moore on Osiris Jones and Memnon in Hound & Horn, Times Lit Supp leader, Virtues of Abundance, September 1937, and voila tout. Appraisals have been rare or brief or nonexistent whether in periodicals or books on contemporary poetry: in me you behold an almost unique phenomenon, a poet who has acquired a Reputation, or a Position, or what have you, without ever having been caught in the act—as it were, by a process of auto-osmosis. At any given moment in the Pegasus Sweepstakes, in whatever Selling Plate or for whatever year, this dubious horse has always been the last in the list of the also-ran,— he never even placed, much less won, nor, I regret to report, have the offers to put him out to stud been either remunerative or very attractive. Odd. Very odd. Of course, the pulitzer, but that was for a selected volume, not a book—not for Memnon, or John Deth, or Landscape West of Eden. . . .   as always, Conrad

191: TO JOHN GOULD FLETCHER[a]   Jeake's House Rye Sussex
April 4 46

Dear John: Your letter much enjoyed, and very good to hear from you, and here, too, which makes it seem quite like the good and not forgotten days, when we all wondered from month to month who next would be flung to the wolves by the knights criterion of the round table and their Parsifal.[1] Dear me, what a long sentence. . . . Rye is relatively undamaged, but looking pitifully shabby and down at heel. The Mermaid a ruin, and Lamb House windowless and boarded up, and the small garden studio gone, and here and there groups of houses vanished; but in the main it looks much the same, and the better for not being too damned trim. It has become a thriving fishing port, with 60 boats—which gives it a new honesty, all to the good. And England is in the main like that too—there's a new and different democratic energy of purpose in the air. Something very wholesome. Gentlemen no longer afraid to work with their hands—that sort of thing. . . .
    I was so glad to have your approval about my stand for

1. These *Criterion* dinners became at times, C A and Fletcher thought, occasions for the assassination of literary reputations. Eliot would be the presiding "Parsifal." For an account, see *Ushant*, pp. 232–33.

publishing Pound—I was taking my sole income in my hands, I may say, for the royalty on those two anthologies in the Modern Library is our lifeline, and [Bennett] Cerf could easily let them go out of print to punish me, if so minded. Not that I hesitated for one second—it was really ridiculous of Cerf and Commins, and I was quite astonished by them: I assured them they were just being fascists themselves; and when they agreed to print the "note" where the poems should be I predicted that it would be the noose that would hang them, as indeed now it has, and sooner than I hoped. Of course that symposium in PM was precisely the opening I was waiting for: I knew that all the thing needed was a good breeze of publicity, and Opinion would do the rest, without further help from me. Now that it's over, no word from Cerf to me: I don't know whether he hates my guts or not: but probably: as the thing must have cost him quite a penny. But useful publicity too, perhaps the anthologies will sell. Mind you, all the time this was going on the two *small* anthologies in the M Library, with the Pound poems still *in,* were blithely selling everywhere, quite unbowdlerized, but also quite unmentioned by Cerf. A wonderful bit of two-facedness.

You were right about the Shapiro book: I didn't *like* it as much as all that: I merely thought it important as a turningpoint and summing up.[2] Also, I ran out of space and time (for we were packing to leave the U S at the moment), and I therefor never got round to my chief complaint, viz., his view of the poet's function— namely, that he practically has none, or is at most a harmless byproduct and amusement. On the whole now I'm just as pleased that I *didn't* go into this briefly at the end of a review, for I wouldn't have done it justice, and to my mind it's of transcendent importance, as indeed the poet is; for I see him as the advancing consciousness and conscience and genius of mankind, the forerunner, firebringer, orderer and releaser; the one who by finding the word for life makes life possible and coherent, and puts it within the reach of all. The scientist and philosopher and mathematician do not make *whole* statements, because they leave out the feelings; it is only the poet who, by adding the feelings, or rather by transmuting his knowledge *through* the feelings, makes, at each stage of man's development, the *whole* statement; he

2. C A's review of Karl Shapiro's *Essay on Rime* (New York, 1945) was in *New Republic* (December 3, 1945).

always has the last word, because it is always the first—the poet was and is the one who invents language. Which is tantamount to inventing experience, or awareness. I'm sure you agree with me about this?

I'm delighted to hear you are writing again. Good hunting. As for me, I'm trying, but so far in vain, to write a novel; but the theme is difficult, perhaps beyond me, or not seen clearly enough; I can't get it to go; I can only hope that as it's the only thing that at all attracts me it may at last give itself up and consent to be netted and brought to the surface, fins, tails, poison-sac and all. My memory is now so bad—A dreadful handicap, for I can't carry things over from one day to another, or not with any certainty. Old age—yes. Though otherwise I really don't mind it—in fact, I think I enjoy it! Do let me hear from you again.   affectionately, as always   Conrad

192: TO MALCOLM COWLEY[n]   Jeake's House Rye Sussex
                               May 27 46

Dear Malcolm: . . . I did see Tom E at lunch last week, who told me that Ezra's letters are very obviously demented, and very melancholy reading. Tom is off to N Y on a business tour for Faber—looking older and thinner, I thought, but in good form. As we usually do, we kept carefully off any reference to each others work: the only literary mentions were of Orwell, who it seems is someone One Ought to Meet, and Dunstan Thompson (my former pupil) who astounded Tom and everyone else in London by getting to know All the Right People in two seconds flat. Which doesn't in the least surprise *me*. I had a pleasant day and night in London, meeting sundry folk, and among others Dylan Thomas for the second time, a delightful fellow, full of good humor and gusto, and a fine drinker. He thinks of going to the U S, which I'm not so sure is a good idea, but who knows? He might emerge unscathed. You don't say anything of your progress on the Hist of Am Lit—how does it go? I thought of you and it a few months ago when in reading a biography of Mayne Reid (an old passion of mine, Reid) I found a very interesting chapter on Poe, with a spirited defense of him against the contemporary charges of drunkenness etc. —Reid saw a lot of him in Philadelphia. Do you know the thing? I have no idea whether it ever was noticed or used, and thought of doing an article on it, but as that now seems unlikely I pass it along to you—Capt. Mayne Reid, His Life and Adventures, London, Greening & Co., 1900. It quotes an article by Reid from his magazine, Onward Magazine, 1869. Very interesting, as a more or less eye-witness and contemporary whitewashing of Poe, specifically a defense against Griswold. Might be a useful titbit? —Onward Mag was published in the U S but if you can't unearth it or the biog. let me know. —We were quite stunned yesterday to learn that the play, Mr Arcularis, is actually being presented at Cambridge July 1st, for a tour of 4 weeks in the sticks, then to the Lyric Theatre, Hammersmith for 4 more, then, if possible to get a theatre, to the West End—we are going to try to borrow enough cash to get to the opening night, lest there never again be another performance. Exciting. Who knows, maybe we'll sell the rights to a misguided movie magnet! Other news—Nicholson & Watson are doing me a Selected Poems, nothing but short things, about half of it from T in the Rock, and the Soldier is about to appear. And I've just sent off to Bernice B a new long poem, THE K ID—a highly peculiar opus of 500 odd lines with which I am disposed to be pleased. I don't know how to describe it—it's a epicule in doggerel, I think—a spiritual history of the U S in a capsule, with the Kid as symbolic hero and Wm. Blackstone as prototype. I began it five years ago when I was having my teeth out, came across my notes tother week, liked them (fortified by nostalgie—the Am. scene always looks so good from here!) and finished it in three or four weeks concentrated but euphoric misery. Christ knows whether it doesn't stink, but *I* kind of think it's fun. All very unexpected, and may entail of course another postponement of the Col. Poems. —Looks as if we'd have to stay here till spring next year—still a great deal to be done to the house before we can profitably rent or sell, or make up our minds about it: and besides, we want a little time in which to *enjoy* England, for so far it's all been hard disagreeable work, cleaning, painting, etc., and neither of us well, and we're now just beginning to lift heads and look about. Very beautiful too—but my god how the bureaucratic regimentation and perpetual red tape gets you down here—england is being turned into an ant-hill, there is no doubt about that, and even the working class shows signs of being sick of it. . . .   Conrad

193: TO MALCOLM LOWRY^{ch}   Jeake's House
                                                     Rye Sussex
                                                     Sept 4 46

My beloved old Malc: What wonderful joyful news that you've
at last twanged the umbilical chord and cast your Inferno [*Under
the Volcano*] off into the blue for weal or woe—and that it is for
weal I have never had the tiniest surd of a doubt. Good, good, good
and then good again, my dear fellow, and only of course what you
deserve, that the book should be simultaneously taken in both
countries. I hope you are going to send me one? As a matter of fact,
and as J D[avenport] has already no doubt told you, we knew of its
arrival here, through the old grapevine, and were already therefor
whetting our glee before your letter gave us the news more personally and specifically. And now, I can't wait to see it, and to
bathe in your beautiful sinuous changeable-shot-silk prose. But how
good too *all* your news is—do you mean you really went to see old
miasmal Cow'shorn cuernavaca again? Your reference is so oblique
and as it were parenthetically elided that I can't quite be sure it
wasn't merely an intention or a dream, or an eliotine velleity. If
true, if fact, how I envy you: both Mary and myself have so often
pined to see it all again, but without the physiological and psychological miseries that then beset us so persistenly. Ed too: I wish you
could see what *he* has kept of it: on our diningroom wall, over the
refractory table, scene of those prodigious alcoholic pingpong
matches, hangs the world's largest pen-and-ink drawing: eight feet
by five of purest beautifullest dreadfullest Mexico: a hooded leering
figure in the desert foreground, seated by a fire of sticks, on which is
a cauldron of dry bones, is about to throw a stick for an emaciated
cadaverous bitch, with enormous swollen dugs; the bitch regards
the stick-thrower sidelong with an ironic nerts-to-you experession
which is quite appalling: at their feet lie other fragments and shards
of bones, and a few (they look, like the crumbled skeleton of an infant) have been gathered into a wooden bowl. But, back turned to
this sinister pair, who are about to perform their sceptical and evil
communion, a classically serene figure, hooded too, glides away
towards the eternal magical hill-town that rises from the eternal
barranca and jungle, and the twin-towered cathedral, and the bitter
black mountains above it, and the afrit-black bitter clouds that

brew above *them*. The whole landscape is magically sinister and beautiful, and altogether it's probably the finest thing Ed has done—we're buying it on the nickel-a-year-for-life principle, as you might imagine. —As for these chicks, you see us in the throes of trying to decide whether to sell the house, or rent it, before going back to Brewster, with the contingent question of where, more or less permanently, to live: too difficult and costly to live transatlantically, in our present earnings-bracket, so what to do? . . . Brewster draws us, howsumever, and I feel this time that I somehow don't get my roots down into the english thing, and I fear I won't again.?? —too old. I like it, but don't quite belong. I've worked—did a queer pome, THE KID, which is a sort of spiritual history of the U S (old Blackstone, and Anne Bradstreet, and Boone and Crevecoeur and Thoreau and Appleseed and the Quaker martyrs and Kit Carson and Billy the Kid and then Melville and Willard Gibbs and the Adams brothers in starlight (Brooks and Henry) (all ending of course with Emily Dickinson?)?? the "Kid" idea as the american eponymous hero, whether as pioneer of the inward or outward wilderness, and done in a loose octosyllabic couplet ballad-like form, giddy and slangy in parts, doggerel in others. . . . it was promptly turned down by Duell Sloan and Pearce (just as the Soldier was) as "rating below my best work": and not only that, but they intimate they don't want me to *print it at all* before they get out my Collected Poems next year! To which I'm replying in the immortal words of mr. eliot, they can butter their asses and bugger themselves, and I'm looking elsewhere for a publisher, and hope to find one. . . . Also, behold me a playwright. No doubt J D told you of it. One Diana Hamilton made a queer bad little play out of Arcularis, which, revised by the Co. of Four at the Lyric Theatre, Hammersmith, went on tour (opening at Cambridge, the Arts), and while on tour they having discovered that I was in England they came to beg me to work on it. Seems poor Diana, who had had a cancer operation, and now dying of cancer of the brain, and drinking herself silly, was incompetent to do so; so I accepted: and at Brighton, Bristol, and Cardiff did a travelling shake-scene, stitching-in purple patches, revising, re-inventing, and trying to make sense out of the incredible psychological hash their combined efforts had made of it. More or less in vain. The leading man and Diana's producer husband ganged up on me, each for reasons of his own; Diana drifted in and out reproachfully, drunk and unhappy; and the time was too short for proper rehearsal; but the thing was a *shade* better when it opened *on my birthday* at the Lyric, Hammersmeef, where Mary and Joan and Jane and I attended. Fun. Taught me a very great deal, from which if I live long enough I hope to profit. The reviews were so-so—not too bad, not too good, with a savage and very funny onslaught by old [James] Agate. But though it had done well in the provinces, it flopped dismally in town, and ceased with scarce a sound at the end of its run ten days ago. I think now I'll try a play or two of me own! —We plan to leave in Nov. or Dec., if we can manage it,— for N Y and Brewster. Let me have a line before that?   and our loves to you both—Conrad

194: TO JOHN GOULD FLETCHER[a]   Jeake's House Rye Sussex
Dec 6 46

My dear John: It gave me a great deal of pleasure to have your letter—you are one of the people I most miss here, and I so often wish you were in England or London, though God knows not at Sydenham. Alas, just as I wish Harold Monro were in Devonshire Street, and John Freeman in the Anerley Road, and Robert Morss still with Ginn and Company in Queen Square. And our dead Paul Nash, who died last July, in Rye or Iden—you and these were my friends here, and not one is left; I live a queer sort of posthumous existence, my friends now, the few I have, being in a younger generation, those of Malcolm Lowry's era at Cambridge, 1929–33—John Davenport, Alan Hodge, Norman Cameron, Gerald Noxon (now in Canada), Stuart Legge, Len Lye (gone to U S) and so on—and they are good fellows, and gifted, and I like them immensely—Davenport is a most generous and delightful person, an admirable friend—but they are not the same thing. Are there limits to what one can give and take in friendship? I suspect so. I find I really mourn these dear people, and that nothing can replace them for me, not quite. Paul, in a way, most of all—we became very close during the last ten years, though latterly we seldom wrote and in the war years of course didn't see each other—but I think our visions, whatever one means by that, corresponded, so that I was, a very little, the poet in him, he a very great deal the painter in me. He was the most *English* genius and the genius most conscious of English landscape painting, with all of its moods and tenses miraculously and calligraphically and *lovingly* caught by that all-seeing hawk's eye of his. I loved him dearly and I miss him dreadfully; for without him England doesn't any longer seem to me to be quite itself. . . . We went to Oxford in the spring and had tea with him, a nurse in attendance—pathetically frail, an intense light burning brighter than ever through the thinnest of clay, his eyes more beautiful than ever, too—an extraordinary radiance and joy. He showed us, ominously, a collection of photographs of all his life's work, chronologically arranged; and what a life's work—even *I* had really no conception of its tremendous range, both in subject and style, yet inevitably evolving from one stage to another and all of a piece—the whole history of a tremendous *love.* I'm sure he knew he was beyond life—in fact he spoke of it. He died in his sleep while on a "holiday" to the south coast. . . .

I'm sending you a copy of the English edition of The Soldier. It differs a little from the American. I'm so very pleased that you like it, and Crepe Myrtle: the latter has evoked not a single comment since it appeared, and the former, as you know, very few, and very guarded. I don't mind much—Used to, but no more. I was always outside the main "thing," and this worried me when I was younger; now I see that it has its advantages. Linscott told me two years ago that [Horace] Gregory had told *him* that he was going to be "rough with Aiken"—perhaps my review of himself and [his wife] Zaturenska in the N Republic had annoyed him. But I really don't care what he says, and am not even curious to see it. I never met him. Just the same, I think it was most awfully generous and kind of you to write him about it—thank you. And thank you much more for telling me that you like these new things: beginning with the sonnets, I have been turning myself inside out, or is it outside in? anyway, moving over to an objective-subjective instead of the subjective-objective; the Eclogues, Soldier, Mayflower, and Crepe Myrtle carried it farther, and I've just done, this year, a poem called The Kid which perhaps carries it farther still. . . . The Kid is *light in tone,* dares a little to be *fun,* and—(though it's a sort of potted spiritual history of America, with the eternal sandlot "kid" and badlands "Kid" as its symbol, and William Blackstone as its first hero, as Melville and Willard Gibbs and the Adams brothers are the last)—eschews the portentous, declines to be rigid or pseudo-intellectual or Kierkegaardian or solemn, cuts corners, simplifies, and rollicks its way in carefree octosyllabic couplets as apparently innocent as a backwoods ballad! These Linscotts and Tates, with their blinkered passion for late-Beethoven-or-superheterodyne-Eliot-quartettes—! They'll be the death of poetry, if we don't look out—or at any rate the death of *us*. Not an atom of unwarped *innocent* judgment or clear-eyed taste left in the lot of them. They don't, as the lowly [Witter] Bynner once remarked of Harriet Monroe, know a poem from a broomstick. Yes, the Auden influence has been lethal: I respect the guy, but I can't like him. The poetry of undigested intellectual formula, with its ever-so-casual off-hand psychological-economical-sociological aggregates, and its typically homosexual fear and shame of love—to think that we should be delivered over to *this* generation for slaughter! Though I suppose the tumbril is a tumbril, no matter what it looks like, and a ride is a ride, whoever it is that takes us for it, and *their* turn, to be thanklessly used as literary fertilizer, or spiritual compost, or crammed into oblivion, just as certain.

As a matter of fact, I'm not so dismal about it as I perhaps sound. I enjoy it all immensely, and propose to do so *con brio* as long as I can eat, drink, and keep my eyes open. . . .   as always, affectionately, Conrad

195: TO MALCOLM LOWRY[ch]   Jeake's House
Rye, Sussex
Feb 23 47

My dear old Malc: your book is magnificent, magnificent, magnificent. I'd have said so much sooner, but I'd been expecting a letter to accompany it, and waited, alas in vain, for that; but now, first comes a wandering jew of a Christmas card, which has been everywhere from New Orleans to Brewster, before flapping the Atlantic; and scarcely less battered and travelled, a postcard from Port au Prince in Harry Murray's and Hart Crane's Haiti; and as both of them are months old I therefor begin to despair of a letter, and launch one myself. I did, however, write to your publishers, and I did send them as soon as I could, a pitifully inadequate blurb, which I can only hope was not far too late and in any event useless: I had then not finished the book, but as book and Reynal & H's letter had themselves taken six weeks to arrive, I thought a quick contribution might be better than none. I said then in my letter to R & H that I had some misgivings about the book qua *novel:* I think I still have, perhaps: though as to that I shall wait till I have read it again. But mind you I don't mean that as a material complaint at all, for as a piece of literature it is a genuine bona fide first cut off the white whale's hump, godshot, sunshot, bloodshot, spermshot, and altogether the most aiken-satisfying book I've wallowed in for a generation. My god how good to be able to relish the english language again, to have it all vascular with life and sensation, as quiveringly alive shall we say as a butterfly on a dunghill—! It is all so beautifully and *easily* done—the elisions and transitions and ellipses and parentheses and asides and time-notations and recapitulations and minatory fingerposts—how infinitely satisfactory to a writer to see all *that* so incomparably well done and understood! And that, only the beginning; for of course in the end it's the richness and perceptiveness of your observation that really feeds the book and makes it, the unsleeping eye and ear, whether inward or outward. O baby, o baby, o baby, it's marvellous Malc, and I hug it to my bozoom. —Of the characters, of course it's all too easy for me to see the Malc-constituents (and dare I mention now and again the aiken-constituents) that go to their makeup: but the Consul you make wholly real and superb; even for me, who can see wheel and lever at work: yes, the great genial drunk to end all drunks, the Poppergetsthebotl of alcoholics! he will become famous. The others, I'm not so sure of; Hugh's constituents are again for me privately too easily traceable, and he never becomes quite real or wholly seems to have a function,—perhaps a second reading will show me wrong. Yvonne too remains for me a little shadowy, and the psychological *reasons* for it all a shade obscure: one is never quite sure whether the alcoholism induced the infidelities, or verser vicer: and this weakens one's sense of the tragic by preventing one's believing that it is necessarily inevitable. I think too, good as the scene is (and by gosh it is) the death of Yvonne is possibly a dramatic or dramaturgic mistake, being itself so much a climax—it tends to double one's image somehow when one comes to the so much more important and (holy great cow) so absolutely superb final scenes of the Consul's betrayal, self-betrayal, infidelity-and-suicide-in-utero, and Blackstone-crucifixion-Indian-absorption-and-death-in-the-barranca. O my my my what a scene all this last is— unforgettably splendid, genius in every page of it. But better without the horse and Yvonne—? Yvonne just off? away? late? lost? on her way? But let me read it again. —Well, the book should, and will, make your name illustrious: up you go to the very top: and we

278

can only hope that it will make you a fortune too. Here, how-sumever, I find myself worrying as to whether the Rank and Vile will be patient enough for your slow unwindings, rich divagations, descriptive tempo: maybe they will: their own loss if not. You will probably, too, run up against ignorant pigeon-holing with Lost Weekend. But this sort of thing needn't worry you. All *you* need to worry about, now, is what to do next! Though even that, I think, won't really be necessary. You've been and gone and done it.

We're stuck here, trying to sell poor old Jeake: I don't like to say it; but there it is. Better so! And as soon as it can be, home to Brewster, I hope before summer. We're sick with melancholy, and all the attendant worries and frets and anxieties, and this unhappy people and land weigh upon us too. We'll be here long enough to have a letter from you—so let's have it? And in the meantime our very much loves to you both, and hail to
UNDER THE MALCANO
or
POPPERGETSTHEBOTL!!!
Conrad

196: TO MALCOLM COWLEY[n]   Jeake's House Rye Sussex
April 2 47

Dear Malcolm: . . . How one gets prodded and pushed, when the Young Critic begins to chirp on the hearth. Life becomes gradually more complex—I find myself feeling very stupid in the presence of *my* dear bright children, and very misguided and oldfashioned and WRONG, and in the end I just have to go off by myself somewhere in a corner to be simple. But to be thus simple under pressure isn't quite as happy as the lost state of being *simply* simple, alas, and to that innocence I suppose we can't any more look forward. Dear Jesus, this inchmeal business of dying! the tedious insistence of the old machine on your paying proper attention to its little details of obsolescence! The somatic buttons that begin to hang by a thread, and then are lost, and forever! I don't mean Jesus—I mean Christ. I mean I'm going on 58 and hate it like hell. —But this is perhaps the English winter—the great frost, the great floods, the great hunger, and the great thirst. Not to mention the great poverty, which of course is always with us, but just now at its worst. We are selling this beautiful and deeply cherished old house, but o god how difficult it is, not only to make the decision, and cut away from a lifetime of vascular attachments and geistliche echos, but to make the actual transaction (no purchaser has appeared yet) and get away with some of the money. . . . I have a dreadful feeling that some last minute hitch or regulation will cap the whole year of frustrations and obstructions and end by leaving us both penniless and houseless. I'm now reduced to selling all my first editions to raise the cash for our daily bread and gin. Prufrock takes us through Tuesday, North of Boston Wednesday, Ash Wednesday through Thursday, and Ulysses I hope and pray through Easter. I thought I'd feel badly about it, but am surprised to find I don't. What are first editions? One's own books, of course! —Well, anyway, we are desperate to get back to America and Brewster, and to escape from this land of gloom and muddle. I want to hear someone really split his sides with laughter, and I want to be able to get drunk, as a Lady arrested in Hastings the other day said, "in my own home." When it will be god knows: it might happen fast, and we want, at any rate, to be in Brewster by June. . . . The literary news is chiefly that just as I shake the dust of Rye from my American feet after twentyfive years of more or less fruitless endeavor a sort of aiken boom seems to be building itself up—the usual ironic time-lag. I have become a kind of literary sow, or littery, with no less than ten titles coming out. —A new pome called The Kid, a vol. of selected short poems, And in the Human Heart, Brownstone Eclogues, Time in the Rock, Conversation, Collected Short Stories, and Blue Voyage, Great Circle, and King Coffin put together in an omnibus with a preface by Graham Greene. It's quite indecent, and I'm glad I won't be here when the shooting starts. . . .   and our loves as always   Conrad

197: TO MARY HOOVER AIKEN[h]   RMS Acquitania
                                                 June, 1947

Well my Sweet, here it is Sunday morning, and rolling like billow-O, and I've had a whacking breakfast of prunes, sausage and bacon, tea, roll and marmalade—while stricken females dashed successfully or unsuccessfully up the stairs. Those who were unsuccessful were at once followed by a steward, like an acolyte, who sprinkled sawdust from a soup-plate as if it were incense. I've never on any ship seen so much vomit. It lines both sides of the corridors—

only a footpath in the middle remains clear. This, and the living quarters, and the toilets are dreadful. 36 in my "room"—it is a stable. The washroom is more like a cattle-yard—filth and papers everywhere. Luckily, I found the Grade A lounge and bar first-off, and established myself there, and have sat there in a coma ever since, speaking to, and spoken to by, no one. —The most solitary voyage, *and the dullest,* I ever had. BUT, the food is excellent— chicken, no, capon—sausage—*real* grapefruit—veal, good fish, steak and onions—well-cooked and plenty. So I've been, as G[ordon Bassett] wd say, a-building myself up, and today feel a shade more energetic and aware. What is more, and bucks the morale, the steward says we arrive Tues. night or Wed. morning—5½ days! Marvellous, if true, and I daresay it is. If so, it will almost make recompense for the really hideous squalor—*our* crossing was nothing to it. And be of good cheer my pet—This all looks more and more sensible *and practical* to me, now that I am out of the silken ambience of England and Rye and Jeake's House—I think it was all poisoning me—now it looks if anything *more* beautiful to me, but is relaxing its Fatal Charm—I feel like Ulysses. And so I fare west. Brewster begins to seem more than ever like the Primal Place—We shall see!   All my love my pretty and be well   Pinky

198: TO MARY HOOVER AIKEN[h]

41 Doors & 41 Adores
as of July 7 1937! [July 7 1947]

My sweet my pretty my pet—what, no Mice and Mommers? Nobody up? Nobody awake? *I* was, last night at three, and the night before at three, very odd, and couldn't get to sleep again, either, and so I at last (I think rightly and brightly) concluded that of course it was because I knew it was *eight* o'clock in Rye, and *someone* (most likely meaning me) should be getting up. What more likely. The unconscious at its little tricks again. Or the Id at war with ego. But nice as the idea is, I find it a little enervating, and again, as yesterday, dawdled in bed till nigh nine, to make up in the horizontal for what I lacked in vertical plunge. Heard Mr. MacAnistan driving up in his ramshackle truck (as unpredictable as ever) and crawled out and into my BLUE DRESSING GOWN and across the road, to find your letter of last Thursday, and yummy it was too. I do wish I could see the transmogrified garden—and I do think it's worth it, but I take off my shoes to you. And O dear, I suppose Daniels and Co [the realtors] are right and that we daren't risk your leaving. And it would as you say be folly NOW to go and lose heart and sacrifice a vital part of the safeguard-profit for which we are really selling—if we can stand three weeks we can stand another two months, I fear—though god knows there are many times a day when I doubt it. Last night I walked round the lawn muttering "I can't bear this another week, let alone another day!" And there are a hundred times a day when I come close to feeling that. True, when there are people here . . . I have fun but then it's worse when they go, and when I *am* alone here it's really, without a car or access of any sort, a quite dreadful imprisonment. . . . My main accomplishment was weeding out clearing and digging the rock-wall bed behind the green bed-bench, removing masses of celandine and crabgrass, and uncovering the lost flagstones, and dislodging a rat, which by gosh the clever Miss Mouse came and caught, and ate at once, practically in the middle of a squeak! Very uncatlike. On top of a huge supper, too. . . . But this my dearest and most beautiful Mary is supposed to be a Nanniversary letter—a sort of birthday for us—and I send it off tonight hoping it will get to Jeaky Monday morning. What a divine, good all-healing, all-sustaining ten years out of hostile time—for which I owe you my life, my sweet, and the privilege of loving you. Paul [Nash]'s Sunflower—no, Conrad's Sunflower. I love you with all my heart and am thankful to you as no one ever ever could be. And o my god how I miss you. If you should want to call me from Mop's on Monday at noon, which wd be six here,(?)—or would it be absurd???? anyway, I'll be at the Bar!   good night my pet   Pinky

199: TO MARY HOOVER AIKEN[h]   Brewster
                                                       aug 13 47

My beloved Pide and Sweet   —your long letter of yesterday was followed by Jane's today, with its dismal account of the stripping of poor old Jeaky—O dear god how awful it all sounds, and how glad I'm not there but how sad I'm not there too—to think of winding my dear clock for the last time—and the poor Mouse [the cat] howling—and everything stripped bare again as In the Beginning! How it reminds me of the first times—Jessie, and then the trip down with the Malc and Jerry to *see* it merely, and finding the To Let sign in the window by the hall stairs—and finally and best the

282

arrival with you and Ed, once more of course to a house relatively denuded or at any rate impoverished. Well: I loved and love the house dearly but although at moments I have an odd feeling of being emasculated without it, or at any rate as being somehow without reserves, and my own household gods, nevertheless I am not going to peek and pine: I know increasingly that it's profound good sense. Every day here further convinces me of that. Every day, looking at this and then reading the morning paper with its drear items from unmerry england. And the dear place after all served me wonderful well—I did my work there, such as it is, and it did it for me, to no small degree either, but tout de meme my work is more or less over now, I can let myself out to grass and have FUN for a decade, and god knows there is no fun to be had in Rye. O well, I don't mean I don't still love it in a sense more than I will *ever* love this, and I shall hope to go over every year—I'm already thinking of a brief spring expedition to London, and seriously, too! . . . This letter I will send to Rye—my LAST—because even if it's late I want it to percourse *through* Rye, like the notice on the bulletin board of a Club by a departing honorary member or guest of his thanks and gratitude. . . .   Pinky

200: TO EDWARD BURRA[r]   41 doors brewster
                                           nov 20 1947

Dear Ed: Home from Highanus where we lunched at the Mayflower (second class) after having martinis at the Mayflower (first class). Very tasty too. Excellent martinis made with noilly prat, and then breaded pork cutlets french fried and cabbage. That was me—Mary had new england burled dinner, viz., corned beef, a bit dry it looked. . . . we went to see Singapore, Fred Macmurray and the Sensation Ava Gardner, very attractive wench too, a little on the Paulette G[oddard] model and somewhat soignée but promising I think. A fine imbroglio altogether. We found eels at the 1st National, and pork chops, the eels are got at Yarmouth, very good indeed. We shall fry them. But holy mackerel how cold it is these days with no car top—our roof was blown off in last week's hurricane, nothing is left but a mesh of chicken wire through which we stare at Blue Heaven and gradually go blue ourselves. The hurricane was very fine: midafternoon it suddenly howled upon us and all of a sudden we looked out and saw that our biggest spruce had snapped

283

in two and the top half was rushing down the road like a giant broccoli in a hurry—the rain was horizontal, and came straight through the walls and round all the windows—drawing room was flooded—common room became a giant shower bath, the roof above pouring steady water through the ceiling—the uproar was magnificent—and alas five old and beautiful cedars all went down in each others arms like ninepins. Of course the power went off, and staid off three days—no light, no phone, no heat (electric furnace) no ice, no water. We were in a state of siege. Made worse for me by the fact that I chose this moment to come down with a mexican dysentery, and of course it was impossible to use the WCs—fortunately we have the Olde Chicke Saleon but o god how draughty it was. . . . Yesterday we lunched with Dolly [Lewis] and Mimi [Voorhees] in S Yarmouth, and Dolly told me about the 60 page letter which Malc wrote her from the ship when he sailed back to England in 1929—she promises to show it to me. Wow. What a Document *that* is. Dolly claims she was always hiding from the Malc in the Purington's barn. Ah those dear dead days. She also says that once when she went up to Provincetown, at the time that Malc and Jan were in residence (?) there, when they went in there was a sheet of music laid open on the piano, title My Dolly, and malc of course drunk on the floor. . . . Nothing has been heard of Genius No. 1 (Alma von Mering) since she went off to Carcassonne. Genius No. 2 is equally quiet in N Y.[1] And John Hay has just rung up to ask me to apologize to Kristi [his wife] for calling the Child (Susan) a Brat. O god. Life on the cape.   yrs   C A

201: TO HENRY A. MURRAY[r]   brewster mass
                                               jan 9 48

. . . Donaldson is I think one of the most golden people I ever did see[1]—I only wish my fear of Fathers and Doctors (and o kee-reist how deep it goes) didn't so effectively prevent my meeting them as I should: everything interferes, and, on top of everything, a funk all of my own. I was scared stiff, and behaved like a three-year-old baby. No kidding. My, what a ruckus my unconscious began kicking up—the dream-life became stupendous—all my dead friends ap-

1. Genius No. 1 was a novelist C A had helped; Genius No. 2 was a poet.
1. Dr. Gordon Donaldson had removed a skin cancer from C A's neck at Massachusetts General Hospital.

peared from every direction, including even Jack, the janitor of Hampden Hall—kittens lost their pelts from the tail upwards, drawing their whole skins off over their heads by nibbling at the inner surface over their noses, and as the shirt was pulled off, the body beneath fell apart in slices of rotten smoked salmon—in a series of such dreams my entire moral System fell apart, and by morning I was a mere tombfull of leftovers. In this far from philosophic state, crammed with death, I walked with Mary through a blinding snow storm to the Harvard Club, and this restored reality a little, and from there to Doom in a taxi. But how marvelous they all were—what could be done for an introvert who had introverted himself into a Knotted Nothing was beautifully done—among angels, Donaldson was an archangel, dispensing assurance and serenity and good will as if they were the very stuff of life: I shrank into my little cocoon on the lethal table, jumped high in air under the first needle of novocaine, sweated like a horse, and watched what I could of the World through the half-inch between towels that was allowed me: as this was a moving fragment of Nurse, I was driven back on self, and the sensations: once or twice so violatingly strange, with such secret etherial little private clicks of Intrusion, that my eye revolved in the direction of a faint, but was halted again on the nurse's shoulder, and the balance restored. Two deep throbs of wonderful revelatory pain—the very center—and after that, Time, rediscovered, slowing down to a human walk again, with D saying that the worst was over, that it was quite a hole, quite a hunk taken out of me, but now putting me together again, and then the reassuring faint kinaesthetic pain of the stitches, each a little more redly etched as the novocaine wore off: if was perfect, the timing, for by the time I was dressed and downstairs to meet Mary, the whole side of my head was in flames. For a moment, when we had found a taxi, my judgment failed me, and I told the driver to take us home, i. e., to the Noxons, St Botolph Street: but only for a moment: then I changed the destination to the Athens Olympia Restaurant, and four Martinis, and all was well. All I can recall of my dream-life that night is a fragment of conversation. "The wish is father to the thought!" "Yes: that's apparent!" Back to punning again, as if nothing had happened. So, you see, dear Harry, it has been a great success. Donaldson viewed me the next day, and pronounced it good: the side of my face, and ear, are still numb; I shave Someone Else, and cut him with impunity; I go back next Monday and Thursday for de-stitching; and there we are. And bless your heart.

Your note came this afternoon—odd you should suggest this lengthening of le cid, for the Brooklyn Eagle critic did too—so have one or two others, including Ted Spencer, who wanted John Jay Chapman enkidded—but me, No, I don't think so, though at one time I *did*, mind you. To the Brooklyn Eagle guy I admitted that I'd had misgivings about the length and proportions—and that I had twice added to it: he too had thought of it as a kind of overture to a Larger Something: but I don't think so. It wants to be a mixture of the light and the Idea, and I fear the slightest overloading with reference and extension would destroy the gayety and quickness: this, I think, the European critic sees better than we do, viz., that we *are* a Kid, seen against the Dark Backward, and that in point of fact we've only been here *two minutes!* —Howsomever, I reserve the right to change my mind, and to take your advice, and you may be Right. But again, I suspect every American will want to rewrite the Kid according to his own Mythos, and why not? Me, I'm comparatively ignorant, dammit, no kidding, and writing the thing in Rye often longed for knowledge I just didn't have. Perhaps I should have waited? but then the impulse wouldn't have been there? O my. . . .   Conrad

202: TO THE EDITORS OF *THE NATION*[ch]   Brewster, Mass.
                                                                        May 14, 1948

Dear Sirs: Randall Jarrell once before left me for dead on the dueling ground which he likes to make of reviewing, and I for one am damned if I will let him get away with attempted murder again (in his Verse Chronicle of May 8).[1] It has come to a point where poetry needs a Public Defender against this self-appointed judge and executioner—and it is certainly time that his credentials were examined.

Everyone knows of course that he can be very witty, and at times very funny, and he gives signs of becoming perhaps a good poet:

1. See Letters 176 and 177. The May 8, 1948, issue of the *Nation* carried Jarrell's one-para-graph review of *The Kid*, calling it "a surprisingly crude hodge-podge of store-bought home-spun, of Madison Square Garden patriotism . . . all banged out in conscientiously rough rhymes, meter, grammar." C A's letter was printed June 12, 1948, with a letter in self-defense by Jarrell.

but I suggest that these are not the only or the best qualifications for a good critic. And if Mr. Jarrell is witty, or funny, it is almost invariably with malice, and with manners that I can only describe as a desire to be personally offensive. (See parts of his inexcusable review of Miss Rukeyser.)

One begins to wonder, in fact, whether Mr. Jarrell is not the victim of some sort of Private Predicament: as if for some reason in himself—perhaps he will take us into his confidence—he is condemned in advance to condemn in advance, and therefore to look with glee for faults about which he can be funny rather than with love for virtues which can be praised. One wonders even whether he isn't *afraid* of poetry, or of those elements of the poetic which elude him, or differ from his own—one wonders whether perhaps it is *only* his own poetry which he can with entire safety admire, lest he find himself all alone in a world a little too big for him. The result is a kind of review which is not only wholly unreliable but wilfully misleading: it is simply not Mr. Jarrell's *aim* to see, or tell, the truth: he is completely irresponsible.

Luckily for his victims, and unluckily for Mr. Jarrell, the truth is in the end objectively ascertainable in these matters, and his exercises in malicious preciosity and highbrow autointoxication will be recognized for what they are: the attempts of one who is himself insecure to keep up intellectual appearances. It is the prevalence of this sort of smart-alec and pretentious parti-pris reviewing that still prevents our having a single good critical paper in the country, one that can be relied on in advance for criticism that is informed without being bigoted or personally biased, which combines an ordered sense of the past with a knowing gusto for the contemporary, and is based on trained perceptions and disciplined taste. And Mr. Jarrell is by long odds the worst example.   Conrad Aiken

203: TO ALAN HODGE^r   Forty-one Doors, Brewster
                                               sept 3 49

Dear Alan: . . . As you may have guessed, the production of Mr. Arcularis at the Provincetown Playhouse on Aug. 8th has kept us busy as two bees, mostly hotfooting it back and forth, 36 miles each way, between there and here, very exhausting. Rehearsals began in July, and by the time of the last performance on August 20th we were pretty dead ducks, and living, if at all, in a sort of coma. But god help us, it was a triumph! A real genuine sensation! the whole of Cape Cod excited about it, in advance too, as a result of the cast's own excitement, so that by opening night there was already a stir—an audience of celebrities, including the ex Attorney General, Francis Biddle, and St. John Perse, who had come all the way from Washington to see it, no kidding! And the play was beautifully produced and acted, and went like a house afire, much to my astonishment: for there were new scenes in it of which the effect *on an audience* was not, by me at any rate, foreseeable in advance. But it was these very scenes which actually turned the trick, thank god: they did just exactly what I had hoped they would: and the result, at least in Provincetown, was a sort of hypnosis of audience after audience which was unlike anything I have ever seen. It even did it with a very tough and drunk Saturday night crowd at the end of the first week, a gang of pansies and lesbians, who were set to break it up: but by the middle of the second act they were literally bewitched. (I report this not with complacency, please, but as an astounded eyewitness to a very curious phenomenon! Everyone agrees about it. Polly Boyden, whom Jane will remember, said it was like the silence of the gallery gods at a performance of their favourite Mozart symphony. It had an almost religious quality.) Well, anyway—there were more curtain calls than they've ever had at the Playhouse and cries for the author, repeated, so I am told, but the author, oddly enough, was nowhere to be seen, for he had hied himself to a low bar not too far away, and had his nose in a Tom Collins, thank god. All very satisfactory. We went up for six performances, making sundry small alterations (mostly cuts, but once, for fun, trying a happy ending) and now we sit with fingers crossed and wait to see whether we can snaffle someone in New York to do it. Movies are nibbling but not really biting. The actors and company are all convinced that it would "go" there. And Edmund Wilson, who saw it the last night, stunned me by saying he was afraid I had a masterpiece on my hands! Wow. So you see, I'm a little off my head. I do wish you fellows could have seen it, though—it was so much MUCH better than the English version, no comparison. . . .

much love   Cahoon

Forty-one Doors, Brewster
aug 29 50

Dear Ed—   well dearie, it's a long time between drinks, etc., but
as you can imagine things has been right hectic in these sticks—the
usual floods of summer visitors. . . . In a way it will be a relief
when all is over and I'm imprisoned in my cage atop the Library of
Cong. Tomorrow a party for the locals, sort of farewell, for which
the Bassett is arriving tonight. . . . Friday we got up to Wellfleet
for cocktails with ex-Attorney General Francis Biddle and wife,
with St. John Perse; somewhat alarming, and may have social Consequences in Wash, where they are quite the grandees. To hell with
it. . . . Well, Dylan Thomas never got here, maybe just as well,
judging from the reports. He spent a lot of time sleeping off his
binges at the Oscar Williamses in their skylight penthouse at the
Battery—Mrs. W, Gene Derwood, seized the opportunity to do a
series of portraits of him, just the head, and the story goes that one
day when he woke up she demanded that he show her his feet, and
on his refusing, hauled off and kicked him so savagely on the shin
that she broke the bone, and he had to be carried on to the boat.
This we heard from [the Richard] Eberharts. But a week later when
I saw the W's they denied it in toto. It also appears that kind
Friends who helped him pack at his hotel, when of course he was
blind to the world, thoughtfully packed about five hundred passionate love letters from all over the country, which naturally in due
course his wife would *un*pack. Good clean fun. In Hollywood he
expressed to Isherwood a desire to meet Chaplin, which being instantly arranged Chaplin then asked him what else he wanted, and
he replied "The most beautiful blonde in Hollywood!" So, Shelley
Winters was served on the half shell. Etc. etc.

Have now been to Wellfleet and back, and with a great conceit of
myself, for St. John Perse, nice fellow, said that "alone in America"
I practiced the whole art of poetry, combining the classic with the
modern, and with a sense of narrative and composition! You could
have knocked me down with a hot dog. He started to say it all,
much more elaborately, in french, but when I foundered he kindly
translated. As you see, a nice fellow. . . .   Conrad

Letters 205–224: October 1950 to November 1961

Through the fifties C A and Mary stayed several times each year in their flat in New York (the "Slumlet"), and in their house in Washington, but they remained "at home" on Cape Cod in "41 Doors." They returned to England—and Rye—three times, the last in 1960. And everywhere C A was writing. Ushant, whose complex form and subject had teased him since 1933, was written mostly at the Library of Congress. The poems in his next two volumes (A Letter from Li Po and Sheepfold Hill) were written in Brewster and in New York. His Collected Poems was published and two new collections—the latter complete—of his short stories. Rufus Blanshard edited a collection, the first since Scepticisms (1919), from C A's almost two hundred critical essays and reviews.

o　　o　　o

The Short Stories of Conrad Aiken (New York: Duell, Sloan and Pearce, September 1950).

Ushant: An Essay (New York and Boston: Duell, Sloan and Pearce, October 1952; Cleveland and New York: Meridian Books—The World Publishing Company, September 1962; London: W. H. Allen, February 1963).

Collected Poems (New York: Oxford University Press, October 1953).

A Letter from Li Po and Other Poems (New York: Oxford University Press, September 1955).

Mr. Arcularis: A Play (Cambridge: Harvard University Press, January 1957; London: Oxford University Press, 1958).

Sheepfold Hill: Fifteen Poems (New York: Sagamore Press, June 1958).

A Reviewer's ABC: Collected Criticism, edited by Rufus A. Blanshard (New York: Greenwich Edition, Meridian Books, December 1958; London: Mayflower Books, 1959; London: W. H. Allen, March, 1961; as *Collected Criticism* [New York: Oxford University Press, February 1968]).

The Collected Short Stories of Conrad Aiken, with a preface by Mark Schorer (Cleveland and New York: The World Publishing Company, November 1960; Cleveland and New York: Meridian Books—World, October 1965; London: Heinemann, May 1966).

205: TO JOAN AIKEN[r]   323 Second St Washington
                                     oct 4 50

Dear Fiddles: . . . This Lib Cong job is thus far pretty much what St John Perse told me it was, "not exactly fictitious, but shall

290

we say slightly imaginary": so little to do that I am bored except when I can do work of my own (which I am finding it more and more possible to wangle.) However, they say that presently it will amount to something more, and largely to begin with the editing of a new series of poetry recordings. Meanwhile, it's largely a matter of receiving visitors and answering peculiar questions and turning down invitations to speak or read. And yesterday and today the wretched business of being introduced to the Staff of the Library assembled in the Library theatre, standing up and making a bow to the multitude. Painful. But I survived. The best thing is my office, generally reputed to be the handsomest in the city, top floor, overlooking Capitol on one side and Supreme Court on tother, with view out to river and country too—all Washington. A fine stone balcony on which to perch, too. And a nice english gal as permanent assistant, who is of course really the Chair of Poetry and does the real drudgery. So you see. I disregard office hours, drifting in at 9-15 in the morning, out for nigh two hours for lunch, then vamoose at 5 to the awaiting orange blossoms. Washington is dull, I think, like something abandoned by a World's Fair, and immense sprawling suburbs, miles of—this aspect is pretty depressing; and the traffic terrifying; and the people reputedly dull, too. But against this are the quite fascinating slum negro quarters, on the fringe of one of which we live,—these are good, various, rich, human, everything. And the trees are truly magnificent, such a variety as never was, most of them unknown to me: I shall have to get me a handbook. Also the markets are nice—we have a fine miniature Covent Garden within walking distance, which purveys everything from brains and chicken gizzards to hard and soft shell crabs and the largest oysters you ever saw: like boats. Delicious too. Also there's a scrumptious fish market where you can buy jumbo crabs right off the boats, and eat your lunch of devilled crab and beer on a balcony overlooking the Potomac. So, you see, it might be wuss, if we don't just get bored to death; or go broke. For it begins to look as if that juicy-sounding $5000 [salary] might damned well be needed: and the prospects of saving enough for a visit to England have dimmed somewhat. But we shall hope and pray. And meanwhile a very superior tom cat, mottled gray, with a classic Egyptian head, has firmly adopted us: comes in every morning for breakfast, sleeps till suppertime, eats again, and having said thank-you and toyed with pencil-under-rug tolerantly, exits till morning. Very good arrange-

291

ment. He got it all taped in 24 hours—practical indeed.
. . .   much love from us both   Cahoon

206: TO JOHN KEMPTON AIKEN^r   323 Second Street
                                              Washington   dec 10 50

Dear Djones: yrs, etc., and right glad to have, and wd have said
so ere this, but as I've reported to Alan [Hodge] I've been laid low:
unused to office hours, and social life, and the pressures that go
avec, I fell to a lowly nasal hemorrhage that went on for a week,
not a drip or ooze but a pour, bled myself thin, and finalement
(we'd been misguided by a bad doc) had to be Packed and sent to
'ospital. Lost 20 pounds, blood count down to sixties etc. etc. but
thanks to it all had myself a rest and am ordered now to thumb my
Nose at the Library, and do so. Psychosoma at its best! Bad. And
costly. Much time for reflection, as I sat head down by bathroom
washbasin, watching life flow down the drain: how futile, brief,
how like a leaf, how all in vain, in vein: fascinating too to watch the
colour of the blood alter: and the fasts and slows: and as I said to
Mary, to think *this* quietist and pacifist should be the first to shed
his blood for his country! To be sure, grandpa Potter preached a
famous sermon from his Unitarian pulpit in New Bedford endorsing
the Draft Law in the Civil War, and then accepted his own summons, and was at the Battle of Bull Run, where he is reputed to
have fished a bullet out of an oak tree beside him, where it had
whizzed itself: but he shed no blood. And here, only ten miles from
that scene, his only (as far as *he* knew, when he died—more were to
come) grandson lost his, how typically of the family, as a result of
work in a library! —The job is supposed to be a sinecure, and I'm
now organizing a rebellion to see that for the future poets it will *be*
so, and *stay* so. But for a while it was hell. Involved, frinst, being
introduced to 1000 employes of the Lib. at a time, twice, in the Au-
ditorium, introduced facetiously as the Lib's "short-haired poet." !
Cute. —Now I do as I please, and am embarked, in office hours, on
that long-postponed novella, or what have you, Ushant. After seventeen years! and so much blood under the spans. And find it as
difficult as I foresaw, and am sorry I left it till so late, and unre-
membering. —Re Tony Bertram. Whose note I saw in Times Lit.[1]

1. Anthony Bertram, a Rye friend of the Aikens and of the Paul Nashes, was requesting information for his biography: *Paul Nash: The Portrait of An Artist* (London, 1955).

There is no doubt in my mind that I myself, with the freudian and other notions, for this was my own preludes for memnon, landscape west of eden (dedicated to Paul—one letter is about this), and time in the rock, period, had a considerable influence on Paul, as he did on me: a very deep osmosis went on between us, and for a long time: I shed into *his* landscapes, and he into mine. During that time, viz., 1930–1935, we were blood brothers, and remained so thereafter, although at a distance. Maybe you would be so angelic as to send *this* on to Tony? And if he wants the letters, I'll gladly send them along to him. The very last are from Oxford, and veritably d'outre tombe, as he himself says: and as he himself *was,* when last I saw him there. What a wonderful creature! Most wonderful of all when he was dying, and knew it: with a luminosity of love and gentleness and *self-estimate* (he went through photos of his life work with M[ary] and myself) which I never saw the like of. Profoundly moving and beautiful, and as true as modest. I think he'll be discovered to be *the* genius of the English landscape. The poetic genius. All of England is there, in that magical shorthand—curious, for it's an x-ray as well as a poetic eye, he loves the structure too. . . . much love to you both in which Mary too   Cahoon

207: TO EDWARD BURRA[r]   323 Second Street Washington
march 9 51

Dear Ed—   your Daily Mail in re tomeliot to hand, and much relished, dear me. I must say I think it was sporting of tom to say it was a good poem, and the fragment quoted really *was* good—but what a tempest in a *pot de chambre.* [1] They should have dug up that other juicy little item from Bleistein, "The Jew is underneath the lot," *that* would have put the fat in the fire—these poets, how they do carry on, to be sure, I more and more think poets are to be avoided whenever possible, they really stink. Especially in large numbers, when herding. They are such incorrigible eager beavers. . . .

. . . Time out at this point for the office phone (where I'm writing) and it appears I'm to lunch with guess who? Charles Laughton and the library staff, to discuss his reading of Robinson's poems at

1. To the charge that one of Pound's *Pisan Cantos* contained anti-Semitic lines, Eliot had replied it was nevertheless a good poem.

an inaugural party here next month for the new Whittall Poetry Room etc. etc. I suppose I daren't mention meeting little Elsa [Lanchester] in Bloomsbury sitting on Tony Bertram's knee circa 1920?

He and Charles Boyer and Cedric Hardwicke and Agnes Moorehead gave a reading of Man and Superman, Act 3. Last night. 3700 listeners, not bad. —I am now resuming this a day later, in the wonderful saturday silence of the library—no work on sats. The lunch with Laughton was fun. A very amusing guy. Seems he owes all to the Sitwell family—when I made a mild crack at Edith it all came out, he was the innkeeper's son at Scarborough, waited on the Sitwells, who finally one day said "You are simply playing the part of a waiter, you are not really a waiter, you're an artist," and invited him out to the manor for tea, lent him books, taught him to read and write and know good pictures from bad, sent him to Italy with a list of what to see, etc. etc. etc. So, was my face red. . . . It was all very gemutlich, but dry; they never serve drinks in ye Librarie, it's a pity; I always rush three blocks home for a couple of quick ones, two Roman Catholic altar-light holders that Mary bought at the five and dime, ruby red, which when filled to the brim with martinis give you quite a welcome wallop. Then back to the Library with a brightened eye and sharpened tongue, nobody knows why! Heh heh. The great excitement *chez nous* is a sudden outburst of radio activity—old Arc on NBC two weeks ago, the Disciple in Canada next week, and Arc on TV by Philco in May,[2] with other prospects pending. . . . I had to go to New Haven for the Bollingen Prize, I was Chairman of the committee, and there met Auden again and this time quite liked him. We've seen quite a lot of R P Warren too. . . . The annual meeting here was fun— Wilder and John Crowe Ransom and Wm Carlos Williams and so on all came to drinks, myself receiving in bathrobe with a fever of 101 and drinking five double martinis, then collapsing. Wilder very amusing. So's Red Warren, with a glass eye, and you can't tell which is which. Our NY slumlet is becoming a regular Salon, we pack them in. . . . Wonderfully quiet after Washington too. There's a scabrous book out about Wash, which I think I'll have to send you. Even gives the whores' addresses, no kidding! What next.   our loves   Conrad

2. C A's play *Mr. Arcularis* and a dramatization of his short story "The Disciple."

Dear Tom: Thanks for your dual-purpose note, official and informal, but I'm sorry you won't be here to lend moral support in the unending guerrilla war with the bureaucrats. My notion of endowed fellowships, which the Fellows themselves endorsed last year, and which appeared to recommend itself to the Rockefeller Foundation—at least, for consideration—and which Huntington Cairns thinks might interest the Mellon Patch—seems now to be somewhat lost in the lower depths of the Library itself; and I hope, at the annual meeting of the Fellows, that it can be thence resurrected. There is also a suggestion, from the Library, that the tenure of the Consultant might usefully be upped to as much as five years. (Perhaps a good idea.) If you would be so angelic as to let me have your views on these two points in the agenda, I'm sure they'd be extremely helpful to us.

Yes, WAKE is a very respectable, not to say sometimes admirable, little institution—a periodical in *every* sense of the word—with some first rate issues to its credit (notably Cummings number). I have warned them that the Aiken number which they contemplate will very likely be the death of them: but it's at any rate heroic. They catch *me* with my pants down, for in my prolonged wrastle with USHANT, that naughtybiography in which you are the Tsetse, and Ezra Rabbi Ben Ezra, my verses have been few and poor. And USHANT itself is too much of a continuum to be anywhere divisible for their purpose. *This* fearful book will come out I expect next fall, unless in the meantime the Atlantic decides to play. If and when, you shall have a copy; and with it will go my prayers that you may not be offended, or that at least you can give me the benefit of a *de veritate* non disputandum! I've had enormous fun with it—a fascinating business, this endeavor to coordinate into one turn of the wheel a whole lifetime of conation; and, without too much recourse to those damned chairs and tables, (as Stevenson complained) to give the effect of LIFE, the pour-in-stillness of LIFE. Jeest. I'm now in that pleasant predicament of looking at a book which quite obviously was not written by me at all, but by two other fellows! And neither of them named Schulz.   As always affectionately Conrad

Dear Old Malc: . . . It was good to hear from you, even if
with the accustomed Chorus behind you, and over your shoulder,
of the whuling Elements, which god knows do seem to be active in
your niche of the world. How do you survive? and do you never
tire? or long, as we do passionately, for something else? Washington gets us down like billy-o, despite pleasant interludes. We had
fun last May, when a very good local theatre-group, who do plays
"in the round" in an adapted cinema—and with astonishing skill—
put on our Arcularis. Panned by the local press, who are a lot of
movie hacks (the reviewers, I mean) but a huge success with the
actors and audiences, and, what's best, very satisfactory to me. . . .
But Washington, no. And the Library, no. I'm this minute deep in
an imbroglio with the top brass of the bureaucracy, who, in the
toils of a millionaire nonagenarian female, who has given them
money, and from whom they hope to filch more, have pretty effectively manacled and gagged the Consultant in Poetry; but he has at
last, after many sleepless nights of sweating conscience, decided to
speak his mind. I did this in the form of a letter to the Fellows in
AmLetters of the Lib. of Cong., whose annual meeting is held here
next month; but as the letter, being official, has to clear the hierar-
chies of Control downstairs, before it's allowed to go forth, I'm
now awaiting the sound of a muffled explosion and the dread summons. All very sickening. None of them know *anything* about literature, none of them have the least notion of a sensitive regard for it
or pride in it, they rewrite (or try to) my letters into their gobble-
degook choctaw (and I rewrite 'em back again), they expect me to
draft letters for the Librarian's signature about matters which don't
concern me, and about which I know nothing, and then return
them to me with a memo to the effect that I musn't address the recipient by his Christian name, which not even his best friends would
dare to do, but by something else: this last, an actual instance, was
what finally took the sanguinary bun, and I'm proposing, at the
meeting, that *this* custom at least be abolished. But you see what I
mean, you see why *we* yearn for other scenes, other climes. New
Zealand: we toy with the idea of settling in New Zealand. It sounds
all right. It's very cheap. It's very Far. It has fern trees, and sea, and
mountains, and the beginnings of a poetry movement. It has a year-

round climate—you can swim or ski on the same day, and you can hunt down your venison, if that is what you want to do, any day in the year. So why not New Zealand? The unanswered question is, how is the gin supply: we shall look into that. . . . But chiefly what I write to tell you, dear old Malc, in addition to thanking you for contributing to that suicidal issue of WAKE, which of course I haven't read yet—your contribution, that is—is that USHANT has miraculously, and all by itself, as in a sort of dreamlike parthenogenesis, got itself written at last—ain't it incredible? I now look back on the curious process with pure astonishment: I read a page or two without in the least recalling what it felt like to write them: it wasn't me, at all, in fact, that wrote it, but an invisible company of tiny visiting firemen. It will come out next fall, Duell Sloan and Pearce—Little, Brown and Co.,—and for once, as Cap Pearce seems to be reduced to a kind of speechlessness of enthusiasm, I dare to hope we may make a few much needed dollars, just when, this job over, we shall most want them. Frankly, I don't know what to think of it. It grew, all by itself, into a New Shape, its own, a spiral unwinding of memory into a spiral projection of analysis: it has a design, and yet it would be hard to say what it is. It seems to me, if I may be presumptuous, to achieve a *kind* of livingness, as of a living presence right beside you, that is perhaps new: or maybe it's a new "order." I dunno—I dunno. It's pretty orful explicit about many things. Yourself included, for you are a fellow named Hambo, and one of the Heros. I pray you won't be offended by any of it: I pray when you read it you will continually say to yourself, this guy loves me, or he wouldn't be so bloody candid about me. But actually, ectually, I venture to hope that you will not *like* the book, but find the treatment of yourself basically and deeply affectionate. What Tom Eliot is going to think is another tassie of tea. I call him the Tsetse, and have already so informed him (no comment from him). And his Retreat to the Church gets what I think it deserves. Will he be a forgiving Christian, a benevolent Martyr, and bless me from the Cross? —As for poor dear Martin, . . . well, I hope he never reads it, that's all, and have warned the kids, in England, that they had better conspire to keep it out of his and Jessie's hands. —And my own erotic career, dear god, dear jesus, what are people going to think of that—? New Zealand, come autumn—under a fern tree, far from the very very madding crowd. . . . Did you know incidentally of Gordon's tragedy—?

For the dear Bassett came down with Gerald [Noxon] for our very first weekend at Brewster last June, and died in his sleep—I found him so when I went to call him in the morning. As he would have wished it—five miles from his family lot in the churchyard at South Dennis, and after a Surfeit of Lobsters, and a life completely without illness. A marvelous fellow, and as one of his teachers wrote me, an irreparable loss. I can't face Boston or Cambridge or the Harvard Club without him: even Brewster now looks a little gray. Alas   heave us a line—our loves Conrad Aiken

210: TO R. P. BLACKMUR[ch]   Library of Congress
                                              February 19, 1952

Dear Mr. Blackmur: The Consultant in Poetry thinks that along with the agenda for the Fellows' meeting on February 29th, should go also some mention of a change in the status of the Consultant vis-à-vis the Whittall Poetry Fund and Poetry Program. In advance of the meeting, I give a brief summary of the events which have led up to this change. Last spring, for the first of the programs under the Fund, it was properly decided that in view of Mrs. Whittall's gifts of Housman and Robinson manuscripts to the Library one of these should be the subject of the first program; and it was agreed on all sides that of these Robinson would be the more suitable. On the suggestion of the Consultant, Cleanth Brooks was invited to give the lecture which was to accompany Burgess Meredith's reading, and to select the poems to be read. But unexpected difficulties arose over the questions, raised initially by Mrs. Whittall, as to whether portions of "Lancelot" should be included in the reading (this being one of Mrs. Whittall's gifts). It was the Consultant's feeling that no pressure whatever should be put on Brooks, either to include the poem for reading, if he didn't so wish, or to comment upon it; and accordingly the Consultant declined to act in the matter. Brooks was nevertheless asked to include "Lancelot"— somewhat belatedly—and refused, on the ground that it didn't fit in with what he had prepared to say, and wasn't, anyway, a very good poem. And that was that.

    Previous to all this, the Consultant had been asked for long-range suggestions about the future programs, but more particularly with regard to the program for 1951–52, and in the summer, while on vacation, in simultaneous letters to the Library and Mrs. Whittall he outlined his idea for this: the establishment at the Library of something comparable to the Charles Eliot Norton lectures at Harvard, with a national rather than merely local aim and significance, and with the further specific proposal that the first winter's program be a series of four lectures on twentieth century American poetry, by decades, from 1910 to 1950. The Consultant suggested that perhaps someone like R. P. Blackmur be invited to give the lectures, and that readers comparable to Burgess Meredith give illustrative readings. (Let it be said parenthetically that Mrs. Whittall was annoyed by the omission of "Lancelot," and has a scunner on lectures anyway!) But on his return to the Library he was informed that it would perhaps be in the best interests of all concerned if in future the administration of the poetry programs be conducted by the Reference Department, rather than in the Poetry Room, but that, of course, the Consultant would be kept informed of such decisions as were taken, and such programs as were arranged. This has been the situation ever since. The Reference Department, with the assistance of Mr. Waters, of the Music Division, administers the program; and, in effect, the Consultant is no longer consulted. As Dr. [Luther] Evans [the Librarian] has pointed out in his letter to the Fellows, this is designed as a temporary measure. But I think, as in a sense a precedent is thus being established, a statement by me is desirable at this point, in order that the Fellows may arrive at their own views about it, and be in a position to discuss it at the meeting. It is obviously an anomalous position that future Consultants will inherit: one in which they will be *thought* to be responsible for programs in which, in reality, they have no hand. It is certainly not a prerogative of the Consultant to criticize the overall policies of the Library. Yet this incumbent of the Chair would be less than candid if he concealed his misgivings at seeing the Library, and in the field of public relations, as this is, permitting its policy to be shaped, at least partially, by one whose judgment in poetry is all too lamentably betrayed by the books which she has provided for the Poetry Room. (They are, in my opinion, a disgrace!)   Yours sincerely, Conrad Aiken, Chair of Poetry

211: TO C. A. PEARCE^{ch}   321 second st se wash d c
                                      March 15 52

Dear Cap: Mary and I have given a day of meditation to your letter, and the suggestion that the announcement in Wake be used again on the jacket [of *Ushant*], and we both feel strongly that

211: TO C. A. PEARCE[ch]

while it is excellent for its original purpose, it ain't quite the meal-ticket for this. For one thing, I don't think "satirical" gives the right impression at all—for that element in the book is small. And this leads off with, as it were, a *mislead,* where instead, I think, some of the other major attributes should initially be stressed, such as—is this a novel? or is it an autobiography? or is it a religious statement? a confession? a philosophy? an analysis of the nature and function of the poet in society? For example, Jean Garrigue, after reading the first two sections, said "This is the novel we've all been wanting to write." For example again, you yourself said in a less prudent moment, "It adds a new dimension to literature." You also compared it to Rousseau, and is it an invention in form, perhaps, comparable to Sterne or Joyce? Is it perhaps the most complete *mis a nu* of 20th century Homo Incipiens? Is the style, the prose, worth mentioning? Is it possible that, as Mr. Barkham said, it might turn out to be a classic? Well, as you see, a hell of a lot of questions, and no answers, but maybe something like this should be the approach. Delmore Schwartz in the current Partisan [Review] discusses the non-novel prose-form that Joyce approached and then turned off from in the Portrait: is USHANT such a new prose-form, with the invention of a new prose rhythm, and spiral design, that makes it possible? I don't know—how *should* I—whether this is in fact the accomplishment, but I do know that this is what I was *aiming* at. And in another sense, I was also aiming at producing a book—statement *and* artifact—so massively complete in itself, and so of its time, its moment, in the evolution of man, that it would obtain an irreplaceable self-sufficiency, even to the point of marking off an era in that evolution, and causing things to "date." (Let me while I'm at it go the Whole Sow!) —Well, now, as I say, we can't holler all that, even if it were true, which we don't know, but it seems to me that it's an occasion for something a shade less cautious than the Wake announcement, and these are merely some of the directions it might take. I don't, again, think it should start off with "Mr. Aiken"—either Conrad Aiken, or Aiken, or even for christ sake Conrad, but *not* Mr. Aiken. I don't think so much stress need be put on the locale—Boston, London, Rye, etc.—for these are incidentals to the structure of a universal, and the book is not about these places but about LIFE. It *is* life. O hell, you see what I mean. . . . Or yet another tack! "Aiken outlined and began USHANT in 1933, abandoned it as too difficult, resumed it only to abandon it

again, but all the while adding notes both for material and design, made a third start in 1946, and finally finished it in 1950 and 1951 while Consultant in Poetry at the Library of Congress." Adding to this the barest of descriptions????? Anyway forgive this maelstrom of egoism, and I hope you can extract from it what you need.
. . .   Conrad

212: TO EDWARD BURRA^r   Forty-one Doors Brewster Mass.
                                      oct 2 52

Dear Ed: Yrs received at breakfast, and us just back from Bean-town, where we spent a night, Mary to visit Butcher Burke the Dentist, and where we had a fine drunk with Walter and Katherine Piston. W's new symphony being performed by Boston Symphony this week. He was in fine fettle, in fact both of them were, and we had fun; ending of course at ye Silver Dollar Bar, where the same old waitress took tender care of us, and the gals danced together on the dais with the hot jazz orchestra outdoing itself, having learned that Walter used to play there a couple of aeons ago when it was called Healy's. . . . Ushant comes out next week, and advance reviews are SAID to be very good. We shall see. Marianne Moore wrote a letter to the publisher intimating that she had been completely OUT-RAGED by it, it sounded as if she'd been f—d by a regiment of Royal Purple Dragoons and left naked in the Grand Concourse of the Grand Central Station. Old Malc, to whom I sent a copy, re-plied with a fine and very funny letter, *some*what hurt, but pretty handsome about it, and saying that he liked it very much. I'm send-ing you one, and hope you won't too much mind the portrait of Nicholas, nor the dedication, in which, with the Bassett, as you'll see, I've bundled in yourself and Mary as well, in memoriam Charlestown (what a winter!). . . . Nor has the Tsetse been heard from either. Ominous, that. I fear the worst. Mario Praz was here the other day, chez Bugs Bunny Wilson, and I reminded him of the time at lunch when Tsetse had just announced that he was a royal-ist, and Praz asked him what the hell it *was* to be a royalist, and Tom did the Indian rope trick, vanishing into thin air with it him-self, and in record time. La La—Well, we'll be seeing you, ain't it fun. And meanwhile our loves—   Conrad

Forty-one Doors, Brewster, Mass.
Oct. 17 52

Dear Mr. Stevens: That was a right nice note of yours about USHANT, and I must thank you. Yes, I found the mask imperative—nothing else could possibly have worked. As you say, focus was an inherent necessity, distance had to be kept, or *I* had to keep *my* distance, and this degree of stylization was the answer. Fun, too. —And yes, think what you were spared in unmerrie England, think, think. Not that I would have missed it, however, or didn't—perhaps—benefit by it, who knows. Anyway, we're going back to it for a brief visit next month—but this time just to see grandchildren. —I'd be curious to hear whether any of the stories go over—as you suggest—in the insurance business. That would be a hall-mark. Not that I haven't got some better ones up my sleeve! Again thanks, and again thanks, a lifelong thanks, for the Comedian as the Letter C—I wanted to put it whole into my Modern Lib. anthology, but the bastards wouldn't let me.   Yours sincerely   Conrad Aiken

323 e 33d st nyc 16
oct 12 columbia day 1955

Byootiful inviolable Eileen—   wot a yummy letter that was from amsterdam and all the other hollandisch dams—and wot fun you seem to be bringing to europe, scattering your largesse(?) like confetti, but how much can we believe? are you really there? as Oscar said on the phone, do you mean Amsterdam NY or the REAL amsterdamn? anyway, now your p. c. says you're in PARIS, god help us, and in a bordello, but who with???? and who are these mysterious strangers with whom you bought the rollflex? do tell, we're famished for DETAILS, sich as were you seasick, did you rape the captain or the first mate, did you get your nylons and white gloves back, or denounce the thieves and make them walk the plank, do you like the FOOD, in Paris, or the drinks, and what part of town do you love in? O well, to hell with it all, here am I solo in your city, and every minute of the day, and when I wake up at night, I think jesus why in hell isn't my adored eileen here so's I cd call up and say c'mon les go to the moompitchers and look under the seats for gum or say shithead to the bengal tygers burning bright in uncentral park. VERY lonely I am without you, and if it wasn't going to deprive you of a lot of fun I'd say DO hurry back, dearie, and scatter sunflower seeds or passionflower seeds or bleedingheart seeds on the doorstep of e durtyturd street and our dingy vomitcolored carpet and play the pyanner with that sad sad sad tune of yours and sing with your polychrome eyes. I mean, I MISS you, dollink, did you guess I would? Ain't it funny, in a nod sort of way I think I luv you, even if you know as well as I do nuttun cd come of it, or only a litel, to use your own orthography? Gee wiz. Anyway, Mary is at Brewster painting a cat picture for Hi Sobiloff and putting the house to bed for the winter, and me, I'm on the town, I see nothing but gals, last night I had dinner as the sole male (?) at Hi's with Jo and Edwina May and another gal whose name I didn't collect, very good likker, and then was staggering home along 33rd when a hung cupple stopped me and said are you mr aiken, and I sed yes, so i had them in to drinks (11 p m): it turned out they was poets living at the corner of foist ave, and VERY nice, and we went to the shamrock for beers, only they aren't drinkers (like you) and had coffee, and we read poems to each other and now I have a tripleplated bronze and gold hangover, and am waiting for the tall blond lovely Elizabeth Pollet Schwartz to turn up for lunch—she said to me on the phone, when she rang up last night, Can I *trust* you? What a question. But my heart is broken because the redheaded caedmon [Records] gal, Marianne, left town to go to hollywood to record the golden voice of james mason without coming to see me or even kissing me goodbye, the brat. Oscar [Williams] too is too busy to see me, everyone is away in the country, but just now I was cheered when the catholic school band, the Immaculata, formed up outside with drums and bugles and blue tunics and offwhite pants, and peeraded down to foist ave going the wrong way along a one way street, tsk tsk. My new book is out, but I won't send you one, for you'd SELL it,   Love, Prorid

215: TO EDWARD BURRA^r   New York
                                                        april 10 58

We had an orful party for the Academy of Am Poets, at which Mrs. Bullock rang a cowbell to silence all the Olde Things, and a small scroll was handed to me—I handed it to Mary and ran back and hid behind the bar. My new publisher Bob Smith was there and held out a five dollar bill to me, saying I could have it if I would shout ROOSEVELT at the top of my lungs. After ten martinis I DID say, in the elevator, with Mr. and Mrs. Bullock (she's the president of the Acad), "I think everyone should be warned that I'm a cousin of Franklin Delano R." and there was a stricken silence, and we all bolted for separate taxis. . . .   our loves   Conrad

216: TO EDWARD BURRA[r]   Brewster
                                                               July 5 58

Dear Ed: . . . Celia Hubbard now here, so the pergola season may be said to have started; but no Biddles as yet. Did I tell you that Alexis Leger [St. John Perse] is married, at 71, to a gal of 50? and gone to France on their honeymoon. Love among the ruins. I guess I DID tell you of our likkerish evening with Uncle Tom and Valerie, at the Silver Dollar rock'n'roll jumping joint and then the Red Loin Grill; Valerie refused beer saying she preferred a *soft* drink, an Old Fashioned—and when Tom lost control of his ankles she heaved him into a cab like a sack of potatoes. Did she really think they were a soft drink???? Very nice gal, and quite pretty. Tom in excellent form, and asked after you tenderly. We started off with dinner at the Athens of course. Speaking of which we have at last got a marker installed on Gordon's grave. . . .   our loves Conrad

217: TO JOHN KEMPTON AIKEN[r]
                              Forty-one Doors, Brewster, Mass.
                              Oct 10 59

Dear Djones,   many happy returns of the very day, and blymey to think that you're 46, no less! Time is indeed fugitive. It was literally only day before yesterday morning that your grandmother McDonald and I took turns walking Jessie up and down the upstairs hall at 73 Reservoir Street, Cambridge, and pressing our hands against the small of her back to ease the pain that YOU were causing. And today is just such a day as that was, blue October, with a soft yellow light on the last of the asters and goldenrod. And chicory. That neighborhood in Cambridge, not far from Fresh Pond, had masses of chicory growing everywhere, lovely. Anyway, there you are, here *we* are, and if life is sad and complicated it still seems

pretty damned good—think of living to see the luniks! Wow. Speaking of which, and the curious niceties of abstraction of which man avails himself in his exploration of the outer and inner worlds, many thanks for your [paper on] chelating agents, which is beautiful, fascinating, a totally unknown language, and, like music, leaves me in a kind of enchanted stupor. Very much the effect of Bertie Russell's Symbolic Logic, which Jake Wilbur and I used to stare at until WE were out of countenance. Ain't it all marvelous. . . .   much love   Cahoon
—one wild cucumber seed enclosed illegally.

218: TO (?)ᶜʰ   [1960]

Thanks for your letter, and very interesting that idea is [1]—true too, I think, and I think too that in a submerged sort of way I have always been aware of it. And perhaps I *can* adduce a shadow of evidence that it was something Stevens was *himself* aware of. In 1933 or 1934 I suggested to J. M. Dent, via Richard Church, that they should bring out HARMONIUM in their poetry series, and I was asked to write Stevens about this, or rather, to ask him for a new book—in their perverse way, they didn't want a book ten years old. Stevens in due course replied that he didn't have anything, he hadn't been writing. End of correspondence. In 1936 I first met him at Ted Spencer's, after he had given a reading in Sanders Theatre. When we were introduced, he at once said that he regarded me as the godfather of all his recent work, and that it was my request for a book for Dent that had started him off again. This would certainly fit in with your theory that he hadn't himself known how seriously to take himself, that the comparative failure of HARMONIUM abetted his self-doubts, and that perhaps along with this went a graver doubt as to the value of the poet and poetry, especially in U S society of that period. —Of course, a further element in all this was the fact that the members of the OTHERS group—Williams, Bodenheim, Kreymborg, Djuna Barnes, Mina Loy, et al., by their constant reference to him as a "dandy," may have contributed to this feeling that he was not quite *in it* but somewhere to one side, and with a

1. C A was asked to comment by a writer of a dissertation on Wallace Stevens on the notion that Stevens was uncertain, in the years before his poetic reputation was secure, how seriously to take his own poetry, and that this uncertainty had effects observable both in his literary career and in the poetry itself.

difference—not engaged or dedicated in the same way. And then, of course, with returning confidence, nothing would have been more natural (it was already implicit in MONOCLE) than that he should construct a theory which would justify the whole corpus, even to the extremes of ironic or humorous self-disparagement.   Conrad Aiken

219: TO W. G. SIMPSON[ch]   Brewster Mass
                                                            Dec 12 60

Dear Mr. Simpson: . . . . Yes, I did start him [Malcolm Lowry] off on his poetry binge, but this was at Cuernavaca in 1937: at Karl's Cafe, usually at noon, as often as he was sober enough, and often enough when he wasn't: partly in an attempt to pin him down, interest him in *any*thing: and almost wholly on a merely technical plane. I set him a damned fine series of exercises in blank verse, devised by myself, and extremely difficult, with great emphasis on vowel and consonant control and caesura, etc. etc. etc., and it was out of this that came the line I quote, "Airplane or aeroplane or just plain plane." . . . Of the hundred or more poems I saw, there weren't more than a dozen that were successful statements: but naturally, for me, they were ALL interesting, as coming from Malc, whom I loved very much, and regarded as a kind of son. I suppose ultimately they should all be printed. My point was that just NOW they might do his reputation harm. —As for that conversational device—"————," it may well derive from me, I would think more probably than from Grieg—but then he never told me much about Grieg. He kept his friends in separate compartments: John Davenport and I had to PLOT to meet. I always suspected that the Grieg cult was to some extent one of M's mystifications or mystic identifications, and some colour was lent to this when earlier this year, in a fragment of mss. of ULTRAMARINE (Purple Passage!) I found a batch of early letters, to and from Malc (these unsent) and among them a brief note from Grieg. As follows: "My dear Malcolm Lowry. I am very sorry, but have to work as hell these days. I have got no chance to accept your kind invitation, my nights and days are crowded with work. As a fellow-writer I know you will understand and forgive. Yours Nordahl Grieg." The polite brush-off? Sounds like. Of course der Malc knew no Norwegian, and, as you observe, it seems most unlikely that Grieg would have adopted a device from Swift. (I didn't either, if it WAS from me that Malc got it.) And no, I never knew Grieg. But I did hear enough of Malc's attachment to understand the canonization and identification in PANAMA—which, incidentally, I think, ought to be seen in its relationship to USHANT? Of Malc's saturation in all my own work I imagine I don't need to speak. He knew it better than I did. Just now, looking at the mss. of ULTRAMARINE, what should I find, tucked in among the pages, but an entire page of GREAT CIRCLE, the description of the eating of the father's skeleton, copied out in Malc's neat pencilling—an appropriate appropriation! —And yes, finally Hambo does appear in A HEART FOR THE GODS OF MEXICO, but not elsewhere—or elsewhere than in USHANT. I hope you can't find a copy of THAT, a very bad book. As for your endeavour to stop this Lowry-Rimbaud business, god knows you have my blessing, and indeed I had already felt Verlaine breathing absinthe over my shoulder. As perhaps the wonderful old Malc intended—?! Tiens. I wouldn't put it past him. . . . —John Davenport and my wife and I drove over from Rye last summer to the grave at Ripe—as I said to Margie, R.I.P., with an E on it, for End, or Ever, or what?   All best wishes, sincerely Conrad Aiken

220: TO NATHAN PUSEY[ch]   233 East 33 St., New York
                                           January 24, 1961

My dear Mr. Pusey: I want you to know how profoundly I appreciate the great honor offered to me by the Governing Boards of Harvard University and yourself, and how deeply I am moved by it.[1] More moved, I think, than by any such thing in my life before, which is as it should be; and I can only hope, therefor, that you can understand with what sorrow I must decline. Years ago I made up my mind against honorary degrees—I don't think I need go into the reasons—and declined the first that was offered to me. I'm afraid it would be improper for me not to do so again. But believe me, dear Pusey, with what searchings and regrets.

Privately, might I add that a *part* of my reason (not all) is a lifelong horror of public appearances. It cyant be did. Bad enough

---

1. President Pusey of Harvard, who had been a student in C A's tutorial in 1927–28, urged him in 1961 to accept an honorary degree.

when I was young—it prevented me from staying at Harvard, the year after we met, because I was asked to give a lecture course, and knew I couldn't lecture—it's far worse now. An affliction, and I know I should be ashamed.

Please forgive me, and ask the Governing Boards to forgive me.   With warmest regards and gratitude   Conrad Aiken

221: TO PRESIDENT JOHN F. KENNEDY'S
INAUGURAL COMMITTEE[ch]

233 East 33 St., New York
February 3, 1961

That was a noble injunction of President Kennedy's,[1] and not least interesting for its curious unconscious echo of that now forgotten credo of the I.W.W.'s, or Wobblies, who, I suppose, had taken it over from the early Marxists of this century—from each according to his ability, to each according to his needs. And to recognize the basic similarity in the manifest *aims* of the two conflicting ideals of society is, of course, to broaden one's whole concept of man's position in the state, and his obligations to it. The obligations are no longer as simple as they used to be: consciences are keener than they were, in these matters, only a short time ago. And no one in his senses could now unhesitatingly say "My country, right or wrong!" Everything for our country if it IS right, of course. But it is in the choosing of what is right that we can best exercise our voice in the destinies of not only our country, but perhaps that of the world as well. In its crazy hit-or-miss fashion there can be no doubt that the world is trying to pull itself together: man wants to unite with man. The North Atlantic alliance idea is a sign of this, the U N is another, the European Common Market yet another, and inevitably these concepts involve each time a slight surrender of the sovereignty of the state, a slight step towards amalgamation. I feel sure that Kennedy must often have indicated that his own mind ran in this direction, and that he would himself have been the first to emphasize that in our choosing a course for our county we must always be thinking not only of our country, but also of the good of

1. This letter was written a few days after Kennedy's inauguration, in response to a special invitation issued to "167 creative Americans" to attend the ceremonies and to write their "personal sentiments" for a book to be presented to the president.

all mankind. Ask what you can do for your country and for man. It may be difficult. But it has to be done.   Conrad Aiken

222: TO JAY MARTIN[r]   Forty-One Doors, Brewster
                                          oct 8 61

Dear Jay: . . . As for the autobiographical question,[1] I still think this should be held at a useful minimum—as far as possible. And I still think that *having taken a line,* viz., that only *via* fiction I matured the poetry, with a consequent emphasis on the personal and private experience, you've had to hew *too much* to this line, and to that extent have gone astray. The early poems—symphonies and others—contain just as much of this autobiographical element as the stories: I could go through Forslin, House of Dust, Senlin, Festus, even Punch, and mark many passages that are a direct transcript from life, whether mine or anothers—the loves, the loves, are there too, along with a vast number of other personal observations. From the very beginning, at school and at college, I naturally alternated between verse and prose, and emptied myself as readily in one as the other: I could *experience* through either, and *turn* experience into either. And it can truly be said, I think, that *more* direct personal experience went into the *early* poems than into the later— with one or two such exceptions as the deliberately confessional Osiris. The preludes and Kid and Landscape and Ruby (what about her?) and Li Po and Crystal and John Deth are something else again. So, to the extent that this is the thesis of your book, it's perhaps wrong! I think you should qualify it somewhat therefor. The narrative-psychological thing, however crude it was, appeared, and *prominently,* in the very first poems in the very first book— Youth was based on the actual experience of a friend-of-a-friend of mine. So, I think you should say somewhere that I had *always* been ambidextrous, and that as a result of this the prose and verse had *always* been reciprocally fructifying—possibly then saying that this had particularly been so in the decade from 1920 to 1930. However, if you'll send me a list of the story titles—I ain't got the Coll. here—with a two-line space under, I'll try to summarize briefly the nature and origin of each—as, frinst, "auto.," "invention," "hap-

1. Martin was writing a critical study, subsequently published as *Conrad Aiken: A Life of His Art* (Princeton, 1962).

pened to x," "auto. plus invention," or some such. Seems to me that's all you really need to know, nicht wahr? Silent Snow is NOT as rooted in my own yard as you think—it's the product of an imagination which began with a very small thing and then went very far away with it—it's beyond analysis, even for me. Whereas Strange Moonlight is obviously just the opposite—imagination takes a hand, to be sure, and transmutes it, but the material is deeply and closely personal, and is allowed to remain so. Etc. etc. etc. And let me point out, too, that the "Irene" of Ushant first appears in the last section of Forslin (the brass ring episode), and the Pauline of H of Dust, if you *must* know, came from Maine and lived in an attic room in Dilaway Street—so what?????! In short, the poetry was amalgamating "raw experience," of one sort or another, all along. And this should *not* be ignored or minimized! So there. —Anyway, I think you can *unweave* and then *re*-weave in such a way as to keep a *direction* going, if you see what I mean, without falsifying the facts? I hope so. And after all, Ushant does tell you all you really need to know—names don't matter, nor places, nor times, these are inessential: it's what D [C A in *Ushant*] did or didn't do, what he felt or didn't feel, and then what he thought about it, that matters, and this you have. Selah.   as always

  Conrad

223: TO JOHN AND MÁIRE SWEENEY[r]

Forty-one Doors, Brewster
oct 23 61

it seems deer fellowes that we will be in Blackstone Village [Boston] ye nighte of nov. 10th upcoming, prior to football with Princetown, and it occurs to us that maybe a Mavrodaphne dinner wd be nice, if you was to join us? Leave us know. Could we come to the Blackstone Front for a whiff of juniper, and then go on by intoxicab to Athens and Olympia? We hope! Meanwhile, a departmental ditty:

> You Wannamaker?
> You wanna Hammacher & Schlemmer?
> You wanna Lord and Taylor?
> Then what you need is Saks.
>   yrs the Alt Man.
>   and our loves to both   c

Forty-one Doors, Brewster
nov 12 61

Dear Jay: Thanks for letters and the rewrite. Alas, me no likee
AT-all, as you'll see by some pretty pungent marginal comments!
Forgive the slang-shots, please, but I do think once again you're
way up the wrong tree, and again being positively *perverse* in this
obsession of yours about all the fiction being autobiographical! To
begin with, you're misusing the word autobiographical *passim*. Autobiography implies self-revelation, self-disclosure, the analysis of
oneself and one's history: to claim this for Arcularis or practically
all the others is absurd. The use of a fragment of personal experience, or encounter, or something told one, or a remembered person,
as a jumping-off place for an invented piece of poiesis does not
make that poiesis autobiographical. In this sense, this whole section
on the fiction is mistaken and, for your readers, misleading: the net
result is that I will be given no credit whatever for being an artist,
for using materials of ANY sort and making artifacts of them, and
what's more, of great variety. This vitally important fact you
suppress or misconstrue in the interests of proving your initial *assumption*—which I do not grant anyway—that the fiction played a
special role. You tend to take this assumption as proved, and then
argue from it. Moreover, as this whole section seems to me trivial,
of really no interest to anyone *per se, not* very well stated, and
really on the order of W Winchell gossip, I hope you will take my
advice and drop it out entirely. Instead, put in a page or two on the
subject, but in general terms, NOT taking up the stories item by
item, a dull business, but *relating* them to the poetry—particularly
to the early narrative poems—T and Movies, Youth, Forslin, H of
D, *Punch*, etc.—maybe Tetelestai too—and also to the later narrative poems, Deth, Osiris, Landscape, Ruby, Kid and Soldier. And
two important middle-period poems, Psychomachia and Electra,
written at the same time as Chap. 1 of Blue Voyage and Bring
Bring. This would make much better reading, and if you can bring
out the similarities of artification in the prose and verse it would be
extremely useful. You see, the current you are interested in, as I
have insisted before, was working, or running, *all* the time in both
mediums, from the very beginning. Remember that the Deceitful
Portrait was written in 1917, Tetelestai either that year or the next:
in these you have the germ of everything that follows. What was

being enriched, in both forms from now on, was the *articulation*. And *most* of the fodder of "experience" had already been laid in. . . .   as ev   Conrad

[The following are C A's comments on the degree of autobiography and invention in each of his stories, which he enclosed with this letter.]

BRING! BRING!   Actual experience of Eunice, but of course greatly altered and amplified, and given a Duxbury setting.

THE LAST VISIT   Completely autobiographical.

MR. ARCULARIS   Based on a combination of a dream on shipboard and the simultaneous encounter with the real Mr. A. Fundamentally an invention of the imagination.

THE BACHELOR SUPPER   An invention suggested by going to a bachelor supper in Boston at T Wharf.

BOW DOWN, ISAAC   Complete invention—can't remember ANY sources.

A PAIR OF VIKINGS   Actually happened—I knew them in Rye. Story not changed at all.

HEY, TAXI!   Complete invention, suggested by a taxi driver telling me of a freak trip from Boston to Hanover, Mass.

FIELD OF FLOWERS   Autobiographical. In another country. And besides, the wench dying.

GEHENNA   Invention.

THE DISCIPLE   Invention. Got stuck in it too, had to put it aside for a year before I cd find a way to finish it.

IMPULSE   Invention. In toto.

THE ANNIVERSARY   Invention, but with Uncle A[lfred] as hero, with Aunt E[dith] his wife: story invented, the portrait true.

HELLO, TIB   Actual occurrence, the cat's death; the setting or preceding situation invented to fit it.

SMITH AND JONES   Completest invention!

BY MY TROTH, NERISSA!   Invention, out of chronic acedia.

SILENT SNOW, SECRET SNOW   As I said before, invention, imagination going far afield from a small premise.

ROUND BY ROUND   Invention plus biographical, based on a newspaperman-friend-of-mine's experience, plus my own reporting of an actual fight—middleweight championship, Vince Dundee and someone whose name began with a B.

THISTLEDOWN   True portrait of a gal I knew well, and who's alive, so nameless.

STATE OF MIND   Invention coming to the rescue of personal tension.

STRANGE MOONLIGHT   Invention and synthesis coming to the rescue of disorder and early sorrow.

THE FISH SUPPER   True story, happened to a friend of mine.

I LOVE YOU VERY DEARLY   Found a similar letter in a book I was looking at in someone's library—built it up from there.

THE DARK CITY   Invention, but using the house and family of a friend of mine—story invented, the portraits true.

LIFE ISN'T A SHORT STORY   Complete invention, based on a casual greeting between two strangers in a theatre lobby.

THE NIGHT BEFORE PROHIBITION   Autobiographical.

SPIDER, SPIDER   Autobiographical. Names cyant be mentioned.

A MAN ALONE AT LUNCH   Autobiographical. As above.

FAREWELL! FAREWELL! FAREWELL!   Autobiographical. Verbatim. It's her own name.

YOUR OBITUARY, WELL WRITTEN   Autobiographical, and suggested by the ad in the Times, with embellishments.

A CONVERSATION   Autobiographical.

NO, NO, GO NOT TO LETHE   Complete invention—know no sources.

PURE AS THE DRIVEN SNOW   True story, happened to a friend of mine.

ALL, ALL WASTED   True story, observed from back window of my house in Rye.

THE MOMENT   True story, combination of TWO friends of mine.

THE WOMAN-HATER   True story, another friend of mine, with a famous musical comedy star, name forgotten.

THE PROFESSOR'S ESCAPE   True story, happened to the friend of mine who figures in Dark City.

THE ORANGE MOTH   Autobiographical—with Van Wyck Brooks, papa Yeats et al. thrown in, and the dream was actual.

THE NECKTIE   True Story, the uncle, but nameless.

O HOW SHE LAUGHED!   True story, I was there.

WEST END   True story, told to me by a woman in London, but with many embellishments.

FLY AWAY LADYBIRD   Based on the situation of two people I knew, but with my own ending supplied. It turned out to be prophetic.

BLUE VOYAGE   Self-explanatory, Cynthia and Faubion were real, so was Silberstein and the others, Smith included. Death of Smith is in the quarrel about negroes, by the way—

GREAT CIRCLE   Call it a psychological invention based on biographical and autobiographical elements—everything altered to suit the thematic purpose. Andrew's unhappy homecoming, etc., invented to supply the jealousy motif, the uncle invented ditto. Duxbury put to use.

KING COFFIN   Complete invention, based on a singular character in my apartment house in Cambridge, odd name something like Ammen, and an air of mystery and superiority. And there *was* a Dr. King Coffin living in Boston.

HEART FOR THE GODS OF MEXICO   Hambo and Noni were real, of course, so was Blomberg. The rest invented. Well, cf. Ushant.

CONVERSATION   Based on the episode of the Robin Hood thief and Bodenheim coming to S Yarmouth, and the ensuing conflict with my friends there. And of course my own setting, with alterations. Names cyant be mentioned. The *resolution* of the quarrel was an invention.

Letters 225–244: February 1962 to May 1973

C A had revisited Savannah twice since "the day of the long drive behind the two black-plumed hearses" and found that "everything had waited for him." In 1960 he urged Hy Sobiloff—a business man, poet, and patron—to visit. Sobiloff at once bought the house (at 230 Oglethorpe Avenue) adjoining C A's old home (called 228 Habersham Street in Blue Voyage), restored it, and gave right of occupancy to C A for his lifetime.

Beginning in February 1962, C A and Mary opened their Savannah home for the winters only, until C A's illness made summer returns to Brewster impossible in 1972 and 1973. In March 1962, C A developed pemphigus, a painful skin disease, and in February 1963 he suffered a heart attack (which gave rise to A Seizure of Limericks); his next ten years were plagued—sometimes mildly, sometimes intensely—by their various complications. Neither his flow of letters nor his zest for conversation diminished.

o   o   o

Selected Poems (New York: Oxford University Press, March 1961; Cleveland: Meridian—World, 1964; New York: Oxford University Press, September 1969).

The Morning Song of Lord Zero (New York: Oxford University Press, April 1963).

The Collected Novels of Conrad Aiken (New York: Holt, Rinehart and Winston, January 1964; Three Novels, London: W. H. Allen, February 1965).

A Seizure of Limericks (New York: Holt, Rinehart and Winston, October 1964; London: W. H. Allen, November 1965).

Cats and Bats and Things with Wings: Poems (New York: Athenaeum, September 1965).

Tom, Sue and the Clock (New York and London: Collier Books-Macmillan, April 1966).

Thee: A Poem (New York: Braziller, November 1967; London: Inca Books, 1973).

Collected Poems 1916–1970 (New York: Oxford University Press, August 1970).

Ushant: An Essay (New York: Oxford University Press, 1971, with key to personae and photographs).

A Little Who's Zoo of Mild Animals (London: Jonathan Cape, 1977).

230 Oglethorpe Ave., Savannah
Feb 24 62

Beloved Harry—   we've been worried about you—how ARE you, and where, and what doing—? Do let us have a postcard with an H on it. As you see, here I am, back in utero, feeling infantile one minute and senile the next, a delicious confusion of identities and generations and personae, for my own house is right there next door, the "stoop" of this adjoins the "stoop" of that, and from our back windows we look down into my own back yard, where once there was a chinaberry tree. All just too good to be true, and somehow profoundly relaxing and releasing, everything acceptable. They've done a marvelous job with THIS house, it's lovely, or will be when we can put a few more sticks of furniture in it—we brought the contents of the Washington house with us (I think I told you we sold it, and quite profitably)—but what filled that little igloo leaves this looking somewhat bare—but give us time. We like it all—and Savannah, and the people—so much that I think we will next year spend the winter here. Wonderful how my childhood friends, and my father's and mother's friends, pick us up as if we'd never been away for a minute—the circle continually comes round on itself—as yesterday when we went to the Juliette Low House (Juliette Gordon, who founded the Girl Scouts; it's the national center) to meet a childhood friend of mine from New Bedford, not seen for sixty years, or in fact since I gave her a dozen of my Aunt Jane's roses for her high school graduation, and who should be there but Bee Gordon, now seventy, whom my father taught to speak—he was a deaf-mute, and this was one of the earliest of such cases. Not least fascinating was this fortuitous conjunction of New Bedford and Savannah. Very moving. . . .   Conrad

226: TO JOAN AIKEN[r]   230 Oglethorpe Ave Savannah
Mch 2 62

Dear Fiddles: Yes, here we are, in this most heavenly house and heavenly city, looking out on the old colonial cemetery where I played every day among the brick vaults and marble pyramids and palms and palmettos; and pink azaleas blooming in the median green of the divided street, under tall live-oaks, and from the windows we can look down on my brownstone porch next door, or at the well-remembered stepping stone against which I cracked my left frontal bone while towing a lovely red fire-engine, in which I had a fire going, of excelsior. All a little eerie, I don't know whether I'm going or coming, and of course every corner of the city—it's quite small, the "old" part, and concentrated, and this is part of its magic—has its secret. Yum! Oysters sixty-nine cents a pint to make a stew with—seventy oysters for sixty-nine cents—what more could we ask? Wonderful too how the childhood friends and ONE old friend [Miss Mary Clay] of my mother (ninety, and incredibly bright and naughty—she calls me "old Man"!) behave as if that redheaded vagrant had never been away at all. Jist fascinating. . . . Cahoon

227: TO THE SAVANNAH U.S.O. COMMITTEE[ch]

Forty-one Doors, Brewster
January 31, 1964

One morning in 1898 this small boy who is addressing you, and who was himself then aged eight, was awakened by the sound of bugles outside his house in Oglethorpe Avenue, and was astonished when he looked out to see soldiers pitching their tents on the green. Naturally, he lost no time in going across to see these wonderful people, who, it turned out were the Company K, 4th Illinois. From two of them, Sergeant Williams and Private Knight, he learned that they were hungry. They had been living, they told him, for so long on "tinned mule"—an idea that appalled him—that they were ready for anything. He went back to the house and returned shortly with a paper bag containing the family supply of animal crackers, which were received with enthusiasm, and perhaps a sense of humor of which the boy was unaware.

Well, this is typical of the sort of thing that Savannah has always done for the men and women in the armed forces. Every Sunday dinner at our house was a dinner for these men, and all of Savannah was doing the same thing.

Is it too much to ask that now again we should come forward with our animal crackers?   Thank you. Conrad Aiken

228: TO T. S. ELIOT^r   230 Oglethorpe Avenue, Savannah
                                        Dec 3 64

Dear Tom and Valerie: Valerie's letter came as a great relief to
us, though we had both kept saying to each other, "Tom's done it
before, he has great stamina and courage," but it's marvelous to
know that he's really beginning to pick up. What a thing to have
gone through—and how wonderfully right that doctor was to tell
you to go home! It was *staying* at home, and being allowed to by a
sensible young doctor, that saved *my* life—hospitals are deadly.
. . . Anyway, we're delighted, and hope all will continue to go well
with both of you. And let us pray for no fogs. But o dear we shall
miss our annual meeting in New York and the exchange of Bolos
and lime rickeys at the River Club or Vanderbilt. And I don't know
about our coming to England—the energies are intermittent, the leg
hinges are rusted beyond even the lubrications of vodka (we have
taken to vodka, it seems to agree with us), and the thought of five
days on a ship fills me with dismay. . . .   Much love from us
both   Conrad

229: TO TED BERRIGAN^{ch}   230 Oglethorpe Avenue, Savannah
                                        Jan 28 65

Dear Mr. Berrigan   Thanks for sending me your book, which is
fun, I think, but not quite my cup of mescal: a genyouwine poetic
license doesn't, I feel, allow you to take liberties with syntax; or to
put it in another way, you *take* more liberties than you provide.
Letting fly like this is amusing, but I fear it's a dead end street,
won't get you nowhere: better at your stage to submit yourself
doggedly—or even tigerishly—to the hoops of good old Virgilian
and Dantean Discipline. THEN you'll be in a POSITION to take
liberties, because you'll know how far NOT to go. Dull, isn't it? But
no, it ain't either, for in fact there is NOTHING so completely and
exclusively fascinating as the *control of form*. And the simultaneous
intertwining with it of the Eye—the "I"—the inner voice, that
comes up from undersea. I think you'll find this is so, and I'd guess
that you could do something with it, too. Anyway, get to it, and
good luck.   yrs   c aiken

230: TO HENRY A. MURRAY[r]
230 Oglethorpe Avenue, Savannah
Feb 4 65

. . . The President's Council for the Aging has asked me for Advice
to the Dying—what could be more timely? The merry month of
May is to be dedicated to the Aging. And Mary's portrait of Tom is
to come out in LUGANO REVIEW (new) with a brief reminisce by
self. We disclose for the first time that there is a concealed portrait
of John Hayward [1] in the background. What fun!   our loves and
hugs   Conrad

231: TO EDWARD BURRA[r]
Oglethorpe Avenue, Savannah
Feb 20 65

Dear Ed: . . . Yours that was sent to NYC survived the ordeal
and got here, and wonderful it was, about all these Royal Deaths
and the flummery and mummery they enTAIL. Jeesus. Reminds me
of why I got the axe from Nyorker in 1936, because I led off a piece
about Geo. V's death, with the phrase "The Kiplings and the Kings
depart," old Woodyard having demised in the same week. (I cyant
remember, but I suppose poor Kip got forgotten in the Royal Back-
wash too.) The Nyorker was inundated with fierce letters from old
Colonels and ancient dames, and that was That. (I was about to re-
sign anyway, fed to the teeth.) Yes, of course, I'd forgotten your
Giant Retrospective was scheduled for Fall Production, though I
must say it's un*like* you to stay around for it. . . . Maybe WE can
pull up our sox and Haul Ass, as the Bassett used to say, and see
both it and you. . . . It seems Alan Hodge's name was omitted
from the TIMES list, *and* that he was supposed to represent *me* in
Westminister Abbey [1] and Faber rang up Valerie to inform her, and
then they rang up Jane to say that Valerie was very much touched!
What organization. And WHY East Coker? That seems to me to be
the acme or indurated acne of affectation, so false that you can taste
the brass. I'm sorry he did it—Mt. Auburn would have been far
better. Mary's portrait of Tom is coming out in the new Lugano
Review, with some acidulous comments by me, in the 2nd number,

1. Eliot's friend, whose apartment he shared before his marriage to Valerie.
1. At a ceremony in Poets' Corner for Eliot.

and so is my new poem addressed to GOD, I think I told you, called THEE, I had a cable from them today about copyright etc. But that will come somewhat later. I kind of like the thing, it's *less* than reverent, and I might even have called it, a la Mack Sennett, And Let My Pie Come Unto Thee. Your account of a Voyage to Londres and its complications and consequences makes me wonder why you go there—of course Clover [Pertinez] doesn't drink, nor Eduardo [her son] either, and I can see the difficulties. But gosh I envy you the Rex and them antique fillums. There's a marble angel in Bonaventure Cemetery here, where my pa and ma are buried, which is the SPITTING image of La Bette [Davis], she is laying a wreath on a tomb, and the *gesture* of that arm is PERFECT! We'll get John's [wife] Paddy to photograph it. That terrible Isabella Tate is having a Memorial Reading for Oscar [Williams] next week, and wanted a limerick. What an idea.   love   Conrad

232: TO JOHN KEMPTON AIKEN[r]
                              230 Oglethorpe Avenue, Savannah
                              April 25, 65

Dear Djones: . . . As for us chix, we're in the frantic process of Winding Up: farewell phone calls etc. etc. and last night a cocktail with two absolutely enchanting old ladies who knew my pa and ma and ME, because our colored nursemaid was a friend of THEIR maid, and used to bring us all to play in their garden. But they knew all about the impending tragedy AND added the unknown factor: our Doctor . . . was a drug addict, and wouldn't listen to Mama, or DO anything. So poor mama was caught in a trap: she told one of them the day before she died that he—papa—*counted* the sheets of paper on her desk, to make sure she hadn't written letters to the north. (Of course, *I* knew of this in other ways.) Potters and Tillinghasts should have done something. Gloomy Gus. Just the same, a pair of incredible octogenarians such as only this city can breed. And so witty! And so delighted that we are back! But o so sociologically backward, we had to keep off that. Or try to. But the more we see of these old gals the more we're impressed with the *social* inheritance everywhere. They were bred to it: nothing quite like it anywhere. The obverse, of course, being the Ku Klux Klan, those bastards. I hope we can give them their comuppance.
. . .   our loves Cahoon

—Lovely letter from a mad fan in Monterey who says he's done a monograph in which he pairs BEETHOVEN and me! Wow. I replied that it was nice to be on cloud seven with old Beety.

233: TO THE PRESIDENT'S COUNCIL ON AGING^{ch}

[Brewster, Mass.]
May 1965

It's extraordinary how little I can now remember of Cicero's famous essay on Old Age, which I had to read in Latin at school— but perhaps natural, for what does the boy want to know of old age, or what can he feel about it? All he does know is that grandfather and grandmother are old, and that this is a preliminary to death, that other mystery. He is still himself completely enthralled in what Santayana called animal faith, and of course is not in the least aware that the very act of being born is to be embarked on a process that leads to death: we live our lives, but in a sense we die them too. I find it profoundly reassuring to consider this inexplicable wonder, as I myself grow older: it has the perfection of a work of art. We can do what the doctor tells us, of course. But more important, I think, is that animal faith, our primal love of earth and sky and water and air, and to renew every day our astonishment at being permitted to be present with these, and conscious of them. Ignore the changed face that looks at you from the mirror, it is really the boy who still looks at you there, *he* has not changed; or if he has, it is only in the fact that he has all his life been gathering an inestimable treasure of memory: his own great poem to the universe. Encourage him to go on with it, and every morning, for this is *you*, the one and only never-to-be-replaced *you*, with its own private, but also cosmic, view of the world. Go along with him, and on crutches, if you have to, but let him enjoy it. And he will.
Conrad Aiken

234: TO VALERIE ELIOT^r

Forty-one Doors, Brewster
May 15 65

Dear Valerie: We were so glad to have your wonderful letter, and to feel that all was as well as *might* be with you, after such an ordeal. I was happy too that you didn't mind my remarks in LIFE.

And I think now I can tell you something extraordinary that happened to me on the day that Tom died. I don't know whether you believe in E S P and all that, and I don't know whether *I* do, but anyway I had that morning a very odd nightmare, in which I was on a ship at sea, and feeling ill. But as the ship was entirely motionless—I rationalized in the dream—it can't be seasickness, it must be something else. Then I woke, and found I WAS ill, with a fever, it was all too true. This, of course, was before I heard, via a phone call from Allen Tate later in the afternoon, that Tom had died. Allowing for the difference in time, it puts my dream very close to the time when Tom actually died and I can't help feeling that somehow I knew what was happening—it's very strange. I still had the fever when I was interviewed by LIFE, and in fact was ill all week. I feel sure it was a communication, of some sort. And anyway, I thought it would interest you. . . . Mary's portrait of Tom is in the 2nd issue of LUGANO REVIEW, with some facetious notes by me on the circumstances. . . . And I hope YOU won't mind my reference to our—Tom's and mine—religious differences, which of course I'd said before. Heavenly here now, the very first of spring (very late this year), we came at just the right minute, deciding to ignore New York and the Academy ceremonies, we were both too tired. Very glad we came and sat down. The two primroses from Hastings which Mary smuggled in ten years ago are now thirteen, a plantation! Do let us know how you are. And much love from us both.   Conrad

235: TO JAY MARTIN[r]   230 Oglethorpe Avenue, Savannah
                               Jan 27 66

Dear Jay: Wonderful about all them developments—hope they don't swamp you, or that you DO get a Guggenheim or whatsomever. Particularly good about Nathanael West, etc.[1] This, I think, is a genuine BREAK, and I trust you'll regard it as such, and *temper* yourself for it: as I see it, it's for you a crucial test, it's a subtle and difficult subject, and an important one. You'll need every bit of liveliness and *humor* and *awareness of irony,* not to say of his abandon to morbidity, the latter going along *pari passu* with Holly-

---

1. Martin was beginning the biography, *Nathanael West: The Art of His Life* (New York, 1970).

wood buffoonery, if you're to get AT this fellow. A genius, in my opinion; a great favorite of Ed's, which should give you a line on him (you might write to Ed and ask him what he thinks, for I'm sure Ed would come up with a fetching fierce phrase or two. I always associate West with Raymond Chandler, who had some of the same gift for hitting the exact center of the vernacular (in ALL its implications—social, moral, religious) of that moment in time. I'm chiefly worried about the humor. This was your weakest point in the book on me: I felt you slid right over it: and to slide over it in West's case would be fatal. Take a bath in Rabelais and Voltaire—metaphorically speaking—before you start stepping Westward. And have another look at Tooloose Lowtrek. Kindred spirits. Damned good contract they've given you, too. Better than any of mine. And why NOT some day do a revision of A Life of His Heart? Too much of your [Ph.D.] boss's theories twisting it sidelong, and too little appreciation of the function of the *imagination:* you wanted every mortal thing to have come direct from the sidewalks of life, made no allowance for what the psyche was doing with this, all *its* life, selecting, rejecting, exaggerating, multiplying, denying, and so on: the end result being not the girl you met on the corner but a prelude or a flute-note of a lyric. It's in this region, now, that I think you must take care: here, and on the purely linguistic level, the development of the finest possible ear and eye for the language, o god, the language. But anyway godspeed. I think it's marvelous.   our loves to all   Conrad

236: TO THE EDITOR OF THE
TIMES LITERARY SUPPLEMENT[ch]

230 Oglethorpe Avenue, Savannah
February 1, 1967 [printed February 16]

Sir,   There are so many things that are half wrong, or only partly right, in your admirable leading article on Malcolm Lowry, that I hardly know where to begin. . . .

It all began—of course—when Malcolm as a result of reading my novel *Blue Voyage,* wrote to me at Rye in 1929, and proposed that we meet. In due course, his letter found me at Cambridge, Massachusetts, and, in turn, he crossed the Atlantic to spend three months with me, working together on *Ultramarine. Blue Voyage* he said he knew by heart. He did, too, and it became a great, and lasting, joke between us that he used so much of this—style, devices, etc.,—in *Ultramarine* and in all the later work as well: the influence was permanent. Even the title *Ultramarine* was intended as a reference to *Blue Voyage,* and I suggested why not go a step farther and call it *Purple Passage?* At one point he even copied out a page of my novel, *Great Circle,* proposing to incorporate it, but I said No. (I have this in his handwriting—it is a description of the devouring of the father's skeleton by the son.) Just as the tooloose Lowrytrek was *my* invention, not his. And I might add, for those who are interested, that the entire argument, between the Consul and the other, about Marxism in *Under the Volcano* was a verbatim report of an argument between Malcolm and myself, with the positions reversed: what the Consul says, I said. Your writer observes that Malcolm could DO this. One might say that he was a *tope*-recorder. A great many of my remarks and turns of phrase are embedded in all his books, as also in letters.

And this brings us to another mystery. It has always been said that *Under the Volcano* was written *after* the Cuernavaca period. Not so. I read not only the "lost" novel, *In Ballast to the White Sea,* while we were there, but the whole of *Under the Volcano.* The first draft, but complete, and with a different ending: the horse theme had not then been developed. In short, that book was going to be rewritten for the next nine years. No wonder, given his genius for language, that it is such a miracle of English prose, which, I think, is its chief virtue. He worked on it as one would on a patchwork quilt; every snippet of colour or serendipity out-of-the-way knowledge that he found in his reading (he was always wanting me to send him old copies of *The Dial* and *Criterion*), was tucked in to enrich it, whether or not pertinent. But the novel was already substantially *there* in July 1937.

Well, I can imagine him roaring with laughter about all this in his Ripe young grave in Sussex, and in this I join him. For to have manufactured such a myth, and turned himself into it, was perhaps a feat of literary *trompe-l'oeil* without parallel. He would have been particularly amused, I think, by your writer's quotation of the signature of his first—and so moving—letter to me:

te-thrum te-thrum
te-thrum te-thrum
Malcolm Lowry.

324

For the te-thrum te-thrum is not, as your writer says, characteristic of Lowry, but of me: it is in fact the running-theme of *Blue Voyage,* which he was quoting. And for Malcolm it was all just a great joke, even with the tragedy thrown in, which incredibly turned itself into a great book, or a great melodrama, as I said to him in a letter. And it *was* a great joke: his whole life was a joke: never was there a gayer Shaksperean jester. A fact that I think we must remember, when everyone is saying What Despair, What Riddles! Nonsense. He was the merriest of men. . . .   Conrad Aiken

237: TO EDWARD BURRA[r]   Forty-one Doors, Brewster
                                           sept 21 68

Dear Ed: . . . I'm afraid my pal Humphrey ain't doing too well—but then, as the entire press is Republican, you never know. Don't know whether I told you I'd been drug into politicks, by joining the writers and artists for H—next thing I knew, the Chairman [Eugene Istomin] was here, with a Hall of Fame baseball star, Frankie Frisch, the Fordham Flash, a marvelous man, frightfully funny. And I was wheedled into making a statement on behalf of the wrys and ars, a democratic credo, which came out in a full page of the NY Times. Fry me for an oyster. Cost them $12,000: they got only a handful of replies, and ONE thousand. Now Dump the Hump as the rebels call him has been violently received in Boston where he appeared outside Filene's Bargain Basement—booed and shouted down by an organized gang, Hitler style. He handled it very well. I still feel he has a chance, if only they'd realize he is the only qualified man. God, if Nixon gets it, we'll leave the country. I hate that character, and wdn't trust him for a second with a bitten farthing. . . .   our loves—Conrad

238: TO GRAYSON P. McCOUCH[h]
                                 230 Oglethorpe Avenue, Savannah
                                 Dec 24 68

Christmas Blasphemy 1968
Beloved Old Bird: Lovely to have your card, and to know from that and from the Middlesex report that you and M[argaret] are still, *hardy seats,* riding bareback—good god. While everyone is

dying around us—poor old Dilly the latest. What a pang that gave me, as I'd finally had to refuse to correspond with him—and you, old Spartan Aztec angel, intervened on my behalf. (He went up to see Zinc Elliot instead. I was thinking about this tother day, and the time when Zinc and Whosit Barker reported a lewd conversation, conducted in the presence of two gals, in which they claimed they'd discussed their Friend, John Thomas, that little red-head—have you seen J Thomas lately—you know, that little red-head? Chuckles, chuckles, etc. etc., and mystification of course (?) for the gals.) I've been telling the Middlesex gang some home truths lately, in the course of refusing to give them money; about the boss. Just said that we hated each other, and that this crimped my career at M. True, too. It was you, and the other fellows, Avvy [deForest] and Jack, and poor deserted Penny, that made up for it. And Heber Howe and May. Joe Killorin, who's editing my letters, wants to see you. It's a marvelous idea. Brukdown hotel, five minutes walk from us, where we can book you. And o how good to see you fellows.   Much love—Conradin

'Twas the night before Christmas	But in came the Kings
And Mary forlorn	And other such things
Waiting for Jesus	And alas poor old Joseph
Our God to be born	Who was wearing a horn.

C A

239: TO EDMUND WILSON[y]
Brewster
Aug 13 69

Dear Edmund: Well, I didn't expect you to like it much, but then, I'd said it to you in private several times—notably on the occasion when I took Erich Heller up to see you, very funny that was, you may remember, so I thought no harm.[1] But butterflies in the stomach, or bats in the belfry! That was a triumph, it scared the b-jjesus out of me, flew right into my face where it fluttered affectionately, then went to heel. Lovely critter, which I will treasure. —Wish I cd see you, but I'm immobilized with diseases, and can't get round much. Heller says he'll come in the fall, Maybe then???   as always aff., Conrad

1. In a *New York Times* interview on his eightieth birthday C A mentioned Edmund Wilson as "a wonderful example of a critic with no style or taste." Wilson promptly mailed C A a jack-in-the-box, containing a black butterfly as the "jack."

240: TO ALFRED ANDRIOLA^r　　　Forty-one Doors, Brewster
　　　　　　　　　　　　　　　　Aug 26 69

Dear Mr. Andriola:　　I was delighted to have your letter, and honored too, and further honored by your suggestion that I speak to the Council about comics. I only wish I could, or had the strength to write something for you, but I've been in poor health for several years, and have to limit myself as to peripheral activities. And speechmaking was alas left out of my "built!" Your own Kerry Drake has for long been one of my favorites, of course. But I have always, since the Yellow Kid in my childhood, and Krazy Kat at college, been an addict, and not only that, but a great believer in the comic strips—both comics and non-comics—as being of tremendous importance as a social force. This cannot be underestimated— the comics reach people who are in other ways inaccessible, and it's extraordinary how quick the comic artists are to seize on social wrongs and weaknesses and expose them in a way that really gets home to the people who need to be got home to! Marvelous, and done with such unerring skill. As for me, I read a great many. I take the Washington Post not only because it's a great paper, but also because it has five pages of precious strips. As for which ones I read, well, I keep an eye on them all, from Apt 3 G through M Worth to Dateline Danger, Snuffy Smith, Lil Abner, the whole shebang, not forgetting The Phantom. Here on the Cape I take three papers a day, to get my belly-full. Do quote this letter if it's of use. And thanks profoundly.　　With best wishes—Conrad Aiken

241: TO JOSEPH KILLORIN^r　　Forty-one Doors, Brewster
　　　　　　　　　　　　　　　Aug 7 71: 2 Whole Days Past 82

Beloved Joe:　　Yours with glorious contents received with joie de boivre or sumpn like that, and misspent in the directions you intimated as most profitable or potable anyway, including a pair of deevine lobsters, from which we had been abstaining, we had it as we liked too, with NO COMPANY, except a surprise *breakfast* visit from brother Rob, all the way from Providence in a downpour. He never thinks to warn us. And glad to see him, and his bottle of tanquerary much! But otherwise, twice to the beach with thermos, our booze companion and our baby tran-sister, who loves to listen to losing ballgames. That's what life is like when we can get it

under control, which this season is well nigh imposs. Have to fight them off, and too often b—well cyant. . . . (This old machine is all stuck up with itself, owing to dogdays or bitchdays, the question-mark has to be put back in place by leger de main, tiresome.) Otherwise all goes mod. well, just unquietly aging in the woods, with the usual round of nightmares, with a nice new word thrown in tother night, brickabrackadaisical—it was all about china, not Nixon's visit to, but those dainty pieces with place-names on them. Jake[Wilbur] is fine, and it goes well. . . . But old age . . . I'm getting cross, cantankerous and, above all, peevish, the kind of gutter that Uncle Tom poked. More than ever when the O. U. P. ad of Ushant arrived, describing it (as TIME did 18 years ago) as a *roman à clef!* In the NY Times. What genius for malefaction they maintain! Leaves me speechless. I woke up today thinking of it with horror. What can you do with people like that—? O well—They at least produced a pretty book, and the pics, I thought, came out fine. And Betty Vaudrin [of O.U.P.] says it appears that SOME reviews are in the offing. —Joan comes here in Nov.—which will delay our trek southward, I fear, but we have no dates. Physically, this is doing the old body good, I can walk at night at the marina, a third of a mile, though I get no practice on stairs. Up to you, kid!
. . .   Our boundless love to all and every—Conrad

242: TO JAMES RAIMES[r]   230 Oglethorpe Avenue, Savannah
                            April 14, 1972

Dear James: Forgive delay, but you must know by this time I aint well, and reading through the Lowry book was almost too much for me.[1] In fact it *was* too much for me for I feel, and so did the others who read it, that it is really a bad book and doesn't do anyone justice, least of all Lowry. I can find no *feeling* for Lowry in it—it all feels like a half-finished hack job made up of interviews with friends of Lowry who were themselves of no importance and with the exception of Davenport had little illuminating to say. I don't think Oxford should be publishing it. . . . It's badly written, disorganized or unorganized and will do Lowry more harm than

1. Douglas Day, *Malcolm Lowry: A Biography* (New York, 1973).

328

good (I can't imagine what Malcolm's wife must think of it). . . . I regret having to say this, or all of it, but Malcolm does deserve better.   Best wishes, as always, Conrad Aiken

243: TO G. B. WILBUR[r]   St. Joseph's Hospital, Savannah
                                     May 8 73

Dear Jake: Very glad to have your letter and about the flourishing floribunda at 2,001 Doors. It seems determined to get us back—reaching after us. But no signs that it can succeed. My feet don't improve, legs neither, and a new course supposed to expedite these matters turned out to be a flop. We could have done better ourselves. But never mind, we weren't meant to live longer anyway. But I'm sorry to hear about your fall, and other mishaps, which seem to have coincided with my own straight backward full-length fall on a cement floor, which though stunning, didn't stun *me*—only stunned Mary. But for me it was the damnedest thing I ever saw. Standing in front of the walker to tie my dressing gown, with two hands off the walker, I watched my body disappear downwards and behind me in a flash, and haven't been the same since physically or mentally. Seems there was water on those coils which begins to account for the strange feelings I began to have 3 or 4 months ago whenever I thought I was thinking. It was no such think, or one of another color. Recovery is very slow and painful—headaches beyond belief all day long and of course multi-watt bruisal damage working its way out—but rather less than you'd think. Fortunately the fall was half-broken by a door ajar. Anyway I guess we'll both have to expect more and better ones. Joe[Killorin]'s in good form and obviously become greatly attached to you. It will do him good to see you again. . . . Little did your mother think that day in spring long ago when she put me in bond to you, namely, that I should see to it that in your old age you should lack neither friends or money! Now what a joke—the golden shoe is on the other foot, thank god. And how sensible you have been with it. In fact you have lived a good life and must know it—all the rest of us do.   Love to you all,
Conrad

St. Joseph's Hospital, Savannah
May 9 73

Dear Old Bird: NO, Old Bird, in every sense of the word. I believe I told you last year that if anything *that* was my last contribution. . . . What would you think of a school where in your senior year you were waylaid in the Headmaster's house by two characters, known as Face Godfrey and Gid Gallagher, upended, your pants ripped off, given the water cure, and then dumped on the floor. I ceased to give a damn, as I would think you should have. It was unforgivable on any and all accounts, and is unforgiven and should go with the list of the Boss's maltreatments of me which you have previously heard. It has taken me a long time to outlive your own private moralism about this. So, forgive *me* and know that, along with Jake, you are among the few people I love and to whom I will be forever indebted for private insights and perceptions to which I would never have had access. In fact, a Hero! —After a fall straight backwards . . . my broken head is horrible, as you know they are, dear old Medico, but we seem to be surviving it, though it is one more hardship for Mary, who has to do all the fetching and carrying, poor lamb. I often think of your mother as that sort of person, and bless you all, and hope you survive.   Love to you and Margaret   Conradin

Letter 245: July 1973

C A died in the late afternoon of August 17, 1973, after a walk "to retrain the legs." He dictated on July 30 to Mary Aiken what was to be his last letter. A Michigan high school student wrote that his teacher had skipped a poem by Aiken in favor of one by Emily Dickinson: "I happened to have a copy of The Morning Song of Lord Zero, *and read the title poem. My instructor replied that Miss Dickinson was accepted as a great poet and that Mr. Aiken was not. . . . I would imagine that you do not fashion yourself the greatest poet of all time, but I, for one, as lowly a critic as I am, enjoy your works."*

245: TO DAVID CRUMM^r St. Joseph's Hospital, Savannah
              July 30 73

Dear David Crumm: What a delicious go-it-your-own way enterprising and intelligent letter about *Lord Zero!* Good for you. No, I don't have any great notion about where I stand as a poet. That will be taken care of by those wiser people who come later on the scene than we do. Thus, as in their turn, those opinions too will be revalued over and over. None of us knows in what direction poetry and the other arts will turn—that's part of the cruel fascination of being interested in the arts as you are, and keeping your head about it. If there is anything good in my poetry people like yourself will find it. That's all we can hope for, and goodness knows it's enough. The effort alone is worth it. Meanwhile let me thank you for standing up for Lord Zero, which, perhaps you would like to know, is one that I myself have a sneaking fondness for. Yours sincerely, Conrad Aiken

Cast of Correspondents

Aiken, Clarissa Lorenz (b. 1899). "Lorelei Two," or "Joan," or "Jerry," or "Créach." Born in Milwaukee, a musician and part-time journalist, she interviewed C A in 1926. They were married February 27, 1930, lived in Rye, and were divorced in 1937. In Boston she teaches music and has written *Junket to Japan* (Little, Brown & Company, 1960) and an account of her life with C A (not published).

Aiken, Jane. *See* Hodge, Jane Aiken

Aiken, Jessie McDonald (1889–1969). "Lorelei One." C A met her in the fall of 1911 walking by Fresh Pond in Cambridge and married her on August 25, 1912. They had three children, John, Jane, and Joan. C A left his family in January 1927 and was divorced in 1929. Jessie then married Martin Armstrong; they lived in Sussex and had one son, David.

Aiken, Joan (b. 1924). C A's youngest child, a writer from the age of five—like her sister Jane, she has specialized in gothic novels with contemporary settings and in books for children which have received wide recognition.

Aiken, John Kempton (b. 1913). His career has centered on chemical research and development, but he has also written the novels, *World Well Lost* and *Nightly Deadshade*.

Aiken, Mary Hoover (b. 1907). "Lorelei Three." Born in Pennsylvania, her father a civil engineer, she was raised in Washington, D.C. A painter—particularly a portraitist—she studied with Hawthorne, Luks, and in Madrid with Quintanilla. C A met her in Boston in 1936; they were married July 7, 1937, in Cuernavaca.

Akin, Emily Ford. "Small, heroic, brittle, fierce, blue-eyed," C A's grandmother was the mother of William Ford Aiken (C A's father early reverted to his grandfather's spelling of Aiken) and of Grace Akin Tillinghast ("Aunt Deena" in *Ushant*, who was married to William Hopkins Tillinghast, "The Frightened Uncle"). C A paints her portrait in *Ushant*, pp. 101–06.

Andriola, Alfred. The creator of *Kerry Drake*. As president of the Council of Newspaper Comics, he presented to C A in 1969 a portfolio of original comic strips by the members of the council.

Anthony, Mrs. Benjamin H., mother of "Cousin Ed," in *Ushant*, with whom, in New Bedford 1901–02, C A had "collected" ships as they haunted the wharves (*Ushant*, p. 95). The Anthonys considered adopting C A, and later hoped he might become editor of their New Bedford *Standard*.

Bassett, Gordon (1890–1951). A friend from Harvard days, in whose memory C A dedicated *Ushant* and wrote "Another Lycidas." He died while visiting the Aikens on Cape Cod, "where he was born, and grew, and knew / as if it were a legend learned by heart / each name each house each village."

Berrigan, Ted (b. 1934). American poet. His books include *The Sonnets* (1964), *Many Happy Returns* (1968), and *Red Wagon* (1976). He is represented in many anthologies and received a Poetry Foundation Award in 1964.

Blackmur, Richard Palmer (1904–65). Worked in Maurice Firuski's Dunster House Bookshop in Cambridge, where he met C A. He was self-educated and a free-lance poet and critic until 1928. He later became a fellow of the Institute for Advanced Studies and professor of English at Princeton University.

Bryher, Winifred (b. 1894). Novelist. The pen-name for Winifred Ellerman Macpherson. She was, with H.D., an ardent proponent of psychoanalysis for artists and a friend and patron of Freud and of Hans Sachs in Boston.

Burra, Edward (1905–76). Highly original painter of the social and spiritual underworlds. His home was Rye, where he came to call on C A in 1931.

Childrey, Robert. A student engaged on a "project," he had asked C A to explain himself and his work.

Cowley, Malcolm (b. 1898). Historian, critic, and influential editor of American literature. He was a junior at Harvard when he met C A in 1918; they remained friends and regular correspondents.

Crumm, David. A student in Goodrich, Michigan, who wrote a letter to C A in July 1973, eliciting what was to be C A's last letter.

Eliot, Thomas Stearns (1888–1965). Met C A at Harvard in 1908, and they were soon exchanging poems and discussing "how to find a new poetic language. . . . A fascinating and difficult adventure, in which Eliot, a year older than Aiken, but more than that in worldliness, was an older brother, and sometimes a stern one" ("Memoir" to *The Clerk's Journal* [New York, 1971]). Their relationship through the years was complex, often—to C A—painful, but he "had never loved any man more than Tom." Stephen Spender said Eliot "once told me that he had always felt disturbed and unhappy that . . . Conrad Aiken had had so little success as a poet. I've always thought that he and I were equally gifted, but I've received a large amount of appreciation, and he has been rather neglected. I can't understand it. It seems unjust. It always worries me" (*T. S. Eliot: The Man and His Work*, p. 51).

Eliot, Valerie. T. S. Eliot married Valerie Fletcher, who had been his private secretary at the publishing firm of Faber and Faber, on January 10, 1957.

Firuski, Maurice (b. 1894). Now owner of the Housatonic Bookshop in Salisbury, Connecticut, he opened the Dunster House Bookshop in Cambridge, Massachusetts, in 1919, and at once met C A there.

Fletcher, John Gould (1886–1950). Like C A, he had quit Harvard a few months before graduation. He returned from Europe in 1914 to Boston, having already published five books of poems, and lived next door to C A. They began a friendship of mutual encouragement for their poetic projects and debate about the future of poetry. Fletcher returned to London in 1916, where C A saw him often over the years. In 1932, shortly after C A's attempt at suicide, Fletcher flung himself from a window and was committed to Bethlehem Hospital. C A undertook to rescue Fletcher from Bedlam and help him return, for good, to America in 1933. They met only two or three times again before 1950, when Fletcher drowned himself.

Flint, F. S. (1885–1960). A founding "imagist," who produced two well-received volumes of poems in 1915: *Cadences* and *Otherworld,* and afterwards published almost no poetry. He also translated from many languages.

Freeman, John (1880–1929). C A met Freeman in London in 1920 when he was a poet with five published volumes and a successful insurance executive. C A hit it off with Freeman and visited or corresponded regularly with "Gentle John" and his family.

Frost, Robert (1874–1963). After C A refused in 1923 to participate in the projected journal *New Leaves,* Frost suggested playfully a stately literary correspondence between them—like Adams's and Jefferson's—with a view to posthumous publication (Frost to C A, August 1926). But later their paths seldom crossed.

Hodge, Alan (b. 1915). Married Jane Aiken in 1948. Joint editor since 1951 of *History Today.* He met C A about 1937 and became one of the group of his younger English friends.

Hodge, Jane Aiken (b. 1917). The second child of Jessie and C A, she wrote an epic poem at the age of five, "The Playlanders," whose ending dream-song concludes C A's *Ushant.* She has been a journalist in New York and London and written many novels, as well as a biography of Jane Austen.

Killorin, Joseph (b. 1926). Callaway Professor of Literature and Philosophy at Armstrong State College, Savannah. He met C A and Mary when they moved to Savannah, where he saw C A several times a week over the years.

Linscott, Robert N. (1886–1964). Advertising manager and then editor at Houghton Mifflin in Boston from 1904 to 1944; editor at Random House in New York from 1944 to 1957. He and C A became close friends in 1917 and corresponded very regularly until the late thirties.

Lorenz, Clarissa. *See* Aiken, Clarissa Lorenz

Lowell, Amy (1874–1925). A dominant figure, from 1912 until her death, in the poetry movement in America—especially in Boston, where she befriended and encouraged young poets like J. G. Fletcher and even C A, although he was adamantly anti-"Amygist." When C A—in England in 1922—planned his anthology of American poets she told him he was the only American in Europe who had "lifted his finger" to bring American poets to the attention of the English (Lowell to C A, April 18, 1922).

Lowry, (Clarence) Malcolm (1909–57). He memorized *Blue Voyage* and "The House of Dust," and in 1928 begged C A to become his guardian and tutor. Lowry came to Cambridge, Massachusetts, in August 1929 for two months to work with C A on *Ultramarine,* and over the next years made regular visits from Cambridge University to the Aikens in Rye. C A said: "We were astonishingly alike in almost everything, found instantly that we spoke the same language, were uncannily *en rapport,* and it was therefor the most natural thing in the world that a year after he came to me, when difficulties arose between him and his father, I was able to act as mediator, and, as a result of this, for the next three years acted *in loco parentis. I became* his father. Time and space were to interrupt this, but never to change it" (manuscript in C A Collection, Huntington Library). Lowry appears as "Hambo" in *Ushant* and in *A Heart for the Gods of Mexico.*

Mackechnie, Margaret and Robert (1894–1975). Artists who lived in Rye, they were friends whom C A saw frequently.

Martin, Jay (b. 1935). In 1953 Martin, a college freshman, wrote C A for advice about writing poetry, and C A "adopted" him: they became close friends. Besides his major critical study of C A and a biography of Nathanael West, Martin has written studies of American literature and a life of Henry Miller.

McCouch, Grayson P. (b. 1888). "The Old Bird" in life and in *Ushant,* was C A's classmate and friend through Middlesex and Harvard; he became a specialist in neurophysiology. C A saw him whenever possible throughout his life. Among his friends at Harvard he could trust "the Old Bird first, as obviously and always the most understanding" (*Ushant,* p. 106).

Monro, Harold (1879–1932). Promoted energetically the cause of poetry in London from 1912 to 1932 through the Poetry Bookshop and a series of periodicals: *The Poetry Review* (1912), *Poetry and Drama* (1913–14), and *The Chapbook* (1919–25).

Monroe, Harriet (1860–1936). Founder of *Poetry: A Magazine of Verse* in 1912, which made her, as critic and editor, an important force in the "poetry renaissance."

Murray, Henry A. (b. 1893). Psychologist and teacher, who met C A in 1927, as he was about to become director of the Harvard Psychological Clinic; they became fast friends. Murray's advice to C A in several personal crises was "just right and damned important to me at the time," and his gifts of money at critical times— especially in the thirties—were "life-savers." Murray's interest in Jung and in Melville was shared by C A.

Parks, Benjamin S. A Los Angeles attorney appointed by Arthur Lowry to act as Malcolm's guardian and legal agent from 1938 to 1940.

Pearce, C. A. (1906–1962). Of Duell, Sloan & Pearce, became C A's publisher with *Conversation* in 1940, and remained so (except for *Skylight One* and *The Divine Pilgrim*) through *Ushant* in 1952.

Perkins, Maxwell (1884–1947). From 1910 was editor (and later officer) of Charles Scribner's Sons and the shaping guide of Wolfe and other novelists. He published the first three of C A's novels and rejected the last two.

Peterson, Houston (b. 1897). A critic and teacher of philosophy who wrote "a study in serenity" on the thought of Havelock Ellis (1928) and then undertook— with C A contributing information about himself and his work—"a contrasting study in complexity and chaos, with the poetry of Conrad Aiken as my . . . principal theme." *The Melody of Chaos* was published in 1931.

Piston, Walter (1894–1976). Composer, took his A.B. from Harvard in 1924 and taught there until 1960. He met C A in the twenties; they shared chess and puns and the Athens Olympia Restaurant, where C A loved "to meet with Piston's whole-tone wit . . . while the martinis flow and clams are sweet" ("Another Lycidas").

Potter, Alfred Claghorn (1867–1940). C A's mother's brother, The "Beloved

Uncle" of *Ushant* and of C A's life who was Librarian of Widener Library at Harvard.

Pusey, Nathan (b. 1907.) A member of C A's Harvard tutorial in 1927–28 and president of Harvard from 1953 to 1971.

Raimes, James. C A's editor at Oxford University Press.

Rodman, Selden (b. 1909). Editor, poet, art critic; he had just graduated from Yale when he asked Aiken and others to respond to Max Eastman's attack on unintelligibility in modern literature.

W. G. Simpson. Quoting Lowry as expressing great, somewhat intricate, admiration for C A's works, Simpson asked about the "several hundred poems" which Lowry claimed he had written "under Aiken's tutelage."

Spencer, Theodore (1902–49). Just beginning his teaching career at Harvard when C A tutored for a year in 1927–28. They became good friends, corresponding occasionally until Spencer's death.

Stevens, Wallace (1879–1955). C A thought that *Harmonium* (1923) was the best book of poetry and "The Comedian as the Letter C" was the best poem of his lifetime. In 1952 Stevens said of C A to Norman Holmes Pearson: "There is something about him that keeps him from rising, both personally and as a poet. No doubt this is his gentleness. He seems to be entirely without selfishness and aggressiveness. . . . He is honest, unaffected and a man of general all-round integrity. . . . There is much that is precious in his work. . . . Most of the attention that poetry attracts is attracted by manner and form, which, to him, mean very little" (*Letters of Wallace Stevens,* ed. Holly Stevens, 1966, pp. 742–43.)

Sweeney, John and Máire. Friends of C A in Cambridge, Massachusetts, in the fifties, where Sweeney was director of the Woodberry Poetry Room.

Taussig, William (1889–1955). C A's first roommate at Harvard. Taussig became a stockbroker in Boston; C A depended on him over the years for advice on his small investments.

Taylor, Kempton Potter Aiken (b. 1893). C A's brother who was adopted in 1901 by Frederick Winslow Taylor (inventor of the time-and-motion study and apostle of the theory of scientific management). He became a surgeon.

Taylor, Robert Potter Aiken (b. 1895). C A's youngest brother was also adopted by Frederick Winslow Taylor. He became an investments consultant in Boston and, later, Providence.

Tillinghast, Harold (1884–1958). C A's "ever kind and ever kindling" "Red-haired Cousin" (*Ushant,* p. 144), son of William H. Tillinghast (Anna Aiken's first cousin and C A's legal guardian) and Grace Akin (William Ford Aiken's sister). William and Anna Aiken first met at the Tillinghasts' wedding.

Webb, Eileen. A writer and Parisian model who met C A and Mary about 1955. Commercial postcards (many from Chinese restaurants) peppered a saucy correspondence—on both sides.

Wilbur, George B. (Jake) (1887–1976). Entered Harvard with C A in 1908 and remained, through medical school, until 1916. As an undergraduate Wilbur read Freud in German and translated it for C A, so that C A dated his immersion in psychoanalytic writings from 1909 or 1910. After psychiatric training Wilbur was chief resident at Iowa Psychiatric Hospital and in 1923 set up practice in

South Dennis on Cape Cod, where he lived until his death. In 1926 and 1927 he underwent psychoanalysis with Otto Rank both in New York and in Paris and became the friend and confidant of Hanns Sachs in Boston, then leader of Freudian analysis in America. Following Sachs's death, Wilbur edited *American Imago* from 1946 to 1963. C A said that he and Jake deliberately "analyzed each other."

Williams, William Carlos (1883–1963). By 1917, with *Al Que Quiere!* Williams was an established poet. C A's review in 1934 of *Collected Poems* is an admiring tribute; his review in 1951 of Williams's *Autobiography* describes the deep differences between their views about poetry. Never close—C A thought for lack of occasion—their friendliness was marked by Williams's offering his house for C A's marriage to Clarissa Lorenz in 1930. In the 1950s they met with pleasure, from time to time, at the National Institute of Arts and Letters and at the Library of Congress.

Wilson, Edmund (1895–1973). Became in 1926 an editor of *The New Republic,* for which C A was a frequent reviewer. He lived in Wellfleet, not far from the Aikens in Brewster, on Cape Cod. They met or corresponded occasionally, and a casual, friendly sparring was characteristic.

Index of Works

Index of Names

Persons whom Aiken referred to by first names or nicknames are cross-listed by those names.

Thomas, Dylan, 268, 271, 289
Thompson, Duncan, 221, 254, 271
Thompson, Francis, 140, 251
Thoreau, Henry David, 274
Tillinghast, Grace Akin (Mrs. Will), 180, 333
Tillinghast, Harold, 5, 6, 337
—letter to: 2
Tillinghast, William Hopkins, 5, 333
Time, 251, 256
Times (London), 59, 63, 129, 185, 319
Times Literary Supplement, 251, 269, 292, 323
—letter to: 236
Tinckom-Fernandez, W. G., 222
Tolstoi, Leo, 139
Tom. *See* Eliot, T. S.; McCabe, Tom
Tony. *See* Moreton, Anthony
Tooloose Lowtrek (Toulouse-Lautrec), 323
Tourneur, Cyril, 139
Transcript (Boston), 95, 121, 187
Trollope, Anthony, 140
Tsetse. *See* Eliot, T. S.
Turgenev, Ivan Sergeyevich, 57, 139
Twain, Mark, 179

Uncle Tom. *See* Eliot, T. S.
Untermeyer, Louis, 43, 47, 48, 58, 67, 76, 78, 81, 83, 116, 143, 255

Valerie. *See* Eliot, Valerie
Valéry, Paul, 139, 170
Vargas, Carmen, 112
Vaudrin, Betty, 328
Vaudrin, Philip, xix
Vaughan Williams, Ralph, 64
Vergil, 318
Verlaine, Paul, 98, 139
Voltaire, 323
Voorhees, Mimi, 284

Wagner, Richard, 72
Wake, xiii, xiv, xvi, xxii, 295, 297, 299
Wallace, Robert, 7
Warrender, Maud, 160
Washington Post, 327
Webb, Eileen, 302, 337

—letter to: 214
Webster, John, 108, 116, 139, 173
Weeks, Ted, 238
Wehle, Harry B., 8, 27, 176, 208, 236
Wells, H. G., 59
West, Nathanael, 322–23
West, Rebecca, 128
West Virginia Quarterly, 189
W. H. Allen, 290
Wharton, Edith, 111
Wheelwright, John, 75
Whiteing, Richard, 14
Whitman, Ruth, 244, 248
Whitman, Walt, 22, 59
Whittall, Mrs., 298–99
Whittier, John Greenleaf, 40
Whoreden. *See* Auden, W. H.
Wilbur, George B. (Jake), xvi, 2, 47, 52, 53, 69, 84, 87, 97, 117, 121, 129, 131, 134, 144, 146, 154, 158, 166, 176, 179–84 passim, 190, 191, 203, 222, 229, 234, 237, 305, 328, 329
—letters to: 45, 56, 63, 80, 82, 85, 104, 109, 116, 117, 119, 125, 126, 136, 152, 243
Wilbur, Joy, 47, 53, 129, 135, 237
Wilder, Thornton, 294
Williams, Myron, 16
Williams, Oscar, 289, 302, 320
Williams, William Carlos, 76 *n,* 90, 121, 145, 215, 244, 305, 338
—letter to: 143
Wilson, Edmund, 154, 155, 250, 288, 301, 326, 338
—letters to: 102, 239
Winchell, Walter, xiv, 311
Winters, Ivor, 172, 250, 253
Winters, Shelley, 289
Woodberry, George, 41
Woolf, Leonard, 106
Woolf, Virginia, 62, 78, 107, 140
Wordsworth, William, 8, 11, 133, 139
Wright, W. F., 52

Yeats, W. B., 21 *n*

Zaturenska, Marya, 276